From cows to tigers

Building Noah's Ark

To Barry

From cows to tigers

Building Noah's Ark

ANTHONY BUSH

Anthony Bush

This book is dedicated to my loving and faithful wife, Christina, without whom this journey would not have taken place; and to my four wonderful children who have witnessed so much of it and their spouses and our grandchildren: Hannah, Jessie, Callum, Freddy, Ruari, Lily, Jemima, Dylan, Grace, Orla, Hugo, Samborne, Barny and Connie.

ACKNOWLEDGEMENTS
I am grateful to Christina and to Sammi Luxa for reading the whole text and for their wise advice; also to Steve Robinson for so much inspiration and help in the science sections, and Jon Woodward for his editorial checking and advice and to Ann Widdecombe for her foreword.
The photographs of the Noah's Ark stage were taken by Chris Wilkinson, Adam Beaumont, Jon Woodward, Dave Sullivan and by family members.

First published in 2012 by Moatwell Press

ISBN 978-0-9572021-0-8
British Library Cataloguing-in-Publication Data
A catalogue record for this book is available from the British Library

Noah's Ark Zoo Farm 01275 852606
www.noahsarkzoofarm.co.uk

Contents

Foreword

Ann Widdecombe

On any measure of success and satisfaction I do not suppose people would immediately nominate farming or zoo-keeping as likely candidates. The first is beset by regulation and the power of the supermarkets and the second by environmental and animal-rights groups. Add to the mix strong Christianity in a secular age where overt religious dedication is less marginalised than suppressed and surely the case must be hopeless.

Yet Anthony Bush is a successful farmer who has turned his farm into a zoo where animals live in conditions which set a new standard across the Western world and where children come to learn about creation by being taught to respect and care for all its forms, great and small.

Noah's Ark Zoo Farm has been awarded recognition as a centre of educational excellence by the Department of Education, despite the protests of atheists, precisely because it does educate and, indeed, enthral. Its story has its roots in farming and it is Anthony's wish that this book should encourage the young to think about farming rather than assume that it is all struggle or simply something for a past generation. Nor does husbanding the land entail isolation in the countryside and one of the fascinations of this tale is the way that the author mixes his devotion to his farm with active work in the poorer end of Bristol among down-and-outs or just young people looking for a meaning to life. Then we move even farther afield to East Africa and the Send a Cow scheme. It is this moving landscape, this interweaving of the open countryside, urban challenges and far-off lands which commands the reader's attention.

For me the story of this remarkable man and his achievements has a particular resonance: when I was about nine, he used to visit my family because he was a schoolmate of my late brother. Once he gave me a set of 'jacks', a game which involves grabbing a specified number of scattered jacks within the time it takes a small ball to bounce and be caught, the whole exercise to be carried out with one hand. One feels that this is Anthony's approach to life: gather up disparate projects and deliver with speed.

Any farmer will tell you that farming is not something which can be successfully carried out without the support and involvement of family and here we meet the four Bush children and Christina the supportive wife and devoted mother.

The author tackles the big moral issues of the day: abortion, marriage guidance, attitudes to sex with the same sense of moving scenery (might he have made a good stage designer?) as one moment we are in the Church of England Synod and the next on marches and demonstrations and then the next in theological discussion.

Let me say that the Bush theological conclusions are not always ones I agree with, but his case is always cogently argued and backed with evidence so that it is not hard to see why he is such a good educator and why the zoo has been such a success. It must be right, surely, that children are properly taught the different arguments about creation rather than force-fed only one as if it were unchallengeable and this book gives an authoritative analysis of the conflicting theories.

There is some rather frank stuff about sex here, which is pretty blunt even for a farmer who makes his income from what the lesser forms of creation do out in the fields and which nearly gave me the vapours when I read it. It was rather different at the young ladies' convent school which I attended but the reader need only turn a page or two and it is gone. Phew!

I visited the zoo in 2011 to cut the turf for the huge elephant quarters which will set not only a new but a challenging standard for the care and freedom of elephants. Anthony invited me to feed a tiger so I put a piece of meat on the end of a reassuringly long stick and held it above my head against the wire of the cage. The huge beast reared up to grab it and I almost dropped the offering, briefly alarmed and nearly forgetting that the wire was there. A more gentle giraffe obviously felt about me as I did about the tiger and refused all blandishments to come close. As always when one is close to nature there is a moment of great awe and a sense of the Eden we lost. I have felt it close to lions in Kenya or when, in the same country, I have watched elephants playing by a salt-lick. I have swum with dolphins and wished fruitlessly that there was a common language we could share. I have gazed upon a polar bear in the majestic surroundings of the Arctic and I have crept closer to a butterfly in my front garden. For many children the closeness, wonderful but utterly safe, will be an introduction to the rich wonder of creation.

Read this book, visit this zoo-farm and rejoice.

Ann Widdecombe, March 2012

Introduction

Anthony Bush

Opening Noah's Ark a week before my 61st birthday might sound like insanity. Fortunately it started little and grew. I suppose it filled a public need because 12 years later it received its millionth visitor. However I had not expected the difficulties and opposition to almost every part of its growth, from cows to tigers.

It is many years since my wife and I were asked to write an autobiography. We never wrote it. I have shrunk from telling a life story, because all too many of them are ego trips. I feel more like Clement Atlee, of whom Winston Churchill said with customary, if acerbic wit, 'Mr Atlee is a humble man; but Mr Atlee has a lot to be humble about!' I too feel I have much to be humble about; being the younger son from a long line of peasants, or tenant farmers who have rented a farm from rich or famous people.

This is no rags-to-riches story, because it never started in rags and has never reached riches, except that a farm, started with all-borrowed capital and rented for 35 years, became an owned one. It is a story of ordinary people living through an extraordinary period of British agricultural development; from Second World War horse power to 21st-century computer and satellite technology; the son of a Wiltshire farm manager becoming a North Somerset zoo owner. Based on a strong and loving marriage to my like-minded, exceptional wife, Christina, we had four immensely talented children, who all got married within a few years of each other and gave us fourteen lovely grandchildren in fourteen years; they all have their own stories to tell one day.

This story traces a path of struggle and progress not instant success. It charts the starting of a dairy farm, then nine other organisations and charities before starting Noah's Ark Zoo Farm. One uniting factor to all these is that, as with Noah's Ark, there was opposition to everything that we have done; sometimes extreme and irrational, sometimes surprising, personal and disappointing. And there was no money to do them any way other than basically. But paradoxically, there was also wonderful support and we have had that amazing experience of having others called alongside us at every step, many of whom were far more talented than we are, with more vision to see each job continue. And the funding has always been sufficient.

Polite conversation is supposed to avoid sex, religion and politics. By that definition this story is not polite, because it is full of all three. They have always all seemed to me to be the most important subjects in life, whereas the media tend to treat the trivial as important and the important as trivial. Some subjects I have dealt with at length, such as human sexuality, marriage, family life and Earth's origins, because they have become part of my story by arousing so much opposition and so much support also. As a lifelong down-to-earth farmer there is little that embarrasses me and they all seem to me to need much wider discussion. The sections on marriage, on bringing up a family and on science are each the product of many years of research and speaking publicly. Those pages are intended to be a sort of short-hand text book to save others from doing the same work.

I hope and pray this book will encourage others to broaden their aims and their conversations, prayerfully to look for people's needs and, whatever others think, press on to meet them. In many different ways this world is a mess, but it is a magnificent mess; so much potential, despite quite a lot of people messing it up, there are also so many good people wanting to do good and their bit to help.

Anthony Bush, Noah's Ark, April 2012

1

Early influences · West Farm, Overton

There were five excited passengers in the pony trap, as it clip-clopped up the sunny track onto the Marlborough Downs. Skylarks were calling far above, stone curlews and plovers swooped low over the grassy downland, a dozen different butterflies danced round us in the summer heat. We finally stopped and all stepped down into the fresh-smelling hay field. I was five years old and it was 1943. Only an occasional Spitfire or Lancaster flying a training flight overhead from nearby RAF Yatesbury reminded us there was also a serious war going on.

The field was full of working horses doing their jobs. Two were turning the hay to give the hot sun a chance to give it a final drying. Others were pulling hay sweeps, like giant combs lying on the ground, which gathered the long lines of hay and pulled them to the elevator. Another was pulling a hay rake that gathered the missed hay into a final line for sweeping. Each horse had its carter and there were six or so other men loading the hay on to the elevator and taking it off at the top and lifting it into place to make the hay stack. The thatchers had already started work on an earlier haystack, thatching it with straight wheat straw before it rained. Hay stacks were not easy to make without them leaning and later collapsing. They had to be built in a line near a road or track so that in winter the hay rations could be loaded on to carts each day. The hay needed to be completely dry to stop later spontaneous combustion if the moisture caused heating and, eventually, fire. There were essential barrels of cider that were eagerly consumed by sweating and hard-working pitchers whose work went on incessantly, dictated by the horses on the hay sweeps. And the dust. Dust from the hay was everywhere. There was always rain on the way so everyone was in a hurry at hay making.

As it turned out we were not a welcome interlude on that hot June day. Doody Patchet and her daughter Wendy had invited us to go on a trip in their new wooden pony trap. My mother, my brother John, and I were delighted to go and at our mother's suggestion we were heading for the hay field. We had loaded up a picnic lunch for Dad, who was farm manager of the 4,000 acre farm and had joined the team in the hay field; as well as ourselves. Everyone stopped for a lunch break, especially the horses, so we timed our arrival for just before noon, the Wiltshire lunch hour. Doody was new to pony carts. Her chestnut pony needed a rest after its journey, so she took off its shiny new bridle and blinkers first, so that it could eat from its nose-bag without a bit in its mouth. This was a bad mistake. The pony could then see there was a pony cart too close for comfort, behind it, so it moved forward; only to find that the cart, still attached to it, moved too. The faster it moved, the faster the cart chased after it. The pony and cart were soon at full gallop straight across the middle of the 20-acre hay field. The other ten or more cart horses in the field became immediately very excited, rearing up on their hind legs. They wanted to join in the fun and gallop too. Then loud carters' voices began shouting out using language I had not heard before, trying to calm the Clydesdales and Suffolk Punches down! Our pony raced round the field then returned to the gate we had arrived by and went a bit too close to a stone gate-post and shattered the pony trap wheel. The cart was dragged on one side till it all fell to pieces and eventually the horse stopped, with only the two broken shafts hanging beside it. Peace was restored. The carters were smiling again and all had a laugh about amateurs, who didn't know much about horses, taking blinkers off before unhitching the shafts of the cart. We all had to walk home.

This was my first of about six years of inglorious relationships with ponies. My parents bought a 12-hand, slightly excitable brown pony called Toby, who, because my brother did not want to ride, became mine. I was a reluctant horseman, only riding, and indeed joining the local pony club, because my mother, who had lots of horsy friends, would have been so disappointed if neither of her children had ridden. She bought me a second-hand riding hat, with a thumb mark worn in the velvet where its previous owner, she pointed out, had been very polite and raised it to a lot of ladies. I was to do the same. Toby often threw me off. Sometimes it hurt quite badly. Veterans tried to reassure me that you had to fall off 50 times to be a proper huntsman, and 100 times to be a jockey. My confidence was not improved by learning that my aunt actually died after falling from a horse! A friendly lady, Phyllis Clark, from the village offered to take me riding with her from time to time and I can remember Toby galloping out of control up the Ridgeway Roman road with me hanging on for dear life, while Phyllis galloped along behind trying to catch up with us. On another occasion we were out riding with the Tedworth Hunt, where all pony club members went. After drawing a cover, a fox was found and we all took off after the red-coated huntsmen and hounds as the fox sped off across a sizeable stretch of downland. Toby was soon out of my control again and first overtook the rest of the field of horses, then we overtook the huntsman, who shouted something very rude at me, then we caught up with the hounds before a kindly fellow rider came alongside, grabbed my reins and persuaded Toby to slow down. There sometimes flashed through my mind – what would happen if I actually fell off when going flat out?

I blamed Toby, of course for being too strong for me, which he undoubtedly was. On one occasion we were due to go to a pony club camp, and I was to be lent a beautiful white pony. He must have been good looking, because the height of jump I had the confidence for was the lowest you could imagine; and one day I saw a photographer lying on the ground beside some crossed poles as we jumped it. The next I knew our picture was in Tatler with that ground shot making the jump look higher! There were only two of us at camp able to represent the Tedworth Hunt in the inter-hunt jumping competition, in the youngest class of riders, Tony Buckley and me. We were to jump side by side. Together we rode bravely up to the first jump…and refused together! We rode up again, and…refused again! We rode up on our final attempt and Tony's pony went over knocking the pole down and mine went through his gap! Then we both refused three times at the second and were disqualified! Complete humiliation – but at least we were still alive! And the Tatler picture restored my 'street cred' with all the pony club who had not been at the camp. I have a huge admiration for horse riders, jockeys and show jumpers now. It takes the sort of courage I never had.

I was living a double life at that time, because I can remember joining the anti-hunting League Against Cruel Sports when away at boarding school, but at the same time hunting with the Tedworth Hunt in the holidays and hoping we would catch as many foxes as possible. I think my logic must have been that country people all fought with the fox, because he took hens whenever he could, but the LACS opposed badger baiting, cock-fighting and other cruelties townspeople indulged in. However, my membership lapsed when I saw fox hunting opposed for reasons that did not seem true to me.

We lived at West Farm, Overton, where I was born as a home-delivery on April 8th 1938 at, according to my father's diary, 10.45am. I was overdue and weighed 10¾ lbs. I think I was a disappointment, because my parents several times told me they had hoped for a girl and were going to call me Patricia Anne! They also seemed stuck for a name for me, so I was called after Anthony Eden, the Foreign Minister, who my mother rather liked the look of. My mother was a hard working farmer's wife, but she was also allowed a maid called Bessie to help her in the house and to help look after us boys. Floor cleaning was all done by hand. There were few carpets as they needed cleaning with a 'carpet sweeper', or brush rotating into dust container, whereas sweeping floor boards was easier. Floor rugs were taken outside to beat. All clothes were washed by hand and wrung dry though a mangle, likewise, all washing and drying of plates and dishes was by hand. Clothes needed mending and socks darning to make them last longer. I could darn socks and sew on buttons quite well by 10. No electrical gadgets had been invented, except the radio, to which we listened for the war news and children's stories and later some comedy.

My father had moved to Overton in 1936, to be farm manager to Frank Swanton, his uncle, who had bought 4,000 acres in four farms a few years earlier when land was very cheap in the depression. Heavy farm work was done by horses and steam, but there were some cars and lorries for transport. During the Second World War horses were phased out as tractors came in, not least because a working horse was a hungry animal; it needed 5 acres of land to grow its hay and cereals at the yields of the day. One of my earliest memories is of lines of 50 horses moving out at 7.00am to work the fields. The head carter at each farm started at 5.00am and brought the horses in to feed; then the other carters arrived at 6.00am to groom and harness them for work. Two horses pulled a two furrow plough and did two acres a day on light ground. One horse pulled a one furrow plough. It was hard work; it meant walking 9 miles a day. They stopped for a break and for a nose-bag of food every two hours, and an hour for lunch for hay. They never worked on Sundays. A few farmers who did sometimes work on Sundays were very much frowned on. The transition from horses continued after the war when old American Staff Cars were used for hay sweeping and other farm duties. I well remember sitting beside my father in a khaki Buick car, as he swept long lines of hay to the elevator.

Farm work was very labour intensive. Cows were milked by hand until about 1943, when vacuum bucket milking began to reach the larger herds, like ours. But I can remember as a little boy often visiting the hand milkers at the top of the yard and seeing them spit on their hands or squirt milk on them to start; then, if a cow occasionally put her dirty foot in the bucket, part way through, they would scoop off the worst of the dung and carry on milking! These buckets of warm frothy milk were then carried to the dairy and tipped into a tank, high up on the wall, with muslin filters at the bottom to strain the milk, which came out over a corrugated water-cooled surface cooler and into silver-coloured churns below. The churns were then taken in the brown Bedford farm lorry to the station and transported that day by rail to London.

Bulls were an essential part of dairy farming. Our herd was the dual-purpose beef and milk Shorthorn by breed and a bull was kept at the top of the yard outside our back door with a pen that allowed easy access from the parlour for any cow that was on heat, or 'bulling'. She had a door to her space, which was too narrow to turn round, ready for the bull to mount her for service and safely return to his pen. Dairy bulls were dangerous and had a ring in their nose and a wire connecting it to an overhead cable at all times. This was replaced by a hand-held bull-pole for the herdsman to exercise him, up the lane and back on most days. Extra dangerous bulls required two men and two bull-poles. This was the time for another man to clean his pen and add bedding. It was also my only initiation into the facts of life; we had no sister but I had once seen a little girl naked, who had two little lips between her legs instead of proper sticking-out bits that we boys had. Cows and dogs were the same. I presumed there must be a connection for grown-up sex somehow a bit like the bull, but that was all way in the future and irrelevant for now. For us, boys and girls mainly moved in different worlds. We only came together for active social occasions like tennis parties and pony club.

One of my earliest memories is of causing a great panic one day, by swallowing some beautiful red berries, growing on a small ground plant. They didn't taste very nice, but I was spotted by Harry Scaplehorn, the farm hand who sometimes helped with our garden. He grabbed me, called out to my mother something about Lords and Ladies berries; then stuck his big earth-covered finger into my mouth and down my throat. I was sick immediately and brought up those lovely red berries. He probably saved my life; they can be fatal to children. So thanks, Harry! It taught me that some bad things done to you may be good for you. A little while later, on Guy Fawkes' Night (why did we still commemorate a 17th-century terrorist?!) I picked up a firework and lit it. There was a loud bang and a small part of my finger disappeared, leaving blood pouring out. I have a line on the finger-print of one finger to remind me how stupid I could very easily be. We also kept a big white rabbit called Flopsy. I didn't like it because it bit me. Our terrier, called Dusty, I also discovered was not to be trifled with; she also bit me. They put me off dogs and rabbits for years. I remember going for a walk with my father one day and he was carrying a gun, looking for rabbits; Dusty found one in its tussock of grass and set off in pursuit, about one yard behind, but with no hope of catching it. It ran across our front and my father shot it. I was surprised that my dad dared shoot the rabbit when it was that close to the dog, which was not harmed. Dad was a very good shot, till well into his 80s. Rabbits were a welcome addition to war-time meat rations. At an early age we learnt how to paunch them (take the guts out) and cross their legs to hang them; and how to skin them in about one minute.

The wild uplands of the Marlborough Downs were a magical part of the farm to visit. In spring and summer it was a rainbow of waving wild flowers with rabbits bobbing between the Sarsen stones. Skylarks filled the air with their endless melody and wheatears and stonechats foraged among the flowers as we rode or walked up to the Downs to see the sheep, past the ancient burial barrows. Much of it was cultivated as part of the 'war effort' and on some of this sheep were folded every winter, on swedes or turnips. When the ewes lambed they were put in yards made of hazel hurdles, strawed down to stop them getting muddy. The outside edge of the yards was divided into small pens and half-roofed with more hurdles to protect the newborn lambs from the snows that seem to come each year. Walter Hurcott was the shepherd I knew best. His commitment was total to his 250 ewes as he never left them day or night for the three weeks of lambing. 'Tis bad luck to take yer boots off in lambin' he insisted. His little shepherd's hut on wheels was his home for meals and sleep and his faithful dogs kept watch for the foxes that could have snatched the precious lambs. In the summer the sheep were let out to graze the downland, with dew-ponds here and there to collect rain water. There was an annual delicacy provided by the lambs in late spring, when their tails were docked for hygiene reasons and the males were castrated. The lambs tails and 'sweetbreads' were a welcome addition to rationing. I have a letter written by my mother to my father just before they were married, thanking him for the lambs tails 'which are such a treat'. Times were different then.

Tennis was a major fact of West Farm life. Dad had made a grass court out of part of the vegetable garden and found some netting to surround it. He was a very good player and played with a number of Wiltshire county and similar standard players each week. We were bought rackets at about 5 and expected to play. It is now generally known that there are hardly any natural genius's at anything, but people get good by practice and lots more practice, be it in musical instruments, sport or most other things (10,000 hours seems to be the figure for reaching the top). Obviously one has to like doing it to be that persistent! Tennis was my thing and I used to hit a ball against a wall in the farm yard for hours. I enjoyed it and inevitably improved, but then found myself winner of Wiltshire under-15s when 12 and 13. My parents had me coached, to help me stay ahead of my contemporaries. Although I later captained my school tennis team and played in Army tournaments, for my Oxford college and had a Somerset county trial, I could never give it the time it needed to get to the top. So by 22 when I started farming, I was down to one or two games a year for the next 40 years. The practice wall was key to my early success and I never again had one after we moved from Overton in 1949, until I built one for our children in the early 1970s.

2

Prep School, 60 Miles Away

St. Peter's School, Weston-super-Mare was where first my brother and then I were sent; for me it was at eight years and one month old, in May 1946. I hated having to leave the countryside we loved so much. Newts and fishing in the stream and ponds, making bows and arrows out of hedgerow hazel, collecting wild flowers of dozens of species we knew well, watching birds so much that we knew almost every species of British bird and its song, made home close to paradise. Boarding school at eight might well be called child abuse now, but at the time it was supposed to teach you to be tough and independent. As our Ford 10 approached Weston Super Mare there was a certain spot where my brother John and I would both start crying; I could still point out this spot today. 'Come on, stiff upper lip, chaps' was my father's usual response; my mother would say 'you know you love it when you get there, darlings'. My first day I was drawn into a fight with a bully who attacked John. He discovered that two Bushes were not a wise contest and became a friend of ours instead.

But the school offered excellent and varied activities and kept us busy from morning to night. Some of the best staff were officers returning from the war; Major Bartlett and Captain Lankester were two of these. Everything was compulsory – boxing, swimming in an unheated open-air pool, cricket, hockey, soccer, rugby, athletics of running and jumping, gym, and cub scouts. I remember the wiry, tough Captain Lankester was the boxing master and held a cushion against his stomach for us to practice punching, goading us to punch harder. A tournament was held every year for a boxing cup. We usually 'fixed' the fights for an agreed winner, to save too much pain, but my last but one year I had grown tall for my year and was promoted to fight a bigger boy, with whom I had no such arrangement. I got beaten up badly. For some reason at the end of each summer term there was naked bathing for one session, but we all had to discreetly jump in backwards in case a local girls' school passed at that moment and looked over the wall! My mother had taken us to swimming lessons, so I was one of the fastest swimmers and won a race. I recall this to my surprise, as I have tried to avoid swimming ever since; being cold and wet for a long time has never seemed an enjoyable option.

A few of us who wanted them were given small allotments of a garden. Although my father had been a very keen gardener providing us with lots of fruit and veg for the house, it was at St. Peter's that I learned for myself how seeds grow and can then easily be eaten by various enemies; also what a wide variety of very different flowers could come from very similar looking seeds. Our vegetables contributed to the school's menu. I remember leaving some small radishes at the end of the summer term and on returning, found them to be about six inches across; and very hot and unpleasant to eat! We also had holiday competitions to do, which our parents, both being very competitive, enjoyed doing; exhibition trays of something (one of mine was a moss garden), or a general knowledge quiz, of which the answers were worked out in the holidays, but we had to remember for an exam when we returned. Fortunately I won one of these; my mother had been known to ask 'why did you only come second, darling?'

We also had prayers every morning and church on Sundays. My mother had taught us to say our prayers and read the Bible, using Bible Reading Fellowship notes. We had been taken to church each week since birth but were not allowed in Sunday School, probably because we would thus mix with the 'village children' of our work employees. At work all men were equal to my father, who worked as hard physically as anyone else, and spoke to them with quite a Wiltshire accent. But at leisure he sounded posher and we kept our distance. We were church people, others were chapel, or perhaps nothing; though at Christmas and Easter nearly everyone was something. The war had got people on their knees, as everyone feared for their lives and a possible invasion in 1940. An Overton memory is of U.S. Army manoeuvres in April and May 1944, when there were sometimes dozens of military vehicles lined up outside our farm entrance. We children used to go up and down asking 'got any gum, chum?' of the American G.I.s; and always being given sweets and a cheery comment. We did not understand what was going on, and what lethal dangers lay ahead for them all; but one day they had all gone and we heard that the D-Day landings had taken place. From then on our parents and us looked at the papers every day to see the arrows on the map of France and how the allies were doing. The King had called the nation to prayer the night it all happened. Prayers were said in church.

All this gave me an assumption of God, who clearly made all the amazing creatures I was discovering and was someone to pray to. However, a relationship with God was not spoken of. My parents took us to church every Sunday, which seemed very boring, but most people were there. I remember my father joining in the General Confession each week (we all did), and thinking 'at least he knows he needs to say that!' But my parents were mainly good-living, sensible and frugal. Occasionally they had terrible shouting arguments and I rushed out of the room. They were good examples and role models to us and had a formal religion as a foundation. St. Peter's was similar; we covered familiar stories of Jesus and his teaching. We learnt of the seven deadly sins remembered as PALE GAS: pride, anger, lust, envy, gluttony, avarice, sloth. We often said the prayer 'teach us good Lord to serve thee as thou deservest; to give and not to count the cost; to fight and not to heed the wounds; to toil and not to seek for rest; to labour and not to ask for any reward, save the joy of knowing we do thy will.' Such sentiments helped us endure the rigours of boarding school and war-time rationing, and had no doubt prepared our predecessors for joining the forces with the difficulties that involved. I was also very superstitious. I lapped up all the superstitions that I could find; then told other boys, in order to have a sort of hold of fear over them. I even invented a pseudo-Christian ritual of crossing myself during the prayers three times to make me extra holy. I can totally understand other religions of the world where 'holy men' invent rituals and tell other people to do them, which can be passed on and elaborated over many centuries. God had better be impressed! That was all that He was getting of me, anyway.

I was also quite a violent boy; often into fights. But as I was tall for my age I was not usually challenged after a while. But I had a keen sense of justice, I hated bullying and dealt with the bullies; I also looked for retaliation and revenge if I was wronged. Boarding school tended to be a bit of a jungle, with the strongest on top.

Inevitably, boarding school meant boys sleeping in adjacent beds and some experimental homosexuality. Officially the school was strongly opposed to it, but did not mention it. But there was communal bathing twice a week by rota, mainly completely innocent, but nakedness was observed and circumcision divided us into cavaliers and roundheads. I remember drawing a picture of two such organs and passing it to another boy, with 'you' and 'me' on it. It was spotted by a teacher and I was very severely dealt with – to my astonishment. Six of the best with a cane, that usually drew blood – nothing unusual in that for me; I was not particularly evil but high spirited and often thinking of slightly risky things to do. I was beaten eight times in all – a school record at the time! But this time I was threatened with expulsion and the beating was with my trousers down. The school was also warned about me at an assembly from which I was excluded. I don't know what was said, but I did become a bit of a hero for a while, which was some compensation. Ironically I thus became an early producer of pornography, which I was later to oppose with vigour! I always felt the whole incident was outrageously unfair. It was a traditional morality but without reasons. Nothing could be done about it; it was the system we were in. Beatings one minute, forget it and get on with life the next. There was no point in getting bitter and twisted.

One memorable so-called spring term was the record snowy year of 1947. It began snowing in early January and stayed till near the end of March. For us school children it was a bonus. Normal rugby was off, because the lines were under the snow. Instead we made forts out of huge snowballs and made slides across the playground – though this was banned after a while because it wore out our shoes. We also learnt about chilblains, feeling the coldest we had ever been when outside and how wonderful it was to warm up on the school radiators. Little did we realise how close the country was coming that winter to post-war bankruptcy, and with not even enough money to buy American wheat to feed ourselves bread was rationed.

There was also quite a wide difference in material goods owned by different boys. Being a private school some parents could only just afford the fees, but others seemed to have loads of money to spend on extras; often these were 'only child' families. I remember feeling very jealous of lots of boys who were bought Dinky Toys. They could race these toy cars and lorries along a low wall round the playground. I felt very left out, being one of the few boys without a single Dinky Toy. My parents sent us *The Boys Own Paper* as being of far more educational value with limited money! One day I went to another boy's locker and stole one of his twenty or so Dinky Toys and went out to play with it. I didn't think he would notice one less. I had, however, completely underestimated my conscience! I felt incredibly guilty as soon as I had taken it and, feeling guilty, there was no fun in playing with it. I crept back to the locker and returned it. This has been a lesson ever since: I will find the fun diluted by guilt, and will have to put it right later! There were, however, lots of rules I continued to break – probably just because they were there – and breaking them usually brought admiration.

On one occasion I was playing in an empty dormitory, throwing a ball against a wall between two windows and catching it, faster and faster. Suddenly it flew out of one of the open windows and I heard a shout. I peeped out and saw the headmaster, who was interviewing two parents, was rubbing his bald head and looking up! I shot out of the room and down the long passageway, while I heard heavy footsteps running up the stairs. I did not quite make the corner to safety; he saw me! 'Bush, come to my study at six o'clock' – another beating followed! The headmaster's wife was kind but also formidable. I remember her taking good care of sick boys, but also teaching us how to resist coughing. It was a voluntary act, she insisted. This control came in useful later in the army.

My exuberance at that time led me defiantly to shout out worse long strings of bad language than anyone else and being shushed by other boys in case teachers heard! This interlude, when I must have been 10 or 11, did not stop the headmaster making me a prefect at 12, in the hope perhaps, that as a poacher-turned gamekeeper, I might be able to stop other younger boys going astray. Unusually, I also was soon de-prefected. If boys did not behave at night, rather than report them or give them Latin lines to write out, I had another method of imposing discipline. I had written out hundreds of lines of 'unicum arbustum haud alit duos erithacos = one bush will not shelter two robins', or 'tempus fugit = time flies' with little reforming value. So instead, I instituted 'running the gauntlet'. This involved all the boys standing on the end of their bed with a pillow and bashing the offender on the head as he ran as fast as he could down the length of the dormitory. It was a deterrent and quickly over; but it was also illegal (probably because it was a bit dangerous!). Unfortunately it was not soundless. I was caught in the act by the Head and 'de-preed' for a month. I also remember one holidays at about that time, smoking a cigarette from Dad's cigarette box and found it so disgusting that I can now say I gave up smoking (and swearing as it happens) when I was 12. Both seem mainly designed to make your mark and shock the sensitive and I was about to discover other ways of doing that.

St. Peter's was a good school both academically and for its wide interests. Some boys later became famous, like Roald Dahl, before my time, and the actor John Cleese, two years' younger. My cousins Richard and Paul Barber were both sent to St Peter's; they have reached the top of the farming and horse racing world. My brother John was High Sheriff then Lord Lieutenant of Wiltshire, chair of some big organisations and is an OBE. The school gave me a good preparation for my next one, Monkton Combe School, where my father had been until the recession of 1928, when my grandfather could not afford the fees. Dad left at 16, to work on the farm.

3

Monkton Combe School, near Bath

I DID NOT PERFORM PARTICULARLY WELL ACADEMICALLY AT ST. PETER'S, BUT did well in sport, being in all the sports teams and being athletics victor ludorum one year (when the boy who probably should have won it was off sick!); whereas at Monkton the reverse happened. I had just failed to get a scholarship to Monkton but, urged on by my competitive mother, I wanted to prove I was worth one. I suddenly took off academically and won the year academic prize by quite a big margin two years running; but I only just made each year's team at the major sports. I would like to have rowed but my parents strongly discouraged me as they thought it would not be socially useful later on. My tennis was continuing but it was not played at Monkton. The School gave an excellent all-round education with a large number of clubs and societies to belong to out of classroom hours: I joined the Printing Club and learned to print letter heads and cards, the Field Club, for studying wild life, the Astronomical Society which had the largest school telescope in the country (a four-inch refractor), the Field Sports Society to whom, my diary records, at 13 I gave a short lecture on Gun Dogs 'about which I knew nothing!', the History Society, the Junior Debating Society, which ran a parallel general election in 1951 and 1955, and the Christian Union, to which half the school went each week. The school also did all the exam education that was needed to pass into Oxford, Cambridge or other universities.This included Latin, which I hated but passed at O-level (with 37%!).

We did some quite spartan things at Monkton which was also preparing us all for National Service – something that most of us would do when we left. Every morning all boys had to have a cold bath that had been run the night before, with a house prefect supervising to make sure that we obeyed the 'shoulders under' rule. Only if there was ice on the bath would we be excused. Dormitories were anything from six to twenty in a room. In my early years there was still rationing. I had often been with my mother to the grocer or butcher where our ration cards were cut out with each purchase. Our Monkton food reflected this, so porridge and vegetables and bread were not rationed but items in short supply were, like meat (4oz of bacon or beef), eggs (one per week plus powdered) limited sausages and offal, like kidneys and heart, a 2oz butter a week (soft in the summer heat) along with a pot of jam that had to last a month.

If the food was not enough for our energy needs, even with the 3oz sweet ration which we could buy at the tuck shop, there was extra bread-and-dripping at 9.00 at night. Because many of us must have been growing fast, this was very welcome. Girls were totally absent and the women were old enough to be our parents, except for the assistant matron and the headmaster's secretary with whom lots of boys fell in love from a safe distance. I can remember in my last year when I was a prefect, thinking of rather a lot of reasons for talking to the head master's secretary.

Fagging was an institution. There were general fags who had to answer 'fag calls' from the prefects' room; these were required to cook the prefects' toast in front of an open fire, wash up for them or, more often, to hump chairs about for events. There were also private fags who had to clean a prefect's shoes and dust his room; a foretaste of having a batman in the army. When I eventually became a prefect I needed to choose a new boy to be my private fag so I looked through the list of those coming and noticed the son of the Archdeacon of Cyprus was on the list, Martin Adeney. I thought he might become quite influential one day, so it would be fun to say he had been my fag. As it happened Martin went on to become the BBC industrial correspondent in the '70s at the time of the miners' strike. I used to amuse my children by shouting at the TV screen, 'Martin, come and clean my shoes!'

The major thing that happened to me at Monkton was to encounter God. The school had a strong Christian tradition and lots of boys seemed to have something different about them; they seemed to be happy, but serious about life and more caring than I was used to. I was among the most mischievous, tending to lean towards the naughty and adventurous for excitement. At Monkton any wrong-doing was implicitly frowned on, but life was not boring, it was full of interest. My own experience had been of an outward form of religion, and I thought about God mainly on Sundays; I considered it a Sunday ritual to go to church, at least most weeks, but did not even attempt to discover God personally. I prayed from time to time, of course, but God was remote and out there somewhere; I needed to do religious things, a bit like a superstition, to make sure I got all the favours and good luck possible. Interested He might be, but He certainly was not close.

One of my contemporaries, aged 14, was a Baptist and was a great help in taking me to Christian Union meetings. My second year some Young Life Campaigners came to CU and one fiery young preacher, Don Summers, gave an appeal to take God at His word, because Jesus was calling us to a friendship. He suggested everyone needed forgiveness and could be forgiven by asking – that was why Jesus Christ had died in our place, to take the punishment for everyone's sins. He suggested we should ask Jesus into our lives because He loved us personally and would make a difference to every part of it. I was a bit suspicious of dramatic appeals and stayed in my seat. But later in my dormitory I knelt beside my bed (lots of boys did that every night to pray) and asked God, who I knew was out there, to forgive me and to come into my life, to be involved with everyday stuff, change me and use me.

The result was dramatic for me. I knew something had happened inside and I knew at last that I was forgiven for all of the bad things I had done. It was a huge relief; life was no longer about struggling to balance the books, to do some good things to balance the bad. I knew now that Jesus' death on the cross paid for everything and that now He wanted me as a friend and a servant, saying sorry when I messed up but moving on. I began to realise that He is with me all the time; that He will never leave me abandoned. Extraordinarily I found I wanted to read the Bible and to remember it, to live by it and please God and be useful with my life. Before this the Bible had been part of a ritual, now it became clear to me that it was God's word to His people, including me, written by dozens of different ordinary folk in a space of two or more thousand years. It was God revealing his heart to us all. I read it from cover to cover. It made sense together, though many bits of it were still difficult to understand. Now life had a reason other than just to get the next excitement out of it.

My sexual confusions dropped way down the list of important concerns, at least for a while. Most surprisingly the desire for immediate vengeance dropped off; I no longer needed to get my own back. I became sure that God had a plan for my life that I needed to discover. As the school was Church of England I signed up for Confirmation classes but Dudley Clark, the chaplain, refused me and said my life did not look as though I was ready. I was shocked but realised there were areas I needed to sort out, mainly being high-spirited, a bit cheeky and naughty. I was confirmed a year later. One routine that began at Monkton was the 'quiet time'. The whole school had to be quiet for 10 minutes from 7.15am, for boys to read their Bible and pray before breakfast at 7.30. The habit, now expanded, has remained a vital part of my walk with God.

To my surprise, my church-going mother was very anti all this new-found Christian stuff. Perhaps I was less enthusiastic about the round of cocktail parties, bridge and point-to-point racing they wanted to take us to. Perhaps a different set of spiritual values was beginning to show during conversations at tennis parties and dances with the children of their friends; whom we were expected to get on really well with. I had discovered such good news that I was wanting to share it. I was already noticing a big difference between Christian boys and girls and non-Christian ones. Whatever it was, she began to say quite often 'never mind, darling, you will get over it when you get older'. It made me wonder whether she and my father had a more intimate relationship with God once, which they had lost. After many years, at least 30, she began to see that Christian marriage and child-rearing worked and was good for everyone, compared with ritual religion, which was not easy to pass on and in so many cases did not keep friends and their children from divorce and family break up. My father was definitely more sympathetic with all that we did, both then and in later life; but I think my mother finally was too. I certainly prayed for them from then on.

During my second summer holidays from Monkton, aged 15, I received quite an initiation into girls. My mother had arranged for me to go to France on an exchange for a month at 14 and again at 15. This was to help me pass French O-level. We took six O-levels at 15. The boy I exchanged with came in June/July for a month and my mother nobly showed him round and looked after him for a month, while our term was still going on; then we both went to their family holiday home in Brittany. To be plunged into an French life was good for my French and an eye opener, too. There were three boys and three girls in the family. Two of the boys were older and we played quite a lot of tennis, I could more than hold my own on the tennis court. I learnt the tennis jargon and a few French swear words too. As I had recently become a Christian I wanted to go to church. The family showed me the local Catholic church where services were in Latin – good for my Latin, but not much help for my spirituality. We also spent a lot of time on the beach. The first year was full of activity, very good for O-level preparation and getting to know the family, and by the second year the girls had matured quite a bit. Two of the girls were twins of 12, and by year two clearly they wanted to embarrass or excite me.

One day as I was rounding a sunken coastal path one of them, who was waiting for me and hiding behind a bush on the sand dune, was given a signal by her sister and started weeing almost beside me, so that nothing of her genitals was hidden when I looked at her! The girls ran off giggling. Later, the other twin came into the family changing cabin, where her brother and I were changing, took all her clothes off and turned in my direction before slowly putting on her swimming trunks and her bathrobe! One day as we were walking towards the house, they asked me if I could carry them both at once, I said I could as neither of them was very heavy; so they each jumped and clung on one of my arms, insisting my hands carry them by the front of the crutch! This was wildly exciting intimacy for me and for them, that I went along with for a few yards, but my excitement was so embarrassing that had to put them down after a short distance! They appeared oblivious of my embarrassment, but giggled with glee. I declined a repeat request. It became clear that, having brothers, they knew about erections and wanted to cause embarrassment! But it was an interesting experience for this all-boys-educated fifteen-year-old, with no sisters; and showed me if I needed it, that I was definitely a budding heterosexual. In fact when I won the form prize that year, I chose a book on anatomy that showed in great detail, among lots of other much more boring things, what girls were like!

Academically I peaked at 15, taking 10 O-levels and doing rather well in a few. I chose maths, higher maths and physics for A-levels; I had got nearly full marks in maths but I did not really enjoy it or, perhaps, did not really click with the teachers. Meanwhile I had been asked to lead the Astronomical Society and the Junior Bible Study. The next year we had seen a mission help lots of boys to faith and, at 16, I was appointed a house prefect and also asked to be secretary of the Christian Union. I did not join the Young Farmers club because farming was one job I was not going to do; we were doing farm work every holidays and it did not seem very interesting.

Monkton believed in muscular Christianity and everyone was encouraged to do their best at all sports. Although I was not brilliant at any sport I scraped in to the year team in all sports at each year until the top level when I was in the second team for each sport, albeit captain of the 2nd XI hockey team. There was also a Combined Cadet Force (CCF) that prepared boys directly for National Service by training us towards Certificate A, which fast tracked us towards officer selection. By my last year I had been promoted to sergeant. By 17 I was house captain of one of the four houses and a school prefect; in fact the rest of my year realised that I was the only boy to be made a prefect, because only four boys were deemed suitable and the other three prefects had stayed on from the previous year. My year responded with a dramatically improved sense of responsibility and other prefects were appointed the following term! As secretary of the Christian Union, to which 120 boys went twice a week, I had to invite visiting speakers. These might be Old Monktonians, sportsmen, politicians, businessmen or vicars, and I was given a book in which each speaker was confidentially graded for the sake of future CU secretaries. I was doing a lot of leading and speaking at these meetings. There were also Sundays to fill, when in those days no work was done or sport was played. When I was 15, I began, with one of the teaching staff and two other boys, as a Sunday school teacher of children at Midford, a village we walked two miles to reach each week. I bought a flannel-graph board and created stick-on pictorial lessons, cut out of a book. One day I was supposed to be teaching three, 12-year-old girls who sat giggling. 'We're in love with you', said one of them. 'Be quiet and pay attention,' I replied, flattered, but slightly embarrassed!

At the end of our last but one year we were due to go to Combined Cadet Force (CCF) camp as usual each summer holidays. I quite liked CCF and had been in the band as one of the four side-drummers. The band was at every annual parade, with about eight buglers, a base and a tenor drummer and four side drummers. We practiced in between, polished our kit and felt important. Summer camp was about learning to be fighting soldiers as National Service was awaiting all of us. We slept on straw mattresses, called paliasses (or chummy-bums) on duck-boards under canvas. There was a mess tent for eating in, primitive toilets, and lots of drill and battle-field exercises on an army training ground using blank cartridges. On this occasion I was due to leave early, as sergeant in charge of the advanced party to get the camp ready.

The night before I was due to leave with the advanced party, I was house prefect in charge of a dormitory. My dormitory had told me they were going for a midnight walk, did I mind? I said as long as I was asleep, I wouldn't even know! Unfortunately the staff member in charge of the house discovered empty beds in my dormitory and woke me. He wanted me to walk in my dressing gown 400 yards and tell the housemaster. The housemaster then asked me to go with him to inspect other dormitories in his house, where he found lots of other empty beds. Next morning punishments were announced, but the boys all thought, completely unfairly, that I had dobbed them in, because I was seen with the housemaster. I was due to be beaten up at CCF camp and I was booed out of the school on the CCF lorry! Fortunately a boy in my year, Malcolm Widdecombe, knew the story and convinced them of my innocence. So I lived. But it was an interesting early experience of unfair and untrue gossip.

During my last year at Christmas, Malcolm Widdecombe asked me if I would go to a houseparty at Capernwray Hall with him. I had known Malcolm since we were 13; we were on-and-off friends and I had stayed in his home and met his 9-year-old sister Ann. She was bright and cheeky but gave no clue that she was to become a Member of Parliament 33 years later and a TV celebrity. Malcolm had not been a hugely popular boy; he was a bit of a trouble-maker, but was quite funny and also had a huge repertoire of doubtful jokes and songs. But he had saved me from being beaten up, so I rather reluctantly agreed to go with him to Capernwray despite it meaning I was going to miss a week of the Christmas holidays at home in doing so. The houseparty was interesting for me but for Malcolm it was a sensation. God met with Malcolm and changed him totally. From being a centre of subversion and difficulty he became on fire for Jesus and a model of cooperative behaviour (most of the time!)

The following term he suggested that three of us should pray for three other boys for a week, and then speak to that boy about the Lord and try to help him become a Christian. All six would do the same the next week, to be repeated throughout the term. In this way about 70 boys had a profound Christian experience during the term, for many of whom it was a time of deep spiritual renewal. Little did I know, but I was also at school with 33 vicars and perhaps even more foreign missionaries and more still lay preachers in different denominations. It was not unusual that Monkton produced boys who became men of great faith and sacrifice. We had often heard actively-serving Christian old boys in chapel and CU, heard their stories and stories about the lives of other great missionary achievers. God uses people and actions in ways beyond our knowing. None of us was in any doubt about Jesus' teaching on heaven and hell, all of us wanted heaven and to rescue as many others as we could from hell. For my own future, I was hearing about the hardships and difficulties accompanied by their joyful faith, of Christians serving God around the world. This began to shape my own sense of service. If these amazing people did these things at God's bidding, how could I aim at less?

But even good boys could get up to mischief. At the end of the school year, when I was in charge of a dormitory of twenty quite high-spirited boys, Malcolm Widdecombe and Ted Longman (a close friend, who shared a study with me) crept in to the dormitory and made me an apple-pie bed (with the bottom sheet folded short as a top sheet). On returning to the dormitory there seemed to be too many boys awake so, suspicious of my bed being sabotaged, I felt inside.

'Every one stand on the end of their bed!' I commanded. 'Who made me an apple-pie bed? You will all stand there till someone owns up.'

'Please, Bush, it wasn't us, it was Widdecombe and Longman' said a shivering voice, eventually.

'OK', I said, 'you and you make my bed'.

Then a voice asked 'can we go and do in Widdecombe and Longman?'

'If I am not here, I won't know about it, will I? I am going to see Mr Watson' I replied and duly went downstairs to the housemaster, Mr Tom Watson to report all was quiet, and have a chat about the day, as we usually did. Tom Watson had been at Monkton himself, at the same time as my dad, 25 years earlier. I liked our daily chats; he was an encourager and I think he was glad to hear what was happening in his house where most of the discipline was left to older boys. Suddenly a huge rampage was heard above.

'What's going on?' asked the housemaster.

'I really don't know, sir', I mumbled, rather unconvincingly as he leapt up the stairs. There he found 20, thirteen-year-olds doing battle with Malcolm and Ted, who were holding their own as Ted was a strapping rugby player and both were over 18! Eventually order was restored.

This was not the first time Ted had tried a prank. School prefects (but not sub-prefects) were allowed to beat boys if they felt it was necessary. One night a boy called Peter Webb had been cheeky once too often so I had him bend over and gave him four whacks with my slipper. The whole house heard the sound of it. Ted didn't entirely approve of beatings and was also often up for a laugh. Two nights later, he did not know where I was and decided to re-enact another beating, so hit the window sill with his slipper four times. Unfortunately at that moment I was with the housemaster, who made a fast exit and caught Ted, much to his embarrassment.

Other than Webb I only ever beat one boy, Peter Akehurst, in the prefects' room with the prefects' cane. It was more a gesture than an infliction of pain. Occasional beatings seemed to improve behaviour in a school that was almost entirely disciplined by its prefects. Peter Webb went on to stroke the Cambridge boat (did I help with his sense of timing?!) and Peter Akehurst became a professor at Keele University. Sadly, both died in their fifties. Ted Longman remained a friend for life, was ordained, married, served in Hackney then St Helens and then inherited an excellent school in Chester from his mother, which he ran as a first-class Christian school for the rest of his working life. We also became godfathers to each other's children. I will mention Malcolm later.

My last year at Monkton was really good experience in organisation. As a prefect I had certain responsibilities like collecting volunteers or conscripts for moving chairs and tables and serving food on open days. I had to deal with chapel absentees too. I found myself made the first captain of tennis. Before this, boys who were bored with cricket could play tennis but were penalised for it by having to do 'pioneers', or assistant groundsman work! This was the first time tennis was allowed as a full sport. As its first captain I had my first taste of organising something from scratch which was to stand me in good stead for the years to come. I wrote off to several schools not far away and invited them to a match, picked our team. We had one good tennis court at Monkton, one borrowed one in the village and a small old one with very short back and sides (called the barber's court). My father was delighted that tennis was now a Monkton sport and collected a team of good adults to play us, including Harold Lee, the British Hard Court Champion of 1931 and Davis cup player (the last time Britain had won it), Wiltshire county player Snowy Horton and four good club players including himself. The tennis club rose to new heights, with fifty members. All courts had to be booked on weekly booking charts and there was a junior tennis team with matches arranged.

As with everything I subsequently organised from nothing, this also met with opposition. The boys and staff from other sports thought it would draw good sportsmen from cricket, rowing or athletics; as we were a small school the teams might therefore suffer. But rather than give up, I agreed not to choose the tennis team from those boys. The appointed staff member gave very little encouragement and we had to get to away matches by public transport – if we could not find cars and staff to take us. I had a small portable typewriter and spent lots of time making notices and team lists. I also typed notices in my role as school prefect, as house captain, as CCF platoon sergeant, and as CU secretary. I seem to remember academic work was the minimum needed to pass my A-levels, as all the rest was so interesting!

My lasting benefits from Monkton were several. Most of all it was there that I was rescued from the dead hand of superstitious religion and introduced to Jesus Christ; a relationship which was to grow and be so important to everything that followed. I learnt too that God was interested in all parts of life and was always ready to help in making the most of each of life's challenges. I also learned much about leadership from good role-models and by being given the opportunity to lead, as well as by being in an environment where mistakes were learning opportunities. I came to discover that time was limited. I would have loved to follow other interests and play a musical instrument but because my parents would not buy me a trombone – my instrument for a term – I had only mouthpiece to practice on! They may have realised that any interest needs time, and I did not have enough of that for all my hopes. Now I really felt ready for the next step in life, when my last term finally ended.

4

School Holidays on the Farm and an Embarrassing Accident

DAD HAD TAKEN OVER THE DUCHY OF CORNWALL TENANCY OF PEART FARM, Norton St. Philip, which my grandfather and his father had rented for four generations. He had realised his dream of having his own farm, on a lifelong tenancy, by 36, which was the average age for farmers to take over farms. He now wanted to die in the house he had been born in. Indeed he did, at 89, still mentally alert and in quite good health and still farming.

Our first holidays had been from St. Peter's, when I was 11, 12 and just 13. Farming had changed little in half a century. Our first two harvests had been with tractor-drawn binders making sheaves, tied in sisal string; which we all helped to collect into stooks or hials of eight standing-up sheaves to dry for a week or two. Grain was cut before it was quite ripe; it ripened and dried in the stook. Then on a sunny and windy day all the stooks were pushed over to dry the butts before they were loaded onto horse-drawn wagons, which soon became tractor-drawn wagons. The butts of the sheaves were always placed outwards, so that any shed grain would stay in the wagon. Our cowman, an Italian ex-prisoner of war, called Lucian, was very strong and sometimes used a big pitch fork to lift a whole stook at once on to the trailer. Lesser mortals lifted one sheaf or two at a time. I learnt to stack these wagons at 12 and then to help unload them onto the elevator taking them on to the rick. Ricks needed quite skilled work, to make sure they widened slightly up to eaves level, and then narrowed to the top of the roof; this was then quickly thatched, with last year's thatching straw.

As we spent most of the year at boarding school with perhaps only one weekend at home per term, holidays were precious. We learnt about other farming jobs by doing them. We fed the pigs with dad, rode on various tractors and field implements and watched other things going on, helping where we could.

Lucian was always friendly. He taught me to milk cows and move electric fences and I watched him do lots of other jobs that later became second nature to me. I have two unusual memories of him; one was of him urinating hands-free as he walked with the electric fence to move it, demonstrating, presumably, that he was a bit of an Italian stallion; and also when he grabbed my arm one day just after he had switched the electric fence on – he held the electric fence in his other hand so that the shock went through me, not him! Lucian had his first child when I was away at St. Peter's and I asked Major Bartlett, who spoke Italian, to translate a telegram message I wanted to send to him: 'Grattione sur la nativita de la vestra filia' still sticks in my mind!

During our second winter at Peart Farm, in 1950-51, my father hired a threshing team to thresh the ricks we had made at harvest time. A big steam engine drove the thresher, which stood next to a corn rick. The thatch was removed and two men started throwing sheaves of corn to the man on the thrasher, who cut the strings with a knife and fed them in. The straw was sometimes saved in bundles for thatching other ricks or cottages, but was usually fed into a baling machine which tied large bales with wire ties. Sisal strings at that time were too vulnerable to getting wet and rotting and to be eaten by rats. Rats were a major problem on grain farms before the days of rat poison. Rats ate through sacks, ate grain, spread disease and multiplied at a huge speed. We had a cousin die of Weil's disease (known as Leptospirosis nowadays), which is carried by rats. Cats and dogs were part of the anti-rat strategy. Rats usually made nests in their own food supply of grain ricks. They were safe there but, unlike mice, they had to come out for water when cats the would catch them.

At threshing we would surround the rick with dogs and people armed with sticks, especially when the rick was reduced to half height, to try to stop the dozens or even hundreds of rats escaping to other places. Terriers were the best dogs, which was why we kept one. They could catch and kill a rat in seconds and be on to the next one. Rat multiplication is impressive: I can remember killing 43 rats from under one straw bale. After threshing, the grain was fed into large, thick and durable West of England Sack Company sacks, each holding 2½ cwt of wheat. It took two people to lift them off the ground (with hands linked together behind and underneath the sack) but a man could carry one on his shoulders. One impressive 64-year old, Charlie Haines, was only 5ft 2ins but could carry one of these bags on his shoulder up 15 steps into the corn mill loft! Younger, bigger men failed. Soon sacks got smaller; then augers (screws first used by Archimedes for water) were invented to do the job.

By 1951 we had our first combine. This needed drier grain so that it could be cut and threshed in one operation. Then on the combine the grain was fed into the same big bags, which were tied tightly with string and dropped down a shute on to the field. These sacks had to be stood on end to let the wind dry them if they were not quite dry enough to store; whenever it rained the bags had to be turned on to their tops to dry out the bottoms, and turned again if necessary until they were ready to load on to tractor-drawn wagons and brought in to the barn. 2½ cwt bags were a three man job: two to lift and another to stack them on the wagon, often with a young farmer's son driving the newly-invented little grey Ferguson tractor, which had first rolled off the production line in 1946.

One day when I was sixteen I was injured. My father had asked my brother and me to help plant potatoes on his new-to-us, second-hand potato planter. This was tractor-mounted, but needed two people on seats to fill the cups with one potato each, which then dropped down a spout into the ground one foot apart, while the machine opened the ground in front and ridged it up behind us. It was a big leap forward in technology. Previously open furrows had been made by a tractor or horse, then lots of people, including us for several years, walked down the rows dropping seed potatoes (the small ones) at about one foot intervals along the rows, from buckets that we carried. There was a lot of walking about with empty and then full buckets, to finish off the long rows. This new planter could cover several acres a day with a driver and two people. As usual I was in high spirits but disaster was about to happen.

Putting potatoes into cups for a few hours gets boring so I thought I would spice it up a bit by letting the horizontal wheel of cups get nearly empty, then grabbing a big handful of potatoes and rushing to fill them all in time. I leaned to the right and stuck my left leg out for balance. It must have got caught in the unguarded machine wheel and I was dragged off my seat amid loud screams from me and from my brother. My father, who was driving, stopped instantly but I was quite badly injured, I thought. My father carried me back to the kitchen where I found to my amazement that my scrotum had been torn open. I must be one of very few men who has ever actually seen his own testicles: there they were, laid bare and apparently undamaged but in need of some good needlework to sew them in again. I had seen hundreds of lambs' testicles, that wartime food delicacy, but I had not expected to see my own. I was of course extremely embarrassed. No one spoke of private parts in those days. All was supposed to be polite mystery.

I was rushed off to St. Martin's hospital in Bath, where I was sewn up and put in a bed. A pretty young nurse soon came along and asked what I was in for. 'My leg', I euphemistically explained. 'Can I see?' she says. Oh no, I thought, men don't show that stuff to girls, let alone pretty ones. I supposed I couldn't refuse the nurse, so I lifted the sheets and looked the other way! She was obviously nearly as embarrassed as I was and said 'Your leg? Why didn't you say?' I thought, what should I say? I just lay there feeling as red as a beetroot with shyness. The episode was repeated a few more times during recovery. I didn't mind telling men I had nearly lost my balls, (they were a well known target area for squeezing into submission in fights at St. Peter's) but girls, especially hearty tennis-playing girls, were not supposed to know such things even existed. Such was the social climate of the day and my reserve after a life of only a brother and at two all-boys boarding schools. My parents were worried that they might never have grandchildren.

I have since discovered that God can control accidents to the millimetre. At about that time General Sir Arthur Smith had come to speak at Monkton Christian Union. He was an abrupt, military man but a shining Christian. 'Don't worry if people think you are cracked for being a Christian; remember cracks let the light in!' he had said breezily. One day during the First World War he had been given a Bible verse and promise by someone in his home church of Psalm 91:7: 'A thousand may fall at your side; ten thousand at your right hand, but it will not come near you.' Later, he was adjutant of his company and was hit by a blast from a shell and carried back to the field hospital. Part of his leg was blown off and part of his back pocket that held his pocket Bible. He looked at the Bible that was partly gone; it was left at Psalm 91:7! He then made a full recovery. If God can protect Arthur Smith's life and Bible to the nearest page, he could keep my fertility.

Peart was a mixed farm of 320 acres. Those were the days of Old MacDougal, when farmers did a bit of lots of things; cows, pigs, hens, turkeys, potatoes, mangolds, turnips, swedes, barley, wheat, oats, grass seed and even flax. Twenty acres were of two woods where pheasants were reared and we had shoots each year. I went through a phase of loving shooting. I would go out with my 4:10 shotgun at 12-years-old and stalk rabbits. Dad taught us to be very careful with guns. Shooting was also a very good social sport in the winter; the shooting season lasted from October to January. About 15 guns and 15 beaters were needed and some good chatting went on between drives and at picnic lunches in a barn; which always included sherry and/or cherry brandy (though the day often started with that); shoots were for pheasants, partridges, rabbits and occasionally hares, sometimes woodcock, snipe, pigeon, duck, a jay, a magpie or a fox. The shoots ended with tea and hot, buttered toast and cakes at Phil and Angela Weeks', my aunt and uncle's house in Laverton, our nearest village a mile away. Shoots, especially on Boxing Day, were also a good family reunion time; when all the cousins and uncles and aunts gathered with other friends.

Pheasant shooting was one of Dad's two favourite pastimes, along with tennis. One winter many years later, my parents had been to China on one of the very first visits allowed by Western tourists. They had so enjoyed it that they invited the whole Chinese embassy to Peart for an outing. The Chinese looked round the farm, then visited a stately home and a farm cottage also. He asked the Chinese Ambassador back again for pheasant shooting. The Ambassador duly arrived in November in the embassy limousine and his chauffeur went to the boot to fetch the gun and returned with an AK47! 'Er, Your Excellency we shoot pheasants in the air in Britain, would you like to borrow a shot gun?' My father decided to put the best shots on each side of the ambassador, and whenever he shot, they should too, and then call out, 'Well done Your Excellency!' The ambassador seemed to love his successful day out, with pheasants falling all round him.

In my early days at Peart I still had my pony, Toby, but the Somerset fields were too small for a gallop; he became too much trouble and was sold. But we still went to point-to-point races, where my father loved to bet. We were encouraged to 'have a flutter' of two shillings at the Tote, on a few races. However as soon as my father stopped giving us extra money to gamble I began to review the economics of this. It seemed to me we very rarely won. My father always backed the favourite, which gave very low odds. He had a system of betting that was supposed to cover his losses by betting a large sum on the favourite in the last race. He almost always succeeded. But I could see that most people lost money. That is why there are so many wealthy bookies. Betting was supposed to add excitement to the race, and it did, but the loss of money lasted longer. It was cheaper to cheer for someone else's horse. So for mathematical reasons I gave up gambling at 12, too!

Besides potatoes, the farm also had a pig herd of about 20 sows, whose progeny at about 9 pigs per litter and two litters a year my father fattened to bacon weight, 8 score 10 (a score was 20 pounds). They were fed twice every day, sometimes by us, and kept in a quite advanced Danish-designed pig house. Every term my father gave us a sow's litter of pigs, which we were expected to sell to help pay our school fees. We also had a large flock of 1,000 free-range hens which meant 900 eggs per day for us to wash. One day, two Alsatian dogs started attacking the hens; Dad rushed out with his shotgun and shot them both but they had already killed about 700; the rest of the flock stopped laying. The owners of the dogs were never discovered. It was a big loss and a reminder of how precarious farm incomes could be.

Each Christmas we fattened a hundred or so turkeys to sell to friends and neighbours; which we learned to kill, pluck, take the innards from and 'truss' ready for sale. We also had the milking herd of about 60 cows; their heifer calves, kept as replacements, that took two years to grow, and a hundred or more acres of cereals, mainly for feeding to the cows. This all became fairly ingrained into us, but most of the work was manual. We hoed root crops by hand, for which the staff were paid piece-work, by the 'chain'. This was a measuring chain of 22 yards long that was used to measure how big an area had been done by each worker. A good worker could double his income for a few days, by coming off hour work for that time and working very hard. Hedges were also trimmed by hand by piece work; similarly ditches were dug and land drains laid that way. All these jobs were hard work, often wet and uncomfortable. On hot days in the summer hay making and harvest took place; these were enjoyable days being out in the field, but back in the barn lifting sacks and bales was all heavy, dusty work and went on for very long days. The 'good old days' as far as I was concerned, had nothing much good about them, unless you could just watch, or write about them. I had decided that one job I would not be doing as an adult was farming. Surely teaching or almost anything else would be more comfortable.

5

The Army

1956 WAS ALWAYS GOING TO BE THE YEAR THAT I HAD TO FACE COMPULSORY National Service. The alternative was prison! Girls did not have to do it; conscientious objectors like pacifists could, with difficulty, argue their way into non-combat activities, and some people managed to escape it for health reasons, or because they found some reason to defer it with study until National Service was over in 1963. But I found it very formative and helpful. It was obviously not enjoyable fun having your life organised from dawn to dusk by people of mixed (or dare I say it, poor) abilities and motives, and earning almost nothing. As someone later said – a background of an English public school and National Service was good preparation for a Third World prison! It made any subsequent lifestyle seem luxurious. But it also taught us how to be low maintenance.

I received my call-up papers at Monkton a few weeks before the end of term. I had to report to the Somerset Light Infantry Barracks in Taunton for a medical and IQ test in early September 1956. My four years in Monkton's CCF qualified me to be fast-tracked to officer selection. The army route to a Commission took me to Basic Training at the Somerset's HQ, which I had volunteered to join, in Taunton. Here we learned Light Infantry drill including marching at 140 steps a minute; we were called to daily events by bugle call and were on various rotas to clean and guard the barracks. We were taught how to lay out our newly issued kit and clean it to a high standard, including spit-and-polishing boots. On a Sunday afternoon I found myself cleaning a huge pile of greasy metal kitchen pans with a poor detergent and cold water. But I had learned from my mother how to sew buttons on, so I helped a young Cornishman to sew on his buttons and wrote a letter home for him; so in return he volunteered to do a night guard duty stint for me, which I felt was a good swap. He insisted no one could be a true Cornishman until he had missed a whole night's sleep!

We had been prepared at Monkton for our first night in a barrack room of beds. From one point of view sleeping in a room with 25 others was not new to ex-boarding school boys, whereas most others felt very nervous about it. But several Christians had returned to Monkton suggesting that it was a good idea to kneel down by your bed to pray each night to show people you were a Christian. There was a warning that sometimes people would throw a boot at you but it was apparently worth it! I duly did this my first night, bracing myself for a boot to land but all I got was someone shouting out 'are you feeling all right?' To which I mumbled yes fine I was saying my prayers. They got used to it, as did subsequent barrack rooms. Sometimes shy Christians were encouraged by this, and other conversations were also started.

I also discovered more about girls. The army had been a steep learning curve of seeing how young men treated girls. My first week in the army, an old soldier (probably 26) announced he wanted to have himself another little virgin that night. The contrast with Monkton where girls were respected but never there, except for the annual dance with Westonbirt (known as Westonflirt), couldn't have been greater. In the army, the 'f' word and 'c' word were used whenever other adjectives could not be thought of, and most people didn't do much thinking. I had a steady really-good-friend girlfriend for six years, whom I had helped to faith when we were both 16. She had been an assumption of a possible wife, but I was keeping my eyes open just in case. I had resolved some time before that I was not going to have sex with anyone before getting married. This was reinforced in the army with graphic film shows of venereal diseases – as STIs (sexually transmitted infections) were then called. Any one willing to be a sex partner with me would almost certainly be a willing sex partner with others and so would be a likely source of infection. Only girls unwilling to have sex could be trusted to be clean of these diseases I thought. But I had also found it easier to gather girlfriends than to lose them (perhaps it was the uniform, or 6ft 4 ins height, or perceived wealth of a farmer's son, or my unavailability, who knows?) so the last thing I wanted to do was to give them reason to cling even closer. And shotgun weddings after finding the girlfriend was pregnant, seemed humiliating and were usually disastrous. But I was prayerfully hoping to meet Miss Right. As I was extremely keen that she should be a virgin and not someone else's used goods, I thought she definitely deserved the same from me.

Where did that terrible myth come from, that losing one's virginity was good or a sign of becoming a man? It seemed to me to be a diabolically damaging idea. 'You don't buy a car without test driving it (try before you buy)' was another total con. In reality everyone expects a big discount on a demonstration model! And that is with the seller sitting in it for all the test drives! No one expects to bite an apple before buying it, then put it back for someone else if the taste isn't right! So I knew it would be hard to be different, but only for a few years. I resolved that being busy was the way to do it.

After a month or so, I left Taunton as a course was due to start for potential officers – ten weeks' pre-officer training at the Light Infantry Training Camp at Strensall, York. Here we learned more about spit-and-polishing boots so they looked like glass all over, clean and iron our kit to even higher standards, how to lay it all out in precise neat piles on our bed every day. We did more fast marching, took our proficiency and marksman rifle shooting badges, and learned the basics of fitness, battle-craft and weapons training, only building slightly on what we had done at school. We also had to prepare to take our War Office Selection Board (WOSB) to be selected as an officer, so we learned how to give a short lecturette of three minutes and how to lead a group of men over a 'command task' apparatus.

One night a corporal being demobbed arrived in the barrack room, after a 'really good time', very drunk and very late. He was carried in being sick all over himself at the end of my bed. My brother had given me his old electric iron without a thermostat, which was used by me and others to press our uniform to a high standard. Someone had borrowed it and left it on the table, standing upright, to get hotter and hotter. Either the drunk corporal or someone else must have knocked it over. We all woke in the middle of the night to find the barrack room full of smoke. The iron was glowing red hot and had burned its way through the protective ironing blanket, through the wooden table and had landed on the floor. There was an iron-shaped hole in the table and blanket! If I needed an incentive not to waste money on drink, that corporal was it! Drink was not a huge temptation, anyway. It was all very well for the demobbed corporal to get drunk but officers needed to prove their conduct was above reproach. The tiny wage we were paid was all needed to get us home on leave or to buy egg-and-chips in the NAAFI shop to supplement our somewhat meagre rations, at a time when we were taking a lot of exercise. Paul Foot, later a well-known journalist was in my intake. We used to have some differences of opinion about lots of things, including the Christian faith, but I liked him. From Strensall we went to Selection Board to decide if we were suitable as officers. I only just made the grade for training as an officer, as I was slightly on the reserved side.

Then it was off to the Officer Training Unit at Eaton Hall, near Chester. It was obviously going to be tougher than soldier training; the army led from the front, officers had to do everything better than the men. Our sergeant majors in charge of us had the surnames Leech, Lynch and Blood, and lived up to them! They were supposed to be polite to us as we were soon to be senior to them. The first night the CSM had said 'I call you "Sir", and you call me "Sir", the only difference is that you mean it!' We had been used to insults. 'Standing there like a long streak of piss' was a favourite one, shouted at our faces from six inches, used on me and other tall men. Others are best forgotten. But here at O.T.U. they added sir at the end! Fitness levels rose sharply, as did standards of smartness of uniforms, webbing and boots. Guard duty was tiring and normal work the following day the worst part of it. We learned the difference between marching well – all in step – and marching brilliantly like the Guards, with heels hitting the ground together. A third of our number were from Guards' regiments. They may have been good at drill, rich and from posh schools, but the rest of us were determined to win the platoon competitions ahead of them – in timed assault courses, rugby, cross country running, football, hockey and the Military Knowledge exam. The timed marches were 6, 9 and 14 miles in full kit (about 60 lbs) to be completed in 1, 1½ hours and 2¼ hours; part of each was at the double (running in step) and part marching. There was an ambulance waiting to pick up those lie-in-bed-after-drinking-the-night-before-rich-kids who did not have breakfast. They fainted and had to re-take the tests later. Times and marks counted towards the platoon competition with an extra day's leave for the winners.

The most dreaded part of training was Battle Camp for two weeks on a Welsh mountain range. It rained almost incessantly, and hailed so hard and long it looked like snow on our camp, while we did platoon battle practice exercises including running and lying on the muddy ground with infantry weapons and live ammunition. Manoeuvres included negotiating the bogs and water-holes covered in grass of that area. I fell into a water-hole and spent the rest of the day very wet. Trawsfynnydd training camp had minimal facilities but at least we could dry out each evening. The worst was when we went to dig slit trenches and lived in them for three days. We dug a covered part of the slit trench with a sheet of corrugated iron and a foot of earth on it, for sleeping under. This was an attempt at preparing for atomic warfare which was a strong possibility at that time. Night exercises, creeping out on patrol at risk of setting off trip wires, were part of it. Our favourite night exercise was creeping out to capture the Guards' officer-cadets, who were usually too busy drinking and chatting to take life seriously. By day, using live ammunition, our enemy was imaginary and I can remember my platoon firing tracer bullets at sheep 600 yards away. The MOD paid good compensation for the dead ones. On field exercise the latrine was a shovel at a distance from the trench. Three pieces of toilet paper were the prescribed ration: 'one up, one down and one to polish'.

At the end of sixteen weeks we had a passing out parade, to which top army commanders and our parents came, and for which we practiced for weeks. We had taken exam papers, which all had to be passed, on a number of subjects from signals and army law, to leadership training, riot control in Africa or Ireland and battle tactics at platoon and company level. As second lieutenants, we would be leading 30 men as a platoon commander, with three corporals and a sergeant some of whom would be long-term, regular soldiers. We were only short-service, but our roles were the same as the regular army. We held the Queen's Commission and had the option of staying longer than the minimum two years.

After passing out of Eaton Hall as a second lieutenant, I was posted to the Somerset Light Infantry, first to test new army equipment at Crown Hill Barracks, Plymouth. The Somerset Light Infantry drilled at 140 paces a minute (double marching was at 180). Since our officer training had been at 120, six of us new subalterns needed a refresher course from the regimental sergeant major (RSM), on the main barrack square at lunch time when other ranks were queuing for food. We started off well: left, right, left, at 140 then the RSM shouted an order that, to half of us sounded like left turn and to the other half sounded like right turn: we split in two, marching fast in opposite directions! We were splitting our sides hardly containing the laughter and wondering what he was going to do. He was alert, however, and shouted 'about turn': we turned; he shouted 'halt': we met. 'Mr Horsefall', he said to one, 'you are turning about like a bloody fairy on a rock-cake' – a remark we thought funny but got him into trouble for so addressing officers in front of the men. The broadcaster Peter Snow was one of the group of six.

Several young officers had cars and two had new sports cars, an MGA and a TR2, bought for them by their parents. I bought a 1935 Morris 8 that I called Auntie Flo. She cost £35 and every available penny to run. I used to drive to Peart in her occasionally and to church, usually the Plymouth Brethren Assembly near Crown Hill. On one occasion they had a lorry on Plymouth Hoe, where some of the men of the church were street preaching. Catching sight of me the preacher asked me up onto the lorry to say why and how I came to be a Christian. It was nerve-wracking but I did it and some of the soldiers must have heard me because it became part of my reputation.

I was quite a strict officer, not knowing quite how lax one could be and maintain respect. On one occasion I was on night duty and called at the guard room to find the guard commander asleep. It was at a time of quite high alert because the IRA had been active. I felt it was my duty to report him and he was subsequently dropped a stripe. I later heard that I was known as 'a Bastard on parade and a Bible off'!

I was at Plymouth at the time when the regiment was meant to be testing new equipment. We wore it for trials at the Royal Marine Assault Course at Lympsham, which was quite challenging. We wore it for route marches and forced marches across Dartmoor, with full kit. One fit, rugby playing, young officer was encouraging his platoon by example by running from the front to the back several times and carrying more than his share of weapons. It was a hot sunny day; about half a mile from the end he passed out and I had to help the MO (medical officer) carry him to the shade where the MO poured two tablespoons of salt with some water into his mouth. He recovered quickly!

Part of the training for new recruits was to be shown films of venereal diseases. VD was widespread among the prostitutes of Plymouth and this sobered us all up as to the consequences of visiting prostitutes. Condoms were available but they carried a severe warning as they had a high failure rate. Catching VD had been a court martial offence in earlier generations, we were told, because it took out a healthy fighting man. Was there a recommended alternative? Yes, keeping yourself healthy and clean for the girl back home (as you hoped she was for you) and/or masturbation. The higher risk strategy of finding an 'easy-lay' at the pub appealed to a few.

The whole battalion was then posted as a Demonstration Battalion at Warminster where we learned to use, then show off, new equipment and fighting techniques to visiting personnel from home and abroad. Finding myself as one of 13 officers and 10 men in my SLI company, I wrote to the colonel-in-chief asking if I could be seconded to the British Army in Africa to join the closing stages of empire in Kenya or Sierra Leone. I was promptly posted to Honiton to be a training officer for basic training for electrical and mechanical engineers (REME). I was also encouraged to play tennis in the Army tournaments, and squash because a member of the Army squash team was in my unit. I even played hockey once. When posted to REME in Honiton, Auntie Flo was very useful. I used to go back to Peart in her each month and to church in Exeter and to Sidmouth Tennis Club, albeit with the commanding officer's daughter, with whom I needed to be very careful as I knew she was in love with me. We kept to tennis, conversation and occasionally croquet.

On one occasion I was driving back from Peart in the dark when my headlights fused. Fortunately I had a fog light wired on a separate circuit and so could keep driving. I also had a torch to hold out of the window to show oncoming cars that I was in a car not on a motor bike! I was within 100 yards of the barracks when a police car caught me. They booked me and my case was heard in my absence. I was fined and got a mention in the local press: 'Army Officer fined 10 shillings'. It was the closest I got to a 'mentioned in despatches'!

I did quite well in the Army Tennis Tournament, at Aldershot and so entered the South West Army Tournament. We put our names in the hat for a mixed-doubles partner and I was hoping for a beautiful young female subaltern. In the event I was disappointed to find myself paired with a rather bossy major, 20 years older than me, but she was rather good at tennis and we reached the final! I still have the silver ash tray to prove it.

Another welcome leisure activity at Honiton was to be invited to strawberries and cream tea by the local Officer's Christian Union organiser, Commander Lee Metters and his wife Etta, at Crediton. They held inter-forces meetings with a speaker, every now and then. Little did I know but my future wife also knew the Metters well as her naval father, Captain Ughtred James was a keen OCU member and took his family on OCU camps. We were to meet the Metters and their children again later.

Most of all, the army was a time of continuing to learn how to lead and teach other young men. I was a second lieutenant, the lowest officer rank but the highest attainable as a National Serviceman. With responsibility came interests: of being entrusted with the future of dozens of young men, of teaching these young men leadership and of being able to build an assault course to train potential officers. My job at the REME training battalion at Honiton was to provide basic training for potential officers, and help men pass their War Office Selection Board and progress to officer training – as I had done. As these were the brightest recruits and as most of them had already done an apprenticeship in mechanics, it was an interesting challenge. They were mainly four years older than me; I had to pretend to be more mature than they were. The course covered square-bashing (drill), fitness, self-defence and assault course work, shooting, and quite a lot of classroom work on signals, leadership, battle-craft and map reading. They also did personal hygiene, which included VD films and warnings, from the medical officer. We taught them to shoot on the range with rifles and pistols and automatic Bren and Sten guns. Difficult soldiers had to be disciplined, in the guard room if necessary. The duty officer always carried a sword at night, but there were other techniques to deal with drunken soldiers.

On one occasion when with my platoon on an exercise I demonstrated firing a smoke mortar bomb and set the heather alight on Exmoor at a dry time of year. We soon had four platoons of men and five fire engines trying to put the fire out before it reached a nearby pine forest. At the end of the exercise I realised I had five thunderflashes, each with the explosive power of a grenade and which we used to throw down as pretend enemy fire near our soldiers, in my leg pocket – just as we were in the thick of the fire! Once, after a day on the rifle ranges, I asked my platoon sergeant to check the ammunition for me. It was an officer's job, and he probably wanted to get me into trouble. When it got to the ammo store three rounds were found in one magazine. I was in trouble. I was marched in to the commanding officer who gave me a reprimand! It taught me not to trust those who did not carry the final responsibility.

Apart from that, I think I did quite well for the army and was given a captain's job (on subaltern's pay) for the last six months. The two years compulsorily given to the army was enormously beneficial to me, in growing from a boy to a man and being offered at such a young age, so much opportunity to lead and to teach. Our spiritual development was supposed to be cared for by the chaplaincy at each barracks. Certainly there were compulsory church parades but the chaplains varied from extremely helpful, at Strensall, to positively embarrassing at others. My private prayer time and Bible reading continued and I can only hope that others noticed a difference.

I wrote the following poem in 1958, courtesy of Kipling, about being an instructor:

If you can keep up interest while around you others fail;
If you maintain your keenness and avoid becoming stale;
If you are really certain that you're stuff has gone across;
That the class has got some value and that time was not a loss;
If you can stress the things that count, not teaching all you know;
To make a great impression on the students down below;
If you paraphrase the pamphlet – use 'hole' not 'orifice',
And use the simplest language in a way the class can't miss;
If you're a certain master of the things you have to teach
And keep down to the brass tacks, within the class's reach;
If your diagrams and models can be seen by everyone
And your class when it is finished are sad that it is done,
And if combined with all these things, you're natural and real;
You're a pretty good instructor – in fact almost IDEAL!

I was demobbed in September and was allowed one free rail pass as a farewell perk. I wondered what was the furthest I could go with it, but my geography was a bit defective and I chose Skye and Inverness as my furthest north destinations! It was a memorable short holiday, though, and I stayed with other army and school friends on the way, visiting Glasgow and Edinburgh and Lochs Lomond and Ness. It gave me an appetite for more of beautiful Scotland, which in those days of slow and expensive travel I had never been to before.

6

Oxford University

Before joining the army I was awarded a place at Worcester College, for 1958 when I was demobbed. It was a beautiful old college, the only one with a playing field within its own extensive grounds; there was also a lake and a wallaby, too (which featured on the tie!). I was to read mathematics. Through my teens I had decided that there was only one job I never wanted to do and that was farming, but teaching maths seemed a good idea – there was a great shortage of maths teachers. And yet my experience of teaching in the army, with a new intake of officer potential every 10 weeks, left me thinking I could not could endure the repetitive side of teaching. When I left the army I could see that farming had moved on in the previous few years and much more of it was mechanical and less tedious than before. My father had also managed to combine farming with other activities like the district council and being church warden, playing tennis, and shooting, and had a busy social life. My grandfather had been a justice of the peace (as had my mother, uncle and aunt) as well as chairing the local Frome Agricultural Show. Of my 20 closest male relatives, 18 of them were farmers, all combining it, despite the 24/7 commitment, with some other things fitted in the middle.

So, arriving at Oxford I felt I wanted to farm rather than teach and probably combine it with Christian youth work with an element of teaching. Maths became a means to an end. It was also a shock: I was horrified at how much I had forgotten in two years of army life. Others reading law, history or politics could start again on equal terms with the new school leavers, but I had to go back to basics and build on it. And mathematicians were alarmingly clever. Worse, I discovered that my college did not have another mathematician in it or even a don to talk to. I had to pedal a mile or two on my brother's old hand-painted bike with only one brake, which he had bequeathed me, for a maths conversation! Every now and then I had flashes of insight but mostly I had just plain forgotten all the short cuts to a quick grasp of the problems posed. Time would undoubtedly sort it out but I had lost motivation and was now certain that I was not going to be a teacher. Meanwhile members of my college were doing all sorts of exciting things like flying aircraft, going to posh dinners, playing tennis and squash, going to Christian Union meetings and college bible studies and chapel. I joined in all of these and quite a lot of bottle parties too. The National Servicemen could be picked out because they did not usually get drunk; they had been there and done that and it was a fairly uninteresting way of pouring valuable money down the lavatory. The dimmer 18-year-olds, it seemed, had to do that right of passage to learn. I was also keeping my eyes reverently open for a wife. At bottle parties I felt I was unlikely to find the sort of girl I wanted to marry: heavy drinkers would be high-maintenance. This left CU, maths lectures and introductions. In fact at Oxford I only found two slight possibilities of wife material, though there were lots of very nice people.

At the beginning of the year we all were matriculated into the university, in Latin and gowns, and became full members under its discipline. At university there were supposed to be lots of opportunities for discussion of every possible topic. For the maturer among us this was one of the best parts of college life; we truly discussed all sorts of subjects, including sex, religion and politics, which were all the more interesting as we found ourselves coming from different sections of society and reading different subjects. Worcester College was a complete social mix from very rich to very poor. We were due to have rooms in college for years two and three, but for year one we were out in the town. I was given a room in an annex of the college called The Stables, which was basically a very cold, old garage building divided into rooms with concrete block walls. It had small windows too high to look out of and had the basics of a bed, a chair, a desk, an easy chair and a rug on the floor. An electric fire and a kettle (alternately, or the fuse would blow!) could be plugged in the single socket that also served the bedside light and my Grundfos tape recorder (new technology), for which I owned a dozen or so tapes.

There were five of us in five rooms of the stables and another five in the house next door. We often knocked on each other's door with an agreed 'I just popped in to say…' which was meant to be followed by 'have a cup of coffee' and a chat to relieve the strain of books. My neighbour, John Buchan, was a medic who invited me to the anatomy/post mortem lab one day at my suggestion to see what he was dissecting. There were various stages of dismemberment of male and female bodies lying on the tables. I heard that a professor had once left his body to research like this and fortunately did not realise that by accident his students would be given his body to work on a few weeks later! Most of the bodies that day, however, were of poor, homeless people and those with no known relative. Apart from the shock of seeing dead bodies for the first time, it was a reminder that we take nothing with us when life is over, and have no control over our own disposal!

Some of us also went to Christian Union meetings, led by people who subsequently became vicars or even bishops, but where the speakers were leading Christians of that time. I also went to the OICCU evangelistic sermons on some Sunday nights, taking interested non-Christians with me, as well as to one of the student churches, St. Aldates or St. Ebbes, in the mornings. Occasionally I went to the more formal chapel midweek, of which the chaplain subsequently became a bishop too.

At the end of the year one we had our moderations to pass. My life had been so full. I learnt to fly an aircraft in the University Air Squadron where I was given the rank of acting pilot officer. We flew from RAF Brize Norton in Chipmunks. If I am truthful, I enjoyed it only a little but as I had joined – and with the Cold War joining was much encouraged – I stayed in. There was the added incentive of a big fat pay packet at flying school in the summer (the equivalent of five weeks' farm wages), and I was feeling poor. In fairness my Dad did pay for essential big things and gave me a small allowance, but it was basic. There was a squadron ball, too, with coloured parachutes draped everywhere and free everything on the RAF, to which I could invite a girl (from near Bristol, in fact) to impress. But the regular training days of navigation and rules of the air were time consuming, with occasional flying lessons. The main flying lessons came at the training camp at RAF Jerby, Isle of Man, in the summer.

When camp time arrived, the flying began in earnest. At first I flew behind my instructor, who was in the front cockpit. I had met a girl skiing the previous winter, who lived in Douglas, so I asked him to do some aerobatics over Douglas Bay, to impress her. He duly obliged. One problem – my straps were not tight. So the loop and stall turns were fine, but when it came to a roll, which had no G force to keep me in my seat, I fell upwards, as it were, into the cockpit roof! Slightly embarrassing till we righted again and I regained my composure. I was sure the girl would have been wonderfully impressed, but did not dare get in touch with her in case she thought I fancied her! So it was all a magnificent waste of effort; but fun – well sort of.

I then did lots of practice with my instructor in the back seat. This was easy because I knew he could get me out of trouble. One compulsory exercise was to master the stall; when the engine is throttled right back, at say 10,000 feet, the plane dropped and fell like a spinning leaf. You had to work out which way the horizon was going round and apply full opposite rudder and full throttle to dive at the ground, then ease the stick back to level off. You just hoped there was enough height left to do it all in! Eventually the time came for me to fly on my own. This was seriously scary. I had taken longer than most to get this far, but take off I must. I was strapped to my parachute (for emergency only) which I thought I knew how to operate but with which I had never jumped. Please God, are you paying attention?

I did my pre-runway checks; called the control tower for permission to take off, moved out onto the runway, revved up towards take off revs, started down the runway gathering speed, 80, 100, 120 and pulled the stick back, we have lift off! Amazing; I was flying alone, free as the wind, look at all those little cars and houses down there, bank left and watch the horizon disappear from the right hand window, apply opposite rudder to stop falling, straighten up, try a little dive and recover, check the artificial horizon and air speed and altitude. But hey, I had forgotten; this was the easy bit, I still had to land! Getting down was no problem, but getting down in one piece was different. Could I remember?

After a few more minutes I decided that I needed to try landing. I contacted the control tower and requested permission to land. I knew my instructor was in the tower, watching every move. I flew round to line up with the runway and began my descent; losing height, flaps down, throttle back, keep the throttle so that the runway was coming towards you at the right speed for the descent. I was expecting to touch down opposite the control tower; lower, lower and finally stall the aircraft the last few inches onto the runway; but oops at the last minute I corrected a slight gust of wind with the wrong foot pedal and landed half sideways. My instructor said he nearly had a heart attack, but I had landed and straightened out just in time. Not wonderful, in fact pretty pathetic, but done! It got better from then on, and I did a total of eight hours flying solo at that camp, well on my way to a Private Pilot's License.

My flying had got behind because of so many other things. I played tennis for my college and with the captain of the university team, Malcolm Booth, who was in my college; and squash in the winter. With a lot of effort I might make a blue the next year. I had also been asked to be secretary of my college CU; there was a possibility of being nominated for Vincent's, the sporting dining club and also for my college dining club. There were some social dilemmas to work through, too. Evangelical Christians of the day had a code of conduct, which involved avoiding the seven deadly B's: beer, baccy, Betsy's, betting, booking office, ball-games-on-Sundays, bad language! Most of them had good reasons behind the taboos, but a negative legalism seemed to be a consequence, which I was against. So I was viewed with slight suspicion. I was keen to be part of enjoying life to the full, but avoiding the usual self-mutilating traps, many were falling into. Some of us had been skiing at Christmas, then had planned a tour of east and southern Europe in August. In fact Oxford had been far too important a place to work too hard! There were conversations to be had at college meal times, sorting out the world, and future options to think through. Maths lectures were not really about the exam syllabus; they were for added interest. But I went to most of them because at least I could meet other mathematicians there, and could ask for help. There was a girl mathematician, too, who was one of the two girls I quite liked.

Everything seemed perfectly arranged for year two, with a room lined up in a prime place in college for the next term. But then…disaster, I failed my Maths Moderations. I was invited to work from home and re-sit the next year but on serious reflection I felt it was no longer appropriate to the direction I was heading. I also wanted to get married; it might just be possible to wait two years but three more and then finding a job was out of the question. My pride had been severely dented, but I had had a wonderful year and met some lovely people, including some very fine Christians and I was relieved that I had not spent the whole of every day working and then failed! I had learnt among other things that Oxford undergraduates, outside their specialisation, are as thick as the next person. This was an important lesson. But where was God in my failure? What was he saying? I was being pruned, as Jesus said we would be, to bear more fruit. A potentially good branch was being trimmed off, was it to allow a better one to grow? As I had gone off the idea of teaching Maths farming seemed the right way to go – to be combined with other things. I had also gone off Maths which, 'though I loved the brain exercise of logic and the elegance of the arguments, often seemed a pointless rambling into theoretical irrelevance.

7

Back to the Farm

Marriage was now a major goal. Sex was everywhere. Promiscuity was growing and though not appealing because of its horrific and painful consequences, sex is a legitimate God-given appetite; essential for the organic growth of the race, as well as the emotional health of people. So where was my wife? I went back to live at Peart Farm where my parents had now lived for 10 years. It scarcely seemed like home as I had been away at boarding school for over eight months a year, then away at school camp or on holiday, the army and Oxford. This would be the longest time I had spent with my parents since I was seven. Working for dad as well as with him was not easy. I had been in charge of 30 men in the army, training them for battle. Now here I was as a farm worker, albeit a sort of heir apparent. Dad was only 47 and had had his own farm for just 10 years. He was still developing it and, with the huge opportunities offered by burgeoning engineering, plant breeding and agro-chemical industries, he could see that my brother and I should be farming on our own. He encouraged us to begin looking for a tenancy. We had no family money to buy a farm but dad had been left a house and field by his father and they could be security for a bank loan.

Tennis and girls were the only things keeping me from boredom at this time. These and going to church – partly to look out for the talent and keep God informed of my request for a wife – and going to a local Bible Study group. I was playing tennis for Lansdown Tennis Club in Bath and had a trial for the Somerset county team. I was also in the process of taking out what turned out to be 22 girls in 22 months! But all with great restraint as I didn't want to mess up my future marriage. What was I looking for in a future wife? It definitely was not just a willing sex partner; I had come across those and thought most men knew the difference between a mere girlfriend and a wife. It seemed to me a nightmare to marry someone and then have a bloke come up to you and say, 'Oh I had sex with your wife once'. Such a bloke might well have slept around so what bugs had he picked up and dumped on my girl? Yuk, it didn't bear thinking about. So that left girls who were likely to be virgins because they were resistant to amorous advances, but polite, cheerful, fun to be with, good looking and intelligent enough – but not more intelligent than me! It was also important that we liked the same sort of company and doing many of the same things but not necessarily all of them. At this stage I also wanted a girl who was fit and athletic enough to hold her own in a mixed doubles; I had played tennis with girls who could hold their own in a men's double – but that might be a threat! Tennis fitness would also have been a sign of being a healthy potential mother to my children, and I certainly hoped for children if my previously exposed testicles permitted!

So I looked around at the tennis club where there were two possibilities. My mother was also keen for us to meet as many girls as possible, including daughters of friends, and so arranged lots of tennis parties on our own tennis court. I was not expecting my future wife necessarily to be a Christian. I realised that some very nice girls had not been in places where God was talked about and might not have had the opportunity to decide for or against Jesus. Perhaps this was my job; I had helped at least one girl to faith already but I knew there were risks: I had come across men who had married non-Christians and been badly held back in their Christian walk, whose children had grown up with a mixed message and gone off the rails. So I always explored a girl's spirituality very early on, putting some off. There was also a question of beauty. Some girls were very nice but had the wrong shaped face or appeared 'less attractive' than others. One very beautiful girl I knew seemed mentally disturbed and very tied to her mother. Beauty was not the very top quality. (I now think we are attracted to someone who looks a bit like us, as a sister or brother might look.) I was also hoping for a girl who might want to be a mother. There was a growing dissatisfaction among girls about becoming the traditional model housewife but farmers found it difficult to manage the long hours in a remote farmhouse without a home-maker to look after headquarters when he was out on the farm. So I was keeping my eyes open. It was a very interesting if slightly scary exercise.

This farming year was an important step in my preparation. My father was a very good, indeed a prize-winning farmer, awarded top prize locally for his overall farming. He continued in the very vanguard of technological improvement and was shrewd at investing in equipment which was useful and labour-saving, rather than impressive. The farmers with the shiniest new toys do not necessarily make a profit. He had selected the new Friesian breed of cattle and was making a good living. Cheap building out of concrete blocks and concrete floors, with a corrugated roof suitably attached, was an important skill I picked up from one of my father's longest serving men, Gilbert Carpenter, along with how to put up a fence to contain cattle and pigs. All these skills were to save thousands of pounds in the years ahead. I also learned the principles of making a profit from farming and how to do the bookwork necessary for employing people and keeping accounts.

During the year a farm tenancy cropped up which my brother John, being the oldest of us, tendered for and was short-listed. We were planning to farm together at first. My brother had missed National Service on health grounds but was academically more qualified than I was, having taken his Oxford PPE with a 2.1. He had then spent time on two other, well-run farms and at home. My father was sure John would get this Crown Commission tenancy. While we were waiting my uncle, John Weeks, who was an estate agent, drew our attention to a tenancy available near Bristol – a run-down dairy farm with no buildings and key money of £4,000 to pay (£50,000 today). This would be paid to the tenant who was in dispute with his landlord over repairs not done. Dad thought I should try for this: it was not good value, I wouldn't get it but it would be good practice.

In the event John was second in line for his tenancy and missed it; mine, because the key money was so high, had only one other applicant. The owner, Lord Wraxall, liked the thought of an ex-army officer (being Territorial Army himself and ten years older than me) backed by a father with a high standard of farming, as his tenant and so he offered the tenancy of Moat House Farm, Wraxall to me. It ticked the boxes of being big enough for a decent living, at 250 acres, with a huge if un-modernised house and proximity to Bristol for youth work one day. God seemed to be leading me – especially in the astonishing way that I been awarded a tenancy ahead of my better-qualified and older brother. I could never have fixed that if I had tried. We borrowed £20,000 (£250,000 today) and moved in.

My brother would marry a girl with an inheritance and they bought their own farm in Wiltshire two years later. Meanwhile Moat House Farm was to be the setting for some remarkable happenings, just close enough to Bristol and a sufficient financial burden to keep me there for many years to come.

8

Moat House Farm, near Bristol

My brother and I moved on September 30th, Michaelmas, 1960. It was a lovely day. The sun was shining. We had our own farm. For me it was a dream come true. Moat House Farm was an ancient farmland site, joining four mediaeval farms of which only mounds in the soil remained, and which had been mentioned in Doomsday Book. It consisted of two, 100-acre, fairly stony hill-tops joined by a beautiful, deep loamed valley. There were lots of overgrown hedges and the whole site, as it was surrounded by woodland, was full of wildlife. The farm buildings were little changed in 150 years and were approached down a winding stone track overlooked by banks of gorse and bracken.

The buildings were almost all of stone. There was an old, cobbled stable building with a hayloft over it entered by a split door for man and cart horse. Next door was a food barn with a long driving shaft high on stone buttresses, from which a big old petrol engine drove various worn-out machines – a chaff cutter, a root chopper and a roller mill. They would have been new technology thirty years before. On the other side of the stables was a stone-built lean-to for a tractor. On the opposite side of the yard were two long cow-sheds with a small hay shed between them, a dairy building at its north end and a sunken midden for storing cow manure beside the south end. There were three other lengths of stone buildings which had at various times housed pigs and calves or been used as storage areas. One was an 18th-century corn storage barn, with an endless pulley system for raising and lowering the grain sacks to and from the loft. They all looked quaint and beautiful.

Reality was soon to dawn. A mountain of work and modernisation lay ahead. The farm had received no investment beyond a six bay round topped Dutch barn for hay and a small concreted yard, for 30 years. There were 15 acres of wheat stubble and all the rest of the 250 acres was permanent pasture. The whole farm seemed alive with rabbits. Two heifers and 60 cows were part of the lock-stock-and-barrel purchase of the tenant's property. Deep cow slurry awaited the cows on their exit from the 10-year-old wooden milking bail on its concrete standing. In some places the sloppy manure was so deep it came above the tops of Wellington boots! The farm was served solely by well water, electrically pumped, by the only mains electricity apparatus on the farm to a reservoir. This reservoir water gravitated to seven water troughs and two other taps for the farm cows with a pipe supplying a WC indoors and outdoors and a kitchen and bathroom in the farm-house. At our first testing of the quality of the water, the report came back 'approximates to sewage'. No wonder we and all our visitors had been ill! We de-horned the cows, which most dairy farmers were doing anyway, for our own safety and to stop cows fighting each other, and shut them away from the area round the head of the well. The next water report was Class 1 (the best possible)! The farm had been connected to the electricity grid a few years before, but only the house had been wired, with a small overhead cable to give power to the water-pump. The rest of the farm lights were still run on an old Startomatic system of batteries with a petrol engine. The milking vacuum pump was also run by this petrol engine. The fencing was so bad the farm was virtually divided into only two fields, with very insecure fences round the entire farm boundary. We had only half enough hay for the first winter.

The landlord had promised £1000 (£12,000 today) worth of buildings to suit our needs and despite our having to buy a dairy herd he did not accept the farm was a dairy farm, so would not pay for the sort of plant necessary for a 1960s dairy unit. In his view it was a sheep or beef and cereal farm and one building was enough. But we needed winter housing for the cows we had been forced to buy, a modern milking facility, dung storage or spreading facility, electricity and water in all the places there was none and a totally re-cropped farm using modern plant species. The 17th-century, five-bedroom farmhouse was full of dry rot, death-watch beetle and woodworm, surrounded by a nettle-filled, dry moat with eight dead cats lying in it! Several open fires were meant to heat the farmhouse and there was a Rayburn coal cooker to heat the water. My brother was to be in charge of the dairy herd with a milker we hired to help. He would need half the farm for this, if we applied fertiliser at recommended rates. I didn't like cows, they were big, smelly, 24/7 animals. Instead I was to start an arable section, growing barley and potatoes on the other half of the farm, look after the flock of 200 free-range laying hens we had bought from the previous tenant, start a small pig unit of ten sows and rear a few hundred turkeys for our second Christmas – all of which I knew a bit about from dad's farm. We had a second man to help and a young student, Michael Pike, who lived in the house with us.

Within a few days the foxes had killed all the hens on a dusk raid, just before we had shut them in, because we had been late getting back from farm shopping. So we insulated the old corn loft and installed 200 more hens reared from day-old chicks on a deep-litter basis. There was one memorable night, a few weeks after we started, when it was raining and had been for several days. On this stormy night in October we had a cow called Strawberry due to calve.

We checked on her late that night; she had calved but had milk fever and had 'gone down' in a small stream in our lowest field called Bullocks Bottom, actually named after a former owner, Mr Bullock, not the beast. We struggled to get her on to a buck rake (used for carrying grass) on the back of a tractor to save her life. It was dark, wet, windy, muddy and a very difficult job with ropes by torch-light (the tractor had no lights) on a slippery bank of the stream, trying to get that heavy cow, who wasn't trying to help herself, out and on her feet. Three of us managed it after we had struggled for two hours and I remember thinking afterwards, 'What have I landed myself in? I am now trapped for years in this job. Do I really want it? I think I actually hate it!'

There was no choice, I was deeply in debt to the bank and had a loan from my father. I owed the landlord rent in a few months' time. The army had shown me lots of wet, cold muddy, uncomfortable situations. Lots of people's jobs are very unpleasant at times. So get over yourself, Anthony, and get on with it!

My brother hired an Italian cowman to do the milking six days a week, an operatic tenor called Nicky who sang to the cows. The second man was inherited from my predecessor, a 64-year-old farm worker called Tom. Tom could drive horses but not a tractor so we sat him on a tractor one day and gave him a brief lesson in stop and start. Tractors were very basic in 1960; the hydraulic lift was only on the most recent and one of our two tractors was without it – this was Tom's. He set off through a gateway and I called out to him to stop. 'Woah there!' he shouted at the tractor, but couldn't remember which pedal to press! He tried this several times, so we figured learning to drive a tractor at 64 might not be his gift. He could do most farm hand-work though, like carrying, sweeping, shovelling, hedging, ditching and wheelbarrow work. One day I was driving a tractor and trailer-load of bales through a rather muddy, bumpy rick yard and Tom was sitting on the top. At one point the trailer hit a bump and a few bales slid off, with Tom ending up head first in a muddy puddle. I rushed to help him as he pushed his face up out of the mud, dripping. 'I'm safe!' were his only words. He was not hurt, just not used to loading bales safely either!

On another occasion, Tom had heard I had met a girl who was an artist. 'I were good at droring when I were at school,' he said. 'I once drored a pikcha of my recter when 'e were milking a cew'.

'Where do you think the picture is now, Tom?'

'Oh in a museum, very likely. Tell ye wot. I'll draw ye a pikcha. I'll draw ye a pikcha of my buggeryjar'. So Tom duly went home for lunch and returned with a picture on the back of a cigarette packet of his budgerigar! Tom was with us for a year, but then left with his sister and her daughter, for a council house and retirement. By that time we had modernised the two cottages; and had put into each a hot water tank and a bath with electric immersion heater. When Tom left, the bath was full of logs. He had gone on taking a bath in his tub in front of the log fire, with water heated in the old wood-heated copper.

A short time after we began farming I was cultivating for a barley crop in a sloping field at the edge of the farm, when a man came running up the field towards me. He was looking very worried and shouted at me 'Quick, help me, my mate is stuck under a tractor.' I quickly took out the pin that held the cultivator in place, grabbed a chain that was pulling some harrows behind it and rushed down and across the road on the tractor with the other man running in front of me. When I got there I saw the disaster. A tractor had been pulling a lime spreader up a steep hill, but the grip was insufficient so the tractor had slid backwards and down over a bank. The spreader had turned the tractor over, trapping its driver under the mudguard. I quickly attached the chain to the other wheel and pulled the tractor off the driver. But it was too late. He was dead. He was a young man of 21, engaged to be married quite soon. Ten or so years later the M5 motorway would be built over this steep hillside.

9

Finding a Wife

STARTING FARMING AT THE AGES OF 23 AND 22 WAS AN EXCITING ADVENTURE FOR my brother and me. However, I was still very much in need of a wife so began praying in earnest: 'Lord, please lead me to a wife'. A girl from one of our cottages, Tom's niece Briar Rose, came twice a week to do the washing up, which we stored at the end of a long table, and to sweep up and clean the worst of our untidinesses. With such a name was she destined to become a Bush? Competent and nice as she was, neither my brother nor I thought so. Within a few weeks I was invited on a skiing party organised by Anros Neill (later Bewes) and her Christian friends. Somehow I felt sure that this skiing trip was going to lead me to my wife. Three long and busy months passed, while we sorted out the buildings, some fencing, some cow stalls for the fresh calving cows and other essentials, then I was off to Victoria Station, London and the Austrian snow. It took about 20 minutes of moving down the train among our skiing party to spot Christina. I had become quite quick at eliminating even very nice girls in my selection of the one who was to be the only one for me forever. I was looking for a beautiful girl, but that was certainly not all, my wife also needed to be strong enough mentally and morally to help me, not give in to me. It would also be nice if she could be the right social background for my mother to be happy, though I would be happy to fight that one.

In the event Christina ticked all the boxes of the above and the much longer wish-list I had been thinking through for the previous years. She was to me the most beautiful girl I had ever met, with a beauty that also lay beneath the skin and in her smile. She was bright but not too intellectual, a strong prayerful Christian whose faith was lived out totally in her life. Importantly, she had done the sort of things that showed her as a potentially brilliant mother – she was a trained teacher, had helped bring up much younger brothers, and knew lots about children. As a bonus she also looked low-maintenance, because she was wearing her father's old skiing clothes! I was particularly wary of highly-painted girls who smoked or drank a lot. She was none of those. She was well dressed and unconventional in a bright pink hand-knitted jumper and well- combed, long hair. And she was clearly very female, slim, curvaceous, pony-tailed, smiley, sexy, sparkly and at the first long look she even looked as though she might like me too. On our third day I told her I thought we would probably get married one day, which she dismissed as holiday feelings and talk. I was impressed at her sanity about my emotional outburst! But our getting to know each other was to face challenges. Not the least of these was that she lived and worked in London, 130 miles from me when cars averaged 30 mph on a good day. She was also a town girl, surrounded by bustle and activity and noise.

Back in England in the following months, between visits we spoke on the telephone. Christina had a beautiful voice, which I loved and looked forward to hearing. She taught art at St. Paul's Girls' Prep School in Hammersmith and, as she worked a five-day week to my six, it was usually she who travelled – coming to Bristol by train where I met her at the station. She only stayed overnight at the farm if my brother or someone else was also there, otherwise she was kindly invited to stay with the Rector, Lawrence Fussell, and his family. She was put to some early tests of being a farmer's wife, holding small pigs while I castrated them! Pigs always make a huge noise until they are returned to the ground but, despite that and the gory bits, Christina seemed unfazed. She fed the hens, collected and washed the eggs; at hay-making she learnt how to drive the tractor while bales were loaded by hand on to a trailer. Her cooking was slightly better than mine, but mine was almost non-existent consisting of boiled and fried eggs and omelettes (we produced eggs and milk so they were cheap). On one occasion I was planning on working instead of going to church, which she was very sharp to disapprove of, almost to the point of her walking out. We went to church instead! I was nuts about her and couldn't wait to see her again. We kissed enough to know we were passionate about each other, but drew firm boundaries about going further. Each of us needed to decide whether we were the right person for the other, for life and sex would get in the way of discovering the other's true character. Neither of us knew we would definitely marry each other until the day we did so because, after all, accidents happen even the day before a wedding and we were both keen to be a virgin at marriage, for whoever we were to marry.

I knew at some point I needed to introduce Christina to my parents. I was a bit nervous about this as my mother usually said of any girl I took there 'What do you see in her, darling?' However Christina disarmed my mother completely. It probably helped that her father was a naval captain, her grandfather was an admiral and her great-grandfather was Lord Shuttleworth from Gawthorpe Hall, now a National Trust house, which satisfied my mother's social aspirations! Christina had also sat and played the piano for a few minutes, which might have seemed a bit forward, but also seemed cultured. Anyway in a very short time my mother whispered in my ear 'Darling, where did you find her? She is like a piece of Dresden China!' I was relieved at this acclamation, because marriage does inevitably join two families. Parental approval is also reassuring; they sometimes see things their children are blind to.

I also needed to meet Christina's friends and parents. Her parents lived in Northwood with three of their six children, a vivacious 16-year -old daughter Jill and two not yet teenage but musical sons, Alan and Ronald. Their other two children Michael and Penelope were already married and living at a distance. I had been told to look at a girl's mother to see what she would look like in 25 years time. Christina's mother was reassuringly good looking and domesticated, despite being the daughter of an admiral; and her father was a kind, sensible and also very musical, CBE decorated, ex-naval captain of an aircraft carrier, now hostels manager in London. They seemed to approve of our liaison. We next went to Ashburnham House to meet some posh friends of Christina's, who were on a working weekend to help Rev John Bickersteth, the new young owner, begin to turn it into a conference centre. This was to be the first of many visits to Ashburnham as it grew in fame and popularity. I very much approved of her posh, yes, but very welcoming friends. I seemed to be accepted too.

In the summer holidays Christina decided to go to France to be an au pair with a French family and test the strength of our affection. I was a bit upset about this, but life on the farm was very busy. We had silage making to finish, hay making, pigs to fatten and sell, harvest to prepare for then finish, and all the while the daily milking and feeding of cows and feeding of pigs and laying hens. Christina rang me one evening. Our phone system was not what it is today. Our telephone number was Nailsea 606, the Post Office was Nailsea 1, the neighbouring school was Nailsea 8; all reflecting the order the telephone authority had reached the house with the phone. We made all calls through an operator. When Christina rang me, the operator told her I was not at home, but was at the local pub! There was actually an NFU meeting there that night and I had just made a call from the pub; the operator must have recognised my voice. So the operator put Christina through to the pub and I was very surprised to speak to her, but very pleased, too! But I was still upset that she had decided to go abroad, and we had cooled off somewhat.

There was also one girl on my list of 22 that I had not completely ruled out of the marriage stakes, so I went to see her. The months with Christina had made the decision very clear, however, and I never saw the other girl again. When Christina came back I made no contact for several weeks till one day I went to the Dairy Show at Earls Court, in October, which happened to be next door to the flat Christina shared with three other girls. She had been invited out by an American who later became a famous theologian, but who wanted a plaster cast of her face. In the event of my renewed interest she dumped him and we were on again. Meanwhile my brother had become engaged to marry his Pam, in late December, in her family's impressive stately home in Clonmel, Tipperary, Ireland, to which we were all invited. Christina initially refused to go to the wedding. It occurred to me to ask her if she would go if we were engaged. She said she might. So that December 1st, 1961, Christina arrived for the weekend at Bristol Temple Meads Station and I proposed to her. We took a joint photo in the photo-booth to celebrate our engagement, to be married in February; much to the annoyance of her new Secondary Modern school in Islington, who had just hired her.

We went to my brother's wedding as an engaged couple. When my brother and Pam arrived home it was to a new house our landlord had found for them a mile from the farm. They were now looking for a new farm to take over themselves.

10

Married at Last

Christina and I were married at Chelsea Old Church on February 24th 1962. She had left a suitcase at a family friend's house next to the church, to obtain official residence for marriage there. She had been at art college in Chelsea and liked the church and area. It was sunny on our wedding day and it also snowed. Most people remember it as the coldest wedding they ever went to, but I was just excited to get it over, scary though the speech performance was. I and my best man Jeremy Murray, an Oxford friend who had been very encouraging of me to marry Christina, stayed at the Savoy the night before to symbolise the end of luxurious singleness. Chicken winglets were the only thing on the dinner menu we could afford (the ends you usually throw away!). I rang Christina from the phone beside the bath!

Our wedding was traditional, meaningful and with lots of our friends and relatives present. The vicar said marriage was like a garden and it needed tending and weeding. I took note because our garden was badly neglected. We promised to love each other till death us do part, for better, for worse, for richer, for poorer, in sickness and in health. We vowed it then and for ever. The reception was 50 yards and a short, very cold walk away, at Crosby Hall. All went well, including the speeches. The family friend toasting the bride and groom had been flattering of each of us, adding that part of Christina's qualities she gained from her father and part from her mother; then repeated the compliment for me. So I thanked him for his speech, the ability to make which he had acquired partly from his father and partly from his mother! Everyone laughed. I thanked everyone for their presence and their presents. We borrowed my best man's car to go away in, after leaving through a milking smocked guard-of-honour making an arch-way of borrowed hay forks and miscellaneous agricultural tools; one of which was accidentally dropped on my father-in-law's bald head!

Having waited 23 years I couldn't wait to get into bed with my new wife. Christina had booked a hotel for five hours, between the reception and the 2.00am flight to Torremolinos, our honeymoon destination. We had decided marriage needed consummating before departure. I had read in a book that the best way to help a virgin lose her virginity was to lay her gently backwards over the edge of the bed. Whatever actually was to happen, I apologised that I might not be any good at it. Christina has said many times that this was the most wonderfully reassuring thing for me to say, as she knew then that I was uncontaminated by other girls and likely to be faithful, because I could control myself. As we expected, our first mutual nudity and sex was enormously exciting if, surprisingly, a little painful. It was low on the Richter scale; there was evidence and proof, if it were needed, of sexual purity and we had done it! We belonged to each other! The honeymoon could only get better. It did.

I had discovered, through courtship, what wonderful things breasts are. The proverb (5:19) says 'let hers be the breasts that fill you with delight'. Now to see them as well as hold them was certainly delightful. I had not fully realised how unique to mankind the added fat in breasts (and buttocks too, in fact) are. No ape or any other creature has bosoms like this, they merely swell up with milk for a few weeks; so clearly they are part of God's special design for mankind, and delight in marriage. Who wants to go off to work if you can play with breasts all day?

And little did we realise that 45 years later brain science would confirm the sense of belonging we experienced at first sex (see chapter 20). It confirms that sex is designed for life-long marriage, not just for procreation, but for closeness, for excitement and for life. The wait had been long and difficult; but the longer the wait, the greater the trust in each other's fidelity we could expect.

Our honeymoon trip was by air to Gibraltar, then a coach took perhaps 20 couples along the south coast of Spain dropping us off along the way. It appeared every one of those couples was having problems. All of them had someone in tears, some of the time. It reminded us what a traumatic event it is to commit to another totally and for life, or perhaps some of them were not committed but wished they were, or perhaps had been living together and thought marriage would somehow be bliss, only to find the same arguments upset them, or the girl was pregnant and they felt they had to get married, and one or both resented it. We were so glad we felt more passionate about each other than ever. A honeymoon, free of interference from in-laws and other well-wishers was very necessary to work on emotional and loving intimacy, which are vital to make techniques of sex meaningful in this exciting adventure. To move from a lifetime of saying no to sex, to one of yes with great frequency and intensity is a big adjustment. It needs time and patience. Perhaps it was for some also a time for moving on from past problems, and in our case a time to talk through all those things that lay ahead and to learn how to pray together. We read through our marriage service again, too.

11

Two into One, Living as Married

We returned from honeymoon to find my mother and her cleaning lady had come 30 miles to try and make our house look habitable for Christina. Just before we had left I had knocked down a wall and opened up a hatch to make an old dairy into a kitchen joined to our living room. There was rubble everywhere and my mother imagined Christina leaving me in floods of tears and going back to London! Christina was built of sterner stuff. We found two old ceramic sinks, including one that calves were drinking from, put them on concrete blocks with water taps into them and two old wooden draining boards beside them. Christina proudly rang her mother to say she had that luxurious and rare convenience of the early '60s, double sinks and drainers! We already had a cheap electric cooker I had bought from our predecessor. I spent what was left of my Post Office savings, after the engagement and wedding rings, on a washing machine. Dirty farm clothes covered in cow and pig dung were more than I thought Christina should have to endure by washing them by hand. I also hoped she would become a full-time homemaker and farmer's wife. The phone rang often and there were things to buy, and sell, for the farm by car, so for her to do a teaching job would have been difficult. After about a month I shocked Christina (but also pleased her) by throwing away the contraceptives, with the result that, as our first child and eldest daughter observed a few years later, 'Mummy, you couldn't wait to have me, could you?' Eleven months after our wedding Lizzie arrived.

One day a few months after Christina arrived, and when she was resting in the afternoon in early pregnancy, there was a knock on the door. Christina crept to the window to look out and saw someone in a peaked cap, who she took to be the gas man. She decided she was too tired to face him. Later she found the visiting card of Lady Wraxall (mother of our landlord) in our front porch! Clearly the gas man was actually the chauffeur who had been sent to knock at the door to announce her Ladyship's arrival! So sadly we missed her visit. But a few days later Lord Wraxall called to see me to congratulate me for getting married, and asked where I had met my wife. On hearing Christina was an art teacher from London he said 'She's not one of those girls with long hair and trousers is she?' Whereupon Christina promptly appeared with long hair and trousers! He was slightly embarrassed and mentioned in the course of the conversation that in the country people found water from the rain water butt was very good for washing hair ! I drew the line at this, knowing what else came from roofs into the butt! But no doubt Lord Wraxall was impressed to discover Christina's great-grandfather was Lord Shuttleworth, a former MP like his own father.

Each Sunday we went to the local parish church, All Saints, Wraxall, where I was soon asked to read Bible readings. Previously Lord Wraxall had read most of them. We, but mainly Christina, started a Bible study-group which moved around from house to house, including once to Watercress Farm, the home of the Vowles family. This became a well-known landmark when, a few days before the son Guy Vowles and his wife Valerie were due to move into it, a fire broke out while they were on honeymoon. An electric blanket had caught fire. It was a shell for the next 45 years because Lord Wraxall, the landlord, was not adequately insured. Meanwhile the church had not been decorated for a generation; some of us formed a working party to paint the inside walls.

I know Christina also found country living difficult, and often lonely. It was quite an event to go out and leave the farm. We only had one car, which could be urgently needed to rush for a spare plumbing, a tractor part or for medication for a sick cow. Farming could not be put off till tomorrow; the cow might die, the good weather turn to rain, the milking not get done by 8.00am, which it was contracted for. Although I came in at every breakfast time, lunch time and tea time, the working days were often long; from 5.30am to 9.00pm and for six days a week, or occasionally seven. On the other hand there was nice countryside all around us, and sometimes Christina could walk to find me on a tractor or bring a very occasional picnic. More often she was trying to build a civilised nest out of our old, damp, worm-eaten, house and with very little money to spend. She wallpapered the kitchen with magazine pages, nailed her old art college nude paintings to the pan-tiled attic roof (to keep the snow out), redecorated most of the house with cheap wallpaper, learnt how to shop for incredibly cheap food, including free second-hand bags of duck-bread from the baker from which we took the best before feeding to the ducks and chickens! She bought bacon bits rather than rashers, she made all our own curtains and furniture covers, and she found all our second-hand furniture from auctions. In thirty years we never acquired new furniture, apart from a double bed which we were given. One person's throw out sale room furniture is another person's antique! We put on more sweaters instead of heating the house. Christina had given up her teaching career, but probably saved a wage by being a specialist homemaker cheaply. For me it was wonderful to know she was usually there; I was always delighted to see her and so very pleased we were married. I still am.

12

New Church in Bristol

SOON AFTER STARTING MARRIED LIFE TOGETHER WE INVITED MY SCHOOL FRIEND Malcolm Widdecombe to lunch, from his theological college, Tyndale Hall in Bristol. I had visited him at the college, once, when I had been in the army and in uniform. Now, he helped me winch down a tree that was standing on our lawn and threatening to fall on the house. A few weeks later, in June 1962, he was ordained and moved to Holy Trinity Church in Old Market, Bristol. Christina suggested we go to his ordination, at which a monk spoke suggesting people should support and befriend their vicar – not leave them on their own. A few weeks later Malcolm wrote to me asking if I would consider being the youth leader at their church, as the present man was leaving. He quoted a dream of St. Paul's and wrote: 'I feel like the man of Macedonia saying "come over and help us"'. I was moved by this request and felt God was calling me to do it. Our local church, All Saints Wraxall, had just held a PCC election and not voted for me, so I asked the local vicar, Lawrence Fussell, if he would send us as missionaries to Bristol. 'Certainly, my boy!' He prayed for us and we were duly 'sent' to Bristol from Wraxall.

The dusty old church hall where the youth club was, in Peel Street, has long since disappeared. It was in an area of east Bristol that had escaped bombing and was full of small, terraced houses of poor working folk and families. The youth club was fun and popular, with 50 or so youngsters coming each Friday night. Many of the members also went to the church, Holy Trinity, Old Market, on a Sunday. In September 1963 Christina (five months' pregnant) and I started as leaders on Friday nights.We introduced more activities and organised the painting of some of the rooms and front door, which had been the same since before the Second World War. The young people loved it and the club grew. Unfortunately the older church folk didn't like the new paint and refused to pay for it. However, a saintly old Christian stepped in and covered the paint cost. Malcolm, as curate, invited all the Christians in the club to meet at his flat on a Sunday night after church. Some very secular club members did not like this and blamed me for allowing a split in the club – a split which I had not even noticed. A year later they narrowly passed a vote of no confidence in me as club leader. The vicar decided to split the club in two and asked if I would lead the Christian young people at a hall belonging to a large church with small numbers, also in the parish and under threat of closure: St. Philip and St. Jacob, known as Pip 'n' Jay.

The new hall was smaller and also in need of a lot of work but one of the Church Wardens there, Eddy Beaver, was especially encouraging to us all. In December 1964 22 of us began the Pip 'n' Jay Youth Club on Tuesday and Friday evenings. We began attending the Church on Sunday evenings. Bruce and Sheila McKay, whose marriage we had attended at Holy Trinity, were key people in the club at this point and they have been leaders in the church ever since. We promptly began work on the hall, in which, as at Holy Trinity, we wanted to make a badminton court. Bruce led the work enthusiastically but injured himself treading on a nail with his rubber-soled shoe. The following spring a piece of rubber appeared at the top of his foot, under the skin! We made the badminton court by demolishing an entrance porch and using every available inch of the large room – altering the stage so that it was retractable over half its depth. No one objected.

The club quickly grew to 120 members with lots of activities and a 'half-time-holy-chat' to help newcomers hear a little of the gospel. Some of the church members at Pip 'n' Jay were very excited at the increase in numbers (the rest left!) and appealed to the bishop to appoint Malcolm Widdecombe, for his second curacy, as Curate under another vicar, and put off the closure. The bishop, Oliver Tomkins, was reluctant because he wanted to send Malcolm to Rodbourne Cheney, near Swindon. I can remember walking into his study in my wellies on my way back from Chippenham Market to explain to him what a brilliant thing it would be for the C. of E. to have new life in an old church in a central position, rather than it becoming a museum to 'visionless ecclesiastics'. When he was still reluctant I wrote to him, as from Screwtape, congratulating him on the closure idea; he replied from Wormwood! Eventually he agreed to appoint Malcolm, doing his second curacy under Roy Henderson, vicar of St. Luke's, Barton Hill, to continue as priest in charge for a trial period – to see if we could get numbers up to 150 in the evening and have £500 for repairs put aside as a joint target.

Bristol has been known as the city of churches and St. Philip and St. Jacob Church had previously been involved in a Christian awakening. The gifted actor, newly converted and ordained George Whitefield, aged 25, was invited to preach one Sunday in 1739 at St. Mary Redcliffe, St. Werburgh's and St. Philip and St. Jacob. The latter was full and a thousand standing in the churchyard. The church hierarchy was alarmed and George was discouraged from preaching in church again! He took this as God's diversion and began in the open air where, with his huge voice, he preached to 20,000 at a time at Hanham Mount and to the miners at Kingswood. Hundreds came to faith in Christ, whereupon he asked John Wesley to come and help. Methodism thus began in Bristol, with those not reached by the C. of E. The New Room was followed by many other Methodist churches. The Baptists had already been active, their preachers commemorated by the Light at Hanham Mount and have continued ever since. The Brethren produced George Muller in the 19th century, who with his wife started huge orphanages and preached in several Brethren churches. In 1905 the Great Awakening that saw 50,000 coming to faith in Wales the previous year, arrived in Bristol. Thousands thronged the streets of Bedminster in a similar finding of faith. The city saw intense disagreements, too, with the Quakers' persecution of the 1680s, and later the strongly held views on both sides over the slave trade of which Bristol was a centre, and the Bristol Riots of 1831 over the rejection of the repeal of the Corn Laws.

Now it was our generation's turn and it was the Pip 'n' Jay Youth Club that grew first. It proceeded to win the Richard Hearn trophy two years running for the best improved club in Bristol. A few youngsters were coming to faith. One had offered for the Ministry. Many of us were attending Pip 'n' Jay Church on Sunday evenings and the attendance and finance targets had been met in less than two years. But Malcolm felt the church, not the club, should be the focus of everyone's efforts so persuaded the PCC to require club members to compulsorily attend church. I was unwilling to enforce this as I felt that, though Malcolm's preaching was good, the services were too boring for all club members to listen to. I would then have to turn them away from club. The PCC insisted. The young people did not go to church and I had to refuse them admission to the club – and so the club had to close. I was very upset as we had put so much into the club for four and a half years and had made so many really good contacts. A whole area of Bristol had had some good Christian influence. I felt like packing it all in – but surely God had to be in this somewhere. It was one of many examples of God pruning me to help make more fruit.

With hindsight it was probably the right decision to close the club: the survival of Pip 'n' Jay needed the bishop's targets to be more than just met and numbers to grow. But we still had to persuade Malcolm to sit looser to C. of E. traditions. Like many conscientious vicars at that time he had been doing all the leading and reading and preaching at all services, but others needed to join in to make services more inclusive and interesting. He agreed. A group of youngsters wanted to start a guitar and drum group to sing at evening services, the service we concentrated on. The Salvation Army had such a group, called the Joystrings. I bought a second-hand drum kit and two guitars and the Pip 'n' Jay Band started, practicing in the Church Hall. We even did some gigs at other places.

Malcolm concentrated on the evening service and was good at keeping us focused on Jesus, at emphasising our need to pray both privately and together as a group. He was also good at preaching for a verdict, so people felt they could bring friends who were interested in God to church. And he invited some good guest preachers.

Christina felt the church needed a book stall. Malcolm didn't like the idea at first, feeling the Bible was the book to concentrate on, but was soon persuaded. Then others began it, with discounted books from a local Christian book shop. There was no Sunday School at morning service, so no one came who had children. In fact almost no one came! The lowest morning attendance I remember, was three, Malcolm, myself and one other! Christina was taking our children to Wraxall church on Sunday mornings, and helping teach them herself. There was only one vestry room at Pip 'n' Jay, so only a crèche was possible. I decided to buy a chicken shed, to put in the side aisle, which could house a small class. Christina then felt she could bring our children to morning service, so after a brief resistance, Malcolm agreed to the Sunday School idea and with one other family as well as ours, the Sunday School began. We called the chicken shed Pip's Cabin, and soon converted the bottom of the tower into a third room. The Reader family's children, recently back from Uganda became, with our girls, the core of the children's work, and others soon joined us.

When the youth club closed I started Action Group. This was a small group of keen Christians who went out every Friday night to pubs and coffee bars, to find some of the 7,000 young people who came to the centre of Bristol for entertainment. We began with questionnaires and found 80% of that generation, the baby boomers born between 1948-52, had been to Sunday School but stopped when they reached 12, bored with church. Almost all believed in God. We then started conversations by inviting people to come to church. We had some wonderful chats, talking through people's uncertainties about God and questions of moral behaviour. At one point it seemed we were each having significant conversations with about 20 young people every night. I led this for the next four and a half years, just as I had the youth club for four and a half years. I never missed a Friday, except Christmas Day. Several of my young colleagues became vicars or missionaries. People we spoke to received Christ in the discos and pubs we visited. Others came to church, where all Pip 'n' Jay members were expected to invite friends and neighbours and where they found a friendly reception, lively music and some interesting and relevant preaching and teaching by Malcolm and others from the pulpit. Under Malcolm's leadership the church grew far beyond its original targets set by the bishop. More rooms were built, then a new wing of rooms, but most importantly thousands of pounds were given away each year for Christian work outside the parish, far more than on the church itself.

13

Expanding the Farm

MEANWHILE, THE FARM WAS GROWING. MY BROTHER AND HIS WIFE MOVED away to their own farm, while we quickly gave up pigs and laying hens in favour of more cows, plus 20 acres of potatoes and 100 acres of cereals. Cows would never have been my farm animal of choice, they were a 24/7 commitment, big and rather dangerous, produced 50 kg of dung and 10 gallons of urine each per day, often all over you, they were very smelly, they got lame or died extremely easily, and were very expensive to replace! But I had been compelled to buy the herd to get the tenancy, the place was geared up for them by now and it was the most profitable part of farming to be in at that time, probably because it was the most difficult. Moreover, I was seriously in debt to the bank. Sometimes you just had to forget your preferences, like no doubt thousands of factory and office workers who chose the job because it was available. The days of specialisation were coming. To be a modern farmer with a good income we had to expand our herd, which meant milking more cows in an acceptable milking time of 2 to 2½ hours, twice a day. We had bought a metal milking bail in 1962 with four milking units and eight cow standings, to milk 80 cows. We put this in a fixed position with vacuum and milk lines to a permanent, self-build dairy made from concrete blocks and with water, electricity and drainage. All of this was designed for good cow-flow from a collecting yard, through the milking bail to a dispersal yard, designed for easy hand-squeegeeing into a tractor-emptied dung tank. There was a loose box attached to hold cows for artificial insemination, which had just begun in a big way as a method of quickly improving cow genetics. Some farmers refused new technology and kept to old breeds and natural breeding but they quickly lost ground in a fast-moving industry. I became the relief milker for the next decade and a half, which involved one day a week, annual holiday and bank holiday cover. I worked on Christmas Day for 33 of my 35 years of dairy farming. It is more stressful for a manager to be the relief milker, but it kept me in touch with the vital needs of expansion and helped me see what buildings and machines were vital and what were not. Successful dairy farming is about attention to the details of diet, milk production, health and repeatedly getting in-calf of each cow, and it is a 24/7 commitment to prevent things going rapidly downhill. The very best quality grass needed to be on offer, field by field, balanced to the daily output of milk by concentrate feeds. Silage had to be made at the right growth stage of the grass and in exactly the right time for best dry silage to ensure top winter yields. When the weather is right we work as long as necessary. For tracking vital fertility issues every cow had a pin on a moving rotating calendar, so that she was put to bull the right day after calving, or else had to see the vet. She was then 'dried off' ready for her next calf on the right day, for a two month rest in a different herd. There were also herds of calves and young cows preparing to join the herd by two-years-old. All these things were also an opportunity to introduce a number of young people to farming and to milking by having them work with me. We all worked a six-day week, which included half a day overtime.

A nine-inch gas main was laid through the farm in 1965, from Avonmouth to Weston-super-Mare. It was a terrible nuisance because it cut through the entire farm and was very poorly fenced by the contractors with what I referred to at the time as two strands of barbed washing line. We had to retrieve cattle from both Portbury and Tickenham, each two miles away in opposite directions. As tenant I was entitled to compensation but only for the cost of the damage and inconvenience we could prove. The landlord had the wayleave money.

The vet came one day to treat a sick cow which was lying in the yard and could not get up. The vet was Norman Page; he was a good and conscientious young vet but I knew he was also an atheist. After his diagnosis it was fairly clear that he was less than certain what her problem was but gave her the best drug injection he could think of. I said, unusually for me as I had never said it before, 'Norman, do you mind if we pray for this cow?' He was paid to stand there; without waiting for an answer I took off my hat, laid my hands on the cow and asked God to make her better. We parted without much more happening. The outcome was that the cow died, but the vet became a Christian! I met Norman a few months later and had heard that he was now a Christian so asked him how it had happened. He replied 'It all began when you prayed for the cow that day.'

We bought our first new tractor in 1969, it cost £860. Up to then we had bought second-hand tractors of various makes; Ferguson, Ford, or David Brown, but we always favoured one dealer, Gallop's of Backwell, whose yard is now a housing estate. Early tractors often had radiator leaks, so expensive antifreeze was not always used. This meant we had to remember to drain the radiator, then fill it again next day. We occasionally forgot and lost two very old pre-war Ford's in two different years, to cracked engine blocks in the frosty nights that seemed frequent in the '60s.

Then the arrival of the hydraulic lift on tractors changed manual farming forever. Back-end loaders arrived first, as a way of cleaning out huge volumes of three-feet deep covered yards of cow bedding, which had been freshly covered in straw each day, at the end of the winter in a very short time. This dung was dropped into tractor-drawn dung spreaders that threw out the manure in wide strips across the field before ploughing. Then came front-end loaders and equipment for them, such as forks and buckets and hay-bale lifting gadgets. Tractor-mounted dung scrapers pushed cow manure into concrete pits in the ground; then tractor-driven augers lifted it into dung spreaders. This sped up the drudgery of all the centuries before us, of brushing cow manure and shovelling it by hand into trailers for further hand spreading with pitch forks on the fields. Field work in the '60s was done on the above noisy, slow, fairly unreliable tractors with no cabs. The right clothes and hat were essential. Old tractors like ours pulled implements that were dragged rather than lifted and took a long time to plough with a two furrow plough, or cultivate with a six-foot wide cultivating tool of discs or cultivator and chain harrows. Bales and sacks were loaded and unloaded onto trailers and into barns by hand. Keen-eyed inventors had all sorts of ideas to ease farmers' routines: tractors grew and acquired fiendishly noisy safety cabs – quiet cabs came next. Field implements got wider and stronger but many of these new ideas just would not work on our stony ground. The fittest survived!

We built more buildings. In 1970 we built a new state-of-the-art, low-jar, herringbone milking parlour with a pit for the milker to stand in to reach cows' udders without bending. This was one of the first in the county designed to milk 120 cows at a time when our herd of 100 was one of the biggest in the county. We put up a silage barn and cow cubicles and dug a slurry lagoon! All these carried a Farm Improvement Grant and, as two of us did all the building work ourselves, cost us very little, mainly simple block work and asbestos sheets. We discovered how to bolt together 14-feet steel stanchions and beams with wood purlins while hanging precariously to ladders, then pouring concrete round the hand-dug foundations and finally nailing the pre-cut asbestos sheets to the purlins.

My cowman John Pickard gave me his notice three times in 1970 because he did not like the new parlour. Each time I tried to find out what he didn't like so that we could put it right. One problem was that I was a foot taller than he was and I had built the parlour so that I had enough headroom. This raised the cows so high John could hardly reach them. John was also an excellent carpenter and made himself some duck-boards to stand on. He had a skin allergy to penicillin, which we occasionally used to treat cows with mastitis. We needed to find long rubber gloves to keep his hands from all water and all cow contact. I was also upset that the best advice at the time was wrong about the depth of the pit that was needed for the milker to stand in. All the jars were designed to fit in this space. As a result we had to have a step for the cows to climb every milking. We endured this for 25 years until we sold the herd. It was one of the many things which has made me sceptical of architects and other experts and since then I have always discussed every building project in detail with my staff, to check that we are all happy about its exact position and how it should work. I have been surprised at how few zoo keepers are consulted about their buildings and how many expensive enclosures are very difficult to use.

I had been doing nearly all the office work myself for the first few years but soon it became obvious that some of the book-keeping and wages should probably be done by a secretary. Two girls, one after the other, helped me in the late '60s but in 1971 a young lady who I had met as the vet's secretary/receptionist started to gather a round of farmers to help out for one day every fortnight – dealing with the accounts, wages and VAT. Joan Rodel was a single mother who had been divorced from her South African husband. She was hugely reassuring, reliable, accurate and easy to work with. Little did I know she would be doing more and more office and accountancy work for us for the next 40 years!

One day, to my great surprise Rees Cash, my landlord's agent with whom I got on very well and played tennis with, came to me with the offer of the 200-acre farm tenancy to Charlton Farm, right next door to us. This was an amazing offer that one would normally leap at but I was expanding the cow herd and the thin soil in which we grew cereals was not yielding well – next door might be no better. The West Country was rainier than further east, so harvest was often wet and difficult. However, the main reason for my lack of enthusiasm was that, having prayed about it, I realised I would have to stop doing all the youth work and church growing and other things off the farm to make the extra land pay. Reluctantly I turned it down. A few years later in 1972 another farm came up for sale of about 100 acres on our other border. I let this go too, but made a mental note that Jesus had promised that those who gave up land for the sake of His kingdom would be given it in this life and in the one to come. Could this happen to us, or was heaven alone to be the place of reward?

I had been elected as Branch Chairman of the NFU in 1967, then as Chairman of the NFU's Group of Branches, under reorganisation. This coincided with an NFU Market boycott due to low prices, when I had to persuade farmers to stay away from all our local cattle markets. This boycott had such total support both locally and nationally that the government was frightened; and passed a law preventing the NFU from taking industrial action ever again, with the penalty of a gigantic fine. Then I found that my successor as NFU Group Chairman had done a shady deal with another member so was not elected to take my place; I was asked to serve an unprecedented second year. The government listened to farmers' complaints about prices, so the late '60s farming recession became a good time for farmers for a few years in the '70s. Most farmers voted Conservative, but usually benefited more from a Labour government. My personal preference would always have been to pick and choose some policies of each party. We never told anyone which our preference was, but I did hear from other farmers that 'Anthony was a nice chap but a bit left wing!'

We were using all the new technology we could to become more intensive and productive. The country needed food, the world needed food. Feeling that my staff and I were all doing a good job I entered the farm for the North Somerset Best Farm Competition and we won it in 1973, were runners up in '74 and won it again in '75. Although this earned us a little local kudos, others grumbled that we won too often. It was also a lot of extra work ensuring the farm was not only at prize-winning productivity (sensible, because this was the same as profit) but also had tidy hedges, good fences and gates and a minimum of muddles and mess. This was a lot of hard work and not necessarily profitable. As I had too many other things happening, we pulled out of the competition. I had also been politically active with the County Branch of the NFU for some years and was elected to be NFU County Chair for 1978, with the extra demands on my time.

14

Lizzie, Born in the Snow

Our children were born in the 1960s. Each one was born of passion and eagerly wanted. Lizzie was born in the snowiest winter of our farming career, only slightly kinder than the all-time cold of 1947, when I was at school.

It started snowing on Boxing Day 1962, when Christina was heavily pregnant and a week from due, and we were returning from visiting my parents. We wondered whether our little Morris Minor would get up the snow covered Clarken Combe Hill from Bristol to Failand then home. We just managed it, but that was our last journey out of the farm by car for many days. By December 31st most roads were partially blocked and snow was drifting to the height of the hedges. The milk lorry, on which we depended to take our milk, had chains on its wheels and we carried the milk on a farm trailer in 10 churns a day, up the farm road. The driver exchanged full churns for empty ones at the milk stand by the roadside gate. On January 1st I found a bulldozer on the main road and paid him £5 to clear our farm road, which was covered to the height of half the hedge. At 10pm Christina, who, with characteristic forethought had just finished printing her baby arrival cards, began to feel contractions. We called for an ambulance and I met it at the top of the farm road. The paramedics decided the road was too risky to drive down as the snow was already a foot thick. Instead they walked along it carrying a stretcher for Christina. In the event, Christina walked slowly through the deep and still-falling snow to the ambulance. I said goodbye to her. It was a bleak, cold and snowy walk back to a lonely house and I was so sad not to be near her at the birth. The following morning more snow had fallen and drifted and the farm road and its hedge had disappeared. I was thankful Christina was in safe hands at the Clevedon Maternity Hospital.

At 5.00am our new milking bail parlour was half full of snow, but the water was running, so we managed to finish the milking by 9am. I then had the challenge of getting the 10 churns on a trailer, the 600 yards up to the road, while the staff fed, bedded down and cleaned out the cattle. The driveway was impassable. Fore-end loaders had not been invented. Hand shovels and a two-wheel drive tractor meant that I could make progress by going across the fields, cutting a fence or two, but I finally got stuck 100 yards from the road. I unhitched the trailer and drove back for a bale sledge, on which we gathered eight hay bales in a pile. I put two churns on this to pull them to the gate behind the tractor, but got stuck. This was one of the two occasions in my farming life when I cried. What was I to do? Why pray when you can worry? I had forgotten to bring God in on this, but promptly did so. Despair changed to hope. By digging at the tractor wheels and surveying a different route I managed to move the sledge and reach the gate. I returned another four times for the other churns, just in time for the milk lorry, 2½ hours after I began. The next day there was a frost so we drove in old wheel-marks and the trailer was not a problem again. A few days later we were driving the trailer on top of five feet of snow up the line of the farm road and above hedge height, which we did for the next three months till the thaw in mid March.

There was a further problem, my worst nightmare was fulfilled. The cowman my brother had hired suddenly decided he did not like the mud in wet November and said one morning 'I am not coming to work this afternoon'. He was required to give a week's notice but his hatred of mud and wet overcame his care about the cows or the rest of us. Cows need milking twice a day; I milked them that afternoon but in the coming days there were turkeys to kill and pluck and distribute to butchers. Then the cowman would not move from our cottage. I had to find a relief milker for turkey-plucking time and over Christmas. He was John Muer, an excellent man who lived in the farmhouse with us for those weeks. I found another permanent cowman but the outgoing cowman needed an eviction to get to the top of the council house list. So I had to evict him. This all had to happen the day after Christina and Lizzie returned from hospital. The cowman's family furniture was in the snow. 'Oh Mr Bush you are so cruel, how could you do this?' 'Because you need a council house and my new cowman needs the home that you are in but have no right to!' This was one of my darker days but John Pickard, who moved in with his wife Pat and two children Druscilla and Neville, started work two days later and stayed with me for 26 years.

I visited our perfect little Lizzie for the first time on January 3rd, the day after her birth (when she was born at 2.10am) on a tractor; having pulled a car out of a ditch and with a pint of milk for Christina. Cars were slithering along some roads, while other minor roads remained blocked for weeks. I visited Christina and Lizzie with a pint of milk every day till January 11th, then the ambulance brought them home and we walked down the farm road. We pulled our car up the field with a tractor and left it near the road for a few weeks. My mother-in-law came down by train and I managed to fetch her in our car, to help Christina look after our precious Lizzie in our cold house. We had managed to make some rooms warm with a combination of log, coal and electric fires. The snow had drifted into our attic through the pan tiles to a depth of 2 feet in places, so when this started to melt due to the heat below, the snow dripped through the ceilings, bringing one ceiling down and running down the electric light cables. So I had to cut a hole and build a trap door into the loft space and fill bags with snow to carry away before it melted! The temperature dropped to its coldest –12.5°C – a week after Christina and Lizzie arrived home but it was wonderful to be together.

15

Annie, by Home Delivery

ANNIE'S ARRIVAL WAS AT HOME, IN THE BEDROOM THAT WAS TO BE HERS FOR the next two decades, on May 7th 1964. She waited till after I had finished the morning milking on relief milking day. This was the first human birth I had attended, even though I had helped dozens of cows to calve and pigs to farrow. I knew the mess would be similar. I came in to find Christina just beginning contractions and the midwife on her way. Christina was lying on the bed taking big lung-fulls from the gas-and-air machine and I was holding her hand. The nurse went downstairs to sterilise the instruments in the pressure cooker and arrived back, giggling, with a bundle of plastic. 'I hope we are not going to need these' she said. The container had melted round the instruments due to the extra pressure cooker heat; the instruments would need cutting out to get at them. Then she paused and said 'Oh! I have forgotten to put my knickers on!' Slightly too much information for me at the time, but it seemed ironic that the baby was coming fast and Christina had not yet taken her knickers off! As I looked at Christina's vulva and the size of the baby's head I thought how in the world is that going to get through there? It did, and no wonder it hurts. Did God warn us in *Genesis* that human birth was going to be painful, to keep us humble? Or prayerful? The astonishing thing is that millions of women every year are so heroic on behalf of the fragile life they are carrying.

Annie arrived and we then realised that the impressive and gleaming gas and air machine had not been switched on at all! I was convinced Annie was going to be a boy, to make our family traditional and one of each. As she so clearly wasn't, it took me a few moments to re-think our family planning. As every dad falls in love with his daughters, this meant I now had two lovely girls to adore. But it also meant that our family was not yet complete; surely a boy was to come? We had taken Lizzie to youth club when she was six months old, where she was doted over by all the teenage girls. We now had two girls to show off and I remember carrying them proudly, one on each arm, to the church crèche each Sunday. The girls also taught me how to be a dad. Not only was I allowed to learn how to hug babies but Christina helped me to discipline when necessary. It is true that little girls can beguile their dad rather easily into getting their own way; I had to discover how to say no, but lovingly. For me the girls were essential preparation for having sons in the family too. The next 20 years were some of the best years of our lives; full of stress from having expensive extra members of the family, demanding in time and energy, but so worth while to see young lives developing with such promise.

16

Our Eagerly Awaited Sons

Our next child should have been born in June 1966 but Christina fell over a turkey perch one evening in early December and had a miscarriage. Christina coped well with the sadness; and I wondered if we would discover a divine reason for it. When June arrived, we found ourselves involved in a relay of a Billy Graham Crusade from London to a Bristol bus station into which had been put many hundreds of seats. We had been trained as counsellors and Christina was especially involved and helped a lady to faith, who became a close friend. I remember being impressed that the Mission had been organised by a group of ordinary people with a GP, David Cunningham, as chairman.

Caspar was born mid-morning on February 28th, 1968, narrowly missing being a leap-year baby. The midwife had again come. This time she was worried about something, and had left the room to ring the doctor as Caspar arrived. I was used to calf deliveries, but was taken by surprise at his speed of arrival: his cord was round his neck and I had to stop him landing on the bed and choking himself. The midwife heard my shouts and returned in a hurry and released the cord; all was well. I didn't inquire about her knickers. Christina was fully prepared; the gas and air had worked perfectly. But Caspar was slightly the wrong shade of pink, so I took him and Christina to Southmead Hospital for observation. While we were there Christina was given a white coat by a young man, so that she could feed her baby. He suggested she did it up at the back, as usual, until Christina pointed out to him that, actually, her breasts were on her front. He was rather embarrassed; hardly anyone was breast-feeding babies at that time, most used bottles. Surprisingly, even 25 years' later, our daughter Annie was told by her midwife that she was only the second mum in her area of Liverpool in 25 years who had breast fed. Things have moved on in the last decade or two.

Lawrence was born in Bristol Maternity hospital on September 24th 1969. He was nearly two weeks late and we were harvesting potatoes at the time. Christina walked up to the potato field, so I brought her back on the bumpy potato trailer sitting on the sacks. In lifting her down I dropped her onto her feet the last few inches deliberately. A few hours later she began contractions! Two home deliveries were considered enough, so we went to Bristol Maternity Hospital in Redland and prepared, with Christina in strong contractions. 'Keep walking Christina' she had been advised by our missionary friends from Thailand, Ian and Rachel Bevington, who were visiting us at the time. Rachel was a midwife who delivered babies from Thai mothers who were in a standing position. I told the midwife that I thought the baby was about to come and that Christina had delivered our last two very quickly; she was the other side of the room and sounded a little irritated when I said the baby was coming. When I called loudly 'It's come!' she believed me and came rushing over. With Caspar and Larry our family was complete. We were so blessed to have children in pairs, to be friends while they were growing up, and close enough altogether that they all knew and liked each other. Our four children were born in a span of six years and nine months.

17

Raising a Family

Despite our busy lives on the farm and in church in Bristol and with the NFU, our children were central to all we did. I was anxious not to be helping other people's delinquents, while creating our own! So I knew I was needed every day as a father. Christina was a fantastic mum, so I felt I was mainly in a supporting role. She decided most things inside the home, while I did the same outside. But as she got up in the night to deal with crying babies (she did after all have the boobs to do it with) I decided to bring everyone an early morning drink. So my day always began, and still does, with a time of Bible reading and prayer, followed at the appropriate time, with my waking each of the children up with a hearty greeting and a tray of drinks. This happened every day of their childhood, unless I was relief milking or away from home. It was a bit disappointing to hear in their later teens 'dad, do you mind if we don't have drinks any more?' I wondered how long they had endured by best efforts through sheer politeness! We also said good night to each of them, in their own bedrooms each night. Christina used to complain that I made them too excited when they were almost asleep, so was not trusted to do this often.

Our children of course also added stress to our marriage. When they finally left home I felt I got a wife back! They inevitably took huge chunks of time and attention from each of us; that is what family life is about. But we also needed privacy and installed a lock on our bedroom door early on. It was on Christina's and my total togetherness that their security depended. When I came back from being away, if they were all present, I would kiss Christina first, then the children. We usually had our disagreements privately, but sometimes they became public; on one occasion we were obviously in a mood with each other, so one of the children said 'why don't you two kiss and make up? Or if you can't do that, at least shake hands!' Which made us all laugh. We were strict about their behaviour and being kind and forgiving. Occasionally Christina put them all out of the room, or out into the garden, locked the door and said they could not come in until they were nice. They would knock on the door and say 'we are nice now', and everyone laughed. Sometimes everyone had to say sorry in turn.

We sent our children to private day school, partly because I was trapped into it by my father with the best of motives. He said he would lend, and then give me, part of the farm start-up capital if I invested the interest in an educational insurance policy for private education. Our local state schools were not very good at that time and we had to drive the children to a school of any sort, as we were so far from a town, or even the village. Christina enjoyed driving the children and listening to their stories and each day's happenings. It took many hours of her time, especially when, for a short time, they were going to four different schools, as well as attending after-school activities of music, drama, sport and dancing. As we did not smoke, drink or gamble – and didn't begin investing in a pension till the children had left school and rarely took more than a week for a family holiday – we could generate just enough funds for a private education provided the farm was more successful than the average.

We did not own a TV until our children went to school but we did a lot of entertaining of our children's friends. Every year we had a birthday party for each of them on the farm. The parties were very popular and usually involved getting dirty and/or wet from playing in our moat. One year Annie invited all her form out in fancy dress, and half an hour from the time parents were due to arrive, we could not see any of them! We despatched a girl on horseback, on the children's pony and walked ourselves to search for them. The girls were all sitting in the sunshine, in a hay field 200 yards from the house making daisy chains, oblivious of the time!

We had bought our girls a pony one year with ambitions that they would enjoy it more than I had. It was however, time consuming and not a great success. It must have learnt to lift the gate string with its teeth as one night it walked out of its field and up the drive on to the main road. The first I knew about it was when a policeman knocked on the door at one in the morning and said there was a dead horse on the road, was it ours? I rushed up with a tractor, to find that it was. I dragged its body off the road with a chain. Three cars were written off but fortunately no one was injured. To our great relief the NFU insurance policy covered us, but that was the end of horses. We then built a cattle grid, to stop a cow ever causing such grief.

We also built a cheap tennis court out of two loads of tarmac and a friendly council pavement-layer, around which we put up some chain link fencing. When the gas main was installed across the farm in 1965, the gas company was due to reinstate a stone wall that they had removed. The old wall was in the wrong place anyway and I suggested that, instead of rebuilding it, they cut a space for a tennis court. We then levelled the ground and laid the tarmac surface. At one point we counted up that we had made facilities for 13 different sports on the farm.

A major source of fun for us all was our ancient moat, for which the farm was named Moat House Farm. As soon as we could afford to we had dug 300 tons of sediment out of it with a dragline and bucket, restored 100 feet of collapsed wall and put a dam across, that was one inch lower than the cellar floor to avoid possible flooding. It quickly filled with water as it had probably originally been built to trap natural drainage from the whole valley in which the farmhouse was built, as well as collect water from the spring that fed it. We found two areas of cobblestones, one at each end of the moat, which were clearly there as cattle standings for drinking. As soon as the moat was restored we bought a small dingy and some paddles, as the moat was not wide enough for oars. We also bought life-jackets as we now had a serious hazard for small children to fall in. But it was huge fun for children's parties. One year all 36 boys of Caspar's form came to his birthday party and 35 of them ended up wet and muddy. We recommended a change of clothes on the birthday invitations!

Over the years I built various apparatus; a rope swing from a perfectly placed branch of a convenient 200-year old ash tree was easy, until one morning ten years later the tree fell down into the moat. I replaced this with an A frame and rope and platforms and a postman's walk, balance beam and a 150-feet zip line over the widest part. Little did I realise that 20 years later some much more elaborate equipment was to follow, but none was as exciting as being over water. Probably the majority of our younger visitors got wet! Especially was this so when we added inflatable tractor tyres in various highly unstable combinations and had weed-bomb fights with the algae that grew in profusion some years!

Most years too, we managed to take a short holiday away, if only for one week. One year we went to Canada to stay with Christina's two sisters, Penelope at Toronto and Jill at Montreal, and their families. We hired a large estate car to take four adults and eight children to travel between them, visit their churches, and visit the Niagara Falls, other tourist sites and some farms and farm research facilities; including trying to plough with two oxen. Another year we went to Denmark and stayed with the lovely Hartzner family of whom their Kim had spent time on our farm. After helping with building work, Kim had memorably written in our visitors' book 'The Vikings concreted the English!' We stayed in Copenhagen for Rene and Ruth's 25th wedding anniversary, and were fascinated to see how they did it; with a dawn awakening of the couple onto their balcony for breakfast, concluding with a six-hour party of food, dancing, more food, and ten speeches, including one from me! We visited ten European countries in ten days on this trip, including what seemed like a daring crossing of no-man's land into East Germany, before turning back.

Another year we had not had time to book a holiday so we hired the last boat available on the Norfolk broads, which happened to be one of the biggest; but we could only afford it for three days. The girls each and memorably caught their first fish with their very cheap fishing lines. The boys loved steering the boat with their sailors caps on. Ten years later we hired a long boat on a canal for a week; another year we were lent a croft in Scotland half a mile from the nearest road and had a brilliant holiday that included having sheep's wool and small frogs coming down the water pipes, from the spring into the bath! We often, and certainly on these last two holidays, took one other non-family friend to help us stay nice to each other. One year I suddenly found that I could get away because harvest was finished, so with a brief prayer, we drove off. When we got to the motorway we said 'shall we go left or right?' We eventually found ourselves driving along a Welsh road and the car in front of us stopped us. Out got some really good friends who were now working in Wales, and asked us to stay with them that night!

My parents owned a flat in Kingswear; so for several years we spent a week having some coastal adventures near Dartmouth. This included, one year, a scary adventure by inflatable boat out to sea (some of us without life jackets), but only 200 yards from shore and on a pretty calm day, before turning round and hurrying back! Daddy was always pushing the boundaries a little, so our girls often repeated the saying 'girls are born as wise old women; boys stay boys forever'. But the children spent most of their school holidays happily on the farm; sometimes with invited friends. In their teens they and their friends helped load all the straw bales at harvest each year and drove them back to the buildings where we all unloaded them. Some loads reached the farm very slowly, because they collapsed and had to be rebuilt! Occasionally a tractor was driven into an electricity pylon or hedge. But it was a good way for each of the children to learn to drive a tractor; and was very useful to me and seemed fun for the children once they were 14 and could legally drive a tractor. They can all claim to be proper farmer's sons and daughters.

At one point, as I became busier with off-the-farm responsibilities my standard of parenting slipped. When we went to Canada as a family in 1972 to visit Christina's sisters and their families we also went to the Peoples Church Toronto, where a young James Dobson was speaking about fatherhood. He recited the following newly written poem/song by Sandy and Harry Chapin, which moved me profoundly. I then shared it with hundreds of people in talks over many years:

My child arrived just the other day,
He came to the world in the usual way.
But there were planes to catch, and bills to pay.
He learned to walk while I was away.
And he was talking 'fore I knew it, and as he grew,
He'd say, 'I'm gonna be like you, Dad.
You know I'm gonna be like you.'
And the cat's in the cradle and the silver spoon,
Little boy blue and the man in the moon.
'When you coming home, Dad?' 'I don't know when,
But we'll get together then.
You know we'll have a good time then.'
My son turned ten just the other day.
He said, 'Thanks for the ball, Dad, come on let's play.
Can you teach me to throw?' I said, 'Not today,
I got a lot to do.' He said, 'That's ok.'
And he walked away, but his smile never dimmed,
Said, 'I'm gonna be like him, yeah.
You know I'm gonna be like him.'
And the cat's in the cradle and the silver spoon,

Little boy blue and the man in the moon.
'When you coming home, Dad?' 'I don't know when,
But we'll get together then.
You know we'll have a good time then.'
Well, he came from college just the other day,
So much like a man I just had to say,
'Son, I'm proud of you. Can you sit for a while?'
He shook his head, and he said with a smile,
'What I'd really like, Dad is to borrow the car keys.
See you later. Can I have them please?'
And the cat's in the cradle and the silver spoon,
Little boy blue and the man in the moon.
'When you coming home, son?' 'I don't know when,
But we'll get together then, Dad.
You know we'll have a good time then.'
I've long since retired and my son's moved away.
I called him up just the other day.
I said, 'I'd like to see you if you don't mind.'
He said, 'I'd love to, dad, if I could find the time.
You see, my new job's a hassle, and the kid's got the flu,
But it's sure nice talking to you, Dad.
It's been sure nice talking to you.'
And as I hung up the phone, it occurred to me,
He'd grown up just like me.
My boy was just like me.
And the cat's in the cradle and the silver spoon,
Little boy blue and the man in the moon.
'When you coming home, son?' 'I don't know when,
But we'll get together then, Dad.
You know we'll have a good time then.'

As someone said 'We learn from history that we never learn from history'. Six years later, I had got too busy again. Larry was about 10 and I must have been spending rather too much time working on the farm and on the NFU and church. He said to Christina one day 'Where is dad? Away again? I feel I hardly know the bloke.' I was so shocked when I heard this reminder of Harry Chapin's song, that I resolved I must spend more time with them, and so I started taking the boys to watch Bristol City Football Club. For several years we watched as many home matches as we could from the family enclosure. We watched them progress through the leagues to the 1st Division, as the Premiership was then called. Then one day it was clear Larry was in danger of being over-fathered, and he wanted to start other things. Their childhood soon passed. Because I was working from home I felt close to all our children most of the time.

One of the best things we did was to spend a long time over meals, chatting round the table long after we had finished eating, about every imaginable subject, earthy, personal, wildlife, politics, we covered most things. We always began our main meal, but often other meals too, by thanking God for it and including other issues very briefly in that 10 to 20 second prayer. We also spent some years reading briefly from the Bible or from a helpful book as an attempt at 'family prayers'. But Christina had the main input into their spiritual lives by praying and reading with each of the children at bed time. And of course we always went to church as a family on Sunday, where really good Sunday school teachers and youth leaders had some very good teaching for them. We were conscious that God has no grandchildren; each of them had to and indeed did, find Jesus for themselves. I also spent lots of time playing every imaginable board and card game with them, while Christina cooked meals. This was an opportunity to teach them how to be competitive, but also how to lose well, without getting in a stew; it was only a game. It was very sad to have them all eventually leave home; we left each of their rooms untouched for a long time.

We had encouraged them all to be independent and to go to university far away if they wanted. They chose Durham, Sheffield, Newcastle and Oxford. We kept in touch weekly but did not expect them to come home till the holidays. During these last years of our children's schooling and university we offered to look after two lovely daughters of a school friend, Ian Bevington, and his wife Rachel. They were lifelong missionaries in Thailand; initially doing agriculture and medical care, later translation and church planting and broadcasting, with an Overseas Missionary Fellowship. Their girls, Carol and Dawn both went to boarding school at Dean Close in Cheltenham and during some short holidays and for days-out in term time, we drove to Cheltenham to bring them back to us for the day to be part of our family. We loved them dearly and they kept our home filled for a few more years. Then, finally, we had an empty nest; but Christina and I did importantly have each other

18

General Synod

In 1967 I had been asked by Roy Henderson our former vicar and friend, if I would consider standing for Church Assembly, the governing parliament of the Church of England. There was a vacancy at a by-election for Bristol Diocese. As the C. of E. seemed stuck in the past and irrelevant to most young people, I agreed, to see if I could make any difference. I stood on a pro-youth basis, visited lots of the voters personally and was elected early in 1968. Aged 29, I was the youngest member at that time. The first thing I did in London was to table a private members motion that church services should be in modern English. I was relieved to see that this caused quite a stir! Enough members signed it and it was soon debated, on November 4th 1968.

I began my maiden speech:

> Mr Chairman, most heartily I beseech thee, as is my bounden duty, that thou shouldst in thy manifold care and governance, vouchsafe to me, that, indicting only of a good matter in concord, I might present as is meet, this motion to thee.
>
> For the benefit of those in the gallery, this is a meaty motion about the manifold on the concord.
>
> I am not trying to get a cheap laugh out of ridiculing sacred language, but just pointing out in intensive form, what newcomers to our church services have to put up with, before they can even begin to come to terms with God...

I then went on to point out that 50% of the world was under 21 and only 8% of Bristol was going to church, even once a month, despite 80% having once been to Sunday school. Language was one of the problems.

There was a short lively debate during which lots spoke in favour, but two ancient speakers objected and said they thought modern language 'tinkles', and, 'you who..' prayers were no way to address God! Sadly the motion was voted not to be decided on at that point. A classic addition to my list of heroic failure attempts! However two years later the Liturgical Commission mentioned the debate as a reason they had decided to bring forward forms of service in modern English for Church services. I was also asked to sit on two of the Revision Committees of services – the Marriage Service; and Morning and

Evening Prayer.

General Synod meets three times a year and is the Church of England's parliament, usually having some Members of Parliament among its number. It is responsible for making church law, reorganising dioceses, parishes, employees, finances and property; for discussing many moral matters which, as the Established Church, its members feel require a Church view. Relationships with other denominations and with worldwide Anglicanism are debated. I tried to attend at least part of every Synod, trying to avoid the criticism of turning up only to speak! But lay members often found it difficult to spare the time so inevitably it came out of my three weeks' holiday a year, usually only leaving one week for the family. There were also mountains of paper to look through as each debate involved a preparation document.

I was a member of Church Assembly and the subsequent General Synod for 17½ years, trying to persuade the church hierarchy not to take itself too seriously, to join in inter-church stuff more, to remember that we also existed for the benefit of young people and other outsiders, to remain Jesus-focused and evangelistic, and to faithfully prepare people for lifelong marriage. I wrote and read out this poem in one debate on inter-communion, dedicated to my broad-church bishop, Oliver Tomkins:

I am the very model of the modern Ecumenical,
With information Baptist, Presbyterian and Methodical;
About the Congregationals I am teeming with a lot of news;
I chat with Peebs and Catholics and I share all their doctrinal views.
I take my dose of Voice, which with the Tablet, keeps me regular
I keep all evangellyfish from spikes and make them secular;
I view with tolerant benignity, within the bounds of dignity,
those matters charismatical I fear may prove scismatical.
I'm truly in the middle, between High and Evangelical,
An Anglican and model of the modern Ecumenical.

It met with enthusiastic applause!

While on General Synod I had some intriguing opportunities. Bishop John Robinson was there, who had just written the book *Honest to God* doubting the virgin birth and resurrection of Jesus and seemingly, too, the closeness of God in our daily lives. I met him in the lobby and asked him if we could have a chat. He said 'come with me while I go to be photographed at my publisher'. I got in his car; he drove. He asked me to look out for a parking meter, so I said I usually prayed that God would lead me to one. Just then he stopped to turn right and was promptly hit in the back of his car by another. I immediately spotted an empty meter space just ahead in the side road and we pulled into it. To me it seemed an interesting little sequence of events; he saw I believed God was with us all the time, even answering prayers for parking meters. He may have needed bumping to the same conclusion!

In 1971 a famous pornography trial took place and there were three editors of *Oz* magazine on trial for producing an obscene cartoon of Rupert Bear. I decided to ask an ordinand friend, Peter Hallett to come to London with me during Synod and we would take Richard Neville, and the other two editors out to lunch and try to help them. One of the editors came with a colleague and we had a really good discussion about a wide range of subjects including porn and God. They gave up their magazine later that year. The next Synod I found myself on the floor of the York General Synod swapping pornography with the Archbishop of York, Donald Coggan, who was also a member of the House of Lords. I had been sent a copy of *Oz* and he had been sent *The Little Red School Book*. The latter originated in Danish social dissent. It was written in the format and size of the Chinese leader, Mao's *Little Red Book*; but encouraged children to take drugs and alcohol and abandon sexual restraint. I wanted to contact the main UK distributor. I arranged to meet him in a café in London and bought him a coffee and we had a good conversation. He was a former Baptist, who had fallen away. I felt so much could be done if only we could get together with people with different ideas and talk issues through. This certainly happened on Synod at that time, where there were quite strong divisions in the church. I tried to talk things through with opponents, which may have been my biggest contribution. Public debates are not always the best way of changing hearts and minds, though sometimes they can be informative and useful, and a way of coming to a vote and a decision.

I had tried quite hard to persuade Synod to be more generous with Clergy salaries. I used the similarity with agricultural shepherds, who also worked long hours and lived in tied cottages and often needed a vehicle at work. I spoke in two debates on this. I am pleased to say salaries rose. Little did I realise that both my daughters were to later become vicars' wives! Marriage was another subject I was concerned about, and spoke about in Synod. The C. of E. had and still does have a lot of opportunity to prepare people for good marriage, help people with marriage difficulties and to send good or bad signals to weak marriages, by both its marriage preparation and its remarriage policy.

The church was called to show it believed in lifelong marriage; it was one of the key and revolutionary teachings of Jesus, at a time when divorce was widespread. He taught that adultery was forgivable, but it was seriously wrong.

Jesus' aim seemed to be for repaired and loving lifelong marriage. If hearts were not hard, this was the way to a contented old age. I tried to persuade my colleagues to take all marriage preparation opportunities seriously, including after the wedding, to resist remarrying divorcees as if nothing had gone wrong, because there might well be hurting former spouses and children looking on, even if at a distance. Remarriage in church therefore was not appropriate, most especially where a former spouse was left alone and that marriage was theoretically mendable. On the other hand every second or more marriage needed God's blessing, so we needed to come humbly for that blessing, when a second marriage had taken place, asking for forgiveness and fresh help to make this marriage work really well, especially with the complexities of a former one to deal with.

The St. Paul's riots in Bristol took place in April 1980. As a member of General Synod I was very concerned about the deteriorating inter-racial feelings around the country and in several cities. The Bristol police had raided the infamous Black and White Café, known for its drugs and drink. As they carried out several crates of illegal booze one of the police joked with the onlookers 'we're going to have a good time at the station tonight'. It was not, however, taken as a joke, but as the final act of a police force that was perceived to be corrupt and too heavy handed. The subsequent riots that broke out injured 19 police and did lots of damage. As a Synod member and as an assistant minister of Pip 'n' Jay, nearby, I felt I should go with a friend to visit the café. My friend was late and I went inside to see if he was there. Having entered I didn't think I should leave straight away so I went to the bar and asked for a coffee. I spoke to a man with a leg in plaster and he replied sharply in a Jamaican accent 'Move away from me, then'.

I was so surprised I asked 'I beg your pardon?'

'I said move away from me then', he replied again.

I moved away from him! I then noticed that I was the only white face in the café, and most were Rastafarians smoking ganga. I could also feel what each of them must have felt sometimes in all-white company – as if everyone hated me! And this was from just one remark and from being the only person with one coloured skin in a group of another colour. My friend then arrived and we joined a group of Rastas to discuss lots of things, including Emperor Haille Selasse, their God incarnate figure, because he was supposed to be descended from Solomon and the Queen of Sheba. We also discussed the riots and social grievances. They were very friendly towards us. I used this event on Synod, and in discussion with the local police.

A short while later, a friend and policeman at Pip 'n' Jay, Billy Burns, was shot in the face at point blank range while bravely arresting an armed robber in a car while he himself was unarmed. He had broken the driver's window with his truncheon and grabbed the driver, but had not seen Stephen Corsa-Acqua, an armed and dangerous wanted criminal, lying behind the front seat. Billy was lifted off the floor by the impact of the shot and landed unconscious on the ground. His colleague saved his life by flicking his tongue back in place as it was suffocating him. I was phoned about it because Malcolm, his vicar, was away at the time and I was the best he had for an Assistant Minister. I called at Trinity Road Police Station, to ask to which hospital Billy had been taken. A *Daily Mail* reporter was there asking the same question, so he asked if he could come with me. On the way he enquired about Billy and how I knew him. I said I was going to pray for him and I hoped Billy would not have his faith in God shaken through this incident. He waited for me to come out from the ward as journalists were not allowed in.

I found Billy, with his wife Maggie at his bedside. Although Billy could scarcely speak because of his injury, he was clearly thinking his life had been spared by a miracle. The bullet had hit the exact line of five teeth, each with enamel stronger than steel. The teeth had all been shot off by the bullet, which stopped at his neck bone. The injury was bad but certainly nowhere near fatal. I told him I felt God had saved him for very important things and that he would 'stand before kings' to talk about it. The *Mail* reporter later asked me if Billy had lost his faith. I told him about his miraculous escape, and thankfulness for a spared life. Billy indeed became famous for this amazing event. Within a year Billy and Maggie sent Stephen Corsa-Acqua a friendly Christmas card. Twenty years later when Stephen was about to be released from prison, a meeting was arranged between Billy and Stephen to demonstrate Billy's forgiveness. Stephen was profoundly impressed and on his release began a project with Billy, going to schools to talk about prison and policing. A couple of years after the shooting, Billy and I were to be linked in another important job, as I will reveal in chapter 27.

My final attempt at reforming the C. of E. was to table a Private Members' Motion requesting that Canon Law be changed to allow (but not compel) informal dress to be worn by vicars and readers who led C. of E. services. It was forbidden to wear anything other than clerical robes. Whatever we decided about reorganising church structures and finances, the public face of the church was usually at its services. Out-of-date clothing looked like an out-of-date organisation. The motion received about 85 signatures at each Synod at which I re-tabled it, but never enough to bring it high enough up the list for a debate. Most people preferred their fancy dress. Many churches do not conduct services in robes now. There is more flexibility than in the C. of E. of the '70s and '80s. When I had first been elected it was the canonical (legal) duty of each vicar to ensure services were in old-fashioned language and dress. Yet still, 42 years later, it is to the shame of some congregations that some churches remain as alien to the outside world as they did then. A few people can keep the majority out by maintaining an exclusive club in the name of religion. They will have to answer for it one day.

One tiny contribution that I made to modernising Church government was at my first appearance at a debate. I arrived feeling hot and took my jacket off and sat down. I then had to be introduced as the only new member of the Assembly who had been elected at a bye-election, so had to stand and acknowledge the polite applause. I realised at that moment that I was the only person out of perhaps 500 present, who was not wearing a jacket. A senior member in front of me turned round disapprovingly and murmured 'are you feeling hot?' Which I affirmed. 17 years later I noted one day that not one person was wearing a jacket in the summer sessions!

I decided in 1985 that I would not stand for the General Synod election. I felt it was now more another person's job than mine. While there are important things to be done in the C. of E. to use all the opportunities of being the Established Church in every parish, there were even more important things to be done in trying to help the 90% of people outside any church, who were hurting and lost and had no idea what life was about beyond trying to be as happy as possible.

19

Growing Church
A Dead Body, Down-and-Outs and Healing

Pip 'n' Jay meanwhile, having achieved its targets by 1969 was in a place in the city centre where down-and-outs gathered. Malcolm felt we ought to start a soup run to help these homeless folk receive a little love and reassurance that they were not forgotten either by us or by God. We might be able to persuade some of them to stop sleeping rough and book in to the Church Army or Salvation Army hostels, or the government hostel further out of town. But we needed to find these rough sleepers. I offered to lead a little group to go on our first search one night, so that afternoon and on the way back from farm shopping in Bristol, I was passing a derelict house in Hotwells, and thought I would see if anyone was in it. I pushed the door, but it did not open more than a few inches. I made a mental note to return that night. When we did and climbed in by a different route, we found a dead body stopping the door from opening! We went to the police straight away, who looked at us suspiciously. They rang Malcolm at his home for confirmation that we were doing official work, then let us go. The press took up the story and Pip 'n' Jay's down and out work took off with publicity and donations! Soup runs continued for several years and were taken over by others.

Under Malcolm's prayerful leadership Pip 'n' Jay has also been a centre for renewal for the wider church. Some time before all this began, in 1965, I first heard of charismatic renewal and speaking in tongues when my tax inspector called at the farm. I noticed he had a Christian symbol as a badge; then he mentioned a speaker at Buckingham Baptist Church that night called Dennis Clarke, who was speaking on being filled with God's Holy Spirit. After work that evening I went to the meeting and felt God challenging me to go deeper with Him. I came home and next evening after work I went and sat on the new nine-inch gas pipe that was being installed across the farm and prayed to be filled with the Spirit. I was immediately reminded that God wants to fill clean vessels and there were three people who might well hold a legitimate grudge against me. The first was the cowman and his family whom I had evicted into the snow. I might justify it, but I felt God telling me to apologise. So I wrote and had a forgiving letter back. There were two others who I had said things to that I regretted; so I wrote two more letters! A year later Christina and I went to a Christian holiday week where John and Diana Collins, later to begin such formative things at Holy Trinity Brompton, were speaking on the same subject. They prayed for us both to receive God's renewal. A significant experience followed.

When I later saw Malcolm I mentioned all this to him, who had also heard about this renewal. He humbly knelt down and asked me to pray for him. Malcolm's ministry was full of times of his own seeking God for more, then helping others to find that too. His small number of, if obvious, weaknesses were far outweighed by his great faithfulness. Renewal came to the whole of Pip 'n' Jay's PCC and leadership. I remember when praying one day, I seemed to be given a strange vision of the Pip 'n' Jay church building, with little flames round its walls and Malcolm was struggling with a big cross in the churchyard, then he suddenly worked out what to do and flew to the top of the church with the cross, whereupon the flames sprung higher, not consuming but lighting up the building and cross. A few weeks later Malcolm started a series of sermons on the Cross of Christ. There began a long period of tremendous renewal and growth when every week people came to faith, or were healed and were greatly helped.

Although Malcolm was the main preacher, especially in the evening, I had become a Reader in 1969 and started helping to lead services most weeks and preached once a month for several years till others joined the Reader team. As a consequence I received invitations to preach at many other churches and youth groups, usually much more often than at Pip 'n' Jay, many of these being on weekdays. On one occasion at Pip 'n' Jay I had to speak about the letter of James, chapter 2; not favouring the rich over the poor. I borrowed an old man's mask from my brother and just before the sermon, dressed up beside my car in the churchyard as a down-and-out, of which there were several at any one time in the churchyard. I put on my old army greatcoat tied with string and put a cider bottle sticking out of my pocket, the mask and an old hat. Then I stooped and walked slowly into the church with a stick. As I walked up the aisle I tried to push in to several pews but was resisted; when I was approaching the front, the lay reader leading the service looked very worried and mouthed to the wardens 'take him out!' I crossed to the pulpit and stood beside the front pew, whereupon an old almost blind man, called Percy, from a very humble background drew me in beside him. When the hymn stopped, I started climbing the pulpit steps, with my stick and cider bottle. There were some gasps of horror. I stood there for a moment, then took the mask off and asked everyone to sit down, while I read 'supposing a rich man in fine clothes and a poor man in shabby clothes come in and you show special attention to the man in fine clothes...have you not discriminated...and become judges with evil thoughts.' Although the congregation applauded the disguise, the point was taken. One lady said 'If I had known it was you, I would have let you in.' Exactly.

On another occasion I had to talk about marriage, two becoming one. I took in a blow lamp and a big space heater. I quoted a Korean custom of bride and bridegroom each taking a candle, lighting them to show they each had individual lives, hopes and dreams, and then each lighting a third candle and blowing out their own; here were two becoming one. This was a lovely illustration I said, but suppose the wife wasn't just a candle, but was like this blow lamp and the husband like this space heater; full of ego and self-centeredness and selfishness. What hope of lighting a candle from these and two becoming a meaningful one? Sometimes humility, gentleness and kindness had to come before marriage unity was possible.

We had used the farm since early youth club days for inviting townsfolk to the countryside. It was a base for some meetings and social events. We invited not-yet-believers or new believers for a meal or to work alongside me in the fields or in the milking parlour, or with Christina in the house. The less mechanical we were the more I could have people working with me. We regularly invited three or four students home for Sunday lunch and built up some long-lasting friendships which were a great blessing to us and to our children. Christina became an expert in simple large-scale catering with big roasts, large baked rice puddings, huge slabs of iced sponge cake and chocolate biscuit cake. We had bonfire parties each year for the church and for friends. We invited classes from the children's schools out to see dairy farming, or harvesting in action. Some problem people stayed the night. Once we found our two little girls cowering behind a sofa because they had heard a motorbike belonging to a lad we were trying to help. We eased him out at that point. Another girl we found was collecting razor-blades in her pillow. We had to find a new home for her, too, this time at Lee Abbey, who were a great help to her over the course of a year. But our own family undoubtedly found it helpful to have less fortunate people staying or eating with us, over many years. In their turn our children later did the same.

One morning at 5.30 I was starting my usual relief milking routine which all relief milkers do for 70 days a year. On this day I put on my sock and put my back out. I had a ten-year history of a bad back, beginning with a tennis tournament at 16 and aggravated as a recruit in the army when we were made to run with a rifle above our heads – after that I was in a metal-ribbed corset for two weeks.

Usually I went to an osteopath, who put it right very quickly. On this occasion there was no one else to milk the cows and 5.30 is too early for osteopaths. So I struggled out towards the cows. When I was midway there, I could move no further. I was in agony. I could not take another step. To our church, with renewal had come teaching about divine healing; God seemed to be healing people miraculously in some places. So I laid hands on my own back and prayed 'Lord you are my only hope, here, please will you heal my back'. I then turned towards the cows, rather than the osteopath. I managed to get one foot forward, then another, then another...by the time I had reached the cows and started bringing them in my back was completely mended, without pain, and I have never had to visit an osteopath again. Hundreds of tons of potatoes and concrete blocks later I can say that God healed me completely. It was not something to boast about but something I learned from: to receive healing for lots of other things over the years. I encouraged others to go the same route – to Jesus, who while on earth, healed all the sick people who were ever brought to Him.* He said we would do greater things than He had done, because He is in heaven, yet in a wonderful way He is also always with us – each of us and always.

In the '70s Malcolm and I each wrote a leaflet. His was called 'Giving is good for you', an excellent summary on how God blesses us when we give our money or time generously. I wrote one called 'Sex is for loving' about the importance of sex being in the context of the lifelong loving relationship of marriage, and avoiding those things that will harm us, like STIs with their potential for sterility, pregnancy outside marriage, abortion with its side effects, and the emotional problems caused by promiscuous sex that leads girls (and boys) into bitter regrets. Many thousands of each leaflet were sold on the bookstall. Mine was later taken by a missionary society and put on their website to attract people from other countries wanting to read English, and thereby discover the gospel. It attracted one of the highest hit-ratings for several years in the early days of the worldwide web, as sex was its first word. It is still top of the Google rankings for 'sex is for loving'.

It was certainly a very busy time helping grow a church and run a dairy farm. Sundays were an essential day off from all but emergency farming matters. However, preaching was done on Sundays. My busiest ever Sunday was when the cowman suddenly couldn't do the milking and I had two sermons to give. So I started milking at 5.00am, finished by 8.30am; had breakfast and went with the family to Pip 'n' Jay where I was due to preach. Then home, lunch and afternoon milking assisted by some of the family to speed things up ready for an evening service and sermon to be preached at St. Peter's, Bishopsworth. As I was very much relying on God for help and inspiration I was careful not to mention how busy the day had been, in case it looked as though I was wanting to look like a hero! With a good preacher Jesus is always the hero.

The rest of Pip 'n' Jay's story would be best told by others. Malcolm and I did not always get on, but each of us had been given things to do, which we

* Jesus healed all who were sick, who came to Him: *Matthew* 4:23-4, 8:16, 9:35, 12:15, 14:14,36, 15:30, 19:2, 21:14, *Luke* 4:40, 6:19, 9:11, *Mark* 6:56.

mainly supported each other in. Tensions arose most over the issue of remarriage of divorcees. Christina and I had seen the value of helping married couples get through difficult times in marriage to the benefit of themselves and their children and as examples of that principle for others. He felt as pastor he wanted to befriend and encourage those who had messed up marriage and help them make a new start. The tensions came when one party did not want to give up on their marriage while the other wanted to make a new start, by being remarried to someone else in church. Inevitably Malcolm and I disagreed in these cases, but that should not have been the cause of greater discord. Malcolm also faced criticism for drinking fairly heavily and smoking cigars quite often. For my part I could not bring myself to be critical of him and therefore legalistic, which was not what freedom in Christ stood for, but to be an example of a different lifestyle. Healthy living was supposed to lead to good health, and barring accidents, longevity. We would see.

These slight tensions between Malcolm and me were apparent to most of the church who had been there for a while. But I heard many years later that some people took these tensions to be having the same effect as in the oyster, where friction can produce a pearl.

Within the church we had a growing team of fast-learning, dedicated believers, too numerous to mention, an exceptional team of Sunday School and Youth Leaders who had been such an encouragement to our own children; and growing teams of musicians, which our own children had joined and benefited greatly from. New believers were being absorbed into both home groups and wider church, or else encouraged to join other fellowships elsewhere. Other churches used Pip 'n' Jay as a place to bring friends to hear the gospel. Pip 'n' Jay was to continue in this role under Malcolm's oversight for another 20 years, setting a fine example in helping people find faith in Christ, raising an astonishing £3m for mission work in total and being a church from which a large number of men and women were called to both part time and full time Christian service, especially to ordination in the C. of E.

At Malcolm's retirement in 2009, after 46 years as vicar, I wrote to him as follows:

> Having seen you last autumn I was expecting the news of your retirement; but now that it is out I just wanted to write to say thank you for your long and faithful ministry.
>
> Having known you since 1951, you deserve a long service medal for that alone. I have a picture somewhere of you and me, aged 18 I think, at Hazelwood, and Ann, too, aged 9 at the time.

> Our Monkton years saw some remarkable blessing from God, especially in 1956, post Capernwray, when you were remarkably used to be a blessing to lots of our contemporaries.
> The years from 1962 onwards were extremely formative for my own spiritual life, which I can date to your asking me (with the words in your letter, 'I feel like the man of Macedonia saying "come over and help us"') to lead the Holy Trinity Youth Club, with everything that followed. It was a privilege to be called alongside you in the development of Pip 'n' Jay from the early days of the Youth Club and tiny congregation, onwards to a full church and everything involved. It was your willingness to buck the trend of priestly control in allowing so many other talented people to share in the development of the church; yet your faithful and consistent preaching of God's Word, that kept us unified in the right direction, all trying to follow the Lord's leading. Your example in leading prayer times, often for all night or half a night was also both a challenge and a blessing.
> I would like to thank you for the opportunities you gave me to be a Reader, from 1969 onwards and to share in the preaching and service leading. Even when disagreements arose in the '80s, you were big enough to keep the pulpit open to allow dissent on the comparatively minor things that divided us. I sometimes wonder why those things caused such sharp division. We were not the first. Paul and Barnabas, and no doubt many others, beat us to it. It is certainly true that from my point of view, man's divisions have become God's multiplications, as we have seen God leading us. We were also relieved that our leaving Pip 'n' Jay, slowly and carefully in 1991, did not harm you all, indeed Pip 'n' Jay has continued to thrive under God, as a testimony to your faithful, prayerful and steady witness and preaching, and your continual encouragement of others to develop their ministry. Your example of open shared leadership has inspired many, and will continue to do so.

At about this time Malcolm received the shocking news of his having terminal cancer of the oesophagus. He bore it well and faithfully continued in worship at the back of Pip 'n' Jay as a member, until his death on October 12th 2010.

20

Marches, Demonstrations and Sexual Liberation

By the early '70s our children and their contemporaries were becoming aware of the world around them and its various influences. Crime had increased by 300% since I was at school in 1955. In particular sexual violence was seriously on the increase. Edmund Burke, Bristol MP 1774-1780 and philosopher, had said 'All that is necessary for the triumph of evil is for good men to do nothing.' As parents and church leaders we felt we should try to do something. The so called sexy sixties were good and bad. They were good in that lots of people started talking about sex. 'No sex please, we're British', had been true about discussing the subject, but of course, sex being a God-given appetite, lots of people had been doing it and getting in a mess. Sex actually comes from the Latin *secare*, to cut or divide. It divides humans into half male and half female. The challenge from Eden onwards has been how to achieve intimacy of spirit, soul and body to make two people one in marriage. Ironically many celibate single people achieve emotional intimacy without sexual activity, whereas prostitution and casual sex and even some poor marriages merely join two lonely people for a few minutes and never achieve what they promise. Most of the mentions of sex in the Bible are in the context of deeper unity between husbands and wives, not for procreation. In particular St. Paul stresses this in 1 *Corinthians* 7. But it was not till the arrival of easy contraception that this could be fully realised, especially for women. The Pill became both friend and enemy of women.

Sex without love increased first in the sixties with the obvious outcome of both divorce and abortion. Political parties are inevitably coalitions of different views. In my lifetime Labour have usually been socially fairer about helping the poor than Tories, but morally weaker in defence of marriage and the family. The Liberals (and Lib-Dems) have been… well, liberal! As it often has done, in the '60s parliament got the social remedies wrong and oh how terribly wrong. Divorce law reform Bill was debated from 1967-1969, described by its opponents at the time as a Casanova's Charter for making divorce so much easier, predicting thousands of extra single parents, abandoned mothers and serial monogamy. Its supporters vehemently denied such a thing would happen and it was passed into law.

It was clear that, despite the pleas by many of us in churches and others, there was to be no provision for either marriage education to help people make wise choices and do marriage well, or for marriage counselling to try to save couples who needed a referee and help in their struggles. Breaking marriages and dysfunctional homes were bound to increase enormously, producing rising crime and suicide rates and inevitable imitating-their-parents divorces in the next generation. It was a shame on those politicians that they could not, or would not see it. Divorces rose from about 30,000 in the early '60s to 110,000 in 1971, and 168,000 six years later. The terrible consequence of this has been exactly as we had forecast. Britain is the single-parent capital of Europe; and dysfunctional families are increasing alarmingly, with the lawlessness and unhappiness that follows. The surprising economic benefit however, was to see a building and housing boom to accommodate single parents lasting for three decades.

At the same time, a sex survey done in the USA showed that the most satisfactory sex was being enjoyed by young evangelical married couples. These were young people who were marrying as virgins, quite young because they did not want to wait long for sex, and intending marriage to be for life, so taking great care in selection of the right person. As we were among them we were keen to keep the subject in the open. Casual sex was promising fun but delivering disaster. 'No strings' sex had hidden strings – of infection or partial attachments, or deceitfulness, or addiction to the habit that drew people into more. Men, both young and older were always looking for sexual opportunities, and conning girls into 'trial marriage' or one night stands. We now know that neurochemicals are released at sexual intercourse in both men (vasopressin) and women (oxytocin) that causes bonding between them. This has been found to be a reason for mental disturbance, depression and suicidal feelings, following the break-up of couples after having sex together. The brain chemicals were partly causing the mess, as bonding was occurring, but not followed by the permanence needed. (*Hooked*, McIlhaney, 2008) Attempted suicides were highest among young people who had been let down after casual sex.

Abortions inevitably were a sought-after consequential option, with David Steel's Abortion Law reform causing a similar trend to that of divorces in the next few years. Abortion would seem an efficient mathematical solution to a social problem. But was that all there was to it? The evidence seemed to show that infertility was one serious consequence that was not being mentioned. There was another more sinister consequence; some mothers were becoming more violent with subsequent offspring, while other women were showing unforeseen remorse and were desperate to get pregnant and put things right, even if their choice of man was very poor. Did God have an angle on it?

Betty Bush with her two sons, Anthony and John

Anthony and John, 1943 ... and 68 years later with John as Lord Lieutenant of Wiltshire and Anthony still wheeling his barrow

Barnard and Betty Bush taking the boys to St Peter's

Peart Farm, 1949

Pony Club Camp, 1949. Anthony as he appeared in *Tatler*

Monkton Combe
School in the 1950s

Midford Sunday
School, 1954.
Anthony is back left

Monkton under-16s hockey
1954. Anthony is middle of
back row

Ann Widdecombe at 9

Anthony with Malcolm Widdecombe at 18

Assault course training, REME Honiton

'Auntie Flo', my first car, a 1935 Morris 8 that cost me £35, and every spare penny

Those that passed Officer Training at Honiton. Anthony is middle of back row

Duty Officer, Honiton

Our driver Bob Wheeler loading the churn lorry, 1962

John Pickard, our herdsman from 1963 to 1988

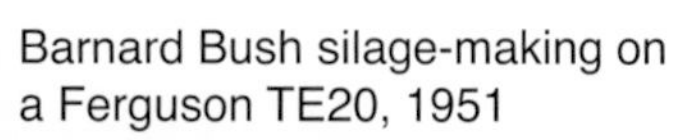

Barnard Bush silage-making on a Ferguson TE20, 1951

'for better, for worse, for richer, for poorer, in sickness and in health'.
Chelsea Old Church, 24 February 1962

The Catholics have a simple answer – it is alive and it is human so it must be protected from conception onwards. Even contraception is wrong to Catholics. They cite Onan (*Genesis* 38:10) as showing God's displeasure at coitus interruptus. But the story of Onan is about his rebelling over God's requirement to raise sons for his brother, not about contraception, and the Bible is less clear about the moment of the beginning of a human life. It says 'You do not know how the soul comes to the bones of a woman with child' (*Eccl* 11:5). We know it is God who 'put me together in my mother's womb' (*Ps* 139:13), so in some mysterious way He chooses which sperm is locked, in an instant, in each conception. But the soul appears to come later by divine fiat. It is less clear how seriously He is offended by such terminations as the morning after pill, the coil and by abortions under a wide range of social circumstances. If a conception has taken place I would not want to risk offending God, so I would want all foetal life protected unless there is a serious risk to the mother's health (and I mean serious, there is always some risk) or the new baby has no hope of sustainable life.

We have a son-in-law who was born a thalidomide victim – with foreshortened limbs. Yet he is a man of enormous talents. It would have been tragic if he had been given the termination treatment so often handed out for reasons of social inconvenience or physical imperfection. Large numbers of would-be parents are denied the possibility of adoption by the easy abortions that have become possible. I would not want to be judgmental either; it is always difficult to seek reform without appearing to condemn those whose actions have made it necessary. Forgiveness and change are essential components of the Christian gospel.

The Abortion Act was also going to prove highly inflationary. It was driven by the sexual liberation lobby and although it was intended to give girls freedom and medical safety, was in practice going to exploit lots of them and ruin the lives of many women and men. So we felt protest was important and joined the Festival of Light in London in September 1971 to celebrate the Light, or good things of life, rather than condemn the darkness. But there was also a sense of warning about the moral anarchy that was inevitably to follow. So as well as a rally in Hyde Park with a march for 20,000 people to Trafalgar Square and lots of speakers, there was a series of beacons lit all round the coast, Spanish-Armada-style, including a one on our farm for several hundred people. This was designed to awaken the moral majority to what was happening and encourage society to hold on to family values. As the march took place one policeman was seen singing with the marchers. 'If you are a Christian, don't you wish you were on this march with us?' he was asked. 'I am', he replied, 'and

I'm being paid for it!'

My response to this moral confusion was to discuss it with other Christians and to organise a march to protest against the opening of four sex shops in Bristol. In Denmark some friends of ours had campaigned against sex shops by blanking out the explicit window displays in brown paper with LOVE IS PURE painted across the paper. This surprisingly led to the tradition of nearly all sex shops blanking out their own windows.

Nudity should never be an issue. Half the world are male and half female, each half looking very similar but for a few centimetres. In the Garden of Eden they were naked but not ashamed, before something happened to make God manufacture the first clothes. Perhaps he wanted to spice up their lives by increasing the mystery, or protect them from thinking about little else, including whether their bits were up to average; or all of these. Objective unashamed beauty is wonderful if it could remain just that. But innocent nudity can be skewed by promiscuity, selfishness and greed, which feed lust and seduction exploited by pornographers. This mushroomed in the '60s for the next three decades; then it moved from the top shelf of newsagents to the internet. One pornographer had declared that the purpose of pornography was to stimulate a male erection, which he said is a skilled art. Nudity had always been allowed in art, even erotic art, but here was incitement to promiscuity, sometimes with sadism too. Our concern was that single men, having been sexually aroused, would not be content with solo masturbation, which for some reason was derided ('you sad wanker'), but would look to harassing young girls, or worse, rape.

Public opinion was concerned lest children should be encouraged to use pornography, or of course in case children were the victims of pornographers. They were naïve, as if those over 18 were not being influenced. A women's movement, 'Reclaim the night', happened a year or two later but did not seem to attribute the dangers that women were increasingly experiencing to widespread pornography. Much later, a 2008 survey of 1,000 American Christians by ChristiaNet.com, showed 50% of men, 20% of women and 37% of pastors said they had an addiction problem with pornography. Microsoft announced that 60% of all internet traffic was sex related, which some by 2012 put as high as 80%; the figures were clearly much higher outside church than inside. The arrival of huge social networks and web sex has encouraged people, especially men and boys, to become addicted to images without the ability to relate to real people, or to build or maintain their own lifelong families. Many will be heading for a lonely old age unless they find help.

1,000 people joined in this anti-sex-shop March in November 1975. We assembled on College Green and marched with banners saying 'love is pure', ‘marry your best friend’ and ‘husbands, love your wives’, ‘sex is for marriage’ and many others. We marched through the centre of Bristol and out to Old Market, past three sex shops. On another day we held a protest against one sex shop, which locals joined in large numbers. This shop closed as it was near a residential area in Horfield. Another we protested outside was, I discovered, being run by a former member of our youth club! He rang me later, apologised for his wife throwing a bucket of water over me (actually a near miss!) and promised to close; he did. The other two remained open, despite our demonstrations.

We found pornography dumped on the farm, beside favourite parking places. Vicars I spoke to found it dumped in church yards. It was clear children were not being protected from it. The film and soft porn industry is built on pretence; actors pretend to have good sex and then pretend the often unrealistic consequences. James Bond is a celluloid zombie, whose actor has no feelings that are not pretence, and no realistic consequences. A plethora of so-called porn stars are paid to have casual and loveless sex, empty orgasms and short-term excitements yielding long term loneliness. I feel sorry for those trapped in its grip, and sorry for those who believe its impossible instant-success message, or are harassed as a consequence. The reality was that promiscuous sex was only possible, especially for girls, with large doses of alcohol to deaden their normal restraints and make them willing to do what they knew they were likely to regret.

Temptation was not well understood. It encourages us to do something *just because* we know it is wrong and likely to harm us and/or others. This was true about lots of things: driving too fast, drinking too much, spending too much money, or having casual sex. They seemed more attractive because they were likely to be regretted. There is a character called Amnon in the Bible, who had sex by force with his half-sister, Tamar, presumably because of overwhelming temptation. This was despite her protestations that she was sure her father would have allowed them to marry. Then, we read, after sex was over, ‘the hatred with which he hated her was greater than the love with which he had loved her!’ How up to date and often repeated is that? Lust somehow destroys people. This must be part of a spiritual and addictive side to pornography, too, which may need God’s help to be set free from and stay free from; then, like any addiction, to find support and accountability in staying free.

There is of course a positive side to sex shops in so far as they encourage married people to be adventurous with all the delights that sex can offer. I could never understand why erotic lingerie was not more widely sold. God clearly made man to be delighted by and sexually stimulated by the sight of a naked woman. It also helps young men to be attracted to women. As a pornography shop keeper once told me 'if that ever stops we will be as extinct as the dodo'. But pornography also creates expectations in men, which their own woman is not always willing or able to satisfy. Married men can carry stimulating mental pictures home to the bedroom, and impose them on the real situation. If this becomes mental adultery, or coercion it must harm a marriage. (See chapter 22). So I wrote a leaflet called 'Is Pornography harmful?' with 14 reasons for yes, which was published and sold through Pip 'n' Jay Church.

One of my staff at this time thought he would be a bit provocative and put up a calendar of nude girls in our workshop. I said 'why have you put that up, Gilbert?' 'It's beautiful and it's art' he replied with a twinkle. I said I agreed with him, but if it was so beautiful please would he take it home and put it up in his sitting room so that his wife could appreciate it too! He grinned sheepishly and binned it. Gilbert was one of my longest serving staff members. He had once had all his teeth removed because he could not stand the dentist. He had a large and very nice family and had a colourful time here, twice he attacked me violently, not to damage me, but because he was not expressing himself well. It reminded me that a battered wife has often won an argument with a less verbally adept husband, who had then thumped her in frustration. Gilbert became a Christian halfway through his time with us, partly through the work of the Salvation Army. The next day he walked the mile to work that he had previously driven in his car illegally, because he had no driving license. He could not pass his driving test, despite many attempts. He was teased unfairly by some of the other staff for becoming a Christian. He then soon passed his test. He was always a good worker and a trusted, frank and honest colleague. He retired in 1986 and died soon afterwards.

Our church and Malcolm in particular felt that, following the successful protest march, it would be a good thing if we should have a positive march, for Jesus. The following Easter I was ideally placed, being on General Synod, to contact church leaders, including the bishops, and we held a Jesus March with a Salvation Army Band and 2,000 people, from Clifton Down Station, round the centre ending at the Cathedral. A few years later, when my daughter Annie was 18, she and some other young people felt it was time for another Jesus March, so she and I but mainly she, invited all the churches to turn out for another, this time about 1,000 people attended. This was formative for Annie as it led to a lot of inter-church event organising, of public nativities and pageants 20 years later, near Liverpool.

This protesting only took a few Saturdays, of course. There was the main job of farming and bringing up our family. We believed in keeping our own children busy and happy; each one had their own talents to develop, of music, sport, dancing, and drama. We did lots of barn dances, barbecues, bonfires and firework parties, sometimes with large groups staying in the barns and house. It would be interesting to know how many hundreds of children visited or stayed at our farm over those years.

Our girls were in a lively youth group and music group at Pip 'n' Jay in their teens. Their young music group had sung and played in a Songs of Praise BBC broadcast from Pip 'n' Jay in the late '70s, in which they lacked a conductor. For some reason no one else was available so I volunteered, but my skills were so clearly minimal I was hidden from view behind a pillar! One day when Annie was about 14, she arrived at breakfast with a song she had just composed 'Who's the King of the jungle'. Over the next few weeks it was sung and developed in their music group and became very popular in church and beyond. Over the next few years it quietly spread through the church network, until it was published in a song book under 'author anonymous'. Christina immediately set the record straight, with Annie's name; but Annie knew that Lizzie and the others in the music group had added ideas, and has put most of the royalties she has been paid towards helping other, more deprived young musicians. One day about eight years later, our son Larry and his Antonia were very surprised to hear the song being sung on a railway platform in Czechoslovakia! It has since spread round the world and been a blessing to thousands, and even faith-forming to some.

21

Farming in a Rut

AFTER 15 YEARS IN A JOB IT CAN GET VERY REPETITIVE, ESPECIALLY DAIRY FARMING for 24 hours a day, 7 days a week, 365 days a year. With a herd of 120 cows we put the cups on a million teats every three years. At one time I knew every cow just by looking at its udder. As I have mentioned, each cow produces 50 kilos of dung and 60 litres of urine every day; this meant scraping 10 tonnes of slurry per day into the lagoon and then spreading it at a later date. Many farmers, including me, buy new things to try to remove the worst of the routine jobs, or even because they are bored and want something new. The new things may not be helpful in increasing income or saving time. There came a time when I was so bored that I actually asked God one day if something exciting could happen on the farm.

A few days later my neighbour rang me to say my Hereford bull was out with his cows, would I please take it away immediately. The police would often turn a stray animal off the road into the nearest field, without enquiry. I quickly gathered up two staff and we set off to move the bull. I carried a pick-axe handle, as I usually did and as we had done on night duty in the army. When we got to the field we quickly separated the bull and put him out on the road, to drive him back to his field 400 yards away along the road. He had wide horns and I thought what good condition he was in. As we walked him along, a motor bike came round the bend towards us, took fright and drove up the bank to avoid the bull! We eventually arrived at the correct field gate and turned the bull into it. I then realised that my own bull was already in the field and this bull, looking almost identical, was in fact another neighbour's! My two blokes were outside the field, smiling, and only I was in with the bulls, which by this time were attacking each other violently with their heads down, within a ring of admiring heifers. I thought 'Courage, Anthony, do something!' So I rushed screaming loudly at the bulls and hit them both very hard on the back of the head, to give them something to take their minds off each other, then I banged the visitor on the bottom, shouting, to get him moving back towards the gate. He was so surprised he did not hesitate. The gate was opened and we returned the bull to the field he came from. The farmer then had to find its true owner.

That week end on the Saturday, we were due to have some visitors. At midday I discovered that two cows had been fighting and one had lifted another over the one-metre high bar and into our slurry lagoon, of half a million gallons of cow manure. She was swimming around in 9 feet of liquid dung with only her head out of it; eventually getting stuck in the crust 20 feet out into the middle. How were we to get her out? What should I do, Lord? One half of the lagoon had a crust on it about one foot thick, but not strong enough to walk on. So I decided to put a ladder on it supported horizontally by someone on the end, while I climbed out along the ladder with a rope, to the cow, which by this time was tiring. I tied the rope with a careful reef knot so that tightening it would not strangle her, under her head and well under dung level. I was up to my elbows in cow manure, which I was familiar with, long before the days of rubber gloves, which would have been no use anyway. Our visitors had by this time joined us as spectators as we fetched a tractor with a fore-end loader, ready to try and lift her out. I had discovered on two earlier occasions that you can actually hang a cow by its neck for a short time and it will live. First we pulled the cow to the edge of the lagoon, then re-tied the rope on the tractor end and hoisted the cow by its neck, which looked as if it would pull its head off, out of the slurry and onto the bank. The cow was fine. Everyone cheered. We hosed the cow down and she turned from brown to black and white, and returned to the herd with very little harm done. Cows have a pecking order in a herd; disputes only become fights if two of them disagree about their social order. That cow will have learnt.

A week or so later we were due to take the children on holiday to a houseparty. I was also due to be doing the calling for some barn dances at the first night's entertainment. At that morning milking we realised that instead of there being four tonnes of rolled barley in a bulk feed bin, nothing was coming out, so it must be empty. What could we do, it was Saturday? I took off the auger conveyor from the bottom of the 20-feet tall bulk bin and looked inside with a torch. There was some cow food inside but it was old and hard and had formed a wedge round which the other feed had been running for a while. I tried dislodging it with an iron bar and hitting the outside of the tank but it was stuck fast. I wondered how safe it was to climb inside but when I put my head in, the ammonia was so powerful I thought I would be gassed. People did kill themselves with methane and other gas poisoning. Could I ring the fire brigade? Probably not popular on a Saturday and anyway, what could they do that I couldn't? Could I just leave it? Certainly not! It was essential for the herd to have their 250 kilos per milking or the milk results would be a disaster. We wanted to be away on holiday by midday, to be at the barn dance.

All the family was the solution. I would go into the bin with a polythene water pipe in my mouth to breathe clean air. Larry, the youngest, would hold a piece of gauze over the end to make sure I didn't breathe anything I shouldn't. Lizzie, Annie and Caspar and a visitor would shovel away the food that I was going to dislodge with a fencing bar. I climbed in and started hitting the rolled barley pile. Suddenly the whole lot collapsed around me and fell out into the gap below, taking my pipe with it. I was waist-deep in barley. The children were all shovelling hard to clear it out of the way, and I heard Annie call out 'are you alright, dad?' They had seen 'Little House on the Prairie' where the dad is stuck in a collapsed coal mine. I called out 'Keep shovelling!' When I'd climbed in the bottom of the tank the methane, which is heavier than air, would have partly dropped out of the hole and the barley, when it fell out of the bottom of the tank would have drawn in new air from the top – so I could breathe. After a short while they cleared a space for me to climb out. We soon put everything back together and were on our way. The children, especially Lizzie, had to brief me about the barn dance calls on the car journey; we had run out of time to rehearse. I then recalled my prayer that God should make something exciting happen. I thanked Him for rescue and for excitement and asked if I could return to something a little more boring.

One morning at about this time someone we knew well and who was a Christian rang at breakfast time to say that her husband had just walked out on her. Two children's futures were at stake. We were stunned; in fact I was furious about it, but clearly could not reach this man in his car to speak to him. So we paused at the breakfast table and I can remember praying 'Lord, please stop him, if necessary by force!' and really meaning it. Later that day we heard that ten minutes after we had prayed, this man had been involved in a car accident in which his leg was broken and he was taken to hospital! His wife joined him at his bedside and they were reconciled. I wrote to tell him how we had prayed and when. His marriage has appeared a strong one ever since. A number of our friends have been through stormy marriage times; some have had to face the consequences of adultery and how to restore the marriage. Adultery is never easy to forgive. Being and saying sorry, and forgiveness from both spouse and God seem to be essentials to this restoration process.

Sometimes the weather produced dramatic interest. In 1978 we had our second really big snow. About a foot and a half of snow covered all the fields. I remember taking Larry on a tractor to feed the outside herd of 30 heifers with their hay. We drove up our usual track, only to find that four feet of snow had drifted across it making it impassable. So I cut the fence and we went an alternative route round the public roads. The roads were completely empty; but an unused side road with a foot of snow on it had just been cleared, one lane wide, by a bulldozer. We used the single lane and drove into our field. I started wading, with huge effort, through a foot of snow to find the heifers in the next field. I saw them a quarter of a mile away and called them. They saw me and realised I had food for them; and came trotting effortlessly through the snow! We threw out the hay to them very quickly. I knew we need not thaw out the water trough, because in 1963 our heifers had drunk snow for three months. We have never had such a big snow since 1978; even if climate change is a reason, then I have to admit it is a big relief not to have the inconvenience.

22

Marriage Preparation, Repair and Sex Difficulties

CHRISTINA AND I HAD BEEN VERY CONCERNED THAT OUR YOUTH CLUB MEMBERS were growing up, getting married and their marriages were threatening to fall apart. We felt there was a need for marriage counselling. The secular counsellors were not trying hard enough we thought, and some churches, including our own, were in danger of remarrying people to the next spouse without trying to keep the first marriage together. Others were saying they had homosexual temptations in their marriage, others transvestite temptations, yet others wanted to change gender. In the effort not to seem judgmental about past failures, which is also extremely important, the whole Christian emphasis on forgiveness and repair and best practice was in danger of being lost.

One couple came to us and said they had both divorced their spouses and their church was praying about marrying them. We said we did not approve and wanted them to revisit their first marriages to try repair. They did not listen to us and their church married them. A year later they came to us again and said they both wanted to go back to their first spouses! They had discovered that the grass looks greener on the other side, but forgot it still needs mowing. Another lady came to us and said her husband had asked her for a divorce because he had said he had *never* ever loved her. A year later he came back to her and said he wanted her back, because he had *only* ever loved her. Such are the emotion-led actions of the day.

I knew from my work on revising the Marriage Service on General Synod that the English language is limited. For example the Greeks had five words for love; we have one, so need to add adjectives. The Greek *Epithumea* meant sexual love; *eros* meant romantic love; *storge* meant familiarity love, like loving old shoes; *phileo* meant friendship love; and *agape* meant love measured by sacrifice. This latter is the love that God tells husbands to have towards a wife – sacrificial love. The very firm line taken by some church people against remarrying after divorce, all stems from the words of Jesus Christ Himself (*Matt* 5:31-2, 19:3-9; *Mark* 10:1-12; *Luke* 16:18) where He said, to everyone's astonishment at the time, that remarriage is adultery except in a few possible cases. Jesus was reminding us how very important vows are. The prophet Malachi (2:13-16) says that God remembers these vows which are for security into old age. Consequently the New Testament writers teach us how to rekindle our first love, regardless of our feelings (*Ephesians* 5:21-33, 1 *Peter* 3:1-8).

It seemed the whole country needed to learn how to stay married. Sex is a great incentive for good behaviour in marriage but if people are love-cheats and ignore promises to be faithful then social tragedy will follow. There was a massive need for learning good behaviour, saying sorry and finding forgiveness so that love and romance could return. Businesses are built by working hard at them, so are marriages and so are families. In some marriages one party has moved too far for reconciliation. The church is then in a dilemma. In the emphasis on forgiveness and new starts that is essentially part of the Christian message there are also those, perhaps the children primarily, who were going to be hurting because the marriage has broken up. This could become anger against the church if it is the church that ends all possibility of reconciliation by conducting a remarriage.

Christina and I spent many evenings during the 1970s and '80s seeing couples for marriage counselling. We worked on the assumption that most couples in Britain had fallen in love with each other before they married, so what had gone wrong that they needed counselling? The Indians have a saying 'Your marriages start hot and grow cold, ours start cold and grow hot'. Usually we saw a couple together, then I would take the husband to another room to try to unearth the real issues and propose a course of action for repairing the marriage. I tried to find out why he had felt the girl had been so right to marry, what had gone wrong, what he thought was to blame, what were the good things that were worth trying to save. Christina did much the same with the wife. If a third party had come into the marriage it made things much more difficult, but was not always fatal to the marriage. Adultery was rarely the *cause* of break up but was usually the *result* of a break down in the relationship.

Christian faith always made repair, forgiveness and better behaviour enormously easier. God helps people. He is not just a force to pray to, He actually helps us do things we find difficult. The Bible gives lots of guidance on marriage. A broken marriage was often a reason for a proud and arrogant husband becoming humble enough to look for God. At one point I had prayed with more men to receive Christ through their broken marriage than for any other reason. If marriages came to us early enough and took the counselling medicine, we found we had a huge success rate. We also did a lot of speaking to different groups about making marriage work including, of course, having a healthy sex life. Sex is not the most important part of marriage but it is usually a good indication of its health.

One day a former employee of ours came and asked would I testify that he wasn't as bad as his wife was making out in their divorce settlement. I asked him if he really wanted a divorce. He said, 'No, but she wouldn't have me back now because I was living with someone else for two years'. I asked if he would like me to go and ask his wife the same. He agreed. I asked her the same question: did she really want a divorce? She replied 'No, but he wouldn't have me back because I lived with someone else for two years'. They had a date that evening and have remained happily married for 20 years since.

In 1974 we set up, with some lovely couples, the Bristol Family Life Association (BFLA). It had three aims: to encourage the media to be responsible about family values of language, violence, sex and marriage, to encourage marriage education in churches and schools and to repair marriages. We were not a charity because charities cannot be politically involved. I employed an excellent part-time secretary, Eileen Simpson, for farm letters as well as to help me with this largely postal work. She put a small poster up in our office saying 'We aim to speak the truth in love', echoing a Biblical thought. To her surprise she even had to round up the cows occasionally, as well as dealing with phone calls.

Eventually our efforts towards marriage counselling were put into a formal small organisation we called Marriage Repair (known as the Marriage Garage). We tried an experimental fortnight, in which Christina and I put an ad in the personal services column of the *Bristol Evening Post*, which read: 'Marriage Problems? Don't despair, ring...' our phone number. To this we had four serious enquiries, all of whom some Christian couples who were friends of ours in Bristol were able to help significantly. So we went more formal, with a more permanent arrangement for Marriage Repair, headed up by our friends David and Christine Mitchell at its centre using their, they felt, God-given and memorable own phone number 44111. This was linked up with six other couples in a similar way to doctors at the time, on a rota to receive calls and give immediate help, and a duty receptionist to pass the clients' numbers to me. I had a list of visiting counsellor couples (who were only briefly trained by our own experiences, but who all had good marriages) to visit clients. We found immediate success in helping about 80% of enquiring marriages to stay much more happily together. I wrote a leaflet 'So you are thinking about divorce', with a summary of what a couple could do to remain hopeful of repair and the telephone number to ring. We distributed thousands of copies. Later, in 1985, David gave up his solicitor's job for a year to set up Network Christian Counselling as its first director on a more professional basis, which is still going strong today. I was the first chairman of trustees until 1991 when they found someone better qualified.

The BBC and ITV were increasingly allowing swear words as if their script writers and comedians had just discovered them. The words I had grown out of at 12 seemed so exciting to apparently repressed broadcasters. It seems to me that swear words are mainly used to shock people. If one set of bad words gets normalised and fails to draw objections, the comedians, script writers, and other 'telebrities' move on to alternative words. So the rest of us have to draw the line and remain shocked to keep them happily using the ones they think are big. I explained their meanings to our daughters when they reached about 10 and asked about them from school. I told them all the words are descriptive; 'fuck' is of 16th century origin, meaning to have sexual intercourse; 'cunt' is from cunnus the Latin for female genitals; 'cunt-struck' has been used from the 18th century to describe a sex-obsessed man. 'Bugger' or 'buggery' is an alternative word to sodomy, or anal intercourse, often used of the criminal act of homosexual assault. To take these words out of context seems to help some people express their irritation or anger, or to add humour (they can be funny). But in my view they should remain out of public use, so that worse ones are not used. I have never tolerated bad language on the farm. It is a sign of selfishness and lazy thinking!

So we all in BFLA surveyed bad language on TV and at the same time the portrayal of sex on TV. We found that 80% of TV sex was outside of marriage and 20% inside; this seemed to us as guaranteed to lead the country into further moral chaos. We pointed this out to them. They noted the Bristol phenomenon and that lots of letters were coming from Bristol; and responded by reducing the mentions of sex but increasing the occurrences outside marriage to 90%!

Hey, broadcasters, has anyone done any thinking lately? – What is wrong with sex? And what is helpful about encouraging promiscuity?

'We are reflecting society', they said.

'So you would be if you showed the detail of battered wives or knife crime! How is it helpful?'

'TV doesn't affect people's behaviour, so stop worrying'.

'Oh, so advertisers on ITV are all daft money-wasters?'

No answer: too many of them were in what a Chief Constable at the time described as the moral cesspit, so to hell with responsibility!

Sir Hugh Carlton Green was Director General of the BBC until 1969 and had a picture of the campaigner, Mary Whitehouse's face on a nude woman's body in his office. The broadcasters seemed incapable of intelligent debate on the right place of sex on TV. Mary Whitehouse had a slightly different agenda – to reduce sex, violence and bad language – and was doing an important and brave job, she was also very articulate on TV and feared by those with a poor argument. We were members of her NVALA and I spoke at meetings for her sometimes. I even went with Mary and others to the House of Commons to meet the new Tory leader, Margaret Thatcher, but Maggie Thatcher had married a divorcee and said she thought marriages with problems could not be saved. Many in her party disagreed with her, but all political parties are coalitions, of varied views. On one occasion I went in Mary Whitehouse's place to Marlborough College to talk about Christian standards of morality. The Head reminded all of us at the end that those standards also included forgiveness for past mistakes where that was necessary – an easy thing to forget. I ran out of time trying to get through to broadcasters, so left them to others as other matters seemed more pressing. We eventually handed over BFLA to Care Trust and Care for the Family and I felt I had to move to other things.

At about this time the press rang Malcolm Widdecombe, knowing he was supportive of these same family values, asking for a Church voice on the opening of a new garage, using topless garage attendants. 'What are you going to do about it?' he was asked. 'Pray for frost!' came his quick reply. The press loved it. It was probably as well that they had rung him and not me. I might well have said that it was not tits that were the problem, but morals. I had hundreds of naked tits on my dairy farm, they come in all shapes and sizes, so it is partly for reasons of comparison that women willingly keep them covered in this country, if not in lots of other countries. Our sexual behaviour was a bigger issue.

Christina and I visited lots of schools at that time, through the '70s and '80s, to encourage kids to prepare for marriage by abstaining from sex before marriage, as we had found so worthwhile, ourselves. We had a slogan 'marry your best friend'. This was in stark contrast to the majority portrayal on TV and film of people who leap into bed with an almost complete stranger, ridiculously writing-off the idea of a slow steady progress with an opposite sex friend as 'Oh I only like you as a friend'. We encouraged teenagers to have lots of inclusive friends, rather than a single exclusive one with whom they were expected to have sex and then get bored. We often got the 14-16 year olds to write down what they were looking for in their ideal husband/wife. The boys would write at the top of the list 'big tits or big bum'; the girls would write 'kind, sensible'. Were the girls ever going to find anyone marriageable? We now know the answer for thousands was no. Too many single mothers have kicked their men out as being useless to family life. With so much of the media encouraging 'no-strings sex' and promiscuity, what hope have most young men of becoming marriageable? Why is there no marriage and family education? Why is that less important than geography and history?

I spoke to each of our girls' schools and to youth groups where our boys were. When Lizzie asked me to her secondary school, Cotham Grammar, it was to speak to the Christian Union on 'Sex is for loving'. She went round the school putting up notices while an embarrassed member of staff took down as many as he could, presumably he was embarrassed at the word sex. In the event the classroom was jam packed, standing room only, and we had some good frank discussion, which went on long after I had left.

At least I felt I had spelt it out clearly to our children and some of their friends. The arguments seemed obvious: if you wait to have sex until marriage, you avoid unwanted pregnancy, abortions, sexually transmitted infections with their inherent sterility problems; you avoid the emotional turmoil of bonding through sex and then breaking up. Masturbation did not have these problems, it avoids harming others. Apart from sex there are also a million other ways of having fun!

The Brook Clinic was totally against us in their efforts to encourage contraception. They said we were kill-joys, especially for warning of the dangers of sexually transmitted infections (STIs). How weird was that? They have now seen the error of their ways. However, the failure rate of condoms, we pointed out, was bound to prove inflationary. If you encourage 100 couples to have sex with a condom, when they would not have had sex otherwise, you will make 15 extra girls pregnant whose condoms fail with average use 15% of the time (not the 'perfect condom' 2% failure use). And so it was; teenage pregnancies rose year by year. 'Contraceptives may not work well but they certainly pay' was a journalists comment on the funding of the Brook and FPA, who sadly still do not seem to realise this link between girls learning how to use a condom, and the consequent proportion of failed condoms. Most girls also reported disappointment with first sex and regrets over it. Western promiscuous culture, often driven by middle-aged women and men, is exploiting our young people. It was as though the media and those do-gooders were grooming young girls for sex, by giving them a false picture of it instead of the reality.

Fast-forward 40 years and the downward spiral of social problems continues, with the viral STIs that are rampant and spreading by promiscuous oral sex. The BBC3 'Dangerous Pleasures' season of 2012* reported that the often symptomless Human Pappiloma Virus (HPV) has spread to 80% of sexually active people of age 25 in the UK, which has become the most promiscuous country in the world. It is passed on in the internal skin of mouth and vagina, leading to cancers of the mouth, especially in young males who can catch it more easily than girls. Vaccination is available free for girls; boys have to pay £300. This programme reported nearly half a million new STI cases in the UK in 2011, of 25 different sorts, and commented that condoms can help control some, but

* BBC 3 'How Sex Works' 2/3 16.1.2012; BBC 3 'Is Oral Sex Safe?' 19.1.12

not all STIs. Infertility and cancer can follow if STIs, especially Chlamydia which is often invisible, are not treated. The BBC also reported 60% of people regretting losing their virginity too young,** over half were drunk at the time.

This anti-girls culture was actually turning the clock back. In 1864 the Contagious Diseases Act was passed in knee-jerk response to 29% of the military being infected with venereal diseases (VDs), as STIs were then called. But the Act required women and girls found near barracks to be examined for VDs and, if positive, to be committed to Lock Hospitals for many months, even for life. The Act outraged women of the day and became a rallying point for women that eventually led to the suffragettes. Women (and men) saw it as a disgracefully unfair way of allowing men to behave badly at their expense. It also sparked off Ellice Hopkins' White Cross chastity movement and others. The Act took 22 years to repeal.

I often joked in speeches at that time 'an optimist is a man who marries his secretary and thinks he can continue to dictate to her'; 'It is true that love is blind, but marriage is definitely an eye-opener' and 'Love begins when you sink in his arms and ends with your arms in his sink'. Some people were attempting an alternative to marriage and choosing cohabitation. Some were persuaded by a stronger partner whom they hoped might marry them one day, others did not fully trust a person as a marriage partner so thought living with them might help them decide – and the sex might be fun in the meantime. It has not turned out as some had hoped. It is difficult for officialdom to track cohabitation because by definition it is private, whereas marriage is public. The Office of Population Censuses and Surveys (OPCS) first published figures in 1989 (Issue 58). It was soon known that 75% of cohabiting couples break up, and of those cohabitees who went on to marry, 50% break up, as opposed to 30% of people marrying without living together. So the total sum was stark: only 12% of those who lived together before marriage would survive together into old age, as opposed to 70% of those who started with marriage. Many years later (2011) the website CIVITAS reported 'Living together leads to living alone' and that unmarried partnerships last under two years on average; less than 4% of cohabitations last 10 years; cohabiting couples are more likely to cheat on each other and be unfaithful, will be economically worse off, have greater health problems and the women are more likely to be abused; those having children will break up even quicker.

A couple came to us one day wanting to divorce. They had lived together before marriage and had felt forced to marry when she became pregnant. They

** BBC3 'Cherry Healey, Like a Virgin' 20.1.2012

both resented the marriage and she was convinced his pre-marriage sex with her meant he was being unfaithful now; he wasn't. She refused to make love to him and lots of little things increasingly irritated them both. They had previously felt passionately attracted to each other. Now they needed to apologise for using each other without commitment before their marriage and start again. They did. Some vicars began introducing prayers of repentance and forgiveness for former cohabitees getting married who wanted to clear away the past and start as new. Living together was clearly very different from marriage.

We felt this news needed sharing without being judgemental about anyone. Perhaps we could use it to try to teach the best behaviour for future happiness. Similarly with divorce, those getting divorced are statistically more likely to experience a second divorce if they remarry. We enquired of a registrar at Bristol central register office who told me he was remarrying between 6 and 12 couples *to each other again,* after divorce, every year. These had all encouraged us in our efforts towards marriage counselling and towards marriage education. Meanwhile, the media were using story lines of living together as a problem-free option; children were being encouraged to walk straight into the fire.

In our schools work we were often given the worst reception by teachers who were homosexuals or cohabiting heterosexuals. They felt understandably threatened, but should have wanted excellence taught in the area of relationships. It was these teachers who eventually stopped our invitations to speak. I have felt sorry for homosexuals as under different circumstances I could have continued as trapped by my earlier personal experiences. Had I not become a Christian and been at a boarding school where homosexuality was strongly discouraged I might have been different. Every teenage boy's sexuality is ambiguous. It is called growing up. My mother took an unusual step for me when I was 18. Perhaps she had been talking to her friends and found some of their sons were promiscuous or visiting prostitutes ('nice' *girls* did not sleep around) and was therefore worried about my lack of sexual exploits. Anyway she arranged for me to see a Roman Catholic psychiatrist called Dr Reeves in Bath, who specialised in helping men out of homosexuality into heterosexuality. He was having a high success rate.

Dr Reeves had found that people were being damaged in their normal emotional growth process; so some boys stopped developing from the same-gender friendship phase that all boys go through at 8-16, into normal heterosexual friendships and attractions by their mid-twenties. This might just be late development; everyone is different. He found the delay may be increased or a person's progress damaged by losing a parent through death or divorce, by a homosexual assault, by heterosexual assault, homosexual peer pressure, an over-possessive parent or a variety of other events. He searched for such a point in each of his clients and helped them to see its effect and move on from it. He was finding that those with homosexual tendencies could be helped to have heterosexual attractions. Understanding and wanting the opposite sex and their different and designed-to-fit-ours sex organs became part of that process.

I agreed partially, but not entirely with Dr Reeves' solution. He encouraged the men to get hold of nude pictures of girls, appreciate their total beauty and allow themselves to be attracted to it because God made males to be attracted to females, and then to imagine himself having sex with the girl. While I felt there was a lot of truth in the attraction argument, I was aware that Jesus has said that looking at a woman to lust after her was the equivalent to adultery. And Jesus said adultery harmed us. It did seem important to know what anatomy girls had, to allow oneself to feel attracted to that, for the very positive reason that God made male and female humans to want each other. As the ultimate pinnacle of His creation He made us sexual beings (see chapter 42).

Kenneth Reeves was showing homosexuals could become heterosexuals by therapy. He knew he was a minority opinion and was disappointed that it was not more widely attempted. It is consequently my opinion that most homosexual inclination in both sexes could be helped to heterosexuality by sensitive courting and spousing. This means looking for an opposite sex 'best friend' and allowing the physical attraction to grow by caring, listening, understanding and most of all loving, in the unselfish use of that word. Sexual interest can grow out of friendship, where everything is talked about. This search for an opposite sex soul-mate may be long and difficult and does sometimes take many prayerful years. We have many friends who did not marry until their late thirties or older. Many homosexuals and heterosexuals wish to remain celibate. However, where there are homosexuals going into schools telling youngsters that if they have homosexual thoughts they are homosexuals for ever, these people may mean well by wanting young people to have friends, but if they are encouraging sexual activity they are seriously wrong and doing the equivalent of grooming the young for sex in the same way that the heterosexuals I have mentioned are guilty for encouraging promiscuity.

The church has a problem over homosexuality. No one should be judgemental, especially if a homosexual calls him/herself that because of temptations only. No-one, homosexual or heterosexual, is guilty for having a temptation (often called a tendency) and all should feel welcome in church as in society. Sections of the Church have been called homophobic for disapproving of practicing homosexuality. This is because several Biblical texts indicate that homosexuality is not God's best plan for His people, it is not what we were designed for. God made the first humans male and female for mutual joy and delight, called becoming one flesh, and this unity Jesus told us, is for life (*Mark* 10:7-9). It is also a secure setting to produce children. The church is also adulterophobic; it doesn't like marriages being destroyed by adultery. The same Biblical texts are opposed to both practicing homosexuality and practicing adultery. Both are mentioned together in the Old and New Testaments. Moses, writing in about 1400BC, in *Leviticus* 18:20, 22, then again in 20:10, 13, deals with first offences then the consequences, for the nation of Israel in the immoral land of Canaan where homosexuality and adultery were widespread. St. Paul, writing in the 50sAD to the churches in the three promiscuity capitals of the New Testament world – Rome, Corinth and Ephesus in *Romans* 1:24, 26; 1 *Corinthians* 6:9; and 1 *Timothy* 1;10, again dealing with both homo- and hetero-sexual sin. While to the Bible believer both are wrong, people caught up either in these temptations or acts do not need our negative condemnation, they need our positive and compassionate help and welcome, to find a way forward and forgiveness where necessary. Jesus said 'Without me you can do nothing'. St. Paul affirms 'I can do everything through Christ who strengthens me'.

Fast forward to Noah's Ark today and we welcome non-judgementally folk of every belief, orientation, faith, race, age and background.

How to bring up a family

During the '80s and '90s, perhaps because we had four children, I was asked to speak about raising a family many times, sometimes with Christina, but usually she was at home actually doing the work that I was speaking about, and which she had largely taught me to do.

A very brief summary is as follows:

1. A good family starts from a good marriage (see below).

2. Set a good example. Children are imitators, if you swear they will too. They will learn how to forgive, love and be loved and how to stay married despite difficulties, from you. They will learn to have fun, and which things are fun, and what things are worth spending money on, from you.

3. Encourage your children. Don't be negatively critical. It's a mean world, complement them. Home is a refuge for learning. Help an unpopular child with his/her selfishness, bossiness or dishonesty. Help them to discover their talents and to overcome natural laziness. Don't over-push. Go to school events and support them.

4. Talk to them and listen to them every day; they may treasure a sentence for a week or a year. A survey showed the average father spends 37 seconds a week alone with each child, do much better. Discover common interests, let them be part of yours, but don't force them.

5. Use appropriate discipline. Make (a minimum number of) rules and enforce them. Support each other, teach respect of the other parent, no answering back. Don't make threats you won't carry out. Make a punishment fair, don't punish for being a child, only for defiance, then not too harsh or too feeble.

6. Let them bring friends home; organise it; you know what they are up to in your own home, can see your child's behaviour and help them. Help them choose friends, with reasons.

7. Teach God's view of marriage and sex. TV teaches the world view which has proved a disaster. There are eight reasons why sex before marriage is harmful (see chapters 5, 20, 22, and below).

8. Watch their intake of TV and limit it, have times for watching good TV or films together. TV, internet, and magazines can harm them as badly as road traffic can. Discuss the reasons with them. Encourage lots of other ways of developing their talents and spending their leisure time; spend time with them doing this.

9. Have a curfew, discuss it with them, enforce it, explain why; children make wrong decisions because they are trusting and innocent, then get hurt. Beware of allowing friends into bedrooms; 50% get pregnant in their own home.

10. Pray for their conversion. Talk to them about it. Take them to a helpful church and youth group, or Christian family camps and holidays. Let the Lord who is in your life (if He is. If not, you can ask Him to be) be in your conversation; remember they will copy you, not do as you say. Pray for their protection, guidance, development and problems.

11. Don't give up; you will look back with pride when you are old. It is much more time consuming, much harder work and much more expensive, than

you want it to be. So many of our friends have children who went off the rails, had bitter regrets; often because they did not make time or were not strict enough about the above. We were often criticised for being too strict but doing the right thing is so worth it.

We have had a long campaign inside and outside the churches to enrich marriage. Lots of people do not get married. Many because they choose singleness, others because relationships went wrong, or they did not find a person they wished to marry. However, the majority of people marry so we wanted to encourage people who want to marry to have a good marriage for life, to enjoy sex at its best for as long as possible. Perhaps because Christina and I have had so much fun together, we hope everyone can make love up to two or three times a week up to their forties and fifties and at least once a week in their sixties and seventies. Every couple will have their own expectation or possibilities, so need to agree together. That means real agreement, especially in illness or weakness that causes abstinence for a while.

The 2,000-year-old Jewish Mishnah used to teach about the importance of sex. The Jews mainly had arranged marriages, often when a girl was 12 or 13. They declared the conjugal act to be the duty of the husband not his right, like providing food and shelter, the conjugal act was her 'onah'. A wife could sue for divorce if deprived of her onah. The Mishnah laid down how often this duty was to be performed. Men of strong constitution, working from home: nightly. Labourers working in the same town: twice weekly. Merchants travelling longer distances by mule: weekly, and so on. His intention should not be to satisfy his personal desire, but to fulfil his obligation to his wife. Many years later research showed that a female orgasm produces an increase in blood-flow and oxygen to the brain, and is considered to be very good for the health of a woman.

Here are my top twelve tips for a long and happy sex life, within a long and happy marriage, for young people who are thinking about it, and older people trying to spice it up. Repairing a badly damaged marriage takes much greater effort, and perhaps outside help and mentoring:

1. Marry your best friend. They need eventually to sexually attract you as well. They must be kind.
Don't marry until you are sure this is a person you can be pleased with all your life. (See 10)

2. Don't have sex until marriage. It will mess up your brain chemicals. It may give you STIs, or a pregnancy, and make you feel second hand. It may put

you off married sex too. It has weird results.

3. If you have had sex with someone else before marriage get it cleaned up: start at the STI clinic, then ask God to forgive and heal the damage. Ask your present or future spouse if they can forgive you.

4. Talk to each other. According to Willard Harley's 15,000 person survey – a woman's top needs from a man are: affection, conversation, honesty and openness, financial support and family commitment. A man's top needs from a woman are: sexual fulfilment, recreational companionship, an attractive spouse, domestic support, admiration and encouragement. Sex on Friday for a woman begins on Monday! Only TV characters do sex without talking. Explain how it feels and what would make it better. Men can be lazy at talking.

5. Don't hurry sex. It has to be learnt like everything else. Women want intimacy of mind, agreement, love, before sex is possible, unless they are drunk, or nymphomaniacs, and not good wife material!

6. Be adventurous; anything is allowed as long as both people like it. Cunnilingus, fellatio, leaping from the window sill dressed only in a bus pass! Instead of VIAGRA pills, try the Very Intimate Attention Gives Rising Affection prescription. If the massage parlour offers exotic, manual assistance, why shouldn't the marriage bed? Sometimes only manual sex is possible.

7. Sex can hurt; check the reason, pray and deal with it, medically if necessary. Pregnancy and sickness (or impotence) are times when kindness, sensitivity and patience will be needed by both spouses. Personal hygiene is very important. Breaking wind at either end can have a negative effect!

8. Don't go to bed angry with each other. Say what is wrong; sort it – you are grown-ups now; say sorry. Forgive each other. If it is serious, find a referee; a good friend or the church minister if necessary.

9. Beware of porn. If nudity is not looked at objectively (out there, not in here) it can lead to dissatisfaction and mental adultery. Your spouse is the nude you need. If addicted to porn, ask your spouse to help. Pray together about it, make agreement over internet use and history deleting.

10. Be satisfied with your marriage choice. They were God's gift to you then and still are (*Proverbs* 18:22, *Malachi* 2:14). Remember the old adage 'keep your eyes wide open before marriage and half shut after'. You aren't perfect either, nor would anyone else be. Marriage is wonderful for companionship at all times, especially in old age.

11. Don't give up if you get bored with each other. God tells the husband unselfishly to love his wife regardless of his own feelings and the wife to submit to her husband regardless of hers (*Ephesians* 5:25,22). 'Love is kind, patient and never gives up' (1 *Corinthians* 13). You will need to keep rekindling a healthy love life. An evening out together or a weekend without the children, or just a bunch of flowers can work wonders. Pray for inspiration, and for each other; the whole thing was God's idea anyway (see chapter 42).

12. Avoid the temptations of third parties which usually begin with being over-friendly for a period of time and becoming a threat. Millions succumb with bitter regrets. They can destroy your family, your life-long dream and your example can be repeated in your children. Grass often looks greener on the other side but it will still need mowing. You may end up a lonely old dear.

As church leaders at Pip 'n' Jay and counsellors at Marriage Repair we were being asked all manner of personal questions. One of these was circumcision. Anyone who has read the New Testament knows that circumcision was an issue; quite a big one in fact in the early Church, as it is today in many countries. A question for parents and church leaders now is, is it relevant in Britain today? I had assumed that when God designed male sex organs they were the very best. The foreskin actually contains a wide variety and far more nerve endings than other parts of the penis. It can enhance and increase interest in sex even into old age. On the other hand God loved His people the Jews and gave them circumcision, so perhaps this was even better. Medical opinion was divided. Some described circumcision as like taking away a dead vestigial organ, because the ape foreskin is almost without sensation, but that was a medical myth and just bad science. Humans in this area, like so many others, are completely different from apes (see below). Another doctor said that circumcision was only given to stop the Israelites getting sand in their foreskins in the desert. I was shocked at his ignorance about the text; circumcision took place after they had been through the desert and just as they entered the Promised Land!

So how should we answer that question on circumcision? It appears that foreskins make males more susceptible to temptation, more randy, so God gave the Jews the custom to stop them being led astray into apostasy and idolatry. (It also appears to reduce the risk of contracting AIDS, by about half.) Is this a reason why a largely uncircumcised, secular Britain is at the top of the list for many sexual problems – STIs, unwanted pregnancies, and broken marriages through adultery. Other countries, especially Muslim ones where circumcision is normal, would not even understand the temptations, let alone copy the practices. In our modern world self control would seem more trusting and less intrusive than surgery. So I think that if there is a very compelling reason for circumcision, like a tight foreskin, or racial tradition, it could justify the practice and God will bless those men anyway. Generally speaking contentment with how we are, and a clear morality and God's help with self control would be best. (Female circumcision, of mutilation of the clitoris, is barbaric and disgraceful; understandably only continued by untrusting, jealous, or already damaged people.)

23

NFU Office Holder

MEANWHILE A LIVING HAD TO BE EARNED AND MY FARMING WAS USING AT LEAST 50 hours a week. If I averaged as much as six hours sleep a night through my thirties and forties it was unusual. But I took a lead from Winston Churchill, who throughout the war was reputed to have had four and a half hours sleep a night with a cat-nap at lunch time. I had also been elected onto the Somerset County Executive Committee of the NFU in 1968, which I thought I would give seven years to. In the event I found farming politics interesting and in need of some injection of enthusiasm from the tenant end of farming; many farmers were inheritors of farms from their rich fathers and did not feel the same financial pressures as us poorer tenants. Farming efficiency was therefore usually driven by tenant farmers (or owner-occupiers with a big mortgage). These did not have time for NFU politics. In 1976 I was elected honorary county vice-chairman, with a two year run-in for 1978, when I became chairman. At 39 I was the second youngest to have been elected to the Chair. That year I was paid travelling expenses, but it required lots of time. Curiously my brother was elected county chairman of Wiltshire the same year, the first time two brothers had been county chairmen at the same time, and our Dad, Barnard Bush, was elected mayor of Mendip District Council (aged 66). The three of us had our photo taken together for the press, and my brother and I did a quite funny BBC radio interview that achieved acclaim for a few minutes as 'interview of the week'.

I was also often called upon to comment on farming; I was close to the BBC in Bristol and easy for a film crew to find. As it was the year of the big snows I was asked to comment on how farmers were finding the snow. I told them about some other farmers' collapsed barns and greenhouses and the difficulty we had in feeding heifers and keeping pipes thawed out. Then I added 'But the Lord sometimes sends us these challenges….' Our Bishop of Bath and Wells, John Bickersteth, must have heard this; I met him a few days later on a pheasant shoot, to which my father asked him each year. He was a good shot. He mentioned this Points West interview, and thanked me for it, then asked, as I had already been a Lay Reader in Bristol Diocese for ten years, if he could license me as the same in Bath and Wells? The licensing happened a little while later and I then preached at the Young Farmers Club County Harvest Festival at Wells Cathedral.

As was usual for a county chairman I gave at least one day and one evening per week that year to go to different commodity meetings, like milk, arable crops, pigs, horticulture, poultry, parliamentary, land tenure, finance and livestock; the Bath and West Show Council, the NFU Mutual Insurance meeting as well as chairing the monthly County Executive Committee and the (O&GP) Standing Committee. I had to visit different parts of the county, including snow collapsed buildings, the strawberry growers of Cheddar, who were having their crop ruined by dusty lorries from the quarry, and each of eight NFU Groups in the county, from Minehead to Bath. There were negotiations with industry groups and some local farmers' dances to go to with my glamorous Christina. There were speeches to make including at a dinner in the House of Commons for the eight Somerset MPs and some local farmers. I tried to include a bit about farming and a bit about family and a bit about God in all my speeches and articles. In the House of Commons restaurant I gave a summary of the current farming worries, mentioned the importance of strong families for the future of the nation, and closed with a verse from Jeremiah 6: 'Stand at the crossroads and look; ask for the ancient paths, where the good way is and walk in it, and you will find rest for your souls'. The MP for Taunton asked me for its reference afterwards, as he wanted to use it at a funeral that week.

One of the meetings I attended was with the animal feed industry representatives. They suggested, at one of these meetings, that they had discovered that meat and bone meal could be safely rendered at a lower temperature and thus save the pig and poultry industry several pounds a tonne in costs. Were we happy? Lacking evidence to the contrary we said yes, for pig and poultry farmers to be competitive in Europe. I made a mental note not to feed it to my cows, ever again. Little did I realise that this was the moment we were inviting BSE into our herds, to show itself two years later. And little did I realise that the millers were putting it into our calf food without telling us, under the protection of professional secrecy. I would never have agreed if I had known. Someone in academic circles or in government should have known this was happening. We were supposed to be responding to expert advice.

As my time was needed for General Synod, Pip 'n' Jay preaching and farm and family, it was a very busy year. But the NFU County Chair was also a great privilege; to represent 5,000 farmers as a wide variety of events. On one occasion I was invited with other stake holders to a meeting in the Bristol City Council offices, with Tony Wedgwood Benn, the Energy Secretary, about a proposed Severn Barrage. He was in favour of this as a generator of renewable energy and of jobs; it could carry a road on it and would cost £5 billion with another £5 billion to go on drainage work. The conservationists were gloomy, but I had seen the River Severn at high tide and even then there seemed to be hundreds of acres of mud beside it; they seemed to object to everything different. Now, 30 years on, the Dutch have built bigger dams and we are still talking about it.

Three years earlier I had sat next to Tony Benn in the dining room of the House of Lords when my bishop, Oliver Tomkins, held a dinner at his retirement for MPs and General Synod Members. I quizzed Tony about his faith for a few minutes. After a while he said to Bishop Oliver 'Does one get a DD for being interrogated about one's faith in front of a bishop?' He was pleasant and friendly and one of those people who the press love to hate; I felt it was because he was often right. He tape-recorded every interview because he had been so often misquoted.

This was also the year of the lorry drivers strike, early in 1979, just as I finished my NFU County Chair year. As I was farming near Avonmouth, which was the focus of it, I offered to represent the farmers of five counties and try to keep essential animal supply lorries moving, which were supposed to be allowed through the picket lines. I went down each morning at 5.00 am, sometimes with one of the children, to give cups of tea to the picket line and make sure they did not stop animal feed lorries reaching the farms. Some Mendip farmers had threatened to come down with shot guns to get through if the lorries were blocked, which was a useful handle to keep the pickets cooperative. At the end of the week's dispute the Transport and General Workers Union were so pleased they offered me an office with them if it should happen again. I am glad to say it didn't!

But a few years later I had to drive a lorry across a picket line myself. Our good friend and neighbour Keith Hodgson ran a business in the wholesale fruit market in Bristol. One day he rang me to say his lorry drivers were going on strike tomorrow, could I drive a five-tonne lorry to do some very urgent deliveries to shops that were running out of fruit and veg supplies; some other friends were doing the same. It was due to be a wet day so I thought I could leave the farm. I agreed and duly turned up, found this frighteningly large looking lorry and probably terrorised the citizens of Warwickshire for a day, including reversing with difficulty into supermarket loading bays. They were relieved to see the fruit and veg arrive. When I had finished I drove back to Keith's yard, where I had to drive past a very angry picket line who were shouting 'blackleg' at me and shaking their fists. Keith thanked me and I asked him 'Would you be willing to talk to those chaps who have just shouted at me?' he said 'Of course I would, at any time'. So I walked back to the picket line and said 'What do you mean by shouting at me, I was doing a friend a favour, and probably helping save your job. Why don't you just go and sort it out?' 'He won't talk to us,' they said. 'Yes he will, he has just told me so'. So off they went and the dispute was ended in an hour. Keith and his late wife Rosemary had been among our closest friends since our children were little; often being there to listen or encourage us and just to be fun for us and our family to be with.

Keith returned the favour on another occasion when a friend, David Matthews, who was a teacher at Whitfield Comprehensive School, rang and asked me if I would pretend to be the Duke of Monmouth on April 1st. The sixth form the previous year had removed all the furniture from one of the buildings, the staff wanted to reply in kind. I asked Keith who had rather a posh car if he would mind being my chauffeur, in my Army peaked cap. I wore a suit, with a rose buttonhole and sat in the back of the car; and we duly arrived at the school, drove slowly across the playing field to the end of a red carpeted reception line of teachers I was to shake hands with. I was then introduced to the sixth form who were told the Duke had come to visit two schools as he had been newly elevated to the House of Lords. I was then shown round during which it rained and a precocious little girl lent me her umbrella. Then a boy said to me 'I think I have seen you somewhere before' to which I replied that it was probably on television. Keith came round with me as an excellent 'chauffeur' and gave appropriate answers in role.

After the tour I departed to return an hour later for an 'Any Questions'. The first question was 'What does the panel think of April Fool's Day?' A student answered first and said 'I love it, I wish it could happen every day', then a staff member replied and said 'I hate it; I don't know who to believe'. The Duke of Monmouth then said 'May I say that being part of the nobility has been rather a strain and I am now reverting to being Anthony Bush, my real name'. There was a stunned silence, followed by appreciative applause as the students realised they had been fooled. Then the girl shouted out 'but I lent you my umbrella!' We continued with the quite challenging Any Questions, which included questions on sex and marriage; and was the main reason I accepted the request. The staff sent her ladyship a bunch of flowers! Looking back, it did seem a bit crazy; but our daughter Annie and son Caspar, and some of our grandchildren seemed inspired by it and inflict similar jokes on people on most April 1st.

24

Farming and Wildlife

THE NFU COUNTY CHAIRMANSHIP IS OFTEN FOLLOWED BY JOB OFFERS LIKE the Minister of Agriculture's panel or directorships in allied industries. I turned them all down because, although the money might have come in useful, there seemed other more pressing unpaid needs off the farm as well as keeping the farm growing and earning. In 1980 I was asked to start, voluntarily, a Farming and Wildlife Advisory Group (FWAG) for Avon County, similar to some other counties, to encourage farmers to conserve the wildlife on their farms in the hedges, meadows and watercourses. This was a major area of conflict between town and country; many conservationists felt that more could be done by farmers to preserve our native species. I agreed. Many farmers were ignorant of wildlife, and encouraged by the wartime and post war needs of the country to grow as much food as possible, had accepted government grants to remove hedges and improve productivity. But there were now food surpluses in Europe so we needed to think more about the environment. It actually cost money to destroy hedges, meadows and ponds, so many of these remained intact but overgrown and needing to be improved. There were also a small number of farmers who were very interested in improving their wildlife, especially owner-occupiers, with long-term aspirations.

I was asked to draw together a group made up of one third farmers, one third local government and Ministry of Agriculture representatives and one third from the wildlife organisations. At our first meeting a wildlife person said he thought a farmer who ploughed up a field of buttercups was worse than a town vandal! He had to be informed that buttercups were actually poisonous to cattle, and above a certain density the field became completely unproductive.

It was clear there was work to do on all parties for balanced progress to be made.

In the capacity of FWAG county chairman, I was asked to join two other chairmen from other counties, to give short lectures to Prince Charles and his 30 Duchy managers on conservation issues. My lecture was on hedges, the others spoke on meadows and watercourses. Amongst other things I mentioned that two hundred years previously the conservationists of the day had objected strongly to hedges being planted under the Enclosures Act, as they 'ruined the view and harboured roots weeds and vermin'. But now we had found they were very beneficial to wildlife and even to agriculture. At the end of my talk, the Prince, aged 32 at the time, asked how big I thought a field ought to be. I replied that I thought about 10 acres in a mixed west of England farm. A few years later I was visiting Highgrove Farm and found the Prince was planting and altering hedges. I asked how big his fields were going to be and his manager replied – about 10 acres.

I opened each FWAG meeting with a prayer that I had written. We need God's wisdom in all aspects of daily life and I wanted to show that, to both God and man. My precedent was that Gloucester NFU and all County Council meetings at that time opened in prayer. The FWAG movement organised farm walks to show farmers what could be done and others what was being done to conserve rare or threatened species. It has held annual competitions and distributed ideas and has been a significant catalyst for change of attitudes of farmers towards the wildlife of which we are custodians. But it also showed government and wildlife specialists that there is a price to pay and farmers should not be expected to provide the cheapest possible food as well as spend money on wildlife; especially struggling tenant farmers, and owner occupiers with a mortgage. Thus arose, 15 years later, the environmental schemes that reward farmers for setting land aside and protecting wildlife habitats. It also showed farmers that some techniques, for example frequency and method of hedge cutting, need not cost money. This can make the nation's hedgerows, which are the country's largest nature reserve, much richer in both flora and fauna.

25

NFU Council or Church Growth?

In late 1982 there arose a vacancy to represent Somerset on the NFU's HQ London Council. I was still concerned that the NFU tended to be run by wealthy landowners, because they were the ones who could afford to leave their farms. Tenants like me were under-represented. Europe was a growing challenge, both as competition and as farming colleagues. No one seemed to know what help our fellow farmers were getting in any of the EEC countries, and how to lobby our government and the EEC for a level playing field. An election was to be held and I did not wholly approve of the farmer who was standing; he had just left his wife after 25 years for a younger woman. I let my name go forward for election because I felt the job needed to be done better than it was. In the event the election appeared to be a tie, so the chairman cast his vote for the other man and it was announced. Subsequently the chairman came to me and said on the recount I had been elected by one, should they re-run the election? I was actually having grave misgivings about the time available, because I had just been asked to lead, voluntarily, a large mission at a football stadium at which Billy Graham was to be the speaker. I felt the election was a God-guided mistake, so let the result stand. I often wondered what might have happened if I had become an NFU HQ Delegate. No doubt many farmers dream of becoming President of the NFU, but there was such a lot in farming that needed to be achieved at that time, that needed determination to engage with government. The slide in farming fortunes ten years later came from faulty groundwork in the mid '80s, when farm support systems were changed and the Milk Marketing Board was dismantled. But I felt the state of the church was also dire. Almost no one was trying to help outsiders find faith, so I felt I should run this Mission.

At about this time I found that having been very active all day long with physical work through most of my 30s, I was becoming much more sedentary. I was putting on weight and feeling flabby. I could scarcely do one press-up. I discovered a system of five exercises that are done by Canadian Air force pilots to keep fit in a sedentary job:

1. Arms above head then bending to touch toes 30 times
2. 20 sit ups

3. Lying on front and arching back 30 times
4. 20 press-ups and
5. 500 steps running on the spot, 10 stride jumps, arms spread every 100.

I have done them several times a week for the last 30 years; the advantage to them is that they can be done watching the news on TV, and they are cheaper and much quicker than going to a gym!

26

1984: Billy Graham at the Football Ground

Our own church had for some years encouraged non-churchgoers to come to church and hear about the Christian faith in an un-threatening, modern-music-filled environment. People were regularly coming to faith. But many churches did not have our facility, nor the gifted preaching that Malcolm Widdecombe and other invited preachers provided. Most of the church had become somewhat inward looking and a comfortable club for insiders. Even ours had limited outreach possibilities. Yet one of the vital parts of Jesus' final commands to us was to tell others about Him. What was anyone doing about that? A number of Christian leaders had felt it was time to invite Billy Graham to come to Britain again, at least to England. Billy Graham was the best known preacher in the world having addressed well over 100 million people face-to-face and had, through earlier preaching visits been hugely influential on the life of this country. His first major mission had been held at Harringay Arena in 1954. Christina and her sister and parents had all come to faith in Christ there. I had gone there too, as a new Christian with my parents, and had been very impressed at the clear explanation of the gospel that was given and the large numbers going forward as enquirers. At Billy's next mission in 1966, 100 church ministers had stood on the platform with him, who had come to faith in 1954 and '55 (which also achieved the Wembley attendance record of over 120,000).

There had even been an effect on the whole country due to the missions in London in 1954-5 and 1966. There was a slight dip in national crime figures following each of them. Billy Graham had pointed out that education had been thought to lower crime, lower drunkenness and increase happiness, yet all that had happened was that there were cleverer criminals, a higher divorce rate, more broken families and increased alcoholism. There was a need for the whole nation to find faith in God to put meaning into life and His strength to do the good things we all found so difficult.

Mission England eventually started in Bristol, Liverpool, Sunderland, Birmingham, Norwich and Ipswich, at all of which, football stadiums were hired. I was asked to be the unpaid chairman of Mission England South West. I said I would share the chair by being Director and running the preparations and event, if another chairman could help by being the Chairman of the Executive Committee and support me. Tony Dann took on this role excellently. His wife Jill was a leading member of General Synod and he and Jill had both played hockey for England. He was an Old Monktonian eight years before me, and as a solicitor, helped draw up this charity and two others I helped to start later. He was a wise and encouraging colleague and guided the meetings well.

In September 1982 we started a three-year period of prayer, training and evangelism (helping non-Christians to discover and begin a relationship with Jesus Christ). The stadium meetings were a focus, but we wanted Billy to arrive on the crest of a wave of evangelism, rather than to initiate the wave. We initially found very little enthusiasm for the Mission. The big evangelical churches were already looking outwards and were saying why have an American, especially an old one of 63, and the days of big missions were past. Most of the others did not seem to care. Only the worryingly small number of 15 leaders turned up at our first exploratory meeting. Should we continue to attempt this enormous outlay of hiring a stadium, employing people in a rented office, spend money on publicity, when there was so little enthusiasm for it? The Diocesan Bishops remained very unhelpful and unenthusiastic throughout the mission, as did more than half of C. of E. churches. By the stadium phase, when churches saw it was happening anyway, lots more became suddenly interested, but by then it was too late to benefit from the full mission and its process and method.

The central Mission England leadership were inspirational and helpful; they drew up guidelines of how the mission could be set up and run, especially, for me, Clive Claver, Gavin Reid and Eddy Gibbs were most encouraging. When the final dates were being worked out, Clive Calver, Former head of Youth for Christ and Chairman of Evangelical Alliance, came to me and said I would soon be under pressure to drop the length of the mission from eight days to five, but he strongly urged us to stick at eight. I thought 'you don't know how little support there is for this'; but I said OK I would hold out for eight. Clive was right. Those were depressing days of opposition to most aspects of the Mission. But if God was behind it, there would emerge enough ordinary folk to make it all happen.

Bill and Judy Spencer, who produced a Christian newspaper, were my main encouragers locally, at this time and throughout the three years. They were full of ideas about building the mailing list and informing churches about what was happening. Their newspaper skills helped greatly with our publicity. I had to find and set up an office with staff. Hilary Field was our first employee and excellent office manager, for two years. Very quickly we felt we were being blessed and pushed along as dozens of volunteers and workers offered to help. There were many who had been helped to faith through the earlier missions with Billy Graham, from 1954, '55, '66, and who knew how God could use a preacher to kindle real faith. As with so many things God chooses the little people to get the real work done; this was the same as ordinary people caught the vision of what could happen. I had to find 36 chairmen of committees, called Task Groups; 20 of these were Area Task Groups to encourage local evangelism from Southampton to Cornwall, and from Swindon to Cheltenham and to South Wales. The stadium phase with Billy Graham was to be the focal point of the mission, as it were the icing on the cake. But everyone knew there would be no cake, or outward reaching mission, without the icing. The church was very bad at the marketing exercise we had been given by Jesus of telling the rest of the world about Him.

All Task groups needed to have half their members under 40, a good female representation and from as wide a range of denominations as possible. They had to generate a steady build-up of interest in helping outsiders come to faith; first by encouraging all church people to pray for three non-Christian friends each. The bottom line is that things happen when you pray which don't happen when you don't pray. As soon as these prayer triplets began and people began to pray for their non-Christian friends some of these friends began to become Christians. In some cases all nine people prayed for within a triplet had come to faith within a few months. Then by encouraging churches to expect new members we would begin to prepare, two years on, for the big Stadium Mission. There were task groups covering publicity and the media, feeding news of the mission to the press; another devoted to women and how to use their networking skills; counsellor training of 4,000 counsellors and then the follow-up of new believers. Another was charged with assembling the biggest choir ever in the south west, of 2,000 voices; the Church Life Task Group had to assemble the list of eventually 1,100 churches of 30 denominations, that joined in the Mission, to make sure they were ready to invite and receive new believers. Full-time trainers were provided by some mission organisations to help churches get ready. The Youth Task Group had to convince thousands of youth groups, school Christian Unions and young people that the mission was for them and their non-Christian friends too.

Early in the mission it became clear that there were strong disagreements among Christians. The biggest was between Roman Catholics and some Baptists and other non-comformists. Anglicans like me were used to living with and deliberately minimising various disagreements, trying to concentrate on the things we agreed about which were always bigger anyway. I was keen to try and keep Catholics on board as well as the opposite wing, because 'out of sight is out of mind' and most of the time this worked. At one point the Catholic priest who was leading their involvement with us, a strong Bible believer and charismatic, whom I knew and liked very much, Richard MacKay, gave me a problem. In the papers one day was a picture of his church and a story of them burying the bones of a saint in his altar. I rang him and said 'Richard, what on earth are you doing burying saint's bones in your altar? I have huge problems already because you guys are in this mission; couldn't you show some restraint?' He replied 'Anthony, we are only doing what the early church did in celebrating Holy Communion in the Roman catacombs on the graves of the church members'. As we were all supposed to think the early church was OK, I had to agree it was not as bad as the superstition that it appeared to be.

The RC inclusion was to be my biggest problem. Billy Graham always encouraged their inclusion because everyone needs to hear the gospel. We don't know how far anyone is with God. However, some churches pulled out because we were going to refer RC enquirers to Richard MacKay's network of Catholic Bible Studies. There were to be 800 RC enquirers in the end. At the stadium we had protestant anti-RC protesters, and I had a letter from one of them to Billy Graham, saying he was 'the biggest traitor since Judas Iscariot', for meeting the Pope a few years before! On the other hand one night at the stadium, a man sat in his seat for half an hour after it was over and said to the steward who spoke to him 'For 25 years I have been lied to about that man (by extreme protestants). I can now see that he is a faithful preacher of God's word'. But that was all to come.

About eight months before the Stadium Mission the Billy Graham Association sent us a team member, paid for entirely by them, to help with all the preparations and running of this huge event, which was well beyond the experience of any of us. We were sent Greg Strand, a tall, charming, thoughtful, eloquent married man who settled into the area with his wife for the duration of the stadium phase. I had noticed that BG team members were of very high calibre; they were the sort of people who could have worked at the White House were they not trying to build God's kingdom with the BG team. They had good experience around the world of knowing what to do, but needed our local input to help them achieve the training, publicity and administrative goals that were needed. Greg was in touch with all task group chair people and his authority was equal to mine, so we needed to agree to avoid problems. It was quite easy to agree. We found it so easy to agree that he and his wife became good friends and visited us at the farm. They also came with Christina and me to Badminton Horse Trials, to show them some posher traditional English life.

For the stadium phase the Stadium Task Group was led by Bill Spencer, who had already done so much for the publicity of the Mission. This group had the final job of equipping Ashton Gate Football Ground for its biggest ever crowd since current safety regulations came in. With an extra 2,000 fixed seats on a new temporary stand, 8,000 chairs on the pitch, and 18,000 plastic covered foam cushions for people to sit in the stands (these went, with many other things, to the other stadiums as well). A large platform had to be erected on the pitch to put a music group, piano and organ, visiting church leaders, Billy Graham and his preaching lectern (with a small roof in case of rain), plus his doctor and security. We had to cut huge new entrances into the back of stands to allow easy access by-passing the normal turnstiles, and make extra walkways onto the pitch, so that enquirers could quickly get to the area in front of the platform. These all had to be repaired after the Mission. There was now space for 38,000 people per night, instead of football's 20,000. We needed space on the bowling green under the Dolman Stand for 400 secretaries to work on enquirers' return cards, to make sure they were posted off to churches by the next day.

There were huge car parks to arrange, but the biggest surprise was that car parking for football crowds was so limited that we had to plan to bring almost all visitors by coach and arrange parking each night for 600 coaches. I realised one day that the people coming by coach would be dropped by their coaches on the wrong side of Winterstoke Road and would have to walk across the road and would thus stop other coaches being on time. So we needed a new bridge over Winterstoke Road! I rang a senior Army officer in the Officers Christian Union, Brigadier Neil Carlier in Aldershot; he said he would ask the local TA Engineers if they would like a training exercise. The TA commanding officer rang me and said they would be delighted to build us a bridge, but could we arrange a 10-tonne crane?

So at the morning prayer meeting at the office that day we asked God to help us find a crane. As I left the office I met a man coming in, who asked if there was anything he could do for Mission England.

I said to him 'what do you do?'

He said 'I work with my father, who owns a crane-hire company'!

The bridge was soon constructed, thanks to helpful people on the Bristol planning committee rushing the permission through. It was erected in the middle of the night, as the road had to be closed. This was itself big news and raised the profile of the Mission. We also put advertisements to the mission on its railings. Our Publicity Task Group had already bought £50,000 of advertisement hoardings to put up our theme advert 'Billy Graham, Worth listening to' below Billy's picture, all round the city and outside every church and beside many country roads, as at general elections. Another donor wanted to pay the £20,000 it was costing us to hire the stadium, because, he said, he owed God a debt. Hundreds of others volunteered their working skills or resources.

The stadium phase drew near; a huge team of stewards were assembled and trained to help park vehicles, guide people to their seats, and watch for troublemakers. As entrance was entirely free, we needed stewards to take the free-will offering each night, in hundreds of buckets and a treasury team was to count it ready for the bank, in Bristol City Football Club's special money room. Money did not feature as a big issue in the Mission. God seemed to move people to give at the right time; we hoped at the stadium that non-church folk could ignore the buckets, but Christians would be generous. But we could not say so! In the whole three-year mission about £750,000 was given, of which about one tenth was left over at the end to give to the organisations who had lent us full-time workers. No doubt this sum would seem tiny, especially to a football club these days.

Six members of the Christian Police Association were on duty each night in plain clothes in case there was trouble. We had heard that a protest group were going to take their clothes off and rush onto the pitch! They did, but were caught before they could move. Others were coming from every imaginable cult and religion to try and prey on interested people. I asked the Principal of Trinity Theological College, George Carey the future Archbishop of Canterbury, if they could send a large group of students down to engage these folk in conversation and keep them quiet each night. They did an excellent job. One of them would be my future Nailsea rector, Ken Boullier. The stewards and other leaders had dozens of two-way radios, which had three emergency channels to switch to. On the opening night the first two channels were jammed by a malicious hacker, before the police traced him and closed him down. The electricity was sabotaged the first night but only for a few minutes. The system was then better secured. We fully realised that evangelism is more important than football, so attracts many angry enemies! Jesus himself had said 'they have hated me and will hate you, too'.

When the public meetings happened, in May 1984, the stadium was the most prayed-for place on Earth. Billy Graham arrived with us in weakness, from hospital, but he has a million prayer partners around the world and had himself spoken to more people face to face, than anyone else in history (now

200 million). It was one of my jobs to invite and then supervise the platform party of church leaders and participants in the mission programme, who were to lead in prayer or be interviewed, or pray for the final blessing. I reported to Cliff Barrows, the Meeting and Choir leader, how many coaches had come that night and from where. He then asked me to welcome the crowd each night and to call out the areas that the coaches had come from, like 'Welcome to 46 coaches from Devon!' for some audience reaction. It was certainly the largest crowd of people I had ever spoken to.

I also sat next to Billy Graham each night on the platform. My job was not to talk to him, but to protect him from conversations before he had given his talk. He had visited us on our farm one day and we had shown him round. Christina made lunch for him, his photographer, and two security people, one of whom was a friend of ours and a newly retired policeman from Bristol. This was Billy Burns who I have mentioned, who had been shot at point blank range a couple of years before. I had also welcomed Billy Graham to Bristol when he first arrived, and briefed him in his hotel about the mission. So I knew him quite well. I mainly sat next to him in silence after saying hello each night. One night I leaned over and said 'there are 28 Mayors in the Silver Delegation tonight, Billy' (that was an area for 500 specially invited VIP's, hosted by our Chairman, Tony Dann). To which he replied 'Are they more important than anyone else?' I had to admit they weren't, even though they probably thought they were!

Billy began each sermon with a reflective prayer, suggesting people had come on a search or out of curiosity or by invitation from a friend or because they needed something to fill an empty life. He then prayed that God would come and meet every need. All his sermons were based on the Bible and Jesus' life or teachings, often from a parable or meeting that Jesus had with someone. He preached to each person directly, using many illustrations and examples from peoples' lives and an occasional funny story. Billy often reflected on the emptiness of the rich or the sadness of poverty, or addiction, or family brokenness, but pointing people of every background or difficulty to Jesus, who could save us from the past and change the future and give meaning and purpose and power to live well. On Youth Night or Families night his illustrations were appropriate to those and there were also famous musicians in the earlier part of each night's programme, like Cliff Richard or George Hamilton IV.

Each night Billy ended with his well known 'I'm going to ask you to get up out of your seat and come to the front, publicly – because while on earth Jesus always called people publicly – and to symbolise coming to Jesus,' for Him to change us. Then he reminded us all that Jesus required us to repent and be willing to turn away from sin, to receive Jesus Christ as Saviour and as Lord and then become a witness to others of the change Jesus has made, like helping mother with the dishes, or being friendly to a neighbour, and finally join up with a church to help us grow as Christians. He invited all the enquirers to say together a prayer of commitment, then to receive a gospel and a booklet to help them study the Bible for themselves. Their details were then taken by a counsellor to pass on to the enquirer's church of choice for follow-on help.

As I listened to Billy Graham preach the first night, I thought this is the same simple explanation of the gospel, with the same Bible verses and explanation that I have heard lots of people preach; I had preached most of the same things myself. When he gave the appeal to come forward, I wondered if anyone would come. The press had criticised Billy for having emotional music to coerce people forward, so we had nothing; just silence. So it was called emotional silence! Over 2,000 people came forward, plus 2,000 trained counsellors to help them. God was answering the praying of people for their friends and family. Lives were being changed. Some critics could not understand the difference between emotional and spiritual. The difference would be seen in how long the change lasted.

The mission was Bristol's biggest ever event up to that time. The stadium had a crowd of 30,000 each night, a total of 240,000 people including 20,000 enquirers who came on to the pitch at Billy Graham's invitation. Two-thirds were under 25. We did a survey a year later and found that 60% of the enquirers were still in contact with their churches; some churches had 100%, others had none, it depended very much on the way the churches had befriended and helped them. One third might have moved house or college anyway. There were wonderful stories of mended marriages, improved parent-child relationships, the unhappy or even suicidal becoming happy and motivated, long term searchers after God finding their hopes fulfilled. Many of our own family and friends found it a significant event in their walk to or walk with God. We are still in touch with several who came to faith at that time.

Following the stadium mission we laid on events, especially for young people. Many churches were not good at helping them. So we hired the stadium's Dolman Stand two more times in 1984, for music and teaching meetings for 5,000 young people each. Many other churches and groups of churches held missions of their own.

The following year, 1985, some Sheffield church leaders asked Billy Graham to come back as they felt they were in an area that had been missed by Mission England. Videos had been taken of the stadium meetings in 1984 and rushed overnight to lots of other churches to have their own video mission. These had seemed so blessed, that it was decided that Sheffield's meetings should, by the new technology of a TV satellite link and large screen, be broadcast live around the country. The sound would reach someone by satellite quicker than a person sitting at the back of the stadium! I remember spending much of February 1985 making a thousand phone calls to different church leaders trying to set up these links. By June 25th-29th, the time of the Sheffield Mission, we had 15 satellite links in the south west in places as varied as Cardiff's Ninian Park Football Stadium for 5,000 people, three theatres, a sports centre, a school, and nine churches. As a consequence there were about 2,000 more enquirers, including a god-daughter of mine who later became a relief-work missionary. In 2011 at a men's dinner meeting to which I was speaking, its leader told me he and his wife had come to faith in 1985 through the satellite relay in Sidmouth.

27

Farmhouse Fire and other Personal Challenges in the Mission

We had personal challenges in this mission. In June 1983, a year before the stadium phase, our house was struck by lightning, with a huge bang and tremor, perhaps ball lightning, which was reported as seen in the same storm nearby. At the time, Christina was at home with two farm students, but I was at a meeting in Bristol. The house roof quickly caught alight, but Christina calmly rang the fire brigade. Four fire engines arrived quite quickly. I was informed as soon as I arrived at my mission office from the meeting. I came straight home and had the strange experience of rounding a corner of our driveway and seeing the house with no roof, but not being surprised, because for many years I had expected at some point to see that! I stood on the lawn watching the firemen putting out the fire. The firemen hosed as carefully as they could without flooding the ground floor which was not damaged. A news reporter, who had been called, as they are with every fire call out, asked a surprising question:

'Has anything else happened to people working in Mission England lately?' Perhaps he thought bad things should not happen to people who are trying to do good.

I said 'Funny that you should ask that, but last week three key workers all had their cars written off.'

'Do you think there is anything in that?' he asked.

‘Probably’, I said, ‘the enemy is always trying to have a go at us.’

The next day the headline in the *Bristol Evening Post* read ‘Devil attacks leading evangelist!’

Billy Graham was interviewed in Holland; the story of our fire was in 27 newspapers around the world and I was live on Boston Radio the following morning! The theology was a bit questionable but the publicity was excellent! The meeting I had been at was slightly different to the mission, as I had just hired a train to take people to an anti-abortion rally in London. I had personally paid a deposit of £328 for the train, and must have handed it over at exactly the moment our house was hit. To our surprise, the news of our fire triggered some wonderful and loving response from other Christians. We were lent two caravans, which became bedrooms for our boys, one of whom, Caspar, had lost all his GCSE notes and other possessions. Lizzie had also had a room in the attic so also lost everything that she didn’t have with her at university. We were insured new-for-old, so everything that we could remember was covered financially, so we eventually built a new kitchen with the proceeds. We also received lots of help to clean up and temporarily rewire the house. People sent meals, and most surprising was that we were also sent about ten financial gifts; and to the sum of exactly the £328 I had paid at the moment the house was struck. In the event I had to cancel the train and we went in three coaches instead, but, amazingly, the Lord seemed to move people to exactly cover my personal cost.

The Mission was not an easy time for Christina, either; I was away from the farm, sometimes six days a week, with other exciting people, or in the car travelling to meetings all round the west of England. I had never worked every day away from home before. Even now I was almost never away at night, as our dairy farm still needed my daily input as well as the family. After our fire we waited over six months before Lord Wraxall had the roof and top floor repaired; even then it only happened when Christina went personally to him to complain. ‘Mrs Bush you must have fortitude’ he said, to which she replied ‘I have had fortitude for six months and have run out of it’, and burst into tears. Being a bachelor he did not know what to do with a weeping woman so rang his insurers in London and the job started very quickly! Our girls had both left home, at least for term time, Lizzie at university, then off for her year’s language study to Germany and France, and Annie was boarding at Monkton Combe, where I had been (my father, who had also been there, had offered to pay the fees), then off to South America for part of a year out. The boys were at QEH School by day but were a great support to Christina, too. The house was finally repaired for Lizzie’s 21st birthday, when 20 friends stayed the night.

This was also Christina’s time to get back into art teaching at adult education centres. She had been painting and exhibiting for some time, but now my absence from home in the day was an opportunity for a little retraining then gradually to start teaching at several classes a week of sketching, painting and calligraphy in Bristol including at the Zoo and Museum, in Nailsea and also on the farm. This continued for about 15 years until we both felt called to a big venture together on the farm.

I left home each morning at about 9.30am, after breakfast, and after doing what was vital on the farm since 6.00am. I then had the day to deal with the Mission in its office, which eventually located at St. Thomas's, near Bristol Bridge. There was so much going on that I was sometimes referred to as the unofficial Bishop of Bristol. The office had my assistant, two other secretaries, Greg Strand (the excellent Billy Graham team member until the stadium phase was over), and six team leaders using it. Sometimes dozens of people called about various matters. I usually went home at 5.00pm and finished farm work late at night as we were tenants with pressure to pay the bills. The first year, 1983, the year of the fire, we had wonderful growing weather and profits were high, as if we were being rewarded. But 1984 was a drought year and we fared much worse. I found myself spending time checking the cows every night. Some days, especially after the stadium phase, I did not get to the office because of silage making, harvesting and a number of other vital farm tasks. It was also an astonishing and unrepeatable privilege, which was to lead on to things I could never have imagined. It also taught me that I could trust other highly competent people to get on with their tasks without my supervision. Delegation with responsibility is an essential part of leadership above a certain size of organisation. There were over 8,000 high-calibre volunteers in this mission, all excellently guided by their team leaders. I was to need to use these principles again in the future.

28

Worldwide Effects of the Mission

A SURPRISING NUMBER OF SPIN-OFFS FOLLOWED FROM MISSION ENGLAND. Apart from an increase in people going to lots of churches, I found myself receiving invitations to visit churches and after-dinner clubs talking about the Mission, Jesus and evangelism. I was also invited to Amsterdam in 1986 to join a team of counsellors at a training week for 5,000 mainly third-world evangelists, invited from 174 countries around the world most of which Billy Graham had visited. It was a memorable week, with some excellent talks by world-famous speakers, with simultaneous translations into eight languages and some good catering for 5,000 people in several diet groups by KLM Airlines. Lots of time was spent talking to dozens of young men about dilemmas of marriage, faith and dealing with finances. Towards the end, collections were made of the clothes from us wealthy ones from the west, with the call 'we need suits and shoes' even 'we need a wedding dress', etc. At some point I said to a colleague that if I gave away many more clothes I would be walking into the aircraft in my under-pants. To which he replied 'but they need under-pants!'

I did not realise it but I was to meet a church leader there who was going to lead to a profound change in my own and many other farmers' future. Meanwhile the marriage counsellors from Marriage Repair had become the key folk in the Stadium Mission for helping people with social or emotional problems. Jim Craddock from the USA had come over to help train them for this role. The time now seemed right for David Mitchell to formally start Network Counselling, mentioned in chapter 23.

Soon after the mission, Derek Groves, who had been involved in rescue and rehabilitation of drug addicts for many years, and in counselling at the stadium, wanted to start a coffee bar in St. Paul's as a place to which street people with life-controlling habits could come. His former rehab employers were unwilling to sponsor this, so Derek was put in touch with me by a theological student at Pip 'n' Jay and fellow preacher there, called Charlie Cleverley. Charlie told me that in his opinion Derek was a man with a ministry; such people were few and far between, would I help him? I agreed to go with Derek to talk to his employers, but they were unwilling to start a crisis centre.

What should we do? Yet again the majority was against a new idea. However, it looked as though Derek needed a little encouragement to take the plunge into a new charity and ministry. As every Bristolian must have seen and known there were many homeless people on the streets by day and as we had discovered on the soup run, by night. Surely these could be and should be helped? After praying this through we eventually decided that this new venture had to be started and Crisis Centre Ministries was born, with no money, but with Derek as its full-time director. Pete Hitchens, Trudie Lane and others joined Derek and Mary Groves in this hard slog of finding premises for a drop-in café in the right spot and setting it up and running it, with the patience and steady commitment needed to help the street kids and those often avoided by society. These street people were among the most difficult to help as they had often deliberately dropped out of society, rejecting those who had, they felt, rejected them. They had built up anti-social habits sometimes over years, and were unreliable, ungrateful and almost unhelpable. The patient, sacrificial commitment of the Crisis Centre team was inspiring. Theirs was and would be an astonishing story of unexpected provision and life-changing experiences for many over the next 20 years and more. One of our early encouragements, once we had found and bought a house in City Road that was suitable, but which needed to be kitted out as a coffee bar, was to receive a phone call one day from Berni Inns saying they would like to help with some used materials. Their store just happened to be in the basement of the house next door! Thank you, Lord.

I was the first chairman of the trustees until 1991, and tried to support the work by chairing trustees meetings, publicising its work and occasionally chatting to people in the 'Missing Peace Cafe', now called 'The Wild Goose', and going on street outreach. On one occasion going through St. Paul's district, I was approached by a lad and told 'if you don't cross the street now you will get mugged'. I looked ahead and saw two unsavoury looking young men coming towards me, but decided to keep going as I had no money on me anyway. I went up to them and said 'Do you know that Jesus loves you? Can I invite you for a coffee and sandwich at the Missing Peace Café?' They scowled at me and turned away. There seemed to be a strange power in the name of Jesus, which I had heard of before when an American girl had told some of us that she had once been captured and bundled into a car to be taken away and raped. So she had started speaking to the men about Jesus. They took her straight back to where they found her, unharmed.

A short time later a lifelong friend of ours with a strong desire to see marriages start and continue strongly started Marriage Resource. He is Ted Pratt, an Anglican clergyman with wide experience of marrying people and preparing people for marriage. I tried to encourage him to make it happen. He found a talented and lively group of trustees to join in the work, but I did not join the trustees until 1994; they set up marriage counselling services in several places and linked in with many others to tell people where they could find help. National Marriage Week was one initiative. When the Labour government took office in 1997 we were shocked at how quickly they took away funding from marriage counselling, in a naïve, misguided attempt not to discriminate between living together and marriage. They ignored the figures I have mentioned, that living together liaisons lasted 14 months at the time, whereas marriages that ended in divorce lasted 10.5 years. People who live together were seldom trialling marriage; at least one of them was usually rejecting it. That government and the next saw delinquency and crime continue to rise, hand in hand with absence of fathers. All seemingly the result of the country having the largest single parent proportion in Europe. When would we learn to value and help marriages?

Meanwhile, Christina and I had been on a trip to the Holy Land, and had been profoundly impressed at the way Bible stories became more real when earthed in actual places, in Jordan, Galilee, Carmel, Jericho and Jerusalem. We met both Jewish and Arab Christians. We also renewed our baptismal vows in the River Jordan in the company of our friend from many years before, Canon David MacInnes, who was also our party's guide. As we had come from a somewhat Zionist church, Pip 'n' Jay, where we tended to hear pro-Israel speakers (nothing wrong with that if it was peace-making), it was an eye-opening experience to visit friendly Palestinian Christians as well as Jewish Christians, in addition to seeing the obvious signs of hatred and mistrust that were everywhere. But we felt God had moved on; the sites were fossils of the real thing and Jesus was moving in real people in Israel/Palestine, Africa and Bristol now. Though powerful memories remained in empty places and old buildings, Jesus was now in hearts and minds around the world. We were there a few weeks after a former Bristol colleague of mine on Church Assembly, Terry Waite, the Archbishop's special envoy, had just been taken hostage. One of our party was an insurance man dealing with insuring international businessmen. He told us he had advised Terry not to take the latest assignment; and told us that he would either be released after six months or not for five years. It was five years. We were quite careful about which roads we travelled on.

29

Nigeria 1986-88

The year after Mission England ended, after we had taken a break and finished the silage and hay-making, and a few weeks after Amsterdam '86, I received a letter from one of the evangelists from Amsterdam, whom I must have met at that conference. He wrote from Ibadan, Nigeria, asking if I would come to Ibadan, to take part in Jesus Festival '86. I replied that in principle I could come, but could he tell me about the festival. My letter took a month to get to him; his took a month to get back to me, when he replied that they were looking forward to seeing me at Lagos Airport on December 8th! I just had time to travel to London for a visa and return plane ticket; then travelled alone, arriving after a fascinating flight across North Africa at Lagos Airport.

Stepping out of the plane I was hit by heat that felt like a sauna. I had wondered what I would do at the airport as I did not know a soul in Nigeria. I need not have worried because I was met by a row of smiling black faces who were holding up a sign 'Rev Anthony Bush, welcome'! We sped the hour's ride to Ibadan in the old church Mercedes, stopping at military road blocks and passing through thick leafy rainforest, big banana plantations, past abandoned rusty lorries and stalls selling hand carved ornaments, past stalls of meat with flies buzzing round it, or colourful clothes, to the biggest shanty town I could imagine. Ibadan consisted of mile upon mile of rusty metal roofed houses squatting beside earth streets. When it rained the streets turned to mud. Only the main roads were tarmac and these were very busy with traffic and with people selling all manner of food items, hardware, clothing and bottled water, to the cars whenever they stopped. I was taken to quite a tidy hotel, that might have raised one star in this country, but which was the best in that city. I was shown where there was a Green Mamba snake that lived in a hole beside the front door, so I was to be careful not to tread on it. It kept the rats and mice down! I was told I was to be the speaker for the opening night of a festival the following evening, and was given the subject of the talk that I was to give. I wondered how many people would be there – a hundred? Or perhaps a thousand? Mercifully there was air-conditioning in my room and no mosquitoes. I prepared my talk.

I was collected the next evening by my interpreter in the church car. I wore a safari suit, which I had brought from England for the occasion. I found myself first inspecting the scouts and guides – about 500 of them! People had started gathering, only about 20 cars, but the auditorium was huge. It was basically a field with row after row of concrete blocks on the floor as seats. I was told it held 50,000 men, women and children, the men sitting separately from the women and children, who had all arrived on foot, walking, in some cases for several hours. There was an air of expectation for God to be doing things. There was lots of African singing, then I was introduced, and spoke through my Yoruba interpreter, though most of the audience understood English as it is Nigeria's official language. The pastor of the church gave an appeal and lots of people streamed forward to receive Christ. I invited those who were sick, who would like Jesus to heal them, to raise their hand. I had told them how Jesus had healed me. We prayed that Jesus would heal them. Many were healed and came up on the platform to tell everyone what they were healed of. In Nigeria there is no free health care and very few people can afford a doctor. Levels of faith are much higher than in England. During the week many deaf people could hear again, many blind people could see, others who had been lame or with pains and lumps came forward to show and tell people about their healing. Later in the week we heard how one man, who said he had been impotent, prayed to Jesus one festival meeting that he would be able to make love to his wife; later that night he found he could make love to his wife one, two, three times! The crowd went wild with excitement! One night lots of ladies came onto the platform with babies, saying how a year ago God had answered their prayers for a baby, after anything up to 13 years of trying to conceive.

I was asked to speak at five memorable meetings that week; two full nights at the festival and one further gathering at the official opening of what must have been the world's biggest church, about ten miles from that first arena. When I was there it was half built, but due to hold 50,000 people on two floors. That day there were about 28,000 on the ground floor only, also sitting on rows of concrete blocks. At the end hundreds came forward to renounce their sins, including witchcraft and sorceries and to receive Christ. They left their witchcraft necklaces and bangles and other items at the front of the church to be burned. Another occasion was at a meeting for about 400 pastors, to talk to them about marriage and its importance to God and to us. Frank stuff; very important to church leaders. At the end an old pastor stood up and said 'I thought you should know that while you have been speaking to us there have been two soldiers standing behind you. They have been sent to show us that what you have been saying is very important for us.' There were no human soldiers, so I asked my interpreter why, if they were angels, did they appear as soldiers? He replied that Nigeria was a police state, and if the president sent a message, two soldiers stood behind the messenger to show that the message carried the president's authority. This was the only time I had been associated with an appearance of angels.

The final meeting of the week was announced by the pastor, at that opening of the new church on the Sunday. All married couples were to attend at the festival ground the following night. 'It is the command of God that you are there' I was very surprised to hear them told. He seemed to want his church couples told something like I had told the 400 pastors. I was due to be flying home later that night. Although men and women usually sat on different sides of the auditorium, tonight husbands and wives were invited to sit together. 'Another meeting,' it was announced 'has been arranged for all second and third wives in that building over there' so some ladies left. Later I saw the wisdom in this; I had no idea second and third wives might be there! At one point I was to suggest spouses turned to each other and told the other 'I love you'; a very radical thing for Nigerians to say! The talk was Biblical, wide ranging, direct and intimate and was met with prolonged applause at the end, when they were told I was now going to the airport and home to my own family. I reflected as I flew back, that the CAC church, which I was speaking at, had separated from the English missionary denominations because the latter had problems with African, especially Muslim, polygamy. When a man became a Christian believer he was required by the British missionaries to divorce his extra wives and send them home to their parents, if they were still alive. Many Africans found that too harsh, especially as the women were never likely to marry anyone else. So a new denomination was started. However, the intimacy within the marriages suffered. To marry one wife only was taught to be best and normal, but teaching was not being given on marriage, for fear of upsetting those from polygamous marriages. My marriage talk seemed to come at an appropriate time.

There were two other preachers at that festival, both from South Korea and one spoke good English. We moved from the hotel and stayed for some of the time at the mansion of a chief who made his living from importing most of the lorries and tractors into Nigeria. He was a very wealthy but generous Christian, who had a hospitality wing of four spacious bedrooms, that were free of mosquitoes (though I did have a friendly gecko on my ceiling, which presumably helped keep the mosquitoes down!). One night another chief or 'king' came to stay in the fourth bedroom; he was a Muslim with three wives and 20 children and had just married his fourth wife, who was a Christian. When the wife heard three of us were Christians who were speaking at the festival, she asked if we would pray for her to have a baby as it was very important to her marriage that she had one. As it happened Christina and I had prayed for at least ten couples to conceive; all but one had done so. So we preachers prayed for the lady. I have no idea of the consequence. I did have a conversation with the King one day at breakfast, about England, Nigeria and about God, too. He seemed nervous and when our host arrived, the King said to him with a smile 'rescue me from this man; he is a powerful preacher'! I am not sure what he was referring to.

In the course of conversation with the youngest Korean preacher he asked me how often I made love to my wife (clearly some nations are less inhibited than others about the questions they ask!). I quoted a recently published figure that in Britain the average 20-50s couple made love 2.5 times a week, and I supposed we were about at that average. 'That is good', he replied 'but my wife and I… only once a week. She is too busy, except on Saturdays.'

When he heard I was a dairy farmer, the pastor had asked whether I could send him some cows for his theological college as they needed milk. So on a spare day early in the week I went to visit the Institute of Tropical Agriculture, which happened to be in the same city of Ibadan. I also visited the nearby biggest dairy farm in southern Nigeria. This had shrunk from 300 cows in the glory days of abundant oil, to 27. That day showed me that the warm, wet tropics of Africa were unbelievably good for growing crops. They could harvest three arable crops a year, instead of our one, as there was no hint of winter. To us in cold England this was like farming in paradise. So the tropical rain forest would have no problem growing huge quantities of cow food. But the tick burden was high; 90% of cattle diseases are carried by ticks – blood-sucking parasites that transferred diseases from one animal to another. Tick-killing sprays were vital, but corruption throughout Nigeria was a terrible problem; supplies just did not get through. The cows had died of no supplies. The big milking parlour was not functioning, either. The few cows remaining were milked by hand in the parlour, because spare parts were not available. West Africa was not a place we could do development work, while the political situation remained as it was. This seems to be the downfall of Africa; such an amazing continent, but not a peaceful incorrupt democracy anywhere. As if to make a point two officials, on my way through airport security, said 'What have you got for me then?' I said 'I am a missionary, I will pray for God's blessing for you.' They each smiled and said 'Oh, that is the best thing!'

I returned to the festival for each of the next two years, each time bringing other preachers with me. I also brought lots of Bibles that people had donated and a requested typewriter one year. In 1988 after speaking at the festival I had arranged to fly north to some friends in Kaduna, to speak at some meetings there. I also wanted to see some farming, to learn more about tropical farming, including cattle farming and arable crops that included groundnut and root ginger. It was an amazing trip. Muslims had been rioting against the Christians and had burnt down 150 churches. The word got round to the Christians, 'remember the words of Jesus, the Master, turn the other cheek; do not take revenge'. Some pastors had been burnt inside their churches. The Muslims were so impressed with the Christian response that many realised God was helping the Christians not to be vengeful, and were turning to Jesus and coming to the churches; all of which were being rebuilt at least twice as big as before. I prayed with several individuals, including Muslims, to receive Christ and then left for my journey home.

When I reached Lagos I found my friends had forgotten to confirm my return flight with KLM, 48 hours before take off. Bad mistake, but I still went to the airport hoping for a place. There was none; I even walked onto the aircraft to see! So I was turned back at 11.30 pm. As the plane flew off I realised I was literally the only person left on Lagos airport departure floor. I sat down to pray about this rather big disappointment. The next KLM flight was in three weeks and I had no address in Lagos that I knew. What was God doing with me? A few minutes later a customs officer came along and asked why I was there. He turned out to be a Muslim, very interested in Jesus. Twenty minutes later he prayed to receive Christ into his life. He then suggested I went downstairs and applied at Spanish Airlines early in the morning for a flight. From Nigeria the flights are very much cheaper than from Europe. In the morning I found that there was a place, so I bought a ticket and arrived home only a few minutes later than if I had taken the KLM flight. Christina had just been rung by my preaching colleagues to say I might not be home till after Christmas, when suddenly I arrived by taxi from Bristol!

30

Starting Send a Cow 1987-91

Although my exploration of Nigeria in 1986 convinced me that West Africa did not seem to be the place to help develop Africa, I felt that the next challenge to take up was to somehow to take British dairy livestock and technology to East Africa. A close friend, John Perkins, worked for Tear Fund at that time and said to me one day that he knew another dairy farmer who felt similarly. This was David Bragg, from Lapford, Devon, 15 years younger than me. We spoke on the phone and agreed to meet, along with some other farmers at his house: Gerald Alford, a real giant in the pedigree dairy farming industry, Robert Vere, newly returned from dairy farming in Tanzania and Andrew Friend, a very experienced African development worker; all of us were sizeable dairy farmers. At that first meeting in January '87, David's wife Brenda gave us all a marvellous lunch, and we discussed all possibilities, even of Nigeria, but also the problems. Robert was very encouraging, but warned of the extra problems a local African manager had from his friends and family if he suddenly found himself in a well paid job; Andrew was cautious because of all the things he had seen go wrong. We left the whole matter undecided, but decided to keep praying about it.

A few weeks later David Holmes, a Christian Aid worker in Bristol, asked if he could bring a Ugandan bishop on to our farm. Bishop Cyprian Bamwose duly came and asked if we could send him some cows, as Friesians did well in Uganda. I said we would certainly think about it. A few weeks later David Holmes rang again and said he had Francis Gonahasa with him, a bishop's son, and development worker for the Church of Uganda. Francis came with pictures, showing how cows could be kept by well trained, but poor people, keeping one cow at a time. Ticks must be and could be killed. Lots of poor farmers had been already trained by Heifer Project International, an American Organisation, but they had run out of money, so the promised cows had not arrived. I took this information to Devon to our next meeting and we began to feel that this at last could work. We had now had three requests from senior African Christians to send cows; one from Nigeria and two from Uganda. This seemed like God calling to us from Africa, not us imposing an idea. We decided to call our plan Send a Cow, partly because Send a Tonne had been so successful in raising food aid that year. But Send a Cow was an unmistakably long-term development, not just relief aid from a drought. I was asked and agreed to be chairman, provided a director could be found. Gerald Alford would begin looking for cattle, as would the others. A possible director's name was offered of a young farmer near Bath. It would be best if two of us could go to Uganda to see for ourselves if it could work.

The next week I went to see Gerald Addicott, a young arable farmer, who farmed with his wife Ros and teenage children, near Bath. They had some empty cattle buildings on their arable farm. Gerald agreed, after praying about it with his wife and his church, to be director. We divided up the formation jobs. As I had recently set up other charities I wrote the first draft of the articles of association and asked my solicitor friend Tony Dann to set up the charity, when we were ready.

Gerald proved exactly the right man for the job; dedicated, persuasive, energetic, sensible, with a good knowledge of dairy farming from the family farm a few years before. He and I flew to Entebbe in February '88, stayed at the Church Guest House, Kampala, with no air conditioning and a pit latrine to initiate us into the culture! We went by mini-bus to Jinja, where we met Bishop Cyprian again; I preached at his cathedral, with the bishop as interpreter. The bishop then took us to see a cow owner and her very well kept and productive cow. We stayed in Jinja. It was here that another bishop, who had heard that we had come, came looking for us. Bishop Livingstone Nkyoyo, from Mukono had driven 30 miles along pot-holed roads to visit us at our hotel. We were surprised at so much gunfire at night and were relieved that the following day we were invited to stay with Livingstone, back in Mukono near Kampala. On our journey back the reminders of the civil war were everywhere; a 13-year-old boy with an AK47 stopped our minibus at a road-block and demanded to see our passports. He looked at mine upside down and handed it back. We passed tables piled high with skulls and bones of those killed in the civil war the previous year, waiting to be buried because no authority had ordered it to be done. We passed a burned-out rusting tank with a banana plant growing from its turret; grim reminders of the futility of war and the terrible violence of civil war in particular. Arriving at the Bishop of Mukono's house we arranged to meet the Diocesan Development team the following morning at 5.00 am, and walk to meet some of the people awaiting their cows. We met several, mainly ladies, who had been trained to keep a cow by Heifer Project International, an American development NGO. Heifer Project had promised them cows and the women had planted elephant grass, built their sheds and waited a year, but no cows had come. The training looked good. We had seen one cow alive and very well in Jinja, so felt our scheme could work. Gerald had to fly back to his farm but I had arranged to see our friends John and Janet Perkins who were now working in Nairobi for African Enterprise.

While I was with John, I discovered that Bishop Festo Kivengere, Africa's best known evangelist who had narrowly escaped the clutches of Idi Amin and who was John's boss in African Enterprise, was very seriously ill and expected to die of leukaemia at any moment. I asked if Festo had called for the elders to pray for him; and if there was someone who could pray a prayer of faith over him. John went to ask him and he said he would be grateful for prayer. John realised that most of the African bishops were meeting in Nairobi that very week so, on March 3rd, he asked three Archbishops, of Kenya, Madagascar and Desmond Tutu from Cape Town, and also a bishop who he thought could pray in faith for healing, to come and pray with Festo. When they arrived I spoke to them for a few minutes about the revival that was happening in West Africa, reminding them that God had promised to heal sick people who were anointed and prayed for in faith, in *James* 5:15.

I remember saying 'would God's word say "the prayer of faith will save the sick man" if it wouldn't?' 'Amen' they replied. We then all went upstairs to Festo's bedside, anointed him and asked Jesus to make him well. Festo was quickly better and got out of bed that day. By March 17th the doctors were astonished to have to announce that the malignant leukaemia had gone. Supporters around the world were informed. He was going about his normal work for the next two months, preparing his diocese and AEE for a successor. It was a strange and wonderful event for this Somerset farmer to have been present at. Then one day he collapsed with internal bleeding and said 'Even Lazarus had to die in the end'. He died shortly afterwards.

John and Janet booked a Missionary Aviation Fellowship plane for me to hire and we all flew to the north and east to see some large-scale Kenyan cattle farming by ex-pat British farmers. The Nightingale family had several herds of Friesians, all milked by hand very successfully. Then a visit to Robin Slade a CMS agricultural missionary at a state farm of 5,000 beef cattle was awaiting us at the next stop. We finally returned 100 miles to Nairobi, reassured that African cattle farming was easier in the Kenyan Highlands and in the Ugandan rain-forest than in England. It sometimes came at a price. I noticed a field of maize growing in the middle of a wide area of brown dry grass and asked my Nightingale host why so? He said 'about a month ago we had a sudden prolonged storm of rain one Sunday afternoon so I turned out with my seed drill and planted this crop in the rain. It has not rained since. You have to take opportunities when they arise.' No other farmer had done the same.

I needed the reassurance those ex-pat farmers gave me because, as soon as

I returned and all of us Trustees decided to start raising cows and money, every conceivable 'expert' arose to discourage us. Letters to the press, ex-colonials from Africa and NFU members spoke against me at public meetings. Animal rights activists insisted it would be cruel to send cows to Africa. I tried five major development charities to try and avoid setting up a new charity by starting under their wing; they all opposed us. They had consulted all the expert agricultural development advisors of the day who had said 'don't send cattle to Africa, they will all die'. Our reply was 'don't look after dairy cattle in England or they will all die; development advisors in England are not good enough at it! Africa needs this and we intend to provide expertise from professional British dairy farmers to make it work'. The climate was ideal in perpetual summer and the grass growth was so fast every British farmer could only envy it. But they remained completely opposed to the idea. It would have been easy at this point to give up, thinking all our donors would be put off by the 'experts'. But the Overseas Development Agency for the government said that although they didn't think our scheme would work, they would agree to back us pound for pound anyway, just in case it did! By June we had found our first 25 cows, money for air fares, bucket pumps for tick-spray, artificial insemination equipment and frozen semen, and the ODA had agreed to their half, provided we sent out a British worker and a Landrover for him. (It had to be a British Landrover, for the ODA.)

I had learned the importance of marketing in Mission England so we printed leaflets and decided to hold a press day for our amazing and exciting venture! The first one was in March at Moat House Farm, when our son Caspar held a suitcase in one hand and led a cow in the other for the press to announce 'Cows going on holiday to warm Africa'. A Ugandan vet was present to tell how valuable cows would be and how well they did in Uganda. Gerald Addicott and I told of our experiences in Africa. It was soon after Band Aid's Bob Geldof had been berating governments for ignoring the plight of Africans, and it seemed there were a number of people around who wanted to help a good idea for Africa.

For the next press day our first cows, all 2-3 year old heifers seven-months pregnant, had arrived two weeks earlier at Gerald's farm for quarantine and testing. So these were all paraded by their donors on July 4th, in a blaze of publicity, with sun-hats on, ribbon necklaces and with a banner saying 'To Uganda with love'. The local vicar prayed with us for the cows. Then they drove off by lorry to Gatwick airport, where they were loaded into crates, five standing side-by-side and lifted into a Boeing 707 and took off for Entebbe Airport. Send a Cow was on its way! Unfortunately, at Entebbe there was a quarantine farm where there was officially no tsetse fly, it had been eradicated. We had heard that a few cows that landed there were getting trypanosomiasis from being bitten by the fly. So we acquired some vaccine from the Institute of Tropical Medicine in Britain. Officially we were not allowed to inject this in the UK, nor in Uganda, which was clear of tsetse. So we sent two farmers with each load of cows, who had to climb over the cow's backs to inject them in flight! This was one reason why development workers could not keep cows alive, so farmers were needed to do the job. Each of our sons flew out; it was also a wonderful opportunity for farmers and their sons to have some fascinating experiences and to see first hand what the needs were in Africa.

Soon after our first load flew out we held a commissioning service at St. Bartholomew's, Bath, to send out to Uganda probably the first missionary artificial inseminator in the world! Geoff Gates, with his wife Ruth and a new baby, was to be our first full-time cow supervisor and AI man. Strangely, at that service, one of the elders said as we stood round them praying for them, that they were going to go through a difficult time but God would be with them. I had been the preacher and had quoted from Amos 'you were as a firebrand plucked from the burning'. A few days later the Gates' first attempt to fly to Uganda ended in a crash landing in Rome Airport, where their plane broke in half and burst into flames. Amazingly, it broke just behind the Gates' seat, and they were only slightly burnt on their hands and faces. Others lost their lives. All of Uganda's exam papers were on that plane, too, and were burnt. The Gates were taken straight to hospital in Rome where their very caring vicar, David Saunders from St Bartholomew's, went to help them and bring them home to recuperate for a few months. They hit the newspaper headlines, as did Send a Cow. It was a very traumatic experience for a young couple to bear, and they did so with great courage.

We had to find a replacement for them quickly. One of our trustees was a young dairy farmer, Peter Read, from near Oxford. With his family's cooperation he volunteered to go to Uganda for three months in Geoff Gates' place. Despite never having been abroad before, nor having taught before, Peter was an inspired cow worker and teacher. On one occasion he had to introduce a new 'pour-on' tick killing chemical. He called for a local cow to be brought to him. 'How many ticks are there on her?' he asked. 'Dozens', was the reply. 'I am going to pour on 10cc of this chemical on the top of her back, and if there are any ticks left in two weeks I will give you a hundred shillings each'. The Ugandans all rubbed their hands with glee, thinking of all the money they were going to make out of the white man. Two weeks later there was not a tick on the cow. The lesson spread like wild-fire. It was an inspired practical way to teach African farmers, women and men, how and why to kill ticks. And it taught us all that practical lessons work in Uganda.

We sent 300 cows to Uganda before BSE struck. Gerald Alford, with his wide contacts and excellent reputation as a cattle breeder, was responsible for finding the cows. Some were purchased with donated money, others came from dairy farmers as a gift. I sometimes asked a farmer how many cows he had, if he did not know I suggested he might not miss one by giving us one! I found the very rich were too mean but the next layer of wealth down, were the generous ones – especially Christian farmers but not exclusively so. We were invited into schools and to church harvest festivals and to speak at Rotary and Round Tables who wanted to help us. On two occasions I accompanied Peter Read, who brought his quiet pedigree cow called Hester, first to Bristol to two city-centre schools. There it stood on two different playing fields surrounded by dozens of excited children who had never seen a cow before and were totally shocked when it dunged! We explained the scheme to them for a fund raising effort both schools were doing for us. On another occasion we took the cow to Worcester College, Oxford, where our Larry studied and was organising a fundraising event in Rag Week. They had a 'milk race' of the Oxford rowing eight versus a College eight drinking pints of milk one after the other. Hester the cow was made an honorary member of the Junior Common Room, with her picture hanging on the wall there. She was moo-ved by the whole experience, which she found udderly marvellous. They also raised money to send a cow.

In that autumn of 1988, Christina and I went with Gerald and Ros Addicott, at each couple's own expense, to see the first load of cows that we sent in July. We had arranged to go with a BBC camera crew: the story would be a good one for them and marvellous publicity for us. Our arrival was timed to coincide with our second load of cows and so we went to the unloading lift at the edge of Entebbe Airport. It was dark. The cows' pallets were rolled out of the aircraft on to the lift and from there they were lowered to the ground and the cows released into a field at the Government Quarantine Farm. We wondered if they would be tired after their journey but they quickly galloped away into the darkness. Hundreds of black faces appeared from nowhere and were chattering excitedly. Their wide-eyed amazement at the size of the cows, huge compared with their own, is a memory we will keep forever.

We four visited lots of cows and filmed them in good health. We stayed in Bishop Livingstone's house, into whose diocese the cows had been distributed and whom we gladly paid for our stay. We saw the house where Geoff and Ruth Gates would soon be living in a college campus. We visited other schools and colleges and were impressed that old cement bags were being used as sewing patterns for needlework coursework. We saw a school where they had no desks and children sat on the concrete floor. Some schools had no concrete so the children sat on dried cow manure floor, renewed each week. In some schools there was no paper to write on, no books or even chalk, so the children repeated lessons after the teacher. Things were so bad that we resolved to fill up the container transporting our Landrover with desks and part-used rolls of newspaper, pens, pencils and unwanted school books from UK schools when we returned from this trip. Christina especially enjoyed spending time with some women's groups and found Uganda a wonderful country to paint and sketch. Livingstone asked me to preach at the Confirmation Service with 100 candidates, at Mukono Cathedral. We were surprised at the call to the service being not a bell, but a very loud, very African drum.

Three times a year Gerald Addicott allowed his farm to be our quarantine farm to gather the cows for vet testing before export. He also converted an old garage into the Send a Cow office where our first administrator, Georgia, worked alongside him. The local MP Chris Patten came to celebrate one landmark load of cows. He had been minister of the ODA and was very supportive. After BSE we had to stop sending cows from UK but by then there were enough to buy them from inside Africa. By this time the development experts had noted that the scheme was working and several of them, including the head of the ODA, apologised to us for being negative at the beginning. My chairmanship would last three years until better people could take over. I retained the title of President causing some smiles, as the USA had a President Bush at that time, so for a charity to have a President Bush seemed up-there!

It also helped me stay in touch with the wonderful team that now continues under the very committed present trustees and staff, and the CEO, Martin Geake. Martin was God's gift to Send a Cow from government development work – and after an illness. Our son Caspar had met him and told him about Send a Cow when he discovered Martin had bought a house in the village where Send a Cow had its office. God's leading seemed evident as Martin worked at the office first as a volunteer then, when his talents became so clear, as CEO. Now, over 20 years after that first load, Send a Cow maintains its Christian commitment and God-dependency while using the best modern methods and practices possible and giving to needy people of all faiths and none. It is training people and has been sending a wide range of animals and organic farming techniques to Uganda, Ethiopia, Rwanda, Kenya, Lesotho, Tanzania, Zambia and Cameroon, (also in the past Ghana and Sudan) helping many thousands of people annually and raising £4-5 million a year. It had its 20th anniversary celebration in Bath Abbey in 2008, with amazing African drummers and Ugandan children singing and dancing; Ugandans shared and thanked God for the huge impact the scheme is having on their lives in Africa.

In December 2009 I was delighted and honoured to retire as President of Send a Cow as we heard that, after several years of asking, HRH Prince Charles announced his willingness to be Patron. As we already had two excellent patrons, the Archbishop of York and Dame Lynda Chalker, it was decided to offer Prince Charles the post of President, which by his by his tradition he takes for five years.

31

Four Weddings and a Funeral

WE HAD CELEBRATED OUR SILVER WEDDING IN 1987 WITH OUR CHILDREN, then in their teens and twenties, and their friends and ours around us. Little did we realise what a momentous decade of family life lay ahead. It began just before I had left for Uganda, in 1988, when we had Annie's wedding to organise. She had gone twice to South America on mission work at each end of her Sheffield University degree course . She had been introduced to Pete Spiers by her sister Lizzie at Durham University and, unknown to me, he had arranged to join her on her second visit to South America to propose to her. Annie had rung me from Bolivia and said briefly 'Dad, Pete's got something to ask you' (she was a talented dramatist and rarely a girl of few words). 'Anthony, can I have permission to marry your daughter?' came Pete's unmistakeable strong voice. I had been too busy to think this through, in fact I had not been warned that engagement was a possibility. In a moment I had a flashback of Pete, an astonishing thalidomide victim defeating his disability of short arms and one and a half legs, becoming deputy president of Durham University Student Union and given an extra year to do it, with an Archdeacon father, now heading for the Church of England priesthood. But wanting my Annie? Did she agree? Presumably, because she was there and apparently not under duress! So I replied 'if you are both happy, Pete, we are delighted.' I hoped he did not hear my total shock. I heard later that he did wonder why I took so long to say anything!

'Think not that you have lost a daughter, think rather that you have gained a…telephone? bathroom?' Nothing could quite compensate me for losing one of my precious girls. I had been warned that no one would be good enough to marry your children. Pete, however, was steady and reliable and I felt I could trust him not to abandon her later. He was a marvellous orator and a keen Jesus-centred Christian with a wonderful sense of humour and great memory for

Two loads of tarmac and a friendly council pavement-layer: our tennis court

Anthony with Caspar, three Tyndale nephews and Gerald Bonnington on top

Anthony harvesting with Gerald Bonnington 1969

The Bush family, May 1978, left to right: Caspar, Lizzie, Annie, Anthony, Christina, Larry and Venus the dog

'Devil attacks leading evangelist'. Moathouse Farm after a lightning attack,1983. Christina was at home at the time

Anthony with son Larry, Peter Reid and Hester – Peter's 'quiet' pedigree cow – on a fundraising visit to Larry's Worcester College, Oxford

Anthony with Topaz in 1991

Anthony and Christina with Billy Graham

Billy Graham visits Moathouse Farm with Anthony, two farm hands look on

Mission England: the TA install a specially-built footbridge for the crowds

Bristol City Football Club, May 14, 1984, Mission England

The parents:
Fynvola and Jimmy James, Betty and Barnard Bush in 1985

Anthony preacing at the Jesus Festival, Ibadan, Nigeria 1987

A church destroyed by Muslim extremists, one of 150 attacked in northern Nigeria

'Reminders of the civil war were everywhere'. Human remains, Uganda 1988

'The next challenge to take up was to somehow take British dairy livestock and technology to East Africa'. Send a Cow: the first donors with cows, June 1988

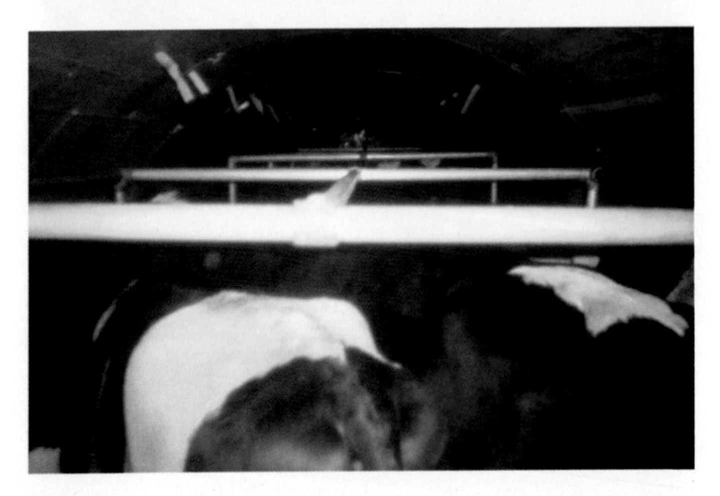

Flying cows: crated and heading for Uganda

The new owner with a donated cow: 'unmistakably long-term development'

Water transport, Uganda 1988

Artificial insemination by scramble bike

1995: Rwandan refugee camp at Goma, Zaire

Anthony welcomes visitors on mission youth night, 1997.
Luis Palau and Cliff Richard wait

In Uganda with footballs from Bristol City and Rovers: 'a few seconds later 50 children disappeared with the football into rain so heavy you could only see ten yards'

jokes. So I felt reassured. They were married at Pip 'n' Jay the next January 9th, then in Wraxall at the Battle Axes Inn for a reception. As I had previously joked that Africans had told me my daughters were worth 28 cows each as a dowry, they presented me with a pantomime cow as an African style dowry, then left in silver space suits for honeymoon, for Liverpool and for ever. Fortunately, I was too busy to cry, and too broke! Since then they have generated love, laughter, drama and four happy children. The thalidomide trust also found them the money for a mill house and windmill they have modernised on Anglesey, for holidays for themselves and for dozens of friends and city folk from Liverpool. Annie also started an after-school club in a very deprived parish, receiving the MBE for it and became an events manager of lots of huge inter-church dramatic events in the area.

Lizzie, our academic all-As superstar, with double language degree at Durham was next, 18 months after Annie. Lizzie had been the trend-setter and guide for her siblings and totally reliable eldest family member for all these years. Now she had met another budding vicar. Both my daughters said often in their teens that they would never marry a vicar. But our lifestyle was very similar but with smells attached, so a vicarage must have seemed a scented relief! Richard Wiffen, an Oxford graduate, was very bright, friendly and had been a rugby playing solicitor who despaired of the futility of pointless money-making. He wanted to make a difference to people's happiness and help them find Jesus. Lizzie did too. She was working for the BBC at the time and he was at Trinity Theological College preparing for ordination. They married from Moat House Farm. Lizzie was driven by me in our unusually clean Peugeot Estate car with ribbons on, married in Wraxall Church where my school friend, her godfather, Rev Ted Longman preached. He reminded the girls (which they did not particularly want to hear!) that they had a vital supporting role in a clergy marriage. Future Bishop Michael Nazir Ali, who Richard had worked with in Pakistan, was there.

They were driven back to the farm by our farm manager, Pete Meredith, behind a farm tractor on a newly painted trailer (which Richard had painted), surrounded by pink-ribboned baskets of flowers that had decorated the church. The reception was in a marquee on the lawn. I remember asking Annie's Peter, now ordained, whether if the wine ran out he and the other 30 ordinands or vicars who were there could do anything with moat water? 'Sorry, Anthony' he replied, 'It's my day off!' I reminded them in my speech that marriages gave children Roots to grow strong, Wings to learn adventure, and Rails for security; I had just given away our Lizzie, our beautiful, intelligent, always busy, sensible, trend-setting oldest daughter. We would miss her terribly. Chester and Ellesmere

Port have been their family and church centre, where they have four lovely children. Lizzie also became active with lots of community and family issues, became a member of the Primary Care Trust, taught languages at local schools and started Assembly Teams going into dozens of schools with visual aids and Bible stories in their huge parish.

Just over two years later, Larry, at 22, announced his engagement to his beautiful Antonia Briggs. They had known each other since 16, then both went to the same Oxford College, Worcester, where I had also been 30 years earlier. He was working in Anglesey Aluminium when he realised that marriage to Toni was the only thing he was certain he wanted in the future. A work colleague had asked him, on hearing about the engagement 'does that mean you are going to live together?'

'No', said Larry 'I think that messes you up'.

'I'm living with my girlfriend; does that mean I am messing us up?'

'Yes, I think so', said Larry.

At which, another work colleague agreed that you weren't a proper man unless you got married. Larry and Toni were married at Chew Stoke Church in August 1992, by Tom Wright, their Oxford chaplain, later to be Bishop of Durham; the reception was at the Webbington Country Club. Toni's father, professor of Russian, David Briggs made a speech. Our financial contribution had been mercifully, much less, for a son, which was just as well; I had not finished paying for our two girls' weddings! Larry had bucked the family trend of farming and bravely fast-tracked to a graduate training scheme in industry; from aluminium he moved to fibre-glass sheets then to Walkers snack foods, until he found his fair-trade ideal as a Director of Traidcraft in Gateshead, while Toni is Education Officer at Hexham Abbey where their family are all members. They have three sweet and lively children.

Caspar had been farming with my father since studying agriculture, singing light opera and being president of the Christian Union at Newcastle University. He had rung me in January '92 to ask if I thought Larry would be upset if he announced his own engagement and wedding so close after Larry's engagement. I said, 'go for it', but did wonder who the amazing girl was who was good enough for him?! We soon discovered why he and his lovely Alice had fallen for each other. They married a month after Larry and Toni, at Malmesbury Abbey, with a reception at Westonbirt School, where Ruari Grant, Alice's father, taught physics; he also played the bagpipes rather well. Caspar and Alice then lived in a farm cottage at Peart, became a farm partner with my father, then a church Lay Reader. When my father died in 2001, he and Alice ambitiously moved the family and the whole herd to a bigger and better Duchy of Cornwall farm in

Cornwall to continue, and then expand greatly, their production of organic milk. Caspar continues as a Reader and then was accepted for ordination training in 2009. Alice is a star hostess with a strong artistic flair and manages their holiday cottages; they have three busy and talented children.

Our silver wedding had taken place a few months after my parents' golden wedding and, just over five years later, all of our four children were married. We now have 14 grandchildren, amazingly almost one per year: seven girls and seven boys, all coming along girl-boy-girl or boy-girl-boy, but never boy-boy or girl-girl! It is difficult to imagine greater blessing. Christina had sacrificed her career and invested her working life in their childhood; what a worthwhile investment.

In between our daughters' and sons' weddings, Christina's dad, Captain Ughtred (Jimmy) James RN, CBE, died at 87. Jimmy had served with distinction in the Navy and in two further careers, leaving us a fine example of energy and cheerful, strong Christian faith to the end. He and his wife Fynvola, who survived him by 21 years, will be remembered for bringing illuminating faith and comfort to dozens of people through their prayerful counselling over many years. Jimmy's funeral at Holy Trinity Nailsea, their spiritual home for just two years, was a cheerful celebration at which his grandchildren memorably sang and danced to the tune 'Heaven is a wonderful place'.

32

Reassuring Happenings on the Farm

DURING THE LATE '80S AND EARLY '90S LIFE WAS OFTEN VERY BUSY TRYING TO FIT IN the chairmanship of five organisations, being a church preacher and doing essential work on the farm, while keeping it among the vanguard of modern dairy farms. We grew fodder beet for about 25 years. These were a cross between a sugar beet and a mangold (or mangel-wurzel) and were a good cheap form of energy, if chopped and put into the cows ration in the right quantities. One year when we were harvesting fodder beet and, as usual, I had a deadline to meet. I was bringing in the last 10- tonne load with my biggest Massey Ferguson 100hp 4wd tractor and stopped on a slight slope to close a gate, ready for the cows to come through at 6.00am next morning. As I closed the gate I was horrified to see the tractor beginning to move forward, gathering speed. It was quickly moving too fast to think of getting onto it. Ahead lay some terrible possibilities, the narrow road had a steep bank on each side that would lead to a certain rolling over of the tractor. The steep banks were there because the farm road crossed a small stream that flowed under a bridge; if the tractor reached the stream, the whole load would undoubtedly be severely stuck for hours. A water trough was another possibility for being hit and crushed, about five metres from the road bank, though that might stop the load getting to the stream. All possibilities seemed horrendous. In a flash I shouted out loudly 'Jesus, please help me; Jesus please help me...' As I watched and prayed the tractor veered off the track, snapping four strands of barbed wire in an instant; it headed for the five-metre space between the trough and the bank. As it drew close to the stream, gathering speed, it amazingly turned left and ran parallel to the water, when a small tree passed between the bonnet and the front wheel of the tractor, bent the footplate against the back wheel and, acting as a brake, stopped the tractor beside and three metres from the stream! I could easily detach the footplate and drive the tractor away, back to the buildings! I was relieved about two things: that my first reaction was to call to Jesus for help and that He had heard my prayer so emphatically – and in a way I could never have thought possible.

On another occasion I was late to speak at a meeting. I needed to fetch a young dry cow from the field to bring her in, to possibly calve that night. I had arranged with one of my staff to meet me at a gate to open it for me to let this dry cow through. I managed to separate the young cow very easily and drive her away from the herd; we walked towards the gate and waited for my colleague to come. He was held up. Time was ticking. If I walked round in front of the cow she would run straight back to the herd and I would be late for my meeting. So I asked the Lord for help. Suddenly I heard some galloping hooves behind me: another cow had separated herself from the rest of the dry cows to join us and furthermore, she had her head down and was fighting the one I was holding. I realised I just had time to run forward and open the gate and return. I did this, then put my stick between the two cows to separate the second one and send her back on her way, and drove the first cow out through the gate onto the track. How amazing to have that second cow sent to help me. Thank you, Lord. I reached my meeting on time.

On another occasion I had to move a herd of 30 lively heifers who had escaped from their field; I was by myself. I had to pass a gap that had no gate to it; it was important that the heifers did not go through the gap or they would be in the wrong field. I asked the Lord 'please will you send your angel to stand in that gap, as I am all I have got here'. As the heifers passed the gap they all turned their heads to look at the gap, but did not go through it. I wondered what they saw. Once again I was on time for my appointment.

33

To Be, or Not to Be, Ordained

In 1990 Christina and I had carefully pulled out of Pip 'n' Jay church, so that no one would know we had gone. Malcolm had agreed that it might be unnerving for many if we had a big goodbye. We had spent a wonderful 25 years there, learning so much; it had been extremely formative for our children, all of whom had been to the excellent Sunday School, supervised so ably by Sheila McKay, then in youth groups with very fine youth leaders. We were so grateful to God for dozens of lovely people, too numerous to mention, who were giving their all to God in imaginative and creative ways, in giving money generously and giving time for foreign and home mission projects, in music and outreach. It was so hard to leave them all behind but we felt we should return to All Saints Church, Wraxall. I had already been licensed as a Reader in Bath and Wells diocese by Bishop John Bickersteth, 12 years before. Following Mission England it was not unusual for me to be preaching three or four times a month in several towns and dioceses. Now, returning to Wraxall where Holy Communion featured more frequently, I was asked by the rector, David Payne, if I would be willing to be ordained, since a lay reader was not authorised to take Holy Communion services in the C. of E. I agreed and the PCC recommended me. The former Bishop of Bath and Wells, George Carey, had just been made Archbishop of Canterbury and so the suffragen Bishop Nigel McCulloch agreed to put me forward to a Selection Conference (ABM). The call had come so far entirely through other people; I had not asked for anything.

It was clear that I would have to study at theological college but, in view of the 17 years I had served on General Synod and my 22 years as a reader (and that I was 52), no more than a year was deemed necessary. In short, I was being fast-tracked by those who knew my history. A new academic year was about to begin at Trinity Theological College. All concerned thought I should begin at Trinity in October, go to the selection conference in November and then, if I passed, continue until the end of the academic year and be ordained the following summer or autumn. If I failed the ABM conference, that would be my problem; I was paying my own fees.

So I started at Trinity, having made sure farm work was manageable by taking on a extra part-time person. I saw the farm staff, including my excellent herd manager, Kevin Burt, early in the morning then left for College by 8.00

for morning lectures. I was let off most afternoon duties at college and so returned to the farm. There were sometimes evenings at college but more often I wrote essays, in longhand, as computers were not for me (though we had one in our latest milking parlour). Unfortunately my conscientious and over-worked rector was not in good health, so he called on me rather a lot to lead services and preach. I preached 42 times that year.

The ABM conference came and went and I passed. I was worried about the way they dealt with one candidate who I felt was decided against unfairly. I later mentioned it to the bishop who interviewed him and reversed the decision. The experience of being at Trinity was truly wonderful. I found the lectures helpful (although was asked by one lecturer to add to some of the lectures because I had been at the Synod debates concerned!) and the students were most impressive: kind and thoughtful. At 52, I was not only the oldest student but older than all the staff! My essays were considered worthy of a 2.1, though my single year qualified me for only a Certificate in Christian Ministry, awarded at a cathedral ceremony. In due time ordination approached and it was assumed I would be ordained in June. My name and details went off to Crockford's, the clergy directory.

Then a new bishop, Jim Thompson, arrived from Hackney. He decided my case was altogether too hasty and proposed a delay for a further reflective year. I duly went off to a monastery for a weekend and kept a diary of reflection and contemplation. My parish duties did not slow down – the rector still was not well – and there were things to do on the farm. My landlord hoped we might leave but we had security of tenure and decided we needed to expand to keep profitable – and that we needed planning permission to build more cow space.

A year later, Bishop Jim called me to see him and said he was not going to ordain me and he did not need to give me a reason. He said something about not liking ordaining characters, who could fill churches, because they just took people away from neighbouring churches. He did not like my theological certainty, he said, and 'I know I will have a storm of protest but I will just have to patiently answer each one'. My parish was outraged and the warden asked if he should raise a petition. I said no, not unless you are sure of 100% support and I suspect you may get only 80%. He agreed. Part of the parish's problem with me was an irony of misunderstanding: some people thought that if I were ordained I would be their vicar and that they would lose their rectory and lawn for fetes. In fact, every non-stipendiary has to go to a different parish. Two vicars later the rectory was sold anyway, because it was too big. I thought the whole thing was so outrageous that it had to be God's work! If a door won't open, maybe God's foot is on the other side, and if the bishop had been praying, as I think he was, and concluded I was the wrong shape for the C. of E., who was I to argue? I heard much later that the bishop had written to protesting people saying that he felt God was calling me to non-ordained work.

My biggest concern was that before ABM I had been on a retreat with Christina and after two days of asking God why He wanted me to be ordained – and of Him saying nothing – I felt He was saying 'I want you to have the authority of the Anglican Church for the work I am calling you to do'. That sentence, that has stayed with me ever since, did not quite say ordination. And yet it was this strong sense of calling that had helped convince ABM my call was real, so was I missing something? Of course, ordination is far from being the only work that needs church authority and anyway, the church is the people and not just the bishop. It was the people who had called, selected and trained me. The work God was calling me to do was clearly now not only within the C. of E., but the C. of E was part of it and my selection and training could not be taken from me. The future might reveal more.

Christina and I did both feel rejected for a while, and confused about the future. It felt a little like Oxford again but this time I had been fully up to the course. It must be God's pruning again. The future had to be elsewhere and I should not be angry or resentful. David Payne moved on from Wraxall in 1992. David, a cricketer, had said to me many times 'Anthony I think you are meant for the big game not the little one – you are like Devon Malcolm playing in a village match'. I did not know whether to feel flattered or insulted but felt ordination might get in the way of something significant yet to happen. Jim Thompson told me I had to move from Wraxall Church. It was unusual to be removed from one's local parish church. I left without protest but I think some locals blamed me for deserting them. John Simons, the rector of Holy Trinity Church, Nailsea came to see me and asked me to join the team at Holy Trinity. His colleague had moved on and a church plant, that had grown from a pub and was now in a Catholic school, was short of leaders. So I joined Trendlewood Church in 1992. Christina was being useful at Wraxall Sunday School so took longer to move. She was more upset with the bishop than I was. I threw myself into Trendlewood life and after six months was added to the preaching and leading group.

There was a lovely team at Trendlewood who were keen to use the freedoms of being C. of E. whilst meeting in a school where they could experiment with different ideas of worship – especially through the excellent music group. I wrote some songs and re-wrote some more, and tried to make the services more accessible to outsiders. Very little outreach was happening. I was doing some school assemblies with Open Air Campaigners, a group led by our good friends

Korky and Annie Davey, who took the stories of Jesus with visual aids and in very understandable ways into dozens of schools in Bristol and the West. My contributions were in secondary schools and were agricultural; I always took a visual aid of wheat or maize grain and whole plants, an egg and a chick into schools to talk about the amazing details of Creation and how Jesus had shown power over nature in his miracles, and that I had found him to be such a personal blessing. I was not allowed to tell children what they should do about God but I could say how I had been helped myself. Some teachers were surprised when the children broke into spontaneous applause at the end. There seemed to be a hunger among young people for news about God.

In 1994 John Simons had proposed people do some prayer walking along their streets, praying for the people in each house as they walked. I could not join in at that time but later I decided I should do a prayer walk all across Nailsea. I felt called to continue with another prayer walk across Bristol, starting at Hartcliffe. I walked down every street, trying to pray for every person in every house, school and factory, from 5.00–7.00 every morning, about 7 miles a day for 100 days. It's surprising who's about at that time of the morning: I was propositioned by two prostitutes and threatened by a pimp.

By the time I had finished, another mission was in sight – but most of my praying was to wait several years for answers.

34

Rwanda

For some months in mid-1994 the news was full of shocking stories of atrocities in Rwanda. It appeared that perhaps a million Rwandans had been killed and nearly another million had run away from the vengeance that might follow. Although I was no longer a trustee of Send a Cow, I was its President. I felt there might be a big need for help soon and, as it was big in the news, people might like to give money to help. I spoke to the trustees and it was clear that they did not think this was a good time to expand, when BSE had just stopped us sending cows direct to Uganda and donations were down. I felt that if we were seen helping so quickly it would raise our profile beyond the three countries we were working in, and increase the support generally as well as for Rwanda. They agreed that I could go at my own expense and gather what information I could for them to work on. They gathered round and prayed for me and Anthony Herbert, the current Chairman of Send a Cow, gave me a letter of commendation to take with me. I felt strongly called by God to go, even if it was dangerous. I decided to insure myself for a large sum in case I was not coming back, so that at least Christina would be a merry widow if she had to be one! Our friends John and Janet Perkins were no longer in Nairobi, but we were well enough known to African Enterprise, for whom John had worked, for them to offer to help me. Their extremely helpful director in Rwanda, Anton Rutayisire, happened, by an interesting coincidence, to be out of the country at that time so kindly put his car and staff at my disposal. I also had a contact in Zaire, where the refugee camp was. I agreed to pay for the car's petrol and for the minders' food.

On arriving at Kigali I was taken to the Hotel des Milles Collines, which I had booked from home. It was extremely smart and had escaped the troubles, as I heard many years later, through the heroism of the Hutu manager who had secretly rescued hundreds of Tutsis from certain death in his hotel. It was now the hotel where everyone in the press or military stayed, so I immediately found the NGO, government and military contacts I needed so, together with a list of contacts provided by a missionary I began to plan an itinerary.

Later in the week I stayed at the Meridian Hotel, which was $50 a night cheaper, but the bed had a broken leg and there were bullet holes in all the windows and in the wall plaster. With the bed repaired I managed two nights there. My two minders came the next day to pick me up and we would go to see several people over the next two days, including two bishops of dioceses and some orphanages and a Jersey cow that was rumoured to be alive still. I was shocked at what I saw on our journeys. Houses had been destroyed. In one place an entire line of shops had fallen over, destroyed by artillery fire in the battle in which the Tutsis defeated the Hutu and caused the mass exodus to Zaire. People were few and very sad. I wanted to see a former cattle breeding centre. As we drove in it looked abandoned: my minders were talking to each other and hesitating. I asked what the trouble was and they told me they thought the area might have been mined. I told them that God had not brought me this far to blow me up in a mine, keep going. They immediately cheered up and said, 'That is right, God is with us'. I took a picture of the empty breeding centre. We didn't explode.

On another occasion we stopped at a school where I asked for the toilet. It was a WC with no seat and infrequent flushes. Absence of toilet paper reminded me that this was a Western luxury, not needed by most of the world who had perfectly good hands anyway. In parts of Africa you view the practice of shaking hands in a new way. A degree of constipation is also useful! On one occasion I was asked to say a blessing before eating: I took a look at the food and thought 'Only God can help me here' and said a heartfelt prayer for blessing!

One day I met a man who had been lined up by the Hutu militia outside his Kigali office and watched, horrified, as people were macheted to death. When they got to him, someone shouted 'its not here it's over there' and they left him standing, perplexed and amazed that his life had been spared. He realised that God had spared his life for a reason, so spent the next few weeks in hiding and trying to rescue his own and other families. I was also taken to meet two other bishops and some development work leaders, to see if Send a Cow could help either now or in the future; in the future seemed the most likely in each case. There was a mountain of reconciliation for each side to climb first, before they could combine for training and cooperative food-production schemes; they seemed grateful that someone had come to see them and to know people in Britain were thinking of them.

I had asked for and received before I had left England, a football from each of Bristol City and Bristol Rovers football clubs. I had realised from previous visits to Africa how popular balls were. I also took 20 tennis balls as gifts. I asked to be taken to two schools where I could present a football in each. The responses were ecstatic. In the second school it was pouring down with rain at the time of the presentation; a few seconds later 50 children disappeared with the football into rain so heavy you could only see ten yards. I have no doubt the football would have been loved to death.

I was taken to the Rwandan border to cross into Zaire to see the refugee camp where the Hutu militia and most other Hutu people had fled. I was met by Philip Betts, my English contact, who was a Christian and worked for the Schluter family commodity company, some of which family Christina and I had known as friends. He took me to see his warehouse. There were about 200 African women sitting on the floor, sorting coffee beans by hand into different grades. They seemed very pleased to see Philip and gave him wide smiles and a big round of applause. I was taken to a Rwandan pastor who briefed me on the visit next day to the refugee camp. I was to address a group of Hutu clergy and church leaders, but must not on any account mention going back to Rwanda. The last visitor who had done so had been the cause of death of several people who had invited him, at the hands of the Hutu militia who roamed the camp. I shared with this pastor a recent Bible study about refugees. It included most of the big heroes from Adam and Eve and Noah via Moses and David, to Jesus and Paul. Being a refugee was often an important character-building stepping stone in God's plan.

The next day I was met by Win Hurlburt, an American and lifelong missionary in his '60s, who spoke eight languages. He drove me in his car into the biggest refugee camp ever created. There were 770,000 refugees in thousands of UN, blue plastic tents in the middle of an extinct volcano. Towards the middle there were eight huge water tanks on legs. Lots of people were sitting doing nothing and watching us pass by. There were feed stations and several huge Portadomes holding the food supplies in barbed-wire enclosures.

We drove past more guards to an empty Portadome, in which about 100 clergymen were waiting for us. They were all in black suits and were sitting on upside-down empty feed containers on the volcanic ash of the floor. We sang a hymn and I was introduced as coming from England. I said I had come to cry with them, I felt so sad about all that had happened. I ran through some things from the Bible that I felt God was saying to them. God has a plan in our darkest times; He will never leave us and wants to keep teaching us. I unpacked the law of love which called us to accept one another, forgive one another, carry each other's burdens; serve, pray for, encourage each other and all in the context of praising God and submitting to Him who is on the throne of heaven. I spoke through an interpreter for about 45 minutes. As they broke into warm applause I felt even more like crying. I was free to go; they did not know what lay ahead. Perhaps some of them were guilty of the genocide, or might themselves be killed in the future, I simply did not know. They were certainly now all its victims.

As we drove back through lines of hostile, sad-looking people, freedom seemed a precious gift. I said goodbye at the border, where I was due to be picked up by my Rwandan minders. While waiting there I saw a lady crossing back to Rwanda and took a picture. Unfortunately I was seen by the border guard and told I was in trouble for photographing a military position! As he led me away to the guard house I grew worried: I could be taken hostage and ransomed. Prison was not a nice thought either, even though English public school and National Service was good preparation!

The Guard Commander demanded I hand over the picture I had just taken. This did not sound like prison, but it meant the whole film must be destroyed. I thought it was just a way of getting money out of tourists, so I put five dollars on the table and said 'would that help?'

'Now you are in bigger trouble; that is bribery.'

I tried explaining that I was on a trip taking photos that would encourage people in England to give money to help Rwanda and showed him my Send a Cow President card. It did no good. I had to hand over the film. It contained most of the pictures of my whole trip, including to the refugee camp! I felt really upset that most of the evidence of my trip had been destroyed – and for no good reason. But God is in charge, I knew, so forget it Anthony. Move on.

My minders then met me and took me back to Kigali. On the way we passed other refugee tents and through the town that led to the gorillas in the Ruwenzori Mountains. Unfortunately I had not allocated any time for tourism things so we returned to the capital. I had a few more appointments, including preaching at a big church in Kigali on the Sunday. There seemed a big response to my sermon there, which was on forgiving each other and receiving God's forgiveness through Jesus. One bishop had asked if we could send him experts at reconciliation. He knew that the future would require people somehow to be able to forgive, then live alongside other people who had done some terrible atrocities.

I made my way to the airport, and on the way said thank you to my host, Anton, the African Enterprise leader, whose car and team I had borrowed. I had hardly eaten anything in Rwanda, so was feeling ready for a rest on the flight home. Christina met me at Bristol Airport and was worried at how poorly I looked. I felt elated but I did not know what had been achieved. Perhaps I was only supposed to cheer up a few hundred people, and remind them they were not forgotten and that forgiveness was essential and possible. Sadly our church did not seem interested enough to ask me for a report. And the fact that most of my pictures had been confiscated, did not help me convince the Send a Cow trustees to launch a special Rwanda appeal, or take any further action then. However, a year or two later David Bragg went to see a bishop from Rwanda, whom I referred him to and a little while later Send a Cow started there in a big way.

35

The First Gulf War and Another Mission

In 1989 I had been asked to chair the Bristol Evangelical Alliance, a group of churches and individuals of all denominations who were united in their belief in the Bible and in praying that people would come to faith in Christ. Our main activity together that year concerned the Gulf War. Saddam Hussein had invaded Kuwait in August 1990 and the whole country was worried about the possibility of war. We decided to hold a prayer meeting on August 24th in Bristol Cathedral and invite all concerned folk to join us for prayer. The Cathedral was full.

This was not my first sermon in the Cathedral, that had been at the thanksgiving service for Mission England in 1985, and I had also preached at two other English and two African cathedrals.

I reminded the congregation that we were in a long tradition of praying for our nation and armed forces in time of war. A tradition which, at least in living memory, had begun in March 1918 in the First World War when, despite recently-invented tanks and newly-arrived Americans, defeat looked likely,. The big advance by the German Army was halted as soon as a day of prayer was announced and this turned to victory, through collapsed enemy morale, almost immediately the Day of Prayer was held. King George VI called the nation to prayer in 1939 at the outset of the Second World War, followed by 13 other national days of prayer (see appendix 5.) Some of these were followed by remarkable deliverances such as at Dunkirk and the Battle of Britain and the low British casualties at the D-Day landings.

I had been opposed to the Falklands War and when the Argentineans invaded on April 2nd 1982 I wrote to the government asking for negotiation instead. The fleet sailed anyway, on April 5th, and some of us resolved to pray daily for the protection of those serving. Over 100 ships, including the naval auxiliary, and many thousands of men and women were involved. During the conflict the British Task Force lost seven ships, but significantly a further 19 of our 42 Royal Navy warships were hit by bombs that did not explode. These events of deliverance seemed to have saved us from defeat in the South Atlantic. God often calls His people to prayer.

As a likely Gulf War drew closer we decided to meet every week from January 4th, first in Bristol Cathedral and then in the Lord Mayor's Chapel until hostilities were over. We held our final thanksgiving on March 1st. We were thrilled that week-by-week, our prayers for minimum casualties on both sides had been answered: only ten of our coalition forces died in the land offensive and far fewer Iraqi conscripts than at first looked likely. It is always a mystery as to why the Lord allows such bloody wars and what plans there are in the consequences. Lincoln saw the American Civil War, which Churchill described as the bloodiest of all wars, not as an accident of history but as 'a terrible visitation at the hand of God'. Prayers in wartime remain a challenge to the faith of millions.

I finished my two-year chairmanship of Bristol EA in 1991. As a consequence of this and of my earlier role in Mission England, in 1996 a group of former Mission England leaders approached me and asked if I would chair a mission to Bristol with the American evangelist Luis Palau, for four days in June 1997. In 1984 Luis had led a Mission to London at the same time Billy Graham was in England. I knew him to be an evangelist of integrity with a more flexible approach than Graham, but very much less known. He had a twenty- or thirty-something family of boys who kept him young and youth were a very important part of his mission.

I needed to see Luis in action before I could support his mission with enthusiasm, and so I flew to Chicago in May 1996. There was a lot of emphasis on fun and activity on stage, with Christian celebrities and faithful gospel preaching by Luis. The Chicago mission was not well attended because not all churches were keenly supportive. A huge church just outside Chicago called Willow Creek was partly responsible, as for years they had been offering weekly opportunities for non-church folk to get a flavour of church. 5,000 people attended once on Saturday night and twice on Sunday morning. The story was well known in Britain and so some of us visited one Sunday. An orchestra and choir introduced the service and a drama group performed a playlet with a message. The pastor spoke well and there was a final song for everyone. It was over in 55 minutes and the changeover of 5,000 people was impressive, with large cafés, huge car parks and very friendly staff.

Back home, our churches had largely stopped evangelising in the last 12 years. And as there was no 5-10,000 seat arena in Bristol (the size of venue we wanted), we decided to hire the football stadium again. This time we put matting across the middle of the pitch and a platform on it, facing towards the newly-built, 4,250-seat Atyeo Stand. There was to be a mega-fun factory led by experienced children's workers as part of the programme.

Luis was good at after-dinner speaking and so lots of dinners were arranged; we also offered him to Newport churches. I remember going to see the Bishop of Monmouth and hearing his enthusiastic endorsement of inter-church evangelism whilst having coffee in the kitchen with him and his wife Jane. Little did I realise that this man, Rowan Williams, would soon become Archbishop of Canterbury. Luis was also invited to Bath and to an open-air meeting in Taunton. The whole mission undoubtedly reminded the churches of our responsibility to tell the world about Jesus. Several thousand people, young and old, would discover that vital relationship with Jesus and though the mission finances were covered, I did not feel God had fully answered my prayers for local people as I had hoped. Alpha courses began to take off more seriously at that time. I could not have dreamed of what was about to open up for us within a few years.

36

Three Animal Diseases

1. Foot and Mouth

I COME FROM A LONG LINE OF PEASANTS ON BOTH SIDES OF MY FAMILY. (Historically a peasant was a tenant farmer, so I can claim peasanthood.) As I have mentioned, at one time, out of my 20 closest male relatives, 18 of them were in farming. You can't be rude about any nearby farmer, because you may be speaking to a relative! One of my great-grandfathers, Robert Swanton, farmed at Mells in the 1890s and his herd contracted foot and mouth disease (FMD) three times. The cattle eventually recovered but productivity was hit hard and Robert nearly went bankrupt. FMD is a disease that affects mainly pigs and ruminants. An eradication scheme was started in Britain in 1911 and infected herds are now slaughtered with compensation. Our government has never been thorough about its prevention. The source of each outbreak is almost always traced back to infected imported meat. Countries like Canada, Australia and USA are far stricter than Britain and have not had an outbreak in many years. During the British outbreak in 2001, a photo appeared in the farming press of suitcases lined up at Heathrow Airport with meat juice oozing out of them all. How many others had foreign meat in them which was packed a bit better?

In my memory, 1954 was a major outbreak in which my father's herd was surrounded on three sides, but he escaped. In the big outbreak in 1966 FMD was heading south from Cheshire; I remember we were holding a half night of prayer for the nation at Pip 'n' Jay and included some heartfelt requests to God to stop the epidemic. The following day it peaked and began to recede. I asked a government vet later what had been the reason for the FMD abating? He replied that he had no idea, it was out of control from beginning to end and they just reacted to each case. He thought ours' and other people's praying was as good a reason as any for it finally coming under control.

2001 was the most costly outbreak of all, at £8 billion. The news broke on Sunday 19th February. A vet at the slaughterhouse at Little Warley, Essex had detected it. The following day we heard that the outbreak had been traced to a pig swill-feeding farm belonging to Bobby Waugh, at Haddon-on-the-Wall, Northumberland. His pigs it turned out, had been infected for several days and livestock from the area had already spread round the country from local markets. The government failed to do what the NFU knew by experience was the only way to get on top of FMD – to call the army in to help with the administration. When a government vet or civil servant asks for lorries or diggers, the owners refuse or put them off. When an army brigadier does the same with an implied threat of arrest, they cooperate!

The government had an election to win and did not want to panic the country. Their selfishness, inexperience and incompetence cost 14 days and most of the £8 billion. What did they know about it anyway? Most of them were at school at the last outbreak, 35 years before; but now, frighteningly, they were running the country!

On the first Monday morning, 20th February, when only the FMD case at the Essex abattoir had been announced the day before, an elderly Christian friend of ours, Ted Woolly, in Wraxall had a dream in which he was taken onto an international passenger jet and shown the cabin food waste being tipped into a container. This container was then taken to the edge of the runway and tipped into a farmer's pig swill bin. He woke, shouting 'you can't do that, there's foot and mouth… ' He thought he was just having a reaction dream to the news, so returned to sleep. A few hours later he had the same dream, which affected him so much that he rang the Ministry of Agriculture in Taunton. A senior official happened to be visiting, who listened to him intently for some while. Two days later the government had ordered all airline swill to be burned from that time on. This dream seemed like divine intervention to prevent FMD coming to the country from several other pig swill routes. Ted told us about his dream, in church the following Sunday.

2. BSE (bovine spongiform encephalopathy)

Mad cow disease, as it is commonly known, affects the brains of cows, but was partially human induced. When it was first diagnosed and linked to Creutzfeldt-

Jakob disease (CJD) the government-sponsored Professor Hugh Pennington suggested 50,000 people were already likely to have been infected, with further tens of thousands to follow. The government then, having initiated a lower rendering temperature for meat offal than the rest of Europe, introduced more draconian control measures than the rest of Europe. A total of 4.4 million cattle in the UK were killed and burned because of this. In the end 164 people died of CJD, including a vegetarian, in the 26 years since the early '80s when it began. At one point I heard that our local vet was in Holland on a study day with a Dutch vet. The Dutch vet found a case of suspected BSE, so he took the Dutch ear tag out and put a British tag in the cow's ear, saying 'we don't have BSE in Holland'. A farmer near Glastonbury imported 20 heifers from France and 7 of them later showed up as BSE cases; yet France had almost no cases of BSE. It was all a great, suspicious mystery. It probably began in UK when, as I have mentioned, using the best scientific advice the temperature of rendered meat was altered. All this was another example of poor science costing us a lot. The huge and special nature of BSE to Britain may have other causes, yet unproven. Organophosphate (OP) compounds that we used to eradicate warble flies are suspected as an additional agent. After the first BSE outbreak farmers stopped losing cows to magnesium deficiency. The symptoms of staggering about were similar, so all of these hypomagnesaemia cases would have been recorded as BSE for many years. Perhaps in France and Holland the opposite happened and BSE was recorded as hypomagnesaemia? We may never know.

3. TB

Bovine tuberculosis has been in process of eradication since the Second World War. We, like all dairy farms had to undergo an annual test for TB on all of our 350 animals to ensure they had not begun to carry the disease. It was essential to ensure animal handling systems were in place to make this easy for us and as stress-free as possible for the cattle. If a cow is found to be positive to her two little neck injections, she is slaughtered and the rest of the herd put in quarantine until a clear test of the whole herd is achieved. No animals may leave the herd until that time. New born calves have to be kept till they are past their optimum selling time, barren cows cannot be sold and more food is consumed. Overcrowding becomes inevitable. There is a big financial penalty in this.

Unfortunately badgers and deer can also carry Bovine TB. Farmers think that cattle and badgers should be given the same supervision and treatment, because badgers scavenge in grass fields and dribble and urinate on grass that cows eat. If TB is detected in cattle, then farmers think that all the local badgers should be tested too. Every badger's sett and fox's earth are known in case rabies should ever land in UK. So why not test the badgers? For some reason dairy and beef farmers are victimised by one cowardly government after another, because there are more voters swayed by emotive language from animal rights folk into saying they like badgers and don't seem to consider the real issue, that badger TB is rising with cattle TB. Even the testing is unfair. In each of the last three tests my herd underwent we had a possible reactor. Rather than roll over I insisted on a more expensive re-test by a different method, the gamma-interferon blood test. DEFRA's best estimate is that their normal skin test is 77% accurate. Which of us would fly if we thought we only had a 77% chance of reaching our destination? The more expensive test is not perfect but it certainly helped us because in each of my three tests the animals were confirmed clear of TB. Eventually, in 2006, the test began to be rolled out across the country. In 2011 it was announced that TB cases had risen from 6,000 in 1998 to 32,000 for 2010, costing the taxpayer £63m and the farmers more; all this and still no clear eradication policy in sight, merely compensation. The issues are complex but it is high time the dairy farmer received more understanding from those who eat breakfast cereals with milk on them.

37

Buying a Farm from Tyntesfield Estate

In 1995 the agent of Lord Wraxall, my landlord, was making fresh enquiries about our farm. This time he offered a bigger sum for us to move. I had been a tenant for 35 years during which time Tyntesfield had shrunk from 26 farm tenants to five. We had just held a 65th-birthday party for Lord Wraxall at the end of a service in his chapel one Sunday, to thank him for being a good landlord and to celebrate with him. Christina had asked all the tenants to bring a cake and had contacted the Wraxall School and the Down's School, whose children made him a card. Ray Llewellyn, the estate buildings manager and some estate staff were there. As the tenant with the longest tenancy I made a speech and read out the names of the 26 farmers who had been tenants on his 21st birthday. Some of the farms had disappeared into the middle of a growing Nailsea.

Lord Wraxall and I had a stormy relationship for many years. He was ten years older than me, and when I arrived, aged 22, I was his youngest tenant.

We both had a military background as officers and had both been to public school – and as I had been to Oxford I was not about to defer to him on grounds of birth, merit was the new ruling class. Nor did he have the money to do what landlords should do by way of maintenance and building, so I tended to just get on and do what needed doing. When my tractor driver Gilbert Masters complained of no porch on his cottage to take off his boots, I asked the agent for a small porch and was turned down. So we just built one anyway. The agent was furious and so was the landlord – Lord Wraxall told me I was the worst tenant he had ever had and I told him he was the worst landlord my family had ever known! Stalemate. We got over it and by the tenants' lunch it was forgotten. The porch stayed.

His lack of money proved difficult as it meant we had to borrow money for the cow buildings and slurry handling facilities and to concrete the yards, but we negotiated a lower rent to partially compensate. I also became quite good at building, learning to lay concrete, put up steel- framed barns and concrete walls – 20,000 square feet of barns in all. Very occasionally Lord Wraxall agreed to do an essential 'roofs and walls' repair or a small capital spend and so when I went to see him to hand over the rent, usually at Lady Day or Michaelmas, I'd ask him for some of it back. He could see the farm was becoming productive: the rent was rising and I got to know him quite well.

On one occasion I went to see him at Tyntesfield House on behalf of another tenant, and sat in the sitting room surrounded by antique furniture and beautiful carved-oak panelling, and on two other occasions when he threw the house open to fund-raising ventures at which his 'Rembrandt' painting (probably 'school-of') and many other valuables were on show. He was generous with his house which was beautifully furnished in Edwardian tradition and which he continued to fill with beautiful collections of glass, ceramics and paintings, inherited and added to and about which he was very knowledgeable. The roofs at Tyntesfield were a problem to him because of their valley gutters. On one occasion after snow there was a thaw followed by a freeze so that the valley gutters froze. Then another thaw came and the remaining snow poured down inside the house and flooded the dining room. He told me how his butler was in tears while he was urging him to roll up the valuable carpet and carry it out to dry.

For a while he lived on his own and did not keep a dog because he was allergic to them. He was burgled twice. The first time he grabbed the burglar, who bit him and got away. The second time he was captured by the burglars who warned him not to set off the burglar alarm. When he defiantly did, he was bundled into the boot of his own car, driven to Portbury Lane and left there, to be discovered by his gamekeeper's family next morning trying to get out.

By 1995, over 30 tenants' annual lunches had come and gone for me at the Battle Axes pub where, each October, Lord Wraxall treated us to roast beef followed by apple pie. I was always pushed to sit next to 'Lordy', to talk to him while the oldest tenant made the same speech about what a difficult year we had all had and how the rents were on the high side. Finally, one year we all fell out with Lordy over a variety of maintenance and rent issues and the tenants' lunches were dropped. I enjoyed talking to Lordy, who was good on art and history and all things countryside and Tory and, as a church-goer, was interested in the happenings at General Synod. He came to a Billy Graham meeting once, where I had introduced the 'Silver Delegation' of posh seats to try and encourage posh people to hear and respond to the gospel. God's prophets had a lot of rude things to say about rich people, so I thought Billy might be the person to tell them before it was too late. By our last Christmas, Lord Wraxall had become very friendly and stayed for cake on Christmas Eve, when he brought round his usual offering of a brace of pheasants as a thank you for tolerating his pheasant shoot. We were sad it was going to be his last.

A few months earlier, when Lord Wraxall's agent wanted to buy us out and sell the farm, I asked him to sell it to us. A modest price might just enable us to carry on dairy farming and pay the mortgage. The future of milk looked bleak to me and I had, with others, tried hard through the NFU to stop the ending of Milk Marque's monopoly buying position. Milk Marque may have had almost all the UK's milk, but it was not the biggest co-op in Europe and it should, by all logic, be allowed to remain in one piece. However, younger farmers insisted that competition could well earn them a penny or two more per litre. How short-sighted they proved to be. They seemed oblivious to the fact that the milk companies wanted to break Milk Marque's monopoly and had devoted £20 million to attract farmers by offering a penny or two more a litre here and there. Those of us with long memories could remember the vulnerability our parents suffered in the '30s, of having to sell one's fragile product daily to an over-supplied market. It seemed to me we were heading for a collapse of the milk industry if Milk Marque was split up. In the end the government ordered its dismantling because farmers were not united. The recession that was about to hit dairy farming was of the Tory Government's making but was supported by younger farmers who would go through it – with many going bust on the way. This was of course the law of supply and demand. Supporters should not whinge now when they see 2,000 cow units taking over from 100 cow units. That is commercial efficiency and possibly better management per cow, too.

I had next to no savings and no exit strategy. We had deliberately adopted a policy over many years of paying for half a person more on the farm than was necessary, to give me time to do the things off the farm that I felt God was calling me to do. Retirement was not an option. So when Lord Wraxall refused my low offer I realised our best action was to agree to his higher price, for which we would need to sell the herd and change to arable farming. The decision was made much easier by the fact that the quantity of milk we were allowed to produce, called a milk quota, had a value. It could be sold or rented out, if not wanted. We had a large quota, some of which we had bought from other producers. For a short two year period this selling value rose from 10p to 60p per litre. A mysterious thing called 'confidence' had hit the milk industry, due to a temporary shortage of milk and lots of people wanted to expand their herd and buy quota to do so. I, on the other hand, couldn't wait to sell.

As 1995 had been a drought year, we on our dry land had very low stocks of silage, so when the landlord said he accepted our offer on the farm, I trusted him and made immediate steps to sell the herd and the crops and the specialist equipment and machinery. We were making ourselves vulnerable to his going back on his word, but after praying about the whole matter both with Christina, and by myself often, we decided God was behind us doing this, that Lord Wraxall could be trusted and we should sell the herd, growing crops, and dairy machinery. Then we should plant wheat on 220 acres that were registered for arable crop growing, letting out the remaining 90 acres of grass on an annual basis.

We had three sales; the first was a cattle sale. Norton & Brooksbank, the pedigree cattle sellers, advertised it, took over our records, produced a fancy catalogue of all 320 pedigree cattle, moved their contractors on to the farm, washed and blow-dried all the cattle, erected a sale ring and sold them. All except one, which we found forgotten with her calf in a loose box the next day! As is usual the cattle were not milked in the morning to make all the udders look bigger and at their best for the sale ring; they had to be milked after the sale before they left. Even the flask of frozen bull semen was sold. My staff knew the sale was the end of their jobs, but I offered them a percentage of the proceeds to stay on. All three soon found new jobs.

The following day was so quiet. Suddenly, after living all my life on a dairy farm (two dairy farms as a child and then 35 years at Moat House) there were no cows! Although I never really liked dairy cows and they had caused me blood, sweat and tears 24/7 for all the time I owned them, I missed them. I felt like crying. All my best and friendliest cows had gone to the butchers at slaughter price. The young pedigree calves, heifers and young cows, which had been among the 5% highest genetic potential in the country, had made very good prices. The one lone cow and calf was our consolation, at least for a week or two.

The next sale was of crops. It took place in a pub with the crops from a few other farms. Different farmers bought the 60 acres of standing maize and 13 acres of fodder beet. The clamp of silage we had made we decided to sell later that winter. Half of it was never paid for; we sold it to a farmer who turned out to be bankrupt. It was my only bad debt in a lifetime of dairy farming.

Our final sale was of the machinery. This is always a big social event in a locality, but usually the farmer is dead. I was 58, very much present and relieved to see spare tractors, feed wagon, and memorabilia of 35 years of dairy farming finding new homes.

I kept two tractors I was fond of. I also kept a trailer, partly because it was the one Lizzie and Richard had ridden on back from their wedding, and partly because I wanted to remove some tired old cow fences to make bigger arable fields and put up two miles of new sheep fence. I had linked up with Sentry Farming, a large share-farming company, who were busy ploughing and planting 220 acres registered as arable fields – registered meant they had grown crops other than grass in the five years before 1990. Six years was too much, apparently. This was a typical piece of badly thought out Brussels and Whitehall bureaucracy that effectively fossilised farming for the next 30 years. From our point of view we had 90 acres that we had to keep as grass forever, when previously we had occasionally, perhaps at six year intervals or more, ploughed up a tired grass field, cropped it with arable and re-grassed it. So we let those 90 acres out to a nearby sheep farmer, annually, in case we needed to use it ourselves. The bigger buildings were to be used by Sentry Farming, who had 1,200 ewes on Lord Wraxall's fields nearby, for their winter housing and lambing from February to April.

So the farm was being productive, but we had not yet bought it. In March 1996 contracts were exchanged and I now had to sell the milk quota to pay for it. Amazingly, for a year the price held and we sold it all well. The value was transferable on to certain business assets of the farm, without capital gains tax, provided we made the right decisions. Our large accountants advised us poorly on this, but in the nick of time I changed to a different, one-man-band accountant. The cottages that had previously housed two of our staff were empty; we redecorated and repaired them with a little professional help and they were ready to rent out immediately. So, we owned a farm with no mortgage, with rental income and a contract farming deal: we were earning more than at any time in our dairy farming lives. It seemed an uncomfortably wealthy situation but a blessing too: as Christians we had always tithed our income, now we could give more.

The buildings were very dilapidated so we thought we should improve the stone ones with new roofs and floors and, with slight tweaks here and there, install toilets and small kitchens and make three office blocks. The windows and doors were so draughty they would not even keep rats out, all the roofs needed replacing with insulated new ones, the floors needed damp proof membranes under concrete, covered with timber floors with carpets.We applied for planning permission for change of use and with professional help for roofs, windows and one floor, began work. We thought what a lot more money we could make from these as offices, than as very out-of-date farm buildings.

We had not considered the bureaucrats, however. A few years before, Christina had registered our 17th-century farmhouse as a Grade 2 listed building to stop the landlord from making changes to it. It was against my advice but I could see she wanted to protect the nest, so I didn't protest. Now it turned against us because every listed building had a curtilage, or area in which other buildings would take on its listed status. I felt it was fair for the buildings along the edge of our garden to be included, however, the authorities wanted all the farm buildings to be curtilage. Try as we might we couldn't get a change. This meant that everything had to remain the same; more fossilisation, and for dubious reasons. We had to produce drawings of all the new windows and doors that we had just put into the farm buildings, which now, presumably, can never be built to a different pattern. They allowed small roof-lights as long as they could not be seen from the listed building. A lot of the work which they thought had been done earlier and thus excused had in fact been done by ourselves. As it is now over 10 years since the deed was done, all of that can stay.

38

A Fresh Call?

Beginning in 1996 I had begun to attend an early morning prayer meeting for men at Holy Trinity Church. We were praying especially for men and for men's things. Why did more women go to church than men? Men may believe in God in similar numbers to women, but were there ways that men could be helped to faith and church made relevant to them? Jesus said that he came to build a church – but were church people insisting on old-fashioned forms of words and practices that were not helpful to men?

Our prayer meetings had surprising consequences over the next few years. One man, Phil Williams, was a very good surfer with an interest in Christian Surfers. He started coming to the prayer meeting when he was in charge of transport at a Sainsbury's depot. Phil wanted to pray with us for help to do the job well, not least because as well as other pressures, there was a demonstration of farmers due at his gate. Over a few months he became more and more certain that he should leave the security of Sainsbury's and start a charity, Christian Surfers UK, to reach surfers for Jesus, and that he should to trust God for an income. Another man, a consultant pathologist Ed Sheffield, felt God calling him to link up with Mercy Ships, a charity that offered operations from a hospital ship at ports in the third world. Soon, Ed was visiting them in Africa and making links to the UK to help with their diagnosis of diseases and tumours; he even received an eye-ball in the post one day! Another doctor, Trevor Dean, felt called to Africa to help with an AIDS programme, to ordination and to work in a deprived area of Bristol. Derek Marsland Brown set up a healing ministry in Nailsea. And my own call came – to set up Noah's Ark.

It now seemed to me that one of the major things that stopped people believing in God was the steady drip feeding of television that suggested nature had arrived by itself, that God was irrelevant and probably not there. The question of why God allowed suffering was another principle reason to disbelieve. David Attenborough has often said that seeing a little boy in Africa with a worm crawling through his eyeball suggested to him that God did not care. My response was very different: God prefers non-intervention because he had given mankind both freewill and the job of ruling the Earth, and yet he is very much present in the world, answering prayers in ways that are often mysterious to us. He has that complex supervisory role of calling thousands of people, like me, to do the caring. Although God had made the world 'very good', as He Himself described it in *Genesis* 1 and 2, Adam and Eve's response was not quietly to enjoy it, but defiance and mischief. So God partially cursed the world, apparently to keep us all busy sorting out the problems that arose. Thus it was now our job to try to enrich Africans and help them kill parasites like eye-ball worms, and not just film their wildlife.

Parasites, diseases, wars, famines, earthquakes, hurricanes all seem to be evils that God has allowed to challenge mankind, through which He brings legitimate employment and uses good people to bring help. Many are avoidable, but the human heart is selfish and often thinks short term. Man builds on earthquake zones too cheaply, or in flood planes and then blames God for weather and earthquakes. Famines sometimes arise from poor national or international food distribution or selfish and belligerent tribal and political leaders. If there is a lack of rain we are told by God to ask for it (*Zechariah* 10:1). God listens to our praying and has the incredibly complicated job of answering billions of prayers each day, of calling people to action and guiding them.

Catherine of Aragon's words 'None get to God but through trouble' carry a truth. To some, suffering is undoubtedly positive and a way of finding God or moving on with Him. Instead of asking 'Why this?' they ask 'What now?' One thing has always been certain: everyone's life will come to an end. In 1800 life expectancy in Britain was 40 years, similar to some Third-World countries now. By 1714, Queen Anne had had 18 pregnancies of which 13 were still-births; four of her five live-birth children died before they were two and the fifth at 11-years-old. Mankind has never shared things well. God, who is all-knowing, alone is capable of assessing the achievements of our lives and rewarding those who have fulfilled their God-given destiny, whether their life lasts a few hours or many decades. I have found Him always faithful – although often slower than I would like Him to be. I am still learning how to listen and discover what to do, including and especially waiting.

For the previous 30 years we had spent a lot of time trying to help marriages and families be strong and happy, to alleviate poverty in Africa and in Bristol and to help people to faith in God. We had also encouraged other very competent people to continue meeting each of these needs. This had usually been away from home. Christina was keen that I should now do something from home which would involve us both.

I had been quite envious of working folk who only worked from 9-5, five days a week with eight Bank Holidays and four weeks' holiday. We self-employed owners of 24/7 businesses found it difficult to take even a few days off. It was still a good life, perhaps better because it was busy. Now there was an inviting option of travelling round the world and doing what retired people do. However, my trips to Africa had put me off going to Third-World countries without a purpose. The poverty I saw made me feel uncomfortable about staying in comfortable hotels, even though they needed our tourist money. I did not feel old enough for golf, bowls or croquet. I felt this small but persistent call to use our farm to help people to discover God, perhaps through His creation? St. Paul assures us that everyone knows God exists through the things God has made, so perhaps unpacking nature could help people? I had wondered about a Noah's Ark theme park, feeling that if we could put Noah in place, people would automatically put God in place. God, after all, was the beginning, middle and end of Noah's story, which was the best known story in the world. We did not need any extra income, nor particularly want the huge amount of work it would involve. Christina and I were both sixty, we had no mortgage, we did not need to diversify and we both were low maintenance. But still the challenge would not leave us: to put this farm, which had come to us through a very short but huge advantage in the milk quota price, at God's service.

Encouraged by our rector, John Simons, I asked a friend at church who was an architect, Trevor Eastell, to draw up some plans for a building shaped like Noah's Ark and incorporating a 5,000-seat auditorium and lots of rooms for animals, leading out onto fields with a car park for 1000 cars and lots of other details. Trevor did some fine drawings at very low cost which we put to the council. We were told they would totally oppose it with four presumptions against us: we were in the Green Belt, in an area of Special Scenic Beauty, in an Area of Archaeological Interest and reached by the busiest motorway exit in the country, to Gordano Services and Portbury docks. I felt God was also in this decision, not least because it would be way beyond our available capital and would mean going heavily into overdraft again.

I asked Mike Clements, our very helpful NFU Group Secretary (and a QEH school contemporary of our sons) what I should do. He suggested we open our farm to the public slowly, bit by bit; that way we would be encouraged by government to diversify and the council could not stop us. It was doing it by stealth, he said. So we spent the next ten years investing £50,000 per year above receipts, growing Noah's Ark. I was alarmed at how much ignorance there was about where supermarket food comes from. I passionately wanted the public to be better informed and felt we could do that, thus also helping our fellow farmers be better understood. We were also very much in favour of children and parents having fun, and wanted to help people have the best possible day out. Thus we hoped our visitors would learn all they could about the amazing natural world God has put us in. Noah's Ark could combine all of these as a theme for the theme park.

39

Science or God?

ONE DAY, WHEN I WAS HELPING A YOUNG LORRY DRIVER UNLOAD TIMBER FOR a cow barn that we were building, I asked him, as I sometimes did to people who casually visited the farm, 'do you believe in God?'

'No,' he said.

'How do you think all this got here?' I asked, pointing to the fields and hedges.

'Oh, it was all out of the Big Bang and evolution. I believe in science', he replied to my astonishment.

I felt both angry and sad on his behalf because his belief fell apart at the next question 'How can anything come from nothing, let alone everything?' but it showed that TV Darwinians like David Attenborough and Richard Dawkins who had been given a monopoly of screen time, had been successful in eroding belief in God. Disagreeing with Darwinism on TV seemed to be censored, even discussion was not allowed.

Yet despite this, at the end of the noughties 'Just under half of Britons accept the theory of evolution as the best description for the development of life, according to an opinion poll.' (BBC Jan. 06) and '40% of public believe creationism or Intelligent Design should be taught alongside evolution in school science' (MORI poll, INSTITUTE OF IDEAS 4th Feb. 09).

Although Darwinians are keen to point out that the arrival of the first life forms have nothing to do with evolution or Darwinism, it is a cop-out, because the fundamental question everyone must ask at some point is 'did life arise naturally or super-naturally?' Did the whole complex web of nature arrive by chance or by design? One of the 20th century's influential atheist thinkers, Anthony Flew, astonished the atheist world in 2007 with his book *There is a God*, stating that he had become a believer in God (albeit only a deist). He had been especially impressed with the physicist who refuted the idea that if enough monkeys typed enough typewriters at random they would eventually produce a Shakespearean sonnet. Its likelihood is one chance in 10^{690} (that is 1,000,000,000…with 690 noughts) so that number of monkeys would be needed; but there are only 10^{80} (or 1,000,000,00….with 80 noughts) particles in the universe. So if chance doesn't work for a simple sonnet, how could it be considered for the production of highly complex DNA and life? It was, Flew thought, more likely that God existed without a cause, than that the universe existed without a cause.

There are very few real facts about the universe that help us with a theory for its origin but Big Bang Theory is the proposal that most people support, though by no means all top scientists. The name Big Bang was coined in 1949 by Professor Fred Hoyle, who did not accept it, like thousands of other scientists (try 'big bang dissent' on Google).

The theory was proposed because of three observations:

1. Most starlight is slightly red, which indicates that stars are moving away from us.

2. There is a Cosmic Microwave Background of 2.7°, showing that space is very slightly warmer than if it had absolutely zero energy.

3. The predominant element of the universe is hydrogen, from which other elements can form, one from another in the hot centres of stars by that amazing process called nucleosynthesis.

I can think of several things which this establishment view is proposing (or at least accepting without explanation) which could not possibly have come from nothing:

1. Big Bang Theory comes from assuming that because the stars are moving away from us they were once closer and closer together, and came from in Professor Stephen Hawking's words an 'infinitely small, infinitely dense' pea which explodes without a cause in one trillion trillionth of a second into a vast ocean of energy, larger than the visible universe. Subsequently a force we call gravity overcame this explosion and caused matter to clump together into galaxies. Then light arrives, by 'a dominance of photons (the zero-mass bits that form light) ten seconds after the bang.' None of these ideas, it seems to me are particularly rational and all make unbelievable claims about the power of nothing.

2. There is much more that is assumed without proof. Atoms form themselves (albeit only hydrogen initially). How? Atoms are astonishingly complex and held together by immensely powerful, constant forces. Atoms consist of protons and neutrons at their centre orbited by electrons. To put it simply the comparative distances are like a fly in the centre of a football

stadium being orbited by others outside the stands. Atoms therefore are mainly space and are held together by forces – nuclear strong, nuclear weak and electromagnetic forces, 10^{39}, 10^{33}, 10^{36} x gravity respectively, and reliably fixed. More recently protons and neutrons have been suggested to be made of various particles called quarks (up, down, charm, strange, top, bottom quarks), electrons are a form of leptons, and bosons, which include photons, are mediators of force from one particle to another. I include some of the technical words to show that all atoms are extremely complex, and they are wholly reliable and able to change into other atoms through that wonderful dependable progression, nucleosynthesis. They are not the sort of things that suddenly appear by their own efforts from an explosion out of nothing.

3. My next doubt is about the galaxies, which consist of a billion or more stars each. For these galaxies to have collapsed under gravity from dust clouds there is a need to invent 'dark matter' which is a purely hypothetical substance, called dark because no one can see it. Dark matter has been invented because without it there is insufficient gravity to hold galaxies together. Despite there needing to be four times as much dark matter as matter (some say much more), it has rarely, and never of a naturally occurring form, been detected. There is a further problem with Big Bang theory, the inflation of the universe should be slowing down but it isn't. So 'dark energy' has also been invented, accounting for 74% of all mass-energy in the universe. These seem to me to be suspiciously contrived.

4. Coming closer to home, we appear to live in an astonishing solar system, some of which I have looked at on our family telescope. The Earth is just the right distance from the sun, which has just the right energy output for us, and the moon is just the right size for tides, eclipses and moonlight of which it reflects back a much lower proportion of sunlight than other planets and moons. There is also this amazing and weird stuff called water which, far from looking like a random connection of hydrogen and oxygen into H_2O, has astonishing properties that appear to be designed to help life, with a huge array of weird and amazing forms in its vapour, liquid, ice, crystals, snow and other marvels on which all of life depends. Even Earth's nine-miles-thick atmosphere with outer protection, although it has changed over time, is completely suitable for life and robust in self-correction. Our Earth is hurtling round the sun at 18.5 miles per second, it spins at over 1,000 mph, and the whole solar system is moving at 7-20 miles per second (in different planes) within our galaxy. None of these look like an accidental consequence of a Big Bang.

5. My next concern about the theory is the biggest so far. It is proposed that the first living thing forms by itself somewhere on Earth, like the 'little warm pond' of chemicals proposed by Darwin. The very simplest life today is not simple. A bacterium has 100 billion atoms in it and the progression from chemicals to amino acids to a protein is complex, and there are 500 proteins in a bacterium. In every bacterium there is also a DNA genome with at least 500,000 base pairs which will need to divide to grow into another bacterium in about 20 minutes. Despite efforts from Urey and Miller in 1955 onwards, it has not been possible for scientists to produce any of the right amino acids for life from such a 'chemical soup'. So it seems to me pure fantasy to suggest a pool of inorganic chemicals could possibly become such a living and ready-to-multiply thing.

6. The next step is no simpler. Evolution is then proposed to have 'kick-started' itself; to change these prokaryotes (bacteria), into other single celled life forms, of much greater complexity and with a nucleus. These are proposed to develop by somehow acquiring even more complexity, including the arrival of sexual reproduction from asexual, into 10,000,000 species of creature in 38 different phyla (or phylum singular, which are life forms, for example all vertebrates are in one phylum).

Without God, it seems to me these are six impossible things to believe before breakfast. How could any scientist believe any of them just happened (without intelligent assistance), except one with colossal faith in the power of nothing? It was like believing that enough whirlwinds in enough scrap yards could eventually make a jet aircraft. Yet how can I blame ordinary folk for believing these people? For several decades a few bullying, strident voices have stirred up the majority to just accept them, on the grounds that the only explanation of origins allowed are with physical causes. To suggest there is a power greater than matter, energy and time, or to mention God or an Intelligent designer was immediately disqualified as 'religion, not science', or labelled Creationism, so that even archbishops are intimidated into distancing themselves from such a thought.

These assumptions also totally oppose the two well established laws of thermodynamics, which are:

1. Energy can neither be created nor destroyed.

2. The entropy, or randomness of a system, increases over time, or order tends towards disorder.

For scientists to believe the unbelievable implied that other agendas than science were at work. People were feeling threatened at the thought of a Creator inventing energy, space, time, all the laws of physics, and life in all its complexity, so they invent a philosophy masquerading as science, whereby 'nothing' does the same as a Creator, given enough time.

When I have suggested that the whole façade is false, to one of its believers, the usual response I get is 'If God made it all, who made God?' To this the answer has to be that He who is outside space, time, matter and energy does not need a beginning. Jesus tells us God is Spirit and showed us a little of His power over nature in His miracles and in the sort of body He had after His resurrection.

As I began to discover these things I decided I had to make it my business to find out much more about Evolution Theory, perhaps more than most people who accepted it; who did not seem to understand the proposals, but merely repeated them. The whole theory seemed surprisingly vague. Over the next few years I visited Bristol University library and watched as many relevant TV programmes as possible. I bought 100 books on geology, palaeontology, phylogeny, taxonomy, anthropology, classification of vertebrates, plants and invertebrates, astronomy, and microbiology (see appendix 6). In addition to these secular authors I have dozens of books and journals by Creation-believers, who include several professors and many PhDs of science subjects. After a conversation with a newly-qualified PhD in evolutionary biology at a zoo conference, he suddenly said 'Anthony, you are the best informed person I have ever met.' This astonished me to the point of dismay as I don't feel particularly well informed, but I realised how few people there must be who actually study outside their field of science. It was like Oxford all over again: outside your field of expertise you are a layman; inside it you are dependent on your teachers.

There was clearly some serious deception going on by scientists who ought to do better. I was trying to be open to the scientific explanations and arguments of mainstream atheist and theist evolutionists, creationists and those somewhere in the middle. A flexible attitude to this subject seems to me to be crucial to encourage positive discussion and debate, after all, none of us has all the answers. How could we use the farm's resources of the natural and agricultural world to gently give people back scientific permission to believe in God?

40

Big Bang or Creation?

A REP ARRIVED ON THE FARM ONE DAY AND STARTED TELLING ME ABOUT seaweed fertilizer. He made a good case for it, so I decided to try some. I bought the smallest possible load, two tonnes, and, using the rep's prescribed amount, spread it in a diagonal strip across the usual lines we fertilize fields with and also in four grass fields. This was a simple scientific test, to see if the cows liked it more and produced more milk, or if the grass grew better, both of which were claimed for it. As far as we could observe it did neither; no smiley cows, no more milk, no more grass and it certainly did not repay the cost.

There were clearly some dodgy scientific claims made to farmers so I was keen to see that the scientific speculation about the past was not equally dodgy. Science means knowledge. Lots of science is wholly legitimate hypothesis (proposal) which, if there is evidence for it, becomes a theory, like seaweed growing more and better grass. A theory is then examined to see if it is confirmed through repetition and observation. It must also be capable of being proved false. If it is found to be consistent, it becomes a 'law' such as Newton's three laws of motion and the laws of thermodynamics.

When we are considering the origin of the universe and its processes, it is more difficult. We are piecing together evidence from a different and distant past. When I used to look at stars through my school's observatory telescope, I was disappointed that so much of the sky was full of little dots of light that needed bigger and bigger telescopes to see them. So much of the story in the sky needed someone else's interpretation.

Then in my lifetime came the Apollo space mission, which completely altered our understanding of the solar system but of which very little is mentioned on TV. I am grateful to Steven Robinson for ground-breaking, honest, thoughtful work using a peer group of scientists as a sounding board over a ten-year period, in unpacking this and developing for the first time a theory of creation. The increasingly popular website www.earthhistory.org.uk is his contribution to the scientific world and one which I have been delighted to sponsor. Just as the ground-breaking work of the Victorian amateur geologist Charles Lapworth replaced that of the professionals like Roderick Murchison; and later Arthur Holmes' proposals on continental drift from 1928-44 were initially considered maverick and are now considered main-stream, so Steve Robinson's proposals are challenging the assumptions of our day.

Actually, something out of nothing, like a big bang, sounds like a creation event; which may be why so many Christians find it credible. This leads to the uneasy truce between scientists who do and scientists who don't believe in God, as if they were saying: 'I will allow you to believe in your God-event, if you will accept that everything happened as if God need not be there after that!' But is it better science to say 'In the beginning there arrived out of nothing a singularity of almost infinite temperature and gravity which expanded into billions of particles then, in unknown ways eventually formed life, which could evolve,' than 'In the beginning God created the heavens and the earth'?

I had been brought up, like many generations of Christians to accept *Genesis* as God's word to His people, confirmed, of course by Jesus Christ as 'which cannot be broken' (*John* 10:35). So what are we supposed to think about the first chapters of *Genesis*? Angry-sounding atheists have ridiculed these chapters and most scientifically-minded Christians are afraid to defend them for fear of being labelled 'creationist' or 'unscientific'. Too often any dissent is met with derision, not argument. I know, I have many emails to show it. If there is room for a theory of origins without a Creator, there should also be room for a proposal about origins with a Creator. Some of the universal questions of mankind must be: why are we here? Where do we come from? Are we here by accident or by design? Is God at the back of all we see?

For a summary of a theory of creation and a reconciliation of *Genesis* 1-9 in the light of 21st-century science see appendix 1. I personally think it is as important to the understanding of our solar system as Galileo's work on heliocentrism.

41

Evolution Everywhere, but not Descent from One Organism

DURING THE LAST 50 YEARS THE SUPPORT FOR 'THE THEORY OF EVOLUTION' has grown enormously. At school we laughed at it with 'your great granny was a monkey' jokes. Some admirers of Charles Darwin said in his anniversary year of 2009, that 'he changed the way we look at the world' and 'he showed that man was descended from the animal world'. While that idea is widely accepted, it has not been proved by scientific data. I think Darwin was wrong, not because there is no evolution, on the contrary, evolution is everywhere from galaxies to bacteria, but because to me the theory has always seemed simplistic; evolution is driven by far more than mutation and natural selection and the continuous links in small steps to a single organism are as lacking as they were in my youth. Darwinism's proposal, that humans are related to apes, is also far from proved, as I show elsewhere.

I have been involved in cattle and plant breeding for 50 years and of course in my own human breeding. It is clear that small changes occurred between the generations. Milk and meat production increase by selectively breeding from the best animals. More significantly perhaps, cattle grow longer coats of hair when they are outdoors rather than indoors in winter – three inches longer. The fur of some species of foxes and stoats grows and turns white when the temperature drops and snow falls. At species level, we look at animals and plants and it is clear that some are like others. Finches appear to be related to each other. All dogs are related and related to wolves; all pigeons are related to each other. Darwin observed these. He used Patrick Matthew's expression 'natural selection' to describe the weeding out of the unfit, but it did not and still does not explain diversity. Richard Dawkins has said on TV that 'the force that drives evolution on is natural selection'. If we think about this, it is clearly untrue. Natural selection can only select, it does not produce the variation from which to select. Dawkins' sleight-of-mouth has deceived many.

I have tried to keep up with biologists, who have classified living things into six **kingdoms** of which plants, animals, fungi and bacteria are the four most people have heard of. (The others are called protists and archaea and recently domains have been introduced, but these are for specialists.) Each **kingdom** is subdivided into several **phyla**, which include creatures with a roughly similar body plan; we and other vertebrates belong to the phylum called chordata. The next biological division is the **class**, e.g. birds and mammals. Next comes **order**, of which one of the mammals' is the carnivore order, subdivided into **families** of cats (felidae), dogs (canidae), bears (ursidae) and others, all of which are again subdivided into **genera** and **species**. Some creationists in the 1750s, like Carl Linnaeus used to think God made lots of creatures at about the genus level. So Linnaeus, the father of modern taxonomy, named the genus as implying origin (as in *Genesis*) within which all were related. Sir Richard Owen founded the Natural History Museum in 1881 as a cathedral to the glory of God and wanted specimens placed in groups of related species. Darwin proposed everything might be related, but cautiously added 'I think' to his tree of life. Who was right?

Charles Darwin suggested the fossil record should be the arbiter which, as he admitted at the time, was a problem. There now looks to be more relatedness than biologists accepted 150 years ago, but still the main body plans make a sudden appearance in the fossil record without any possible ancestor. Official palaeontology text books (like *The Fossil Record*, ed. Michael Benton) record the appearances of families of animal and plant life, and orders of smaller life, as these are known to give rise to related descendants and are statistically more informative and reliable. Those of us who think God is required to breathe life into the first unrelated creatures can accept more variation than that, and often the phylum appears to be that point, as with the cnidarians (jelly fish to hydra), though arthropods (which include the insects) and chordates (vertebrates) may well include several original kinds. The search for the limits of evolution may yet prove a unifying factor between Creationists and Darwinists, for want of better words since we all believe in evolution.

I found in the course of discussions and emails that the big question was: do related changes come by accidental, mindless, chance mutations or by the activation of a pre-existing, front-loaded genetic programme of awesome complexity in the DNA? This question could probably be resolved with current technology. Did God design a few creatures to evolve and diversify into thousands? Or did the novelty and diversity of detail all arrive by viruses and mutations in small steps and over millions of generations, as Darwin proposed? The astonishing intricacy, variety and novelty of the natural world takes my breath away, like the altruism of a defenceless mother duck against a stronger predator, the ability of birds to mimic sounds, the exquisite flight of flocks of birds and bats that seem to think together with split-second timing, the changing of every cell of caterpillars into butterflies; the migration of butterflies navigating thousands of miles (built into the genes) and the urge of the salmon to jump waterfalls – all are annual miracles of reproduction and breeding. The plants that possess moving parts to attract and digest insects; the nest-building ability of the weaver bird, the wren and the long-tailed tit; the hovering rotating wings of the 1.8-gram bee hummingbird and the nervous system of a mosquito – all are awesome. These millions of diverse novel features are passed down the generations without tuition, and make a theory of mindless chance seem to me to be hopelessly inadequate.

In all the matings on my farm as well as those which I have read about, a male and a female, each with their own diversity, come together and the genes are shuffled to produce a unique individual. There are mutations (changes which are usually mistakes) over time. Francis Collins, head of the Human Genome Project, says in his book *The Language of God* (p131) that 'these occur at the rate of one error per 100 million base pairs per generation', so we might have 60 new mutations that were not present in our parents. Most of these would be neutral, and culled quickly if harmful. However, given enough time,

Collins says the tiny number of mutations that are helpful will naturally be selected to produce the novelty and variation that exists in nature. Which sounds very imprecise and hopeful, but Francis Collins, as a keen Christian, would invoke God to be involved in this process. As God can do anything, Collins can believe it. The secular proposal is totally different since in that, chance plus nothing replace God.

Personally I would be extremely sceptical about the time required being available (see chapter 43), as well as about the adequacy of mutations to do the job. DNA has an astonishing correcting mechanism that comes into play at reproduction. Genomes can call on a variety of damage-detection and repair mechanisms, including base excision repair, nucleotide excision repair, mismatch repair, non-homologous end-joining and homologous recombination. A 21st-century discovery is that these repair mechanisms have been described as 'very near to (and quite possibly at) a global optimum for error minimization.' (Freeland *et al* 2000)* They point to being designed by an Intelligence who was aware of the dangers and wanted to give a strong possibility of success, not mistakes for each replicating gene.

Occasionally apparently harmful mutations are temporarily helpful to survival, like sickle-cell anaemia resisting malaria, or flightless cormorants surviving on the Galapagos Islands because there are no predators. However, point mutations, including these, are not helpful generally. For example, on our farm we had a two legged lamb born with no back end; its skin was sealed behind its ribs. It did not live. My brother once had a calf born with five feet, one of them upwards between its shoulders; I saw it a few years later and the foot had not grown, but was still there. A friend of mine had a calf born with hair underneath its skin, the skin being on the outside; it did not live long. 90% of female bovine twin calves from both-sex twins are freemartins, with no uterus. All these are examples of point mutations, or mistakes. There would be many more we did not see in early natural ending of pregnancy.

These are not examples of the sort of evolution that would turn bacteria into people. It is difficult to see what would. Bacteria stubbornly remain bacteria. The computer pioneer John McCarthy said 'he who refuses to do arithmetic is doomed to talk nonsense'. It seemed to me as a former mathematician that we need to be very careful that the sum of our proposals comes to an accurate conclusion.

I was also reading that the very latest discoveries in DNA now point to far more complexity than was thought even very recently. 'Junk' DNA of a few years

* Freeland, S J, Knight, R D, Landweber, L F & Hurst, L D, 2000. 'Early fixation of an optimal genetic code, *Molecular Biology and Evolution* 17:511-18.

ago is now seen to have 'indescribable complexity'. And the problem for those supporting Darwin's evolution-in-small-steps paradigm seems to be not the lack of evolution but the abundance and speed of it; not just in small steps, like cattle hair growing longer, or finch beaks changing shape, but in huge leaps. So for example leaf and stick insects, the phasmatodea, appear first in the fossil record (in the Triassic) without wings, then acquire wings. The acquisition of wings and being able to use them is not an event for small steps; nor is there evidence that it happened that way. Phasmatodea seem to have had the potential for wings and flying at their origin – there is evidence for pre-existent and pre-designed genes being switched on or off. Wings seem to come and go in the different trees of life.

I had read a book by Richard Dawkins called *Climbing Mount Improbable* in which the author suggested a big evolutionary leap to a vertebrate eye from no eye was unbelievable, but there are 40-60 different sorts of eye of varying complexity in nature, so this was how the eye evolved, he thought. However, the questions remain – by what documentable small-step process did each of these useful stages arrive out of no eye? By what process did a simple useful eye change into a more complex one? Take the vertebrate eye – how did it suddenly achieve all its nerve endings coming from the front of the receptors, to combine through the optic nerve and a blind spot, whereas the cephalopod eye from way down in the Cambrian, had the same complex design features (those that had a lens), but its nerve endings come from the back of the receptors. There are other complex eyes, as in the trilobite, in the Cambrian also. Ignorant biologists criticise the vertebrate eye as inefficient and proof of poor design. But Dr Vij Sodera in his *One Small Speck to Man* (p294) says the opposite (skip this if you don't like too much science):

> There is evidence to show that the inverted design of the mammalian eye had very important nutritional and detoxifying functions. Apart from initiating the chemical changes that produce nerve impulses, light also causes damage to the photo-pigment-containing discs within the outer segments of the rods and cones. In response to this damage old discs are broken down and replaced continually with new discs. Any damage also releases toxins, such as free radicals which are continually neutralised by specific enzymes. Each melanin- containing cell of the pigment layer of the retina has fine processes (microvilli) that surround the outer segments of up to 20 rods and cones. These microvilli increase the surface area of contact, and toxins and nutrients pass respectively to and from the capillaries of the choroid through the pigment cells. The supreme importance of the blood supply for the

> proper functioning of the retina is shown by the fact that, weight for weight, the retina has the greatest blood flow of any tissue in the body.
> However the choroid blood supply is actually much greater than the nutritional requirements of the retina so it must have other functions, one of which is protection of heat damage caused by light. It is found that if the blood flow in the choroid is experimentally reduced, the retina becomes more vulnerable to light-induced thermal injury. There is also evidence to show that the rate of choroid blood flow is controlled reflexly in response to changes in intensity of the illumination. So by being closer to the rods and cones than they would be in the simple cup design, the blood vessels are better able to act as a protective heat sink.

Many others have observed that evolution by small steps is not what we find. It has been pointed out that 'sudden appearance' is what happened for '...most major groups of organisms. They appear in the fossil record as Athena did from the head of Zeus – full blown and raring to go, in contradiction to Darwin's depiction of evolution as resulting from the gradual accumulation of countless infinitesimally minute variations.' (Jeffrey Schwartz, 1999. *Sudden Origins: Fossils, Genes, and the Emergence of Species*, p3).

Likewise with plant life. The major plant groups appear as if out of nowhere – mosses, ferns, horsetails, cycads, ginkgos, conifers, gnetophytes, monocots and so on. Darwin would have been profoundly disappointed by this, as he had said that the lack of fossil evidence 150 years ago was 'the most serious objection which can be urged against my theory'. (*Origin*, p265). There are now the same as well as different objections against his theory, but we owe him a debt for pointing out to the creationist scientific establishment of his day that there was much more evolution than they admitted (though their view was guided more by their science than their theology). Darwin refused to be called an atheist, but his beliefs about God remained uncertain and confused, right through to the end of his life. See: http://www.noahsarkzoofarm.co.uk/pages/research/12-charles-darwin/darwin.php

42

Sex and God

A PROFESSOR WAS ONCE ASKED TO GIVE A SHORT LECTURE ON SEX. HE STOOD up and said 'Ladies and gentlemen; it gives me great pleasure' and sat down! Many of us would agree with him.

Sex may be popular, but I have wondered for a long time if it is also one of the proofs of God. Bacteria reproduce without sex. There are far more bacteria than any other creature. They can multiply into two every twenty minutes, so can become many millions in a day. There are estimates of 100 million – 3 billion bacteria in every gram of soil and lots more in water and air; and millions more in our stomachs and on our skin. 9,000 species have been classified, but there are probably far more. There is no scientific evidence for sexual reproduction having arrived from bacteria. So why is there sex? This is such a problem to Darwinism that it is normally ignored, or loosely explained as hybrid vigour.

At an early age I watched a bull mating a cow. He was nearly twice her size and after sniffing her back-end to see if she was 'bulling' (on heat), he struggled to get his front half up on her back, with a leg down each side. Meanwhile she looked as though she might collapse under his weight, but managed to stand. Then out came his wet cork-screw of a gristly, blood-filled penis, which he had to 'screw' into her vagina, about 5 ft from his head and which neither bull nor cow could see. The operation took less than a minute, and with one thrust his job was done. Nine months and eight days later an astonishing miracle happened: a 90 lb wet mass of new life arrived with a splash from a 15-gallon bag of fluid and lay there, for a few moments. It had a unique mix of its father's and its mother's genes. Was it alive? If it blinked and shook its little head, yes. Or, perhaps there was no sign of life, so it had to be picked up by the back legs to drain its lungs, swung and then dropped with an oof! It began to breathe. It was alive! Sometimes it needed a straw put up its nose to make it sneeze then breathe, or mouth-to-mouth resuscitation; and sometimes it was dead. Every molecule is the same in a live calf as a dead one. Clearly 'life' is in addition to the body and would need an initial source of that life; but why sex?

The sheer variety of sex organs, especially male ones is another surprising feature, best understood in my view as design features. Why are testicles hanging in a small bag on the outside of most male mammals, but internal for all birds and reptiles? Even some mammals have internal testes, like hedgehogs, moles, shrews, hippos, elephants, hyraxes (whose testes expand by a record 20 times their normal weight in the mating season!) and monotremes (Echidnas and Platypuses) – and for no apparent reason. Strangely, most mammal penises have a bone in them to help them stay straight enough for mating. The following mammals have the os penis, or baculum: primates (apes and monkeys and lemurs), rodents, bats, carnivores, insectivores, pennipeds (seals, etc) and monotremes. And why are ostriches and the duck family (the anatidae family of ducks, swans and geese) the only birds to have an external penis? In some ducks it is huge – the length of their body! If all the others can manage with a 'cloacal kiss' of organs touching, why can't these? I can see the advantage of the anatidae design for under-water mating, but other water birds, manage on land, so why not the duck family? Anatidae mating can be among the most violent, with the male grabbing his mate by the scruff of the neck and pushing her head under the water, while he mates her.

Amongst our zoo animals some penises have other special design features. Our porcupine's penis normally faces backwards, except for mating. How do they mate? Very carefully. She lowers her spines and turns up her vulva for little more than a cloacal kiss of the birds. Cats have about 100 keratin spines on their penis, thought to stimulate the female's fertility; tapirs have a curved sort of cube on the end; four families of mammals (two with a baculum and two without) fire their urine backwards (retromingence): the cats, procyonids (racoons, coatis, etc), tapirs and rhinos – perhaps to mark their territory; yet, of these, tapirs dung in water, apparently to conceal their position! So its purpose may also be defensive. The elephant penis is dexterous and muscular, almost like a second trunk, for fitting into the female vagina that hangs down towards the ground between her back legs with the opening facing downwards.

There are other design features about sexual reproduction that are not usually discussed, perhaps because of shyness, perhaps because they do not confirm macro-evolution. (This is one of my major complaints against macro-evolutionists, they are so busy looking for similarities that they sometimes fail to research and teach differences.) Reptiles mainly have a hemi-penis in two halves that can be used alternately. The first lizard in the fossil record is the tuatara, now only found in New Zealand; this uses the cloacal kiss of the birds. The next of our modern reptiles, the crocodilians and turtles have a single penis.

There are animal record-holders because of their sex organs; the barnacle is one record holder and has a penis 40 times his body length and he can send it visiting all the females within range, but not move his body. The longest mammal penis is 2.4 metres, belonging to a blue whale; the shortest is the common shrew at 5mm. A surprise is the gorilla, which like other apes has a baculum, or bone in it, but is only 5cm long. (African men sometimes insult other men's organs by saying they are 'built like a gorilla'). The sheer diversity appears to me to need more purpose than mere random mutations.

Many times in speaking about marriage I have quoted George Bernard Shaw's 'marriage is popular because it combines the maximum of temptation with the maximum of opportunity'. The same can be said of animal mating: the animals appear to be eager for it. It does not explain how sexual reproduction came from a-sexual reproduction, but the advantages of sex are huge. There is double the gene pool to add diversity and interest. The risks are also great: the male and female might not find each other, or like each other, or be able to perform in the small window of opportunity – the 'on heat' – that they have been given. With a working zoo we know all too well that a male and a female do not automatically produce young.

When a pair have achieved sexual union, there is the next challenge: the male sperm has to travel inside the female until it meets an ovum, or egg. The sperm is equipped with an extraordinary propeller, or flagellum, made of 39 different proteins and able to rotate at 200 times a second (12,000 rpm, up to moderate Formula 1 speed!). In the case of a bull semen, which is 4 microns in length, it can move 4-21 mm per second, equivalent to a 15-feet car moving at 100-500mph. Human men produce and store 1,000 sperm at every heartbeat, each 1/500th mm long, and can ejaculate 4 million sperm at once, of which only a few reach their destination and only one will fertilise the egg. (The overall distance to travel is the equivalent to 200 miles if the sperm were the size of a human, the ejaculation of which is 15 miles in two seconds!) The egg shuts to other invaders extremely fast after the first sperm reaches it; the fertilised egg then has to implant on to the uterus wall, to grow. All these are areas of vulnerability, but it seems clear to me that our Maker felt the design worth the risks. I find it ironic that humans are researching cloning while God's strategy was high risk diversity, which I suspect He is supervising in ways we can only imagine. Very early in 2007 a komodo dragon at Chester Zoo gave birth parthenogenically. Other creatures sometimes do this and sometimes mate. Yet almost all vertebrate birth, and insect and invertebrate birth (not to mention plants) is by sexual reproduction.

From both our marriage and our marriage counselling work and knowing the challenges for the sex therapist, leads me to wonder if human sex is a proof of God too? From the beginning God made men and women to live together; lifelong marriage was the plan given to Adam and Eve, and it essentially included sex. Jesus confirms this by saying that a husband and a wife become one flesh (*Mark* 10:8). To separate them is to upset God, too. The Biblical teaching is that husbands and wives do not rule over their own sexuality, but their spouse does (1 *Corinthians* 7:4). To help us with this, we have been given a far greater sexuality than any ape or other animal. I have already mentioned that humans alone have added fat in the breasts and buttocks, apparently for attractiveness alone; there are many and large differences between the sexuality of apes and man.

The human male organ becomes erect psychosomatically (mind over body), by seeing female beauty or nudity, or by emotional, mental or manual stimulation and, at this, blood alone is pumped into it. This is unlike apes; the ape penis has a bone in it, called the os penis or baculum to enable it to penetrate the female. Male apes are stimulated by the female's slightly flirtatious behaviour and by smell detection in a very limited heat period of female willingness. (Male apes would, like other animals, also see from her sex organs whether another ape is female, but this alone is insufficient for mating.) Sex is over in 5-7 seconds and is almost always only for reproduction.

Unlike for apes, the human female vulva is at 45 degrees to the angle of the body. Desmond Morris points out in his book, *The Naked Ape,* that for the vulva to migrate through this angle, step by step, is an evolutionary problem. The angle also has significant advantages: human females can cover their vulva from view completely by putting their legs at an angle to their backs. They can also mate with a male from the front or from the back, with equal ease. Human females have among the most secretive of all genitals; not only do they not protrude but they are hidden by pubic hairs – hence the Shakespearian double entendre in *Much Ado about Nothing*, referring to 'nothing' as Tudor slang for female genitals. And human female sexual receptivity is not limited, they can mate at any time; but their fertile time is hidden, unlike the ape. Human females also have a hymen formed of skin, like a few animals, but not a mucous one as some animals have. The biggest difference, however, is that the human female has a clitoris as a centre of the sexual nervous system; a complex organ wrapped round the vagina with a bone in it and with only its tip protruding. This area carries more nerve endings than the male penis and allows a sexual climax far, far greater than any animal. Apes like some other animals have merely a little flap, sometimes erectile, of skin, but it should not carry the same name as it has not the same orgasmic function ('clitoris' is from the Greek for key). So humans have been given unique sexuality that allows, indeed encourages sexual activity at any time and very often, as part of lifelong bonding and a reward for mutual love into old age.

There seem to me to be some design features that indicate that sex is intended with only one person. The neuro-chemical bonding that takes place with sex would be one indicator. Some animals, like the prairie vole, also mate for life and have been found to have the same neuro-chemicals involved. Others that mate for life have not yet been researched for this, but perhaps they should be. The hymen is biologically unnecessary except as the sign of purity that is valued in so many civilisations. The angle of the vulva shows not only that a wide variety of sexual positions are intended, but more modesty is possible than in animals. The hiddenness of female genitalia, as well as the way a woman conducts herself, means that she can easily stop men being visually aroused by her. Sexual attraction has to be more powerful and more fun for humans because of our fears, our reasoning powers and, with longevity, familiarity of many years.There is no limiting 'on-heat' time for humans. God invented clothes but as a later event, after Adam and Eve had showed themselves selfish and disobedient. In a perfect, trustworthy world clothes would not be necessary. Humans can go on having sex, ('making love' is actually what it needs to be, for long-term success) long after the menopause; this probably indicates that it is also good for the mental and emotional health, as well as the longevity, of both parties. In recent times, the world's oldest father was 94 at the time; humans can continue to be sexually active past 100.

My study of the Bible has led me to conclude that we are not made like angels without bodies, or even to act as if the body was less important than the soul. Nor are we made to behave like animals. But God has created mankind of each gender and every race, in His own image. We were meant to see all our similarities before the differences. Inter-human respect is intended to precede all that we do and say, because the image of God is found in the maleness and femaleness of all humans.

43

How Old is the Earth?

IT SEEMS TO ME THAT THE BIGGEST SINGLE NEED IN DARWINIAN EVOLUTION is a very long period of time. If the Earth can shown to be young, evolutionary development will still be clearly present, but the theory that bacteria became people will not work. Surprisingly there is no way of directly measuring the age of the Earth. Its age is normally taken as the same as the radiometric age of meteorites that are assumed to have been part of the nebula from which the earth formed (4.54 bya). Yet there are two icons of earth and sky that challenge the concept of the Earth being billions of years old. One is a look at the moon with its huge-cratered face (see appendix 1); and the other is the white cliffs of Dover.

Almost every day, even on the TV news, we all hear time scales of millions of years repeated so often that we feel it unscholarly to question them. Yet pause for a moment and ask how long is a million years? It is an unbelievably long time, compared with the history we know, of say the first cities of ancient history being built in about 3,000BC. Yet somehow we have absorbed the very old timescale just because it is repeated lots of times. At the other end of the spectrum some Young Earth Creationists propose that less than 10,000 years sufficient for all of Earth's history. If we actually look at some rocks, both of these proposals are seen to be impossible. For example, take a complete sequence of rocks 5,000-metres thick spanning the entire sedimentary fossil record, say from North Dakota as quoted on www.earthhistory.org.uk (article: 'No one wants to be an extremist') and the linked Talkorigins website, and we see the choices are between a deposit rate of 0.00007 mm per day for Dakota's chalk deposits on the Old Earth timescale, or 16 metres per day for the Young Earth one. To my mind each is as impossible as the other; the first far too slow for reality, the second much too fast.

The rocks themselves do not have a birth certificate, but we could examine the sedimentary rocks layer by layer to see if we can work out the time it took to lay them down just from assessing how much sedimentation took place at each period of geological time. Astonishingly, this is not how either secular geologists or Young Earth Creationist geologists are allowed to work. The secular geologists are only allowed to age the sedimentary rock layers by taking the volcanic rocks that are interspersed among them and submitting them to radioisotope dating. While the Young Earth geologists divide the whole geological column by a period of 150 days, or five months, the time they think Noah's Flood needed to reach its full inundation and during which, they propose, all the rocks from the period known as the Cambrian right through to the Cretaceous were laid down. In my view Noah's Flood in the Bible was at its height much quicker than this, perhaps in just a few days.

Old earth evolutionists arrive at the millions-of-years dates, by measuring the decay rate of certain radioactive elements in rocks that have a volcanic or igneous origin. As each radioactive element gets older it loses particles at a certain rate. This can take a very long time:

> All potassium contains a 0.01% (i.e. one part in 10,000) of the radioactive isotope K-40. ('K' is the chemical symbol for potassium. K-40 means that the total number of neutrons and protons in the nucleus is 40. Ordinary potassium is K-39.) The half life of K-40 is 1.26 billion years. When it decays (explodes), the K-40 emits an electron, a neutrino, and the remaining nucleus turns into Argon-40, abbreviated Ar-40
> (website of Professor Richard Muller, Univ. of California, Berkeley)

So a geologist can take a rock to the laboratory, vaporise it, and measure the amount of argon gas that comes out. From that measurement, he calculates how long ago the rock was formed.

These ages assume radioactivity has always been at today's decay rates; but this may not be so. They are also proportional to the speed of light, because the equations describing atomic decay contain a number of atomic constants, including the speed of light. If energy is conserved in a varying light speed process, these constants are changing so there is effectively a light speed term in the numerator of each equation. Thus, the higher the light speed, the faster the decay rate, in the same proportion. Has this speed always been as it is now? We know its present speed, slightly less than 300,000 km/sec, through a vacuum; and that light travels half as fast through a diamond as through a vacuum (and at its slowest, 17 metres/sec, or 38 mph through rubidium cooled to almost absolute zero!). Space is not a vacuum, indeed as I have mentioned it is an energy sea, from which light seems to acquire its zero point energy. If the speed of light is a function of the energy field and the energy field was much greater once, the age of the earth would be much younger (see chapter 55 and appendix 1).

Rates of sedimentary deposits are linked to radioactivity in the mantle and to past thermonuclear fusion in the core, because both of these produce heat. So if the interior of the earth in the past was hotter, more magma would be produced at the mid-oceanic ridges, which in turn increases the flow of chemicals into the oceans (affecting, for example sedimentary build-up) and quicker plate-tectonic movement (affecting mountain-building, erosion and sedimentation). The direct evidence of sedimentary build-up rates suggests that all geological processes have slowed down exponentially over time, levelling off towards present-day rates in the mid to late Holocene, a few thousand years ago. See www.earthhistory.org.uk/creation-theory/speed-of-light for more on this.

I have been shown other well known and serious discrepancies between the radiometric ages of rocks and the evidence of geologists' eyes; www.earthhistory.org.uk/questions-of-age lists several. For example, tidal cross bedding, tidal bundles and tidal rythmites are known, as their name states, to be laid down by tides and so follow a pattern in their strata of sediment laid down by spring to neap to spring tides. These accumulate, for example, at 3-4 metres per year in the Carboniferous of south-west Wales (Couëffé et al 2004).* There are other places that are also better understood as laid down quickly, for example, successive marl-chalk couplets in Cretaceous chalk cycles that are conventionally dated at 20,000 years each to fit with radiometric ages of associated volcanic rock, are far better explained as needing only one year each. Cyclicity in the Jurassic is similar. This would shorten the age of Cretaceous rock, like the Dover cliffs, by a factor of 20,000.

There are in places 30 km thicknesses of Archaean rock, which are supposed to take a billion years to lay down, which means 0.03mm per year. But volcanic rock cannot be laid down that slowly, or even as slow as 100 times faster. These are, of course, part of a scientific quest, not a religious one but they will inform the debate on whether the Earth is nearer 100-150,000 years' old rather than 4.5 billion.

* *Journal of Sedimentary Research*; November 2004; v 74; no 6; Renaud Couëffé 1, Bernadette Tessier 2, Patrick Gigot 3

44

Noah: Truth or Myth?

I first heard the story of Noah and his Ark when I was very young. It is a fascinating story of hard work, rescue and heroism in the face of the ultimate disaster. The story has been used very recently in the zoo world as a conservation idea. Chester and Colchester Zoos have had a major symbolic reference to it, in a building or logo. 'Noah's Ark' keyed into Google yields 5.6 million mentions. Recently the name Amphibian Ark was given to a conservation year. To most people it appears to be a story like Santa Claus. Lots of children's play or learning centres have been called Noah's Ark. It usually has a children's image. But like Santa being based on St. Nicholas, who and when was Noah?

When we opened our original Noah's Ark Farm Centre, I wondered – if the world could see evidence of a true story of Noah, would they see that God is essential to Noah's story? These things can be said about it:

1. The Noah's Ark story is one of the best known stories in the world.

2. The historical and anecdotal evidence of this is in the most ancient traditions on every continent, from China to Mexico; in every story, the element of rescue by divine intervention from a disaster of one man to father the future generations is common. Many other details are very different. Sometimes it is written in stone as in the Gilgamesh Epic, from Mesopotamia in the 7th century BC.

3. The Bible's account in *Genesis* 6-9 is the longest, most detailed and most credible; it is presented as history, not fiction, and includes not only heroic details, but the shocking too, (Noah getting drunk and naked). The story is confirmed and quoted in many other books in the Bible.*

* Noah's name appears as a historical person in the genealogies of *Genesis* 5, 10 and 11 and 1 *Chronicles* 4; then in *Isaiah* 54:9 God remembers His actions in Noah's day and makes a similar guarantee; in *Ezekiel* (14:14,20) Noah is alongside two other heroes of faith in God's estimation. Jesus Christ himself quotes the story of Noah in important teaching, as a historical event in *Matthew* (24:37) and *Luke*'s gospels (17:26), likening it to the coming end of the world as sudden, overwhelming and inescapable. Peter says Jesus visited the souls lost at the time of Noah's Flood between his death and resurrection (1 *Peter* 3:18-20); and in *Hebrews* 11:7 Noah is among the heroes of faith, listed among other real historical men and women.

4. he dimensions of the Ark are astonishingly technically plausible, thousands of years ahead of the marine technology that made such a ship again. Its dimensions are ship-shape, unlike the Gilgamesh Epic which are not, and were not superseded until Brunel's *Great Eastern* in 1858, though the Chinese treasure ships of the early 15th century came close. Noah's ship was unique in that it was built only to float. Other ships are built to move in a controlled direction.

5. In recent years human genetics suggest that there was a Mitochondrial Eve (by examining people's mitochondrial DNA), who was mother of all living humans, who may have come from East Africa (an estimated) 200,000 years ago. There is also a Y-chromosome male common ancestor, thought to have been living, also in Africa, 60-90,000 years ago. These could point to Noah as the male Most Recent Common Ancestor (MRCA), who would have been the father of all subsequent humans. It would also, via the four unrelated women on the Ark point further back, to Eve as the MRCA of all women, so of all humans.

Many people have tried to explain Noah's Flood as a local flood in the Black Sea or at Ur in Mesopotamia, or as a bulge of water sweeping round the world, or leaving traces of a timber structure on the current Mount Ararat. Local floods do not require a huge Ark to be built, and the other worldwide suggestions are not supported by geological evidence. However, our radical proposal, in appendix 1, does seem the only one likely to fit the evidence to the story.

45

The Model Ark

IN 1997 I WAS FEELING CONVINCED THAT BUILDING A REALISTIC, SCALE MODEL of the Ark was something that would not only be an interesting centrepiece of a theme park about animals, but also a good discussion subject. Then if we also put lots of play equipment in place even children might get something out of such a theme park.

So we went ahead and started designing a 14-feet model Noah's Ark. We chose its length to be in scale with the biggest collection of model animals – Britain's, which were on a 1:32 scale. I wrote to the head of the London School of Naval Architecture, Professor David Andrews and asked if a student could do some work on Noah's Ark. I had heard that a degree thesis could be done on an old ship or a new one. A student, Thomas Grafton came to see me; then, armed with all that I could find, went away to see if a 450-feet long timber ship, 75 feet wide and 45 feet high could float. I told him that John West the Christian naval architect of the ss *Canberra* had built that ship the exact size of Noah's Ark. He did his degree thesis and I showed it to a friend, former professor of the London School of Naval Architecture, Charles Betts, who was now head of naval procurement at Abbey Wood, Bristol. Charles looked at it and said that the work was sound and the ship would definitely float in a force-12 gale, i.e. it would ride a 150-yard wave without breaking its back under its own weight. But 5,500 tonnes of yellow cedar, the strongest timber in the world, would be needed. It would also need (stone) ballast to keep it stable and resting in the water at the level suggested in *Genesis* (15 cubits) as being the height the water came above the highest land.

Then at just the right moment some friends, Steve and Chris Stone, whom we had known for many years since Steve had become a Christian at Pip 'n' Jay, offered to help us. Steve was lecturing in plumbing at Bristol Polytechnic and as an experienced builder was offering to help us if we decided to start a Noah's Ark theme park. His wife Christine offered to run the café as a separate business, as they had always wanted to run a tea room. Steve also knew a former model-maker at Bristol University, called Bob Harris, who since computer simulations had arrived had become a plumber. I went to see Bob with Thomas Grafton's plan and my own layout of the floors showing how, after reading a number of feasibility studies, the animals might have lived on the Ark.

Fundamental to this was how many animals were needed on the Ark to preserve all air-breathing life. As I have mentioned, 100 years before Darwin, Linnaeus, the father of modern taxonomy, classified plants and animals by their 'genus', which he thought were *primae speciae* or first creatures that God had made, which had spread out into related groups. A friend, Dr Arthur Jones had done some excellent work in 1997 on a list of all the vertebrate *families* which he thought were the modern equivalent of these genera, and I made a pictorial display of all the air breathing ones. We thought at that time perhaps 500 pairs of animals would have been on the Ark. Others like insects would have would have just arrived, then in due time left with or without permission!

Bob Harris was a cheerful, enthusiastic and very skilled model maker. He started building the model in his spare time, fitting it diagonally across a bedroom of his house in Fishponds. I used to drive over and see it and pray with him about it every two or three weeks. After we had first prayed about acquiring some seasoned wood to build the model with, Bob was delighted to have a phone call one day from a builder friend, offering some timber from an old airing cupboard. Bob considered our prayers answered when the wood was located in the very street where he was doing day-time plumbing work. It was well seasoned and enough to build the whole model. Bob was very careful, and was often excited by the inspiration that came to him over the details. So was I. He built it to take apart and reassemble, at least once, with viewing windows to see the internal layout in the middle at both sides. It looks like a giant barge. There are three floors as the Bible states, and a window, 'finished to a cubit above' or ventilation slot 18 inches wide as some rabbis think it meant, along the top of the roof for ventilation. There are individual pens on slats on the lower floor, for the large animals to dung straight into the bilges. Then there are medium sized animals are on the next floor and small ones with fragile diets and insect food supplies on the top floor, beside Noah's and his sons' family rooms. There are reservoirs for the 2,000 tonnes of water the animals would need, filled by pipes from the roof (*Genesis* says it did not rain before the flood; spring and river water were used). There are also rooms for hay and grain. It is a beautiful model, well constructed and it took Bob over 1,000 hours to build.

46

Preparations for Trial Opening, Unease with Egyptology

WHILE WE WERE BEGINNING ALL THESE PREPARATIONS, IN NOVEMBER 1997, Christina and I went on holiday to Egypt. It is a fascinating history-filled country, where I would love to spend longer. After our interesting Nile cruise was over, we left our group, who were staying on at Luxor, on November 16th, and we flew on to Cairo to see the pyramids and Cairo Museum. It was just as well we did. Early the very next morning, 17th, at Hatshepsut's temple, at Deir el-Bahri, Muslim Jihad terrorists shot and killed 50 tourists. I would undoubtedly have been visiting this temple again had we stayed on with the group.

We were to discover that among the ancient and amazing treasures of Egypt, there also seemed to be a conspiracy to hide information to fit an agenda. We went to Egypt expecting to trace Israel's considerable influence of and dependence on Egypt, as mentioned through 2,000 years of Biblical history from Abraham to Jesus, a history that I knew so well. I was shocked to find no mention of Israel anywhere, and that the Egyptian Christians were being persecuted most terribly. This persecution was hidden from tourists and the press and was mainly through not being given jobs, or being housed in ghettos to process garbage, like the Mokkatam Garbage Village, also known as Manshiyit el Nasr. Church was allowed, but Muslim converts to Christianity had to be baptised secretly. We met a recent convert from Islam, through the introduction of a friend working in Cairo. Converts could be killed if their conversion became known.

I enquired about references to Israel at Cairo Museum and found only one brief mention; the guides told us they did not know anything about Moses, or any Israel/Egypt history. I had just come across two independent Egyptology writers who were each suggesting that Egypt's most famous queen, Hatshepsut, was probably Moses' step mother. Moses is recorded by Josephus as leading an army to Ethiopia, where he marries a princess. He might have been in charge of all Hatshepsut's prolific building work, including her obelisks. A plaque has been found in a temple at the Egyptian turquoise and copper mines of Serabit, an ancient town half way down the Sinai peninsular, that had been translated by Professor Grimes of Munster University: 'I, Manasseh, Captain of the Mines and Chief of the Temple, offer thanks to pharaonic Queen Hatshepsut, because she drew me out of the water and advanced me to high honours'. ('Evidence for Truth: Archaeology', Dr Victor Pearce, Evidence Programmes 1993, p.64.) To this clergyman and archaeologist, Victor Pearce, there seemed little doubt that Moses had been called Manasseh at birth, and had been adopted by the young Princess Hatshepsut.

Could one trust official Egyptologists? Official Egyptology (*National Geographic*, April 2009) certainly records that Ahmose founded the 18th dynasty and fathered a childless Amenhotep I and a daughter Ahmose. This royal daughter Ahmose married the non-royal general, Thutmose I and they were parents to Hatshepsut. Thutmose I also had a son by another wife and called him Thutmose II. Thutmose II had a wife by whom he sired Thutmose III, outside the royal bloodline. Queen Hatshepsut was of the god-like bloodline, so she was first regent for Thutmose III and then reigned with him from c1479–1458BC. These would be about the right dates for her to have adopted Moses when she was a young Princess in about 1526BC, then to protect him as her son until Moses killed an Egyptian, for which, as a rival for the throne, he would probably have been killed by Thutmose III had he not fled to Midian. Egyptology is made more difficult because Thutmose III, sometime after Hatshepsut's death, (or others at that time) had all the mentions of her erased from everywhere he could find it. This is all the more likely if Moses and all the Israelis had just left the Egyptians in economic ruin and humiliation.

There is much more that is hidden. I have always felt it an unlikely proposal to suggest the Mount Sinai where St. Catherine's Monastery is built could be the Biblical one. When we visited it this became even more clear. It is in the middle of a well-used part of ancient Egypt, with Serabit and its mines and temples only a few miles away; there is no part of the Red Sea that could be miraculously crossed between it and Goshen in the Nile Delta. There is no open space for a million people to camp or approach the mountain, undetected by the Egyptian army. So many are now suggesting it is more likely that the Red Sea was crossed either at the middle of its eastern fork, at Nuweiba south of Elat; or at the Strait of Tiran at the south end of the Gulf of Akaba. Adherents to both of these believe Mount Sinai to be Jubal Al Lawz, in Arabia. There is an area of north-west Saudi Arabia now that is called Madian, which could be the Midian that Moses spent so long in, and Al Bad is a modern town with ancient links with Jethro, Moses' father-in-law.

The two possible routes for Moses to have taken would thus have been either towards modern Elat, then turning south to Nuweiba; or following the coast of the Gulf of Suez south to modern Sharm el Sheikh and crossing the Strait of Tiraz there to Arabia. *The Exodus Case* by Dr Lennart Moller makes a strong case for Nuweiba. Others think the under-water photos fraudulent and the crossing too deep, so prefer the Strait of Tiran. Whether these proposals are right or wrong, they are certainly well worth further research, to help Jews and Christians learn from and help Egypt's tourism industry. It is also possible Islamic forces are stopping Israel being mentioned in both Egypt and in Saudi Arabia, but sadly it will have to be done in the very countries where such research is not welcome. I had to act as unofficial tour guide on these matters to our largely Christian group.

Meanwhile, back at the farm, we were hard at work preparing for a provisional opening of Noah's Ark Farm Centre, perhaps for the summer holidays. We had leased out an office, which looked surplus to the visitor centre, to Christian Television Association. CTA was led by a prize-winning TV man and good friend I had known since Mission England days, Crawford Telfer, and his colleagues, Malcolm and Pam. They made videos for missionary societies and Christian teaching videos. Crawford was later to make an excellent video and DVD for the zoo farm. Christina and I had decided that the other offices and their rent was less important and had to be sacrificed for the new visitor centre, so we put the exhibition and finished model in our biggest modernised stone barn, which was now carpeted. The shop and crafts went in another, which Christina was to run.

Steve Stone had assisted me enormously by helping finish one barn and making-good the café building. We also built a toilet block, including a disabled toilet, for which Steve did most of the plumbing. I laid lots of concrete blocks, fitted door frames and hung 32 doors in all. We found that the septic tank to our house, which had been built as a very large one by our landlord a few years before, was adequate – though I was to find myself at the bottom of it extracting nappy liners and sanitary towels from the pump, as did others, rather too many times in the years ahead! We wondered if Steve might even become site manager; but the returns were so low we would be unable to employ a full-time buildings manager for some years.

With an experienced farm worker and shepherd, Simon Nancholas, I built open-air bird pens around two ponds which we dug with a Hymac digger. We also built an outside adventure playground. I wanted to incorporate a circuit of the most exciting play apparatus we had seen, to add to its play value. This consisted of a keep-off-the-floor challenge, children moving from one item to the next to complete a circuit. The Royal Society for the Prevention of Accidents (RoSPA), who we invited to do our annual inspections, did not like the risk of falling from one on to another but they allowed it. We also built a climb-over high wall and a short zip line, somewhat army-style. A container-ship captain and friend, Chris Hughes was a great help in his leave time with this and, along with his wife Mary, in welcoming the public. Chris told me his 300-metre ship had an engine about the same size as our entire café and needed three miles to stop! We also made a car park out of the area in a field where farm machines had been stored. About 100 cars was all that our expectations could reach.

We removed the walls between three old loose boxes, where Guinea pigs and rabbits could be held. We bought two llamas, two rheas, two wallabies and lots of ducks and hens. We also bought two Coscoroba swans, because they looked like a mix of a swan and a duck, to show how the duck family of ducks, swans and geese, were related. We borrowed goats, pigs and horses. We were also aware that the British are the greatest animal lovers in the world and British treatment of farm animals was way ahead of Europe, who only agreed that animals were sentient beings in May 1999, in the Treaty of Amsterdam. During my own lifetime UK farmers had castrated pigs and sheep and disbudded calves, all without anaesthetic, kept veal calves in the dark and lots of animals in small spaces; all of these had stopped in UK long ago. Farm conditions were now controlled by compassionate Acts of Parliament. We wanted to show the best welfare of farm animals to the public as we explained where their meat and grain come from. We offered a free tractor-trailer ride on straw bales to see the crops and animals; and a nature trail to explain wild life conservation.

We planned to open with a trial, two days a week, called 'Summer Open Days' on Fridays and Saturdays, from August 1998. A week beforehand we had no one to run the ticket office! We mentioned at church, for prayer, that we needed a volunteer and a lovely retired couple, Marion and Delwyn Cox, offered. They were to remain key people with us for many years, well into their seventies. We were not allowed to sell tickets so we had to sell programmes that first year, at £3 and £2 each, entry by programme! The programmes were also a map and guide.

We duly opened on August 10th, for 25 days through to the end of October. Our highest attendance was 160; only 1,350 visitors came altogether but people loved it. We had spent about £20,000 and received a gross income of £3000; and running costs of animal food, wages, electricity, insurances, tractor repairs and fuel, etc, had to be deducted!

I had passed my 60th birthday, so could we face putting it all on a proper footing the next winter, ready for an Easter opening? We prayed of course and my rector, John Simons, and the men I was praying with each Wednesday, felt it was still right. John even went so far as asking if all my life and resources were in God's hands or only part of them? Tough question. It was unlikely to earn us a living for a long time, as it would probably always consume more to grow it than it earned, but we had an income from the rest of the farm, which was beyond what we could decently spend on ourselves. It would offer employment to several people and might educate and be a blessing and fun for thousands. In addition we had received so much from farming, and because farmers had received quite a bad press, we also wanted to help food producing farmers now, by explaining to the public where their food comes from.

We still had to work out how Noah's Ark could be most helpful in kindling people's faith.

47

First Full Year of Noah's Ark Farm Centre, 1999

WE NOW HAD TO GET PLANNING PERMISSION TO OFFICIALLY OPEN. THIS WAS slightly embarrassing as we had only recently received planning permission to change the old farm buildings into 'office or light industrial use'. And it meant applying for change of use for some of the land from agricultural use, to mixed agricultural and leisure/ education use. Christina and I were the sole grantees; we had hours and days when we were permitted to be open, to conflict as little as possible with rush hour traffic. We needed planning permission for each item of adventure play equipment, the garden shed which was the ticket office and the car parks and the sign at the main road. The red tape nearly drove us to tears, in fact Christina reached tears at one point with one of the planning officers; but eventually all was well, just a few months after the event! This was the first of many experiences of the council. As farmers we had hardly been aware of planners, because farm buildings for most of my farming life had been exempt, unless very big, in which case my landlord's agent had dealt with it. Planning officers have a different agenda than just being helpful to us; they have people in every parish trying to do things, and others trying to stop anything happening, even in remote valleys like ours where only a footpath runs through it. So there is planning law that both sides need to be aware of. We also discovered people who work in offices work very short hours compared with farm hours, so we had to learn to wait patiently for things to be done.

We decided to open five days a week, Tuesdays to Saturdays, plus Bank Holidays. Christina felt strongly about no Sunday trading, and as I had done 35 years of dairy farming, seven days a week, when the average working life for a dairy farmer was 26 years, I decided that in my retirement I was going to do less. Or so I thought.

In the all-time-record wet January of 1999 we were glad to be indoors making a large drop slide, with lots of play and educational activities round it. Our part-time shepherd and I had built it ourselves to a design that I put together after visiting a number of other play grounds to see what was popular to play on. A drop slide is the circumference of a circle, so a high one looks scary, but is very safe. In our case we could just fit in one of 15 feet before visitors hit the roof of the old cattle building. We built the curve of the slide on horizontal timbers set in concrete blocks, overlaid with several layers of thin ply, then lino. This drop slide we combined with other slides and balancing beams, so that as much activity as possible could happen in the same volume of barn. It all had to be visible by the children's carers and be netted for safety. We themed it the Diplodocus Dive, and put lots of educational peep-holes round a lower crawly way, and marked them as homes for various British animals, like badger's sett, squirrel's drey, rabbit warren etc. Christina painted lots of lovely animals, birds, and even dinosaurs on it.

Anticipating more visitors we made a bigger rabbit and guinea pig handling area. In their former place we asked a friendly local bee-keeper, David Hounsel who was the same age as me, to set up a demonstration bee hive with glass sides to educate the public into the fascinating world of bees, with appropriate display material purchased from the Beekeepers Association. We also made a straw den for swinging around on ropes and crawling through tunnels, which our children had all enjoyed doing so much when they were young. It was a health and safety nightmare, but great fun. We had let Sentry Farming use our buildings from February to April, from 1997 onwards, for lambing a 1,200-ewe flock which spent the summer on the next-door farm. It became a wonderful attraction for our Easter visitors – to be guaranteed to see a sheep lambing. We made plans for schools to come, then divided each school into groups, and three of us each led a group to see and talk about the different animals, as well as visiting the Noah's Ark Exhibition.

I had been to a talk given by Peter Gwyn on how he and Trish had first opened their farm, Court Farm in Banwell, to the public a few years earlier. They had held a big cowboys-and-indians event every year, and then one year left the farm open with a big sign at the gate, expecting people to just drive in. No one at all came, for two months! 'You have to go and get them', said Peter. I was used to marketing for Mission England and so we had a leaflet printed and employed a company to distribute it; Christina put out some hand-written press releases to give the press some animal stories. We also did postal distributions in selected areas.

Adam Stone was our animal manager, in a break in his drama career. His mother, Chris ran the café and helped look after the guinea pigs and rabbits. We bought in some orphan lambs to bottle feed and I bought a six-month-old Highland heifer, called Cloud. Adam trained her and even rode her! I also located a dairy water buffalo herd and bought a one-month-old calf, whom we called Bridget, because that is what you do when you want to cross water – bridge it. At the same time our 14-year-old dog, Topaz, was getting old and so we bought a new puppy we called Barley, to overlap with her. One day Topaz got so weak she fell into the moat and I had to pull her out; she was barely conscious. Barley was about six-months old. I felt Topaz was at the end and in usual farming tradition I very reluctantly shot and buried her. When Topaz was a puppy I had found her ancient predecessor, Venus, dead on the lawn one day, so buried her with a wooden cross at the head of her grave. I had taken her collar off and must have left it on her grave. The next morning Topaz had found Venus's collar and had taken it to bed with her. It was all she had of her friend. Barley, on the other hand, seemed pleased to be the centre of attention; she went on to have 22 puppies in three litters, all of which were adored by visitors, especially young ones who wanted to take them home with them. They usually had to make do with a toy one from the shop instead. Two planned litters sold at a good pedigree price to help pay for some improvements, including one puppy which, to the excitement of some of the staff, went to the singer George Michael.

We discovered how athletic a fox was. A Muscovy duck was killed and another taken from behind a six foot fence with electricity round its base. As the duck was missing altogether, the fox clearly thought nothing of running up the fence with a duck in its mouth and leaping clear of the electric fence below. We asked some local fox shooters to come and help thin down the fox population. They found five one night. A few years earlier Lord Wraxall had employed someone to sit in a hide after 800 pheasants had been killed by foxes. Eighteen foxes had been shot in a month from one spot. We resolved to make fences with a big overhang at the top of seven foot fences in future. Our wooded hill was clearly full of foxes with a high breeding rate.

We had given tractor and trailer rides for many years, taking our children and their friends over the farm and leaving them at a distance, to walk back, sometimes doing a scavenge hunt of nature items on the way. If they were too hearty I would start tipping the trailer on the way, to give them a thrill. The tractor and trailer I had put some bales on in our experimental year, with ropes round it, to carry about twenty people, was scarcely up to health and safety standards. A college student, Andy Raines, had been working with me during his college holidays, fencing and improving the place. He was an expert welder and wanted to start his own engineering works, so I commissioned him to take our old dung spreader apart (it had not received a bid at the sale) and build a passenger trailer on the old wheels and chassis. Andy did an excellent job, the first of lots of metal work he was to do for us in the next few years.

We also built a food and farming exhibition in our old milking parlour. We had concreted over the old central pit, repainted the walls, and designed field crop display boards with pictures, describing the human and animal uses of all the farm crops. Each display had a bowl of its seeds. We found that children loved mixing up all the seeds to confuse people. We covered them with cellophane, and the cellophane was broken open. The public! What a wonderful world it would be without people, especially children!

We loved them, really. In our first full year we received 24,579 visitors, including free under twos and returning season ticket holders. Our gross receipts were £73,000, which, after deducting nearly £11,000 VAT, almost covered our costs, but Christina and I were working all the hours God gave. Christina was the main telephone answerer and four of us carried extension phones; she even answered the telephone while cleaning the farm toilets. She spent most of each day running the shop, which had a craft area in it, and managed all our publicity with the press and local printer. She also booked and vetted a growing team of volunteer helpers, to whom we gave café vouchers for helping. Christina and I shared the out-of-hours telephone-answering duties; we also all shared the education talks. We were trying to introduce God gently but clearly, and I was also talking about Noah's Ark. I was the only person with animal and poultry know-how and was doing some of the tractor rides with some kind volunteers helping. I was also repairing fences and equipment and trying to deal with all the statutory bodies that were telling us we were not good enough – at more or less everything! In the evenings I was working on more displays about the uses of the animals and their physiology and about creation and God. By August Adam was looking for an acting job, doing some of the tractor rides and animal talks, caring for all the animals and supervising animal handling. We also had some volunteer help, most notable of whom were the Wilkinson family who became a major part of Noah's Ark in the years ahead. We also had some lovely extra assistants in the ticket office and shop, as the Stones had too, in the café.

That Christmas we held a nativity play for 400 people in a barn, 'Melchior's Magical Mystery Quest' by Riding Lights Theatre Company. Adam was a key player in this. As Adam had left us for his stage career, it was clear we needed a new and qualified animal keeper, so Christina and I were praying for a suitable person. We rang Lee Abbey, near Lynmouth, one day, because we knew they took on young people for reflective periods of time and put them to work on the farm and estate. They recommended Lucie Guilbert, an archaeology graduate who had spent time on the Lee Abbey farm and had now moved back home to Guernsey, where our friend and Annie's godfather, Richard Seymour was a doctor. Richard had spent lots of time on our farm when he was studying medicine in Bristol in the '60s and had driven tractors and baby sat for us. As Lucie was near them on Guernsey at that moment, Richard and his wife Sarah interviewed Lucie for us and gave us a glowing report. Lucie became God's gift to us as animal manager for the next five years. She arrived in March 2000, and was short, pretty, very friendly and chatty, and very good with animals as she had worked in a pet shop, as well as with Lee Abbey sheep and cattle. She was also a shining Christian and began to take on some of the teaching. Lee Abbey had also been good for her in terms of interpreting her faith in the work place. We also began to be asked to do work experience for Year-10 students, and to take more volunteers. Christina vetted these too and booked them, then handed them over to Lucie, who trained them and organised them well. From the outset we all came together for ten minutes at 10.00 am to discuss news of the day, to read a few verses of the Bible and to pray for the day and its visitors and for everyone's safety and for animal health. Then came a coffee break, which Lucie persuaded me was good for everyone, followed by opening to the public at 10.30 am.

48

Millenium Year and Studying Fossils

THE END OF 1999 WAS DUE TO BE APOCALYPTIC MELTDOWN. ALL THE computers in the world were due to leave aircraft stranded in the air, while all the finance houses went into chaos. Or perhaps they would, or perhaps every thing would be OK. In the event it was just another day. With fireworks. We visited the London Dome, which was great fun and very enterprising. We learned from it that we at Noah's Ark were not particularly good! But we were also nearly a billion pounds cheaper. How do we grow with limited funds?

I had spent most of November and December 1999 working at geology. I bought a large university text book called *The Fossil Record 2,* published in 1995 and costing £450. I had come across its predecessor in the university library. It included a complete record in the form of bar charts, of where every family of every sort of living thing had first appeared in the fossil record, and when it had gone extinct, if it had; it also showed if the same family exists today. It was a complete revelation to me. I was looking for the facts without anyone's gloss on them. The fossils and the layers that they come in, tell the story of the lower layers being overlaid by upper layers (unless the rocks have been inverted). This book left the dating out but just recorded which creature came before another and in which named epoch (like Jurassic, for example).

Several years before this I had become suspicious of the 'spin' that Darwinians were putting on the fossils; making out that there was a continuous tree of life. I had read a completely eye-opening speech by Dr Colin Patterson, Senior Palaeontologist at the British Museum of Natural History, to a Systematics Study Group in America in 1984:

> One of the reasons I started taking this anti-evolutionary, or let's call it non-evolutionary view, was last year I had a sudden realisation for over twenty years I had thought I was working on evolution in some way. One morning I woke up and something had happened in the night, and it struck me that I had been working on this stuff for twenty years and there was not one thing I knew about it. That's quite a shock to learn that one can be so misled so long. Either there was something wrong with me or there was something wrong with evolutionary theory. Naturally I know there is nothing wrong with me, so for the last few weeks I've tried putting a simple question to

> various people or groups or people.
>
> Question is: Can you tell me anything you know about evolution, any one thing you know to be true? I've tried that question on the geology staff at the Field Museum of Natural History and the only answer I got was silence. I tried it on the Evolutionary Morphology Seminar in the University of Chicago, a very prestigious body of evolutionists, and all I got there was silence for a long time and eventually one person said, 'I do know one thing – it ought not to be taught in high school'.

A further statement in the speech is often quoted by Creationists:

> I fully agree with your comments on the lack of direct illustration of evolutionary transitions in my book. If I knew of any, fossil or living, I would certainly have included them. . .I will lay it on the line, There is not one such fossil for which one might make a watertight argument.

Colin Patterson got into trouble for these, so was asked to clarify with Talkorigins, and in August 1993 this was his reply (on their website):

> Dear Mr Theunissen,
>
> . . .The specific quote you mention, from a letter to Sunderland dated 10th April 1979, is accurate as far as it goes. The passage quoted continues ... a watertight argument. The reason is that statements about ancestry and descent are not applicable in the fossil record. Is Archaeopteryx the ancestor of all birds? Perhaps yes, perhaps no: there is no way of answering the question. It is easy enough to make up stories of how one form gave rise to another, and to find reasons why the stages should be favoured by natural selection. But such stories are not part of science, for there is no way to put them to the test. . .But I still maintain that scepticism is the scientist's duty, however much the stance may expose us to ridicule.
>
> Yours sincerely, [signed]
>
> Colin Patterson

So I was approaching this study of the fossil record with scepticism.

I found that for the lowest and very thick layer of rocks (the Archaean and lower Precambrian) there were about 12 sorts of heat resistant bacteria alive; and nothing else. These orders are all extant; they still exist today. Then other tiny single celled creatures, but more complex because they all have a nucleus, were fossilised. A little later, in the Cambrian, there was a sudden appearance of

450 families of creature in the remaining 35 phyla of life. Nothing connected these complex and all sea-creatures, like molluscs, worms of different sorts, sponges and trilobites, with the previous single celled creatures. As Richard Dawkins noted about them in his *Blind Watchmaker* 'It was as though they were just planted there, without any evolutionary history'. In the next layers plants suddenly appear, but not flowering ones, these were plants that all multiplied by spores and were good colonisers of empty land – mosses, clubmosses, and liverworts, horsetails, ferns and progymnosperms. Then appeared the creepy crawly world of centipedes and millipedes, followed by a sudden explosion of insect life; these millipedes, and 15 of the 27 orders of insects (defined as having six legs; most had wings, though not all at this time), appeared in the Devonian and Carboniferous; all the rest are in place by the Jurassic. All of these were air-breathing, because they had trachea in them, so they were from the land, not from the water.

I discovered that some fishes appear next, then four-legged tetrapods with seven or eight toes per limb; later the dinosaurs appear and soon the Archaeopteryx, which is a sort of magpie-sized dinosaur-bird with fully-formed flight feathers that could undoubtedly fly, and some tiny mammals. In the same fossil period as the dinosaurs were duck-billed platypuses and the Gaviiforms or diving sea birds in the Loon family and turtles. Much later came another explosion of birds and mammals and flowering plants. The amazing thing for me to discover was the abrupt appearance of many life-forms. There was lots of evolution happening, like dozens of species of trilobites that changed from layer to layer; evolution was obvious, but to suggest the fossils pointed to a continuous tree of life was contrived to the point of being plain untrue. There was lots of extreme weather going on so that extinctions were happening too. The end of the Permian wiped out 57% of all families of life that had been fossilised up till then. The conditions on earth must have been very unstable and quite unlike today.

Another surprising thing to me was to realise that for something to become a fossil was very difficult. It had to be in the right place at the right time. It had to be submerged by sediment or mud, or perhaps a dry sandstorm; either as a live animal, or as a dead body or a skeleton a few days or years after its death. The animal or plant could of course have been around alive, or dead for quite a while without being fossilised. Areas of the world were ancient, on very old rock, known as Archaean, that had either never been covered in sediment, or had all its sediment eroded away; for example, most of southern Africa and bits of most continents that had once all been joined together in Gondwanaland, before continental drift as we know it, started in a big way in the Jurassic. So lots of birds and mammals might have been living at the time of the dinosaurs, but in different parts of the world from where the dinosaurs were fossilised. Assumptions have been made that may not be true, often on the basis that the rocks and fossils need millions of years to lay down. That, as I have shown, need not be so.

The startling thing to me about all of this was that the whole fossil record fitted a recolonisation order, not an evolution-from-nothing one. Steve Robinson and Michael Garton, two bright, honest and radical thinking geologists, had introduced me to this thought and it really seemed a possibility. I had first met these men at a Creationist Conference in November '98 at Cloverley Hall in Shropshire. It was there for the first time I heard that some Creationists were questioning the traditional Creationist Flood Year interpretation of the fossil record. At that time I thought I could trust Christians to tell the whole truth in what they spoke about. I found that, although I realised Darwinism had lots of spin and guesswork in it, now I was shocked to see that Creationism had too. Steve, as I have mentioned, was particularly helpful in unpacking the evidence and over the next few years we were to work together on presenting this third approach to the fossils, which we really thought would be a breakthrough.

Almost all Creationists up until now, had felt that 6,000 years was enough time for the whole of history; they felt the Genesis genealogies were complete. But the lecturers at Trinity College had suggested the Genesis genealogies were understood by the Hebrew writers as a short summary of a much longer history. At college I had found confusion regarding the first 11 chapters of *Genesis*; lecturers were uncertain whether it was history or allegory and yet were aware that Jesus treated it as history. So I found the new proposal quite a relief as the geological evidence seemed so strong in favour of a timescale longer than 6,000 years; not millions of years but certainly many tens of thousands.

So that winter's study of the fossil record left me in the uncomfortable position of being certain that the Darwinian paradigm did not fit the data, and that the traditional Creationists paradigm did not fit either! I wondered if a few of us had been allowed the beginnings of insight, to begin a search, changing our minds several times, as we stumbled our way into a new interpretation – gulp! With the unpopularity that would bring from almost everyone, again.

The following summer I went on a geology field trip organised by a geologist, Michael Garton. We went to see two quarries near Frome. On the way, Michael showed us Nunney Castle, where a wall had been destroyed by the Parliamentary army in 1645. A modern restoration on top of the broken wall would, under examination, show signs of a pause for several hundred years before the new stone was added to restore it. He told us it was likewise with geology; one layer of sediment is laid down, and then can come erosion, or a pause, and a new layer of sediment laid down. The skill and honesty of the geologist is relied on to interpret how long each of these time periods takes.

We looked at hard grounds (the top of a layer of sediment which had hardened over perhaps a number of years) where Jurassic sediments had been laid on Carboniferous. Any layers representing the intervening periods were missing, probably previously eroded away, but some of these layers are present along with a coal layer in a geological fold at nearby Radstock, where coal had been mined (in fact I had visited a coal mine, and gone down the shaft there when I was 12). As we looked we could see fossilised oysters on the surface of the Carboniferous limestone. Oysters grew under water by fixing onto a surface, on which they must have been growing for 10-30 years to reach the size we saw. Then they had been inundated by Jurassic sediment and their fossil status sealed. Likewise we saw tiny worm activity in the same hard-ground that had also lasted a few years, before being covered with sediment, and deprived of oxygen. This showed first of all, that it did not need millions of years. Nor could it happen under a one year flood. Neither view was confirmed by the evidence (which is academic-speak for 'they are both wrong'!) So we started on a journey, exploring what fitted the facts and what did not.

There is a long way to go before any consensus can be reached. All those who have written books and received funding will defend their positions. 'Hypothesis testing and peer review' sounds all very well; but when peer pressure ridicules dissent and censors out counter arguments, they are doomed to circular arguments and self congratulation. Usually with a new paradigm a younger generation comes to accepts it while the whole older generation has to die off, taking their old theories with them. In the meantime there are lots of other parts of science to explore and develop. In our Noah's Ark Exhibition Steve Robinson helped us put up some new displays setting out Recolonisation Theory for the first time. We drew these up as proposals alongside the two other proposals, of Darwinism and traditional Creationism. It did not stop militant Darwinists labelling us as 'Creationists' and 'brainwashing children' and 'guilty of child abuse' for telling children they have a Creator. Why do they feel so threatened? And sadly, Creationists labelled us as 'compromisers'. Those who should have known better ought to have been pleased to test a new idea.

On the farm we put up more fences, borrowed a pregnant sow from a farmer in Marshfield who sold meat at farmers' markets. We swapped the sow every eight weeks when her piglets were of weaning age. We borrowed more and different goats as they were popular to feed. We installed a permanent trampoline indoors. We also built more adventure play outside, which even more resembled the assault course I had built in the army, moved the climbing wall and made it higher, installed a scramble net, parallel bars and an overhead rope. We installed another zip line, which stopped rather quickly. It was dangerous in fact, especially as we discovered mothers did not mind if their three-year-olds ignored all the warning signs and went flying off the end! Litigation looked likely. We did hasty modifications. I made a recording in the Noah's Ark exhibition, explaining the model and the story and how it applied to us and God today.

We started animal shows in the barn by the sand pit, where we were also handling rabbits and guinea pigs and showing off the sheep and goats. We made a tiered, straw theatre to seat 150 people and led in some animals such as the horse and donkey. I spoke at most of these animal shows and Lucie did the others, replacing the several leaders required for our tours of the different exhibits. Instead, we brought in a cow and a sheep and explained what food and clothing came from them. We also showed how a chick hatched from an egg, and described the uses of chicken, and we brought in a beautiful white cob belonging to our friend Mary Edmunds, along with one of two Shetland ponies we were given, and a donkey, to show the horse family. Using the mysterious cross that is present on all the dun-coloured domestic donkeys in the world (but not on any wild one), we began to explain how Jesus Christ had ridden a donkey as Messiah into Jerusalem and had then died five days later on a cross. The purpose of His death was in our place, so that we could be forgiven and become friends with God and get to heaven. The donkey's cross reminded us of this. This theme was to develop over the next years. The shows were very popular with visitors and we realised there was an important part to play in explaining the uses of the food producing animals.

In this, our second year we had 30,000 visitors. We took £93,000 in total receipts, roughly covering our costs once again, but leaving expansion to come from elsewhere.

49

2001: Tourism's Worst Year

For reasons I have already mentioned, farmers were furious with the Labour Government for their terrible mis-handling of the Foot and Mouth crisis (FMD), which broke in February 2001 (see chapter 36). By March most of the country was under restriction. Because the government in election year refused the NFU request, born of experience of the horrific 1966 outbreak, to bring in the Army to sort the administration out, the infection spread to all parts of the country. Footpaths were closed and most tourist attractions with animals closed. We were meant to have camels, bison and red deer, which could give us publicity. In the end all we could find that was new were some birds. I drove and fetched some white storks and Lilford's cranes from Rhode Bird Garden that was closing down, because their founder/owner had died. This in itself was a reminder that businesses do not often survive after their founder dies; so would ours? We chose these exotic birds because although they look quite similar they are in different biological orders and carried an important message in their design. Cranes are in the same order as trumpeters; they fly with necks stretched out and have a very long windpipe, coiled in a recess in their breastbone, for making a huge trumpeting sound. They are vegetarians. Storks are in the same order as herons; they fly with necks bent under like an S, have a usual windpipe and are mainly carnivorous. White storks are one of the very few species that have no voice; they clatter their beaks together for communication, an evolutionary variation, but not because the absence of a voice along with clattering beaks made them fitter than, say, a heron.

These birds confirm the Biblical suggestion that God made a limited number of 'kinds' of creatures with the genetic potential to spread within orders into a large number of species. Before this we already had in our collection the anseriformes represented by the ducks, swans and geese, and the galliiformes represented chickens, pheasants, and peafowl.

Darwin had written in a letter to Asa Gray in 1860 'The sight of a feather in a peacock's tail, whenever I gaze at it, makes me sick'. How sad; they are simply beautiful. No doubt this reflected his uncertainty about God. It would be hard to try to explain the evolution by small changes through random mutations not only the length of tail, but its astonishing coloured 'eye' placements in five colours (due to five thicknesses of keratin) covering dozens of barbs on several tail feathers. But it is a very strong pointer to evolution from within its DNA, designed by its Creator to spread into such diversity and such beauty.

I wondered how peafowl could evolve within the pheasant order; they seemed such a big evolutionary leap from pheasants, but then at the Gerald Durrell Zoo in Jersey I saw some peacock pheasants, which looked like very short-tailed peacocks. Although the many small steps for Darwinian evolution would seem impossible, for created evolution, with a mechanism in the DNA that switches on or off quite large gene differences this was very likely. The Darwinian proposal that peacocks with the most eyes attracted the most females was proved untrue by a group at Tokyo University, after observing 268 matings over seven years found that 'the peacocks train was not the object of female selection' (*Animal Behaviour*, 74(4), 1209-19, April 2008). This was hardly surprising, as it is well known that a peacock's tail gets more eyes the older it gets (all birds moult all their feathers every year and grow new ones); geriatric peacocks are unlikely to be the most successful ones!

We also installed a bigger animal show theatre made of timber, to seat two hundred, in the same barn as the first straw-bale theatre. We installed a PA and a musical call at the beginning. This show was becoming a major and unique part of our education of youngsters. Lots of leaders of groups seemed to want the farming education and the Christian setting for it presented to their young. As I was doing the school shows myself, with Lucie taking some, I could guarantee the content.

I remember saying one day about the cow and the sheep 'these two animals are related, but not everything is related', to which a man in the audience shouted out

'Oh yes they are!'

To which I replied 'Just because we have 50% the same DNA as a banana, it doesn't mean we are related to one!'

'Oh yes it does!' he replied.

At which point the audience broke into a slow hand clap and I said 'We will discuss this at the end'.

We did. He was a thirty-something, enthusiastic, bacteria-to-man-by-chance macro-evolutionist, with the usual empty spaces in his theory.

Early in our season, as FMD spread, a pig was suspected of having it at Lawrence Weston City Farm, six miles away as the crow flies. All their FMD susceptible animals were killed and because a neighbour of theirs was also renting grass keep next to us, we were also put in a controlled area. It looked like disaster; and all brought about by the selfish vote-seeking Labour government, who had refused to act with urgency. Then the pig that had been killed was found not to have FMD after all! Such was the panic after the neglect. We decided to stay closed until Easter anyway, on April 7th. The FMD restrictions applied to all ruminants and pigs. We decided to move all our ruminants away from the public and then open the rest of the farm, with disinfectant baths for vehicle wheels and for people's shoes. That way even if visitors came from FMD areas, when they had been asked not to, they would not come anywhere near our vulnerable animals. We had been officially encouraged to do so and were requested to trade normally to stop public over-reaction! A few people were furious with us. They thought we ought to stay closed and suffer huge economic losses, because other farmers were suffering small ones; and because all the footpaths had been closed. An unhelpful local councillor was seen nailing a 'closed' sign onto our brand new 8 x 4 feet farm sign and damaging it. Many other open farms did as we did and opened. A few zoos and safari parks stayed closed to protect very valuable animals from long distance travelling visitors.

Numbers were well down on what we hoped and needed, but at least some people came. The local eradication was over in May, but public perception was that it still persisted. People were ringing us in September and asking nervously whether they would see burning piles of cattle if they came to us.

When the FMD restrictions were lifted we brought in the animals we had been planning for; two bison from Chester Zoo, three female Bactrian camels, and some red deer from a deer farm in Brockley. New zoos find it very difficult to obtain animals. I had asked several zoos for a camel, but for reasons that were not known to me at the time none was forthcoming. However, Trevor Lay, the owner of a huge duck aviary and who had supplied us with some birds, also found these camels.

They were Bactrian camels, highly endangered in the wild, which had been in a zoo but belonged to Martin Lacey, a very experienced animal trainer who had worked with good results at several zoos. Martin owned Linctrek, a company that hired out animals for trekking or for shows, TV or filming; and he also owned the Great British Circus. Farmers have less problems with circus than some people, because we put rings in bulls' noses and lead them round a sort of circus ring called an agricultural show, where horses and dogs are also trained to do clever things under the control of their owners. Zoos likewise have a long relationship with the circus. Jimmy Chipperfield's circus founded most of the safari parks: the lions of Longleat for the Marquis of Bath, the Earl of Derby's Knowsley Safari Park in 1971, the Duke of Bedford's Woburn, Sir John Muir's Blair Drummond Safari Park in Scotland, and the American team's West Midland Safari Park as well as providing the lions for the film Born Free. Billy Smart founded Royal Windsor Safari Park, which became Legoland. Zoos love to show off their animals in similar ways to a circus, so many have performing sea-lions, and free-contact elephants to interact with visitors, notably at Blackpool Zoo where the elephants came from Blackpool circus. Other zoos train skunks, coatis, armadillos, parrots and many other animals to educate and entertain the public. Britain would claim the highest animal welfare standards in the world, so all this artificial animal handling is closely watched. Farmers know that there are lots of hypocrites who criticise artificial animal behaviour, but should not do so if they have milk in their coffee, cheese on their toast or keep dogs as pets!

The farm was now better than ever and growing in good reputation in adding hands-on and educational value to a day out. A councillor from Portishead asked the council to stop schools coming to us because we were 'Creationists' (whatever he meant by that). His request was considered by the education committee, some of them knew us well to be mainstream Christians, and his request was thrown out. One of our local papers also seemed against us for several years. The atheist lobby had spotted us and were going to be more active in their opposition. On the other hand we had joined the National Farm Attraction Network, to keep us in touch with other open farms and to help raise our standards further.

We had discovered that our recently built passenger trailer was causing wear and tear on the tractor so introduced a regular inspection by our tractor maintenance company for my peace of mind. Imagine my horror one day, which turned out to be my *dies horribilis*, when I was driving the tractor with 20 passengers in the trailer and it suddenly detached from the tractor and I left it behind for a few yards! As I could not pick it up immediately with the tractor, I suggested the passengers all walk back to the farm with me. On the way we took a short cut through a sheep field, where the ram was lying very still about five yards from us. I said nothing when a visitor suggested he was sleeping soundly, but feared he had just died. He had. Having seen the visitors on their way fairly happily, I then walked to the farm office, only to discover that the sewage drains were blocked and liquid was flowing across our back path! What joy; I could now get the drain rods out and try to find the blockage, which I could be certain was caused by a nappy liner which should have been put in a special bin provided in every toilet.

During this year our car park began to get busy. We had forgotten it might need organising on busy days. One of our cottage tenants, Dennis Anderson, had just retired and had spotted the problem and asked if we would like him to be our volunteer car park attendant. He was God's gift to us. Dennis had recently been through a traumatic time, hit with four whammies; his wife had died, his house had started to collapse into a coal mine, with no insurance to cover it, he contracted throat cancer so went through a laryngectomy and could only breathe through a hole in his throat (and spoke with an amplified whisper), and his business partner defrauded him of his share of his taxi firm! He might have been expected to ask 'why should God let all this happen to me?' The reverse was the case; why not me? He had been our tenant since 1999. The car parking and eventually the coach parking became a big job, so we eventually paid him a part-time wage for that and also to gather the bin bags at the end of the day. He was wonderfully reliable and friendly, though sometimes subject to quite nasty treatment from a small number of the public. Being an ex-National Serviceman like me, we understood each other well. He also came to faith in Jesus during the first year or so of working with us and joined our church. He remained an example of cheerfulness and friendliness despite great hardship. He was called on by the NHS to go to hospital and encourage others who were having the laryngectomy that he had had to learn to speak and fight depression. Dennis worked till the end of 2007 when his health declined. He died in July 2008, aged 72. We missed him enormously.

I created a display that was to get me into trouble with the police. September 11th, 2001 was the day the World Trade Centre in New York was destroyed by two Boeing 767s piloted by Muslim suicide bombers. What was God doing? Are all Muslims bad? I felt I wanted to make a display for adults to read, while watching their children play. I had already written a display on suffering, as it is the number one reason for questioning the existence of God: why does a loving God allow suffering? The Bible seems to indicate that all its great heroes were allowed to experience suffering, most especially Jesus Christ in the lonely road he travelled and in his cruel and drawn out death by crucifixion. So, the Son of God suffered, like thousands of His followers. Suffering can be a growing and learning experience.

Now, I was concerned that secular British people did not understand Muslims. Conscientious Muslims were taught to revere their Holy Scriptures, the Qur'an, as God's detailed and infallible word to them, in the same way as Jews and Christians revered the Bible. We use the German word for our Maker, God, the Muslims use the Arabic, Allah. I wanted to point out to people that Muslim bombers were not evil people, they were conscientious people. Was it not time we looked at the book they felt so conscientious about? When Mohammed dictated the Qur'an he was well aware of Jesus Christ, Christians and the gospels. The New Testament had been written 500 years before Mohammed was born. But there were also heretical Christians and Jews around him, who were in touch with apocryphal writings, not accepted as accurate by the church. Stories from these are in the Qur'an (like the Gospel of the Infancy of Jesus, and the 2nd-century Fable of Egypt). There are instructions also to be both violent to and respectful of Jews and Christians.

So on the one hand the Qur'an says 'We believe in that which was revealed to Abraham and Ishmael, Isaac and Jacob and the tribes; and that which Allah gave Moses and Jesus and the prophets. We discriminate against none of them...' *Sura 3.* But on the other the Qur'an states 'Fight against those to whom the Scriptures were given' and 'if you do not fight He (God) will punish you sternly' *Sura 9.* 'Make war on them until...Allah's religion reigns supreme' *Sura 8.* 'When you meet the unbelievers in the battlefield strike off their heads' *Sura 47.* And as a reward for martyrdom they are promised many times 'gardens...reclining with bashful virgins' *Suras 38, 55.*

I put on my display that Muslims need our help, not our criticism. It is hardly surprising that if these words appear in their holy book they will be taken literally, by some conscientious young Muslims, trying to obey God. That is what Christians do with their Holy Bible. But the prophet Mohammed, though usually a gentle, devout searcher after God, also did violent things in his life, married 11 times, including a 6 year old, and was very different from the loving and forgiving Messiah, the sinless Jesus Christ this country is used to. Many Muslims will feel compelled to obey the violent instructions of the Qur'an and kill by terrorism or suicide bombing anyone who is not a Muslim.

One of our visitors must have told the police that I was in breach of the racial and religious discrimination act, so two police officers arrived and took away the display. A few hours later they brought it back and said there was nothing wrong with it. So I put an additional note saying the police had OK'd it!

As we were Noah's Ark and presumably all religions came since then, I also put up a display comparing all religions. Some atheists sometimes imply that all religions are the same and bad. Meanwhile radicals from Hinduism and Islam are fighting each other and even killing their own relatives if they become Christians! At the same time many ordinary people in those religions are simply trying to find God. It is the religious leaders that are often the guilty ones; in earning a salary or reputation within the religion they try to control others. In past centuries Catholics have killed both Muslims and also Protestant Christians. Controlling priests did not want Jesus' words read by ordinary people, so William Tyndale, the Bible translator, was martyred and burned at the stake. His newly translated Bibles were also burned. Now some older Muslim Imams persuade impressionable young Muslims to commit suicide and murder, and persuade them that they will get to heaven for such an evil. If there is to be trust of Muslims in this country the Islamic community will have to distance themselves from these violent Qur'anic words. In 2011 the *Sunday Times* reported that 36% of British Muslims thought a Muslim should be killed if they converted to another faith, and 37% wanted Britain to be under Sharia law.

The Qur'an is, I believe, a confusing book; much of it is a re-writing of Biblical stories and thoughts of living a good life in peaceful coexistence, but it does also undoubtedly encourage violence towards non-Muslims (therefore by definition converts away from Islam should be killed). There are several passages about Jesus in it. For example the Qur'an describes as 'monstrous falsehood': 1. That God should have a Son *(Sura 1)*, and 2. that Jesus died on the cross *(Sura 4)*. So the incarnation of Christ and his sacrificial death on the cross are denied; those two most important parts of God's rescue of mankind.

I have heard Muslim preachers say on video 'Nowhere in the Bible does Jesus claim to be the Son of God'. This is a distortion or misunderstanding of the gospels. Jesus says privately or in veiled terms He is the Messiah many times,* but to avoid cutting his ministry time short by arrest, He did not say it publicly until his trial, when His outright claim to be the Messiah was why His enemies' demanded His death for blasphemy.** There are three New Testament writers who expand this and explain that Jesus was not only the Son of God, but the Creator of the world, and was redeeming the world He created.***

Despite Islam coming 600 years after Christ, Islamic teachers claim there are 1,200 mistakes in the Bible because, they say, the Bible was lost for 100 years, and reappeared with all these mistakes in it! This is not scholarship but Islamic wishful thinking. It is time the Qur'an was allowed to be examined in the same scholarly detail as the Bible and without death threats for doing so. More people should know that no Muslim may convert from being a Muslim without (at least the threat of) being killed; all men marrying Muslim women must convert to Islam before doing so and all women marrying Muslim men must bring up their children as Muslims. Almost every majority Muslim country makes it very difficult if not impossible for Christians (and other religions) to practice their religion without being killed by extremists with the tacit agreement of the ruling majority. Islam is undoubtedly accompanied by fear and is in great contrast with Christ,

* Jesus says clearly He is the Messiah to the woman at the well in *John* 4:26; and admits He is the Christ (Anointed One or Messiah) in *Matthew* 16:17, *Mark* 8:29, *Luke* 9:21.

** In *Matthew* 26:64, *Mark* 14:62, *Luke* 22:70, Jesus tells the Sanhedrin court that He is the Messiah In *Luke* 23:3, *John* 18:27, Jesus tells Pontius Pilate that yes, He is the Christ and that is why He came into the world.

*** Three New Testament writers state that Jesus Christ was creator of the world: *John* 1:3 'He was with God in the beginning, through Him all things were made and without Him was nothing made that has been made'.
Colossians 1:16 'For by Him all things were created, things in heaven and on earth...'
Hebrews 1:3 'In these last days God has spoken to us through His Son, through whom He made the universe...'

the gentle author of His religion of love.

However, the Jesus of the Christian gospels that Mohammed's contemporaries knew so well still welcomes Muslims today. Many thousands of Muslims are finding Christ, often by praying in their mosque in Jesus' (*Isa*'s) name; a surprising number of them are saying they have received dreams or visions of Jesus. I often tell Muslims that I will pray for them that Jesus will give them a dream. It is Christians' opportunity to help Muslims find Jesus. God will have his way.

Pointing back to Noah and even to Adam, there are memories in other religions of Genesis characters that have become gods; so Zeus and Hera and the Garden of the Hesperides, echo Adam and Eve and the Garden of Eden. And other Genesis patriarchs are worshipped as ancestors also, like Noah as Nereus and Nimrod as Hercules. It seems to me vital that children of every faith are taught all religions, especially Christianity, so that everyone can search for God. He is big enough to reveal Himself to searchers. The Bible will be discovered to stand tall, far above all other scriptures.

Visitors from all cultures and faiths visit us now; we welcome their discussion and appreciate their constructive comments, especially where a genuine search for truth and appreciation of Creation is a common goal. Sometimes Muslim women hand the children over to the men and get out their prayer mats in a discreet corner to pray. Many from a variety of religions and denominations have said how they appreciate a Christian-based centre which is open about its faith and also a very happy place full of wholesome fun. Many years before, our Wraxall rector David Payne, had taught the church about bringing the Kingdom of God to ordinary people in a tangible form. Now, a little taste of Kingdom life was starting to happen, and something we continued to pray for.

My father died on Christina's birthday in December 2001, aged 89. He had stayed fit and alert to the end, still running his Duchy-rented dairy farm at Norton St. Philip, albeit in partnership and with major help in every way from our son Caspar, then 33. My parents had played tennis until they were 87, to a good standard, and had performed well in the village tournament until 85. Dad had wanted to die in the house where he had been born, in 1912. His funeral filled the church to overflowing. My brother gave an excellent, historic tribute, the great-grandchildren sang a pop song with changed words and both Caspar and I wore our lay reader's robes; Caspar led the service and I preached. A funeral is the best possible reminder of our common mortality, and an opportunity to gently remind worldly relatives that there is an important eternity to be prepared for, as well as money to be made here and now. It is also a wonderful opportunity to meet up with all the relatives.

My father's passing was a triumph of good living to the end; he was always positive, never rude about people, cheerful and a pleasure to talk with. His faith was clear and consistent, demonstrating with good deeds what went on within him. He was in hospital for four days. He prayed aloud with me for the only time in my life on his first evening in the RUH Bath, then more or less lost consciousness. One tribute said his passing was like that of a giant oak, that had been relied on for so long by so many. I thank God for his example and his memory. It was only at his passing that I felt I had become fully head of my family. My mother lived on with companions in their rented Duchy farm house until the end of the tenancy the following year. By then Caspar had moved the whole dairy herd and machinery to his new Duchy farm in Cornwall. My mother moved to a retirement home near Bath. By her insistence the home had to have people to play bridge with! 'Use it or lose it' was her expression, and she remained mobile, alert and interested in us all until she died, at 91, in 2004; also in the RUH.

Despite the FMD and atheist opposition, in 2001 our attendance was up by a modest 23% and receipts reached £118,000. Costs of new and seasonal staff were being covered, but there wasa still nothing for expansion, to which Christina and I contributed from the remainder of the farm. Red tape was mounting under a government that felt it was not controlling us enough, so, after the FMD debacle it invented yet more irritating paperwork, making demands for more of our time from its growing bureaucracy, which no doubt the tax payer was paying for. More hygiene with every animal journey was required, more information passed around, but with very dubious benefit to us all. The food chain had been wholesome and efficient up until now, so why add all the paperwork?

50

2002: Growth at Last, Expansion and Accidents

Our numbers doubled in 2002. We had serious catching up to do after FMD, so for the first time we opened for February half term, then for Saturdays only until Easter. We had done a feasibility study in 2001; a small government grant had been offered to farmers damaged by FMD, this was not money for us, but it was to pay someone else, a consultant, to give us some ideas on how to grow and how to manage the growth. I did not take all the consultant's advice, but he did introduce me to the idea of 'people flow' and leaving enough room for growth. We had a former silage barn, 56 x 105 feet and 30 feet high. that I thought we could use as an arena and into which we could fit some substantial play equipment. As we were using it to store the harvest and lamb sheep, we would have to build a new arable barn in a more accessible place. The new barn cost £80,000 out of my dairy farm capital, and we still needed to develop the old silage barn.

We applied for a grant to the Rural Development Authority of £100,000. It took me ages to fill out all their forms and try to guess what good it would do us – this 'making a business plan'. How could I possibly tell whether any extra visitors would come as a result? I must have convinced them I knew more than I did. We were awarded £5,000. For this we have been answering questions from them every year since about how many visitors and jobs it created. The answer was that their £5,000 would have been worthless without the £100,000 that we put in beside it. The doubling of visitor numbers, however, impressed them. No doubt lots of people earned a big salary servicing that and other grants, so it helped justify their work. We were offered a plaque to show we had received their funding. I declined. If it had shown the whole truth I might have accepted.

We had taken on a new enthusiasm for building in 2001because a wonderfully helpful friend of mine, Hugh Pratt, felt that God had a plan for us. An employee of Hugh's joined us. This was Barry Baker, another of God's gifts to us, a skilled builder, plumber and welder with lots of experience on land and even under the sea! He had run his own company and could turn his hand to anything. Furthermore he had huge artistic flare and was an exceptional time manager. He had the amazing gift of being a fast worker and also being a nice person. His first major job was to help build the arable barn, which was already underway. I helped lay more concrete after my 60th birthday than any year before it, which is saying something as we had laid a lot of concrete, including the farm road and all the dairy buildings and yards.

Then in 2002 I designed a three floor adventure play area, with one new and two second hand play slides coming from it on one side and a prow of Noah's Ark ship the other, overlooking a 500-seater arena. The Noah's Ark front was to have windows in it for theatrical use overlooking the arena. Barry was full of good ideas for improving mine, and of easier ways of building. I switched from builder to builder's labourer at 63. Then, during the season, Barry brought in Tim and Max, from his cheerful family of builders and they built the Ark Arena seating, on some metalwork built by Andy Raines. We had the slides finished in time to put them in our leaflet, as the biggest indoor wave-slide in the west! It went an extra wave higher than usual, because our silage barn was so high.

The arena was built for our animal shows, which had outgrown the little 200-person arena we had previously built. By August 2002 we were able to seat 5-600 for our shows. Big doors allowed large animals and even a tractor to come in and move scenery. We had in mind nativity plays for thousands at Christmas also. At Christmas in the year it was under construction, 2001, we had straw bales laid out as a theatre and attracted 650 people to our live-animal nativity. They were sitting precariously on half-built ledges but, thank God, no accidents happened.

During the year I had penned a very much tongue-in-cheek poem to the NFU magazine:

> There once was a farmer near Bristol who worked from first light
> until night-fall;
> Slaved at cows, sheep and wheat, pigs, chicken and beet, but his profits
> were nothing but frightful!
> Then along come inspectors from Whitehall and tell him his
> efforts are dreadful,
> Made him fill up their forms all night until dawn till they near
> took him off horizontal.
> But just before all the worst happened a flash of inspiration
> struck him –
> Quit growing the food as much as he could, be diverse, to a
> tourist attraction!
> Now, at Noah's Ark Zoo creatures come two-by-two and
> playgrounds with hundreds of kids on,
> But the forms all come faster with every disaster; blocked
> toilets and bins needing lids on.

So advice to young sons of the land would be thus: only stay as
a farmer if you really must.
Best – advise them, inspect them, regulate or correct them.
Or be determined or blessed or go bust!

To my great surprise I won a prize for it and received some very smart Hunter wellies and a case for them!

Part of the paperwork that was new to me was also new to the country in recent years – the accident book. Almost every scratch needed now to be reported, recorded, with witnesses, dates, times, positions and circumstances. The American culture of suing was on us. We pray every day for safety from serious problems, and we work hard to keep animal health and playgrounds 'as safe as necessary' to use a RoSPA expression. Every time an ambulance is called we have to send the accident book page off to the HSE for registration. Like any school playground there are minor accidents, as excited children take risks, run, fall over and generally behave as children should. We had six play areas designed for hundreds of children to have fun on.

I had my first experience of being sued, soon after we opened the wave slide. A solicitor wrote to me demanding a new pair of suit trousers, because he had burnt a hole in his present ones going down the slide! I wrote to him saying if I was going to visit a farm I would not wear a suit; if I was wearing a suit on a farm I would not go on a wave slide; if I was going on a wave slide in a suit I would get into one of the bags provided, as was indicated by the slide! I handed it over to our NFU insurers and asked them to resist it robustly. They did.

We have been sued very little, in fact. I am only liable if an accident is my fault. If so, I am insured by the NFU Mutual. They like us to have a playground inspection by RoSPA each year and sometimes come round themselves. One year our trampoline, which had a 'Parents must supervise' notice beside it, was being abused and a child bounced off it and broke an arm. We were told the child had bounced onto a chair. A parent must have carried the chair twenty yards and put it there to save having to help their child climb on to it. The trampoline was working well, the surrounding surface was good and I suspected the parent who sued me had also moved the chair. As the chair only occupied a tiny part of the circumference of the trampoline, the child might not have bounced onto it anyway; perhaps the child was just bouncing out of control and hit the ground. Regardless, I was not responsible for putting workers all round each of our trampolines, we had no authority to control children. Parents were required to supervise, as there were notices everywhere to tell them.

We learned that the free offers by accident lawyers are not totally free; the injured person has to take out 'insurance' of £100 to cover the unsuccessful claims. In my own defence I had to spend two hours in court, including an hour being interrogated by a barrister; but the judge found in our favour. This convinced the NFU that I was not a push-over, so has helped keep our premiums reasonable. The only other insurance case was on a zip line for children, when an adult went on it and a bolt broke, causing an accident. The NFU again dealt with it; they doubted whether it was our fault, but I did not hear the outcome.

Our doubling 2002 numbers brought us up to 72,300 visitors yielding £235,000. This was probably our most profitable year; had money been our driving ambition we should have planned to remain as we were then, with tiny alterations. But we took a different course. We had applied for and received planning permission for three new animal houses, two of them quite large ones for big farm animals. But with what were we going to fill them? On the answer depended their interior design, fittings and cost.

51

2003: Becoming a Zoo Farm Ape Biology, Gypsies

WE AND SOME OTHER FARMS WITH SOME EXOTIC ANIMALS ON THEM (LIKE wallabies, rheas and llamas) had been criticised by some zoos for not having a zoo license. So, smarting under this criticism, we had applied for one, and had been inspected then awarded a zoo license in 2002 by DEFRA, the new name for the old Ministry of Agriculture after the shame and the shambles of FMD handling. We had been made to advertise in local and national newspapers that we were applying for a zoo license, then an inspector came round. Any corrections we needed to make were entered as conditions on our license. Our conditions included mainly more paper work: recording arrivals, births and deaths, making a diary of events, including animal health and treatments, having a routine monthly vet visit rather than just for treatments, improving some fences that were becoming a bit worn, having some special food preparation rooms and meat storage freezers and fridges.

Some of the complaining zoos might have regretted their criticism. It began us on irreversible progress into being a serious zoo. I still considered myself a farmer of 300 acres with a budding zoo on which we hoped to breed some exotic animals as well as continue with our very important education role, now increased by an added conservation element. So we took the name Zoo Farm, instead of Farm Centre. In 2003 we took the opportunity of the zoo license to acquire primates. Barry built as large new primate enclosures as we could fit in, attached to our old dairy building. There were European minimum sizes, with sometimes essential features like water pools and their sizes, laid down for all zoo animal enclosures. We always intend doing much better than the minimum; but they are a guideline. Then we put cotton topped tamarins, from Shaldon Wildlife Park, and black and white ruffed lemurs, because they are so deliciously noisy! Lucie, our animal manager, had badly wanted a pet marmoset monkey, so I bought her a bottle-fed female called Millie and she reared it at home and took it round wherever she went. We then bought a male to go with it and put them both in their enclosure.

We also found a litter of five sugar gliders, because they are marsupials and grow their young in a pouch. They otherwise look like small gliding possums to which they are related. One became very tame, and used to glide from its helper/trainer, Jack, to me, and back again in animal shows. These did very well until a keeper from another zoo told us we were apparently feeding the sugar gliders on the wrong diet. So we gradually changed it to the other zoo's recommendation, and three of them promptly died, including the tame one. It reminded me of dairy farmers who all know their ration is best. In actual fact there are lots of solutions and we now started to be much more cautious about advice. The previous owner is always the best recommendation if the animals are looking healthy. Visiting keepers from other zoos have often given us unwelcome advice or criticism, which is why I try to be as encouraging as possible to other zoos' keepers when I go to them.

We bought two capybaras, whom we called Clarissa and Countryman. We added them to the duck ponds, where they lived happily with the ducks and Lilford's crane, and also two African crowned cranes, the national bird of Uganda, where we had such fond memories of starting Send a Cow.

Although, animal arrivals interest the local press as they have not lived in the area before, there is also huge interest in other unusual animal stories. In July 2003, we had just such a story. We had taken delivery of a new male wallaby whom we named Wally. He was white, because we like some white and some brown to show the contrast and make some of them more visible. Wally was not settling in with his new wives. One day a pig in the next door field dug away with its nose and made a dip in the ground under the wallaby's fence. So Wally escaped and hopped away to the nearby wood. In fact he became a free-range wallaby, hopping in sight of a nearby pre-school who thought, at 100 metres distance he was a large white rabbit. They rang us and we duly 'drove' him, back to his enclosure, where after a while we managed to catch him in a net and return him. The hole had been repaired and I stood and watched him for a while.

Wally clearly did not like some of his wives so this time he hopped to the pig wire that was surrounding his pen. It was six-feet high so I was not worried. Then as I watched he squeezed his whole body through a square in the wire smaller than a postcard. I could scarcely believe it! This wallaby that stood nearly two-feet tall, made himself into a long thin sausage by pushing and shoving; and was on the outside of his field! He then hopped 200 yards to his wood. This time he was in no mood to be driven back. So, seeing a press story, we rang the RSPCA and local TV, radio and papers and Wally became a celebrity. TV cameras on quad bikes were chasing Wally; photographers were creeping round the wood. Eventually we managed to corner him in a thicket; where I suggested a slogan the opposite to the Second World War American soldiers description, Wally was 'under-sexed, under paid and under here!'. The RSPCA tranquilliser darts failed to knock him out. The dose was increased. It failed again. (Wallabies, we later discovered, needed a huge amount of that drug, much more than other animals of their size). Off he went to another part of the wood.

Then we surrounded him in a bigger thicket with a long RSPCA net where, surrounded by RSPCA men and press people and encouraged by a reporter, he ran out, got caught in the net and I grabbed him. We carried him back triumphantly. This time we had put up chicken netting fixed to his pig netting, and he never got out again. He eventually learned to like his females, discovered what to do and sired a dozen babies. But the story of his escape was really good for us. All the local press, TV and radio took it up and the *Sunday Times* published a cartoon about him. This was picked up by US and CBS radio and Christina was interviewed on Canadian radio, where her sister heard her! It was all so good, that we began almost to ask 'what can we let out next?' However, as some less friendly people might imply poor zoo keeping from this story, we thought better of it.

We were also delighted to hear that in our fourth year open, we had been awarded a Highly Commended in the small attractions class of the National Farm Attractions Network 'Oscars' for the whole country.

We added more indoor adventure play, and more and posher toilets in an old feed shed, in 2003, to accommodate the doubling numbers. Our Christian friend, Chris Murray, who runs Pennywell Farm in Devon, had been a huge encouragement since before we opened, telling us what things worked well for him. He suggested we should stick to concrete as a toilet floor surface. He changed to tiles and regretted it as they were high maintenance and could be slippery. He also told us about trying to sell organic and local, good-for-you food in his cafe, but hardly anyone bought it! He had to return to a more popular menu. His farm regularly won awards; he was a good mentor.

We had by now quite a good website, designed by a school student Adam Beaumont, who was to become an even more key person to us later. We included on it all the details of what happened here and times of opening and prices and directions. We also had educational pages and risk assessments. I also wanted to add to the debate on creation and evolution; so we added more educational material, including an article on the differences between apes and man. I also made a display to put up in our primate house. For 'apes' I included the group of primates that my research indicated are definitely related to each other, because they all have three-colour vision; all other mammals have vision with blue and green receptors only, but not red (which means bulls can't see red, only a flapping blue/green cloth!) In Darwinian small evolutionary steps, the vertebrate eye could not acquire both a complete set of red receptors, and also a whole set of extra red interpreting sensors in the visual cortex, at the back of the brain. (Though a mutation could cause a loss, to give colour blindness or two colour vision). The great apes, the lesser apes, chimps, orang-utans and old world monkeys come in this category, perhaps with New World monkeys, too, which have only two colour vision.

There are some obvious similarities between apes and man, such as skeletal features, placental birth, nails instead of claws (albeit very slow growing in apes) and susceptibility to certain diseases. Mice and shrews have more anatomical similarities with each other than exist between apes and man, but mice and shrews are classified in different orders, as they should be. I felt it was time apes and other primates were seen to be in a different order to man. So perhaps God took the ape blueprint and added a huge number of modifications to their front-loaded DNA to make Adam then Eve as the first humans. My friend Professor Stuart Burgess, of Bristol University, whose specialism is design in nature, had awakened me to these differences between apes and man. He has now written a book about them, *Origin of Man*, which we sell in our shop.

A growing number of differences are being discovered, apart from those in the area of sex and reproduction already mentioned, (of the ape os-penis, fat in breasts and buttocks in humans, pubic hairs, highly sensitive clitoris, female orgasm, vulva at 45° in humans), in chapter 42. There was a widely publicised supposed 99% similarity in ape and human DNA; but recent work shows the differences are far greater, even perhaps 30% of gene difference (*Nature* 437:88-93), some other differences are:

> Man has a neck and S-shaped spine, joining the skull from below and so can carry loads on his head; an ape has no neck and a C-shaped spine, joining the skull from the back.
>
> Man has a huge brain of 600-2100cc (Neanderthals were at the top end) compared with a 300cc ape brain.
>
> Man has a complex three-arched foot with a big toe for walking long distances, apes have four hands, no arches and opposable big toes that are like thumbs.
>
> Man's legs are longer than his arms, and taper together for walking along a line; apes have arms longer than legs and waddle, or mainly knuckle walk, many of them can swing through trees easily.
>
> Man had opposable fingers from thumb to every finger, with one tenth of his muscles in his hands, controlled by a quarter of the brain's motor cortex (so we have vast skill potential from musical instruments to writing, painting, sports and model making); apes have only a simple hand grip between thumb and first finger.
>
> Apes have only 30 face muscles for a few face movements, man has 54 facial muscles for tiny facial movement, non-verbal communication and facial recognition.
>
> Humans have a large larynx and vocal chords and lips and tongue all designed for 6,500 languages and singing; apes can only make a few simple sounds (perhaps 100, similar to a raven, or a parrot), but sometimes very loudly.
>
> Men and women are mainly hairless (very short), but have hair in very different places to apes; pubic, long face hair (male only) and constantly growing head hair, but also baldness in men.

There were no compelling reasons for apes leaving African trees and acquiring these differences by small evolutionary steps, nor the evidence that it has happened. Apes remain apes. Mankind has always had these differences. The progression inferred by ancient African bones seems to me very contrived, not least because the earliest men, at Laetoli and Kadanuumuu, precede the so-called missing link of Australopithecus Garhi by a million radiometric years (see http://www.earthhistory.org.uk/transitional-fossils/man). So we proposed that apes and other primates should become a different biological order from man. There is very little that indicates apes are more intelligent than say parrots, dogs, crows, horses or dolphins. However, Darwinians tend to ignore such questions of science because the ape-to-man progression is essential to their philosophical proposal than man evolved from bacteria by random forces. This has to be yet another example of inadequate science, and people seeing similarities that they want to see, while ignoring important scientific evidence. The display caused a lot of interest. When the militant atheists saw it they published it on websites with derisive comments against it. Ironically, they claimed our science was bad, yet they did not produce any science against it, only ridicule, presumably designed to intimidate us.

In the middle of 2003 we had our first encounter with gypsies for some time. We had employed them in the '60s as many farmers did, as seasonal workers to pick potatoes. This time was more sinister.

I was aware that ten caravans had moved into someone else's field with its gate open (bad mistake, but due to a road accident) opposite our entrance. The first we knew of their arrival was of two gypsy boys putting ice creams up their sleeve to try to steal from our café. Later, when we were closed, Christina spotted them at about 6.00 pm trying to force their way into our ticket office. I had just left the farm so she was alone, but with the dog. She courageously shouted at them, and they ran off. She rang the police, who arrived very quickly with a van full of six riot squad officers; they got out to discuss it with me, as by then, I had just returned. While we were standing there I noticed a Ford Transit van coming down the drive; as soon as its driver saw the police it stopped and hurriedly backed away. The police saw that we were having trouble, so said they would go and talk to the gypsies and warn them off and they said they would call by in the night.

As I reflected on all of this I remembered Jesus' words 'do good to those who hate you'. So I rang Lucie and also our helpful friend Rick Wilkinson and asked if they would get up early the next day, Sunday morning, and help me take the gypsies some provisions for their lunch. Rick and I were both up at 7.00 am and met at Wraxall's all night garage store, where I bought them several loaves of bread, butter, cheese, and some fruit and veg and meat paste.

It was a fine, still morning when we loaded it all into the quad bike and trailer. Diamonds of dew were sparkling on the grass as the sun struggled to disperse the morning mist and we drove into their silent field at about 8.00 am. Lucie and Rick were in the trailer. A chorus of dogs greeted us. Then a middle-aged lady appeared with a long kitchen knife, tapping it very obviously on the palm of her hand. I drove up to her and said 'I'm looking for the boss man'.

'I'm the boss man', she replied in a low Irish drawl.

'Good morning,' I replied, breezily, 'we have come from your local church to bless you with some food for your lunch; we are also from the zoo farm opposite'.

The lady lightened immediately, 'Oh that's very kind of you, to be sure', she replied.

As we were unloading it I said to a young man who had appeared and was joining in the thanks, 'Why did your people try to rob us three times yesterday?'

'It wasn't us,' he replied.

'Oh yes it was, we followed you back' I said.

'I'll send them to apologise' he quickly replied.

'No, don't do that', I said emphatically! 'But please tell them that stealing is wrong; and we want to show you all, that God loves you, like He does us.'

'Thank you very much for your kindness; God bless you', he replied.

Later that afternoon he rang me to say that they were moving on and to thank me again for the food. I knew that gypsies have long memories and we would be remembered by that group for years ahead. It is also interesting that kindness brings results where hostility often fails. I know all our neighbours were very frightened for that one night, and wanted the police to move them on quickly. That is not always as easy as it sounds.

Two years later another group of gypsies arrived on the farm on a Sunday afternoon, saying they had just been to the horse trials in Wraxall (which I knew were on that weekend). Christina saw them first; I was with a photographer from the *Evening Post* and a well known Christian, Doug Horley, who had come with his team, to talk about doing a video. The gypsies were very intimidating to Christina and demanded help. They had a flat tyre and asked to borrow a jack and wheel brace. I came over and said I would be pleased to find one they could use. When I arrived back on the quad bike, one of them said 'how much do you want for the socket set?'

'They are not for sale' I replied 'otherwise how would I be able to change your tyre and our own?'

'Have you got any horses for sale?' he asked.

'No, none, sorry'. When they finished changing the wheel, one of them said 'we have a van with a broken axel at the top of your drive and can't leave here until it is mended, but we have found a place near Gordano Services that can mend it for £180, but I can't get to a bank tonight, as it's Sunday'.

'I am afraid you can't stay here,' I said, 'we have hundreds of visitors coming in the morning and you will be obstructing the road.'

'We can't move', he said, 'unless you can lend us £180; I swear on the body of my uncle I will bring it back to you tomorrow'.

I replied 'Well I am a Christian, and I can see you have a problem so I will go and see what I can do'.

I went to the *Evening Post* photographer and a friend standing with him, and said 'I'm in trouble, here' and told them about it, as I took out £180 from my wallet. When I returned I had my back to the photographer; the three men were facing him. They signed a receipt for the money. The photographer took a picture and quickly changed his digital picture card. One of the gypsies must have spotted him, as he rushed over to him and said 'how dare you take my picture, give that to me'.

'What picture?' said the photographer, and showed him all the pictures he had taken on the other card. Eventually with reassurances and thanks the gypsies left. The next day the *Evening Post* editor rang me and asked if he could publish the story.

'Give them today to keep their word, and return the money; I am not expecting it back, but you never know,' I said.

The following day no money had arrived, so the picture was published, a huge one, with the headline 'Daylight Robbery'! Two days later I received a postal order through the post for £180.

I was so surprised I rang the editor and told him. He published the same picture with another story about how surprised I was! I then received a phone call from one of the gypsies asking if I had received the money. I thanked him very much for it. I wondered if they had seen the picture, or even both of them, and whether that had encouraged them to pay up? Perhaps they could not read the articles and thought they were wanted men. It ended well; even though I suspect it was a scam they had tried quite regularly. It may have deterred them from that, at least in this area.

In 2003 we had our hottest ever days, August 6-9th, with temperatures over 30 degrees. Our attendance grew only 2.9%, to 74,400 our lowest increase. While this was a high figure for a farm, it was low for a zoo. We needed to add new things if we wanted to attract more visitors.

52

2004: Mazes, Shires and Rhinos

At about this time we knew several other farm parks were about to close or had closed to the public. Rode Tropical Bird Garden had closed in 2001, then a rare breed centre near Bath. Then came Bee World, near Bridgewater, followed by an open farm at Brockley, followed by Secret World Wildlife Sanctuary, who found the burden of health and safety just not worth the effort, so became a sanctuary only, instead. Then the very successful Old Down Farm Park, under Robert Burnase closed; Animal World, near Burnham, closed and opened again, then the multi-million pound @Bristol Wildwalk closed and later too Cricket St Thomas Wildlife Park. We were reminded of commercial realities and that no one owes us a living. Would we be the next to close?

Chris Stone, who along with her husband Steve had been so vital in the beginning stages of Noah's Ark, decided that she would stop being our café proprietor. She had worked through the very difficult task of providing refreshments for very uncertain numbers of visitors, as we climbed from 24,000 to 74,000. Some days were deserted, others, like fine Bank Holidays, were so overcrowded she could scarcely cope. We had always encouraged picnics, unlike many attractions. Usually a café does not find it easy to make a profit if picnics are allowed. The very difficult skill is to employ only the right number of people. All our café staff have been people to be proud of. Chris was replaced by Wendy Hall whose husband Colin, was a former professional footballer. They were practicing Catholics and Wendy, with Colin's support, did an excellent job as our numbers grew in peaks and troughs for the following years.

During 2003, Christina and I had visited a number of mazes. Longleat has probably the best hedge maze in the world. It was professionally designed and built, and not opened for 17 years. When I went round it I found it frustrating because it was not easy to complete. Many people vandalised it to get out when they were lost! It was also made of yew, which is poisonous to animals as well as being very slow growing, and it had a ticket office when open. Mazes have a long history, including a Christian one in some of the great churches and cathedrals, reminding those who did them about life's different paths and the choices that must be made. We visited a number of maize mazes too, but these had not grown high enough until August and were destroyed for cattle feed in October, with a new one built the next year, usually by specialists who sold the designs. We now had no cattle to eat the maize, so a maize maze was not suitable for us.

I wanted to build a maze and perhaps make it the longest hedge maze in the world. We had an area available; I had always been disappointed not to be able to build a full sized Noah's Ark, so decided to design a maze that incorporated an area the Biblical size of the Ark, with some large animals beside it. I drew it on paper and decided that we would incorporate two dinosaurs (diplodocus and glyptodon) and an elephant, rhino, crocodile and giraffe. In our proposal the fossil record told the story not of the origin of the world, but of recovery after the Hadean/Archaean wipe-out. So a few dinosaurs would have been on the Ark, albeit juveniles that were soon to breed.

We then laid out the picture on to the ground in string (two miles of it!), including drawing the animals. I had never drawn in string before, let alone animals that were much bigger than life size. I wondered if they would be recognisable from the air. I ordered 12,000 green beech and 2,000 copper beech; the copper beech were to be the outline hedges for the animals, filled by green beech. I chose beech for the hedge because it is a native species and the whole site a wildlife conservation area. Also its palatable trimmings would be useful as animal browse and the whole area would be good for reducing our carbon footprint. We were to discover that most of the giraffe's winter browse silage can be made from the maze trimmings in July. A 10-feet high tower would mark the finish, from which all the animals could be seen. I had decided to make it more interesting (and easier for visitors to complete) by making it an educational maze, with 15 branches or brachiations to it, with alternative routes at each branch. There would be a nature question at each of the 15 branches, indicating which path was right, and the correct path of two to five choices would offer a letter to collect. The wrong path brought you back to the clue again, the correct one led to the next question. This would accumulate 15 letters comprising an anagram of a creature, with a small prize for everyone who completed it. Today, the maze can be clearly seen on Google Earth.

We had also built a meerkat enclosure. Fred Beaumont, whose wife, Noelle, worked so cheerfully and efficiently at our ticket office, and whose son, Adam, was helping on computers in his holidays, collected a casualty meerkat from Edinburgh Zoo. These were soon followed by two purchased female meerkats that turned out to be males! Such is the slightly dodgy nature of the purchased animal network. We had made them a moat, with fish in it, wires across the top to deter the buzzards and foxes and an underground pipe for a burrow, through which they travelled from their pen to their heated house. We later swapped the two new males for two females from a zoo training college. One of these also turned out to be male. Oops!

We also installed a simple reptile house at one end of what was previously the old milking parlour, to house corn snakes, bearded dragons and foam-nesting tree frogs. This needed lots of heat and insulation. We were also given a leopard tortoise, which had been fed most of its life on lettuce – the major food that should not be fed to a tortoise. It therefore had a very wrinkly shell and inhibited growth. But we were grateful for it as it was bigger than most European tortoises, and much less stealable because of its size and because it needed heat. We brought the reptiles into the animal shows from then on as interesting additions to our educational message.

At the same time as we were marking out and planting the outside maze (I planted 8,000 trees myself, at about 600 trees per day; more tree-planting after my 65th birthday than in the whole of the rest of my life). I was also planning a three dimensional indoor maze. I had seen one in Cornwall, but was not happy about the hidden-ness of it, from the child-protection point of view. So I decided that from one side a parent should be able to watch a child all the way through, with walls made of 50 mm weldmesh. I sat down with a piece of paper and superimposed five floors on each other and worked out how to do a route via all five floors visiting them all four times on the journey. I then handed the plans over to Barry, who with great imagination and skill built it strong enough to last a century! We put escape doors to almost every section of the maze, so that if a child (or adult) panicked, they did not need to go far for help. It had to fit in with the existing adventure playground at the top and bottom exit/entry doors. It was to be called the Beehive Maze, so I looked up terrible bee jokes on the internet and named each section of the maze after one, like:

Mumble Bee, elocution department
Bee and Queue, building department
Worker Bee Union, for bees wanting more honey for shorter working flowers
Bee Pee Station – Bee cloakroom
Humburger – Bee fast-food bar
Swarmin here – sauna for cool bees
Zzub Zzub club for bees learning to fly backwards
Lone Drone Zone – Bee dating agency
Fuzz Buzz – beauty salon
Bee Gees – singing room
Beetza Hut – café
Jumble Bee – Bee smart with old clothes store
Bee Bee See – Television room
Date-a-bee – counselling and bee-trothal agency

Your honey or your life – Bee self defence classes
Buzz-Bee – Posh hat store for guard bees, etc

We had also spent £25,000 on a fully padded soft play area, built by Zap Leisure, into one end of the Arkiventures barn. We put lots of picnic tables beside it for parents of under 5s to watch their children at play. We installed an artificial blue tarpaulin ceiling; also another area of toy ride-in cars.

Early in 2004 we heard that the beautiful white cob that a friend had kept on the farm, and that we had used in the animal shows, was moving. We needed a big horse, preferably a shire horse. I had tried every possible contact looking to buy one from anyone, but after speaking to about ten different contacts I finally gave up; I put the telephone receiver down and said to Christina 'we need to pray'. There and then we asked God to send us a shire horse.

About twenty minutes later a lorry driver arrived on the farm and asked Christina, at the farm house, where I was. Roy Juggins found me and said 'Would you like two shire horses?'

My jaw dropped open and I said 'You are an answer to our prayers. We only asked God twenty minutes ago to lead us to a shire horse'. Roy went on to say that a few minutes ago he had decided to come and see us, from Nailsea, because his wife, Jeana, was dying of cancer. The shires were both champions of about four years old; but Jeana could no longer show them. She would like them to come together to us, where they could go on being shown to the public. It was a slightly bigger commitment than I wanted, with two big mouths to feed, but I have often found God does not always give us the cheapest solution; but it was the best possible. Two for company, geldings for quietness, and champions for looks. Jeana saw them settled in here before she died. Her funeral was in our church, Holy Trinity, Nailsea, attended by dozens of lorry drivers and horse enthusiasts. I made a horse-shoe shaped wreath of wire and straw, which Christina decorated with daffodils. We placed it by the altar and then it went with the coffin.

We next had the challenge of collecting the shires; they lived on the farm of nearby farming friends, the Triggols in Tickenham, three miles away, next to Tickenham Primary School. Three of us duly set off to walk them back. I was in one car. Christina joined us later in hers. We had told the school headmistress, Karen Sancto, who is another friend and from our church, that we were due to fetch them, and we told the press, so would the school like to say goodbye to them before they left? We found the horses, took them to the school gate and introduced Ari and Boxer to the children, told them a little about working horses, then suggested we all pray for them in their journey and new life. Lucie prayed. At the end, I heard one six-year-old say to another 'That was the best service I've ever been to!'

Lucie and a helper then walked the horses up to Noah's Ark along footpaths and a bridle way, with a little help from me and Christina at the road crossings. When we got to the farm they crossed a big field until they reached our two bison behind their fence. The bison snorted at the shires, who turned tail and fled back across the field to the gate! Great big one-tonne softie cowards, afraid of two female half-tonne bison! They shires been inseparable friends all of their time with us and have given great pleasure to thousands of people. They sometimes cause a little embarrassment by letting down their huge male organs in the animal show or by dunging profusely, a large bucketful at a time, but this gives people a giggle and demonstrates the facts of life!

We had been trying to persuade the local bus company to stop the bus at our gate for the previous two years. Their bus sailed past our gate almost empty most of each day, with a few more passengers at rush hours. We had received enquiries from our volunteers and from visitors. If they came to us by bus they had to get out at Failand and walk a dangerous two miles along the verge of a very fast road. Therefore, no one came by bus. The bus company was unyielding. One day a pretty young fifteen-year-old volunteer called Josie, came to the farm and asked to be dropped at our gate. The driver refused, drove past the gate to Failand and dropped her. She duly walked the two miles back. Christina was furious and phoned Josie's parents, who agreed that we should make a protest. Christina wrote a press release for the local papers. The next day Josie's picture was on the front page of the *Bristol Evening Post* and in the weeklies when they published. Within three hours of the first story appearing the bus company rang us with the promise of a bus stop. The signs duly appeared. We had a press call with the bus company and brought along lots of animals and staff to celebrate the new stop. We had waited 44 years for it and now, at last, not only our visitors, but residents from near-by farms and houses could safely catch a bus.

When my father had died in 2001 and my mother in 2003, they had left my brother and me a small farm between us. My father had left his savings to his six grandchildren and it had been his intention that our son Caspar would farm his land for life, rented from us, his father and uncle, along with the farm he and his father had rented from the Duchy for five generations. The Duchy had wanted to sell this group of farms and had offered Caspar a better farm in Cornwall, so despite it not being our father's intention, the land became ours to sell. When, after complex issues had been sorted out, it was eventually sold, over the course of three years and in bits, I had the possibility of building a bigger pension fund. Or else perhaps God wanted us to put it to work. I felt very certain that, just as we were required to put our newly owned farm to public use, so now we should grow the enterprise and invest in it (not that we were expecting a return). The housing of more zoo animals seemed the right way forward. We had been to see Bristol Zoo's two top men, Joe Gipps and Bryan Carroll; in fact Bryan had been the (albeit cautious) sponsor for us joining BIAZA. I knew they had wanted to open a new wildlife park in a few years time, and there did not seem any point in keeping all the same animals. They said they wanted to keep black rhinos; I said we were planning on white rhinos.

I had been to lots of zoos and now West Midland Safari Park's Wildlife Director, Bob Lawrence, was particularly helpful in directing us to a South African rhino exporter and also showing us how best to look after them. The holding and their drainage seemed to be the issues to deal with. Similarly fencing needed to be strong. We began the work in September, making a fence of 150mm timber poles with a deer fence, connected by four wire hawsers, all the way round their enclosure. Very heavy gates and locks that could not be cut were also installed, then a double electric fence a metre off, of 8,000 volts. The rhinos would always be shut into their yard or house at night. We did not trust animal rights activists, who had a reputation for terrorism with animals. Did they actually like animals, or care about their wellbeing? Or was it just an argument and a cause to fight?

We used one of the four building spaces for which I had applied for planning permission two years before. One, intended for exotic cattle, now seemed ideal for rhinos and so with the same footprint and timber exterior, we built the inside strong enough for three rhinos. We ordered a male and female rhino from South Africa, where they were auctioned each year by overcrowded safari parks, to be part of a consignment ordered by six British zoos and safari parks. We enlarged the drains to solve the problem we had heard about and planned a rhino race to stop and examine the rhinos if necessary. I had never seen a rhino race before, but knew how important cattle crushes were for stress-free examination of animals.

Part way through building our engineer, Andy Raines, arrived with two barriers that had bars wider than recommended by other zoos. I looked at them and wondered if this was a divinely ordered mistake. Fifteen inches instead of 12 meant that the rhinos could put their heads through, and we could treat them somewhat like cattle and feed them on the outside of the pen. Although it would be a first for rhinos it seemed well worth trying. We would need a safety net to keep the public safe, and keep the keepers a little further back, but it could just be an amazing opportunity to appreciate these beautiful animals.

It was. Now the public can actually touch the rhinos through the safety net, and both animals and people seem to love it. I mentioned it to our South African rhino dealer and he said 'I think you have done what we should have thought of years ago!' The race works a treat, too, and we have weighed them in the race, as well as giving them mud baths and other treatments. The rhinos were due to arrive in January 2005.

We had been surviving with an office in our house for the last five years. Christina and I lived a 24/7 commitment to it all, answering almost all the phone calls ourselves. Now Adam Beaumont joined us full time. Since our first year Adam had been a wonderful help during his school and university holidays, and had redesigned our website. Now he installed a computer in a former junior staff room and did all manner of other useful things as our office and marketing manager. Christina had spent time each December working on our leaflet, our main marketing tool. We had taken out a few advertisements but otherwise tried generating publicity from the births and other events on the farm. Now Adam tried more media, created adverts and laid out our new brochure. We took him on knowing he was destined for greater things.

Adam also designed another website – www.earthhistory.org.uk – on which Steve Robinson installed the new Recolonisation Model of geology, for which Steve became our part-time farm consultant on a small salary. I had come to see that Steve was a godly and inspired genius, perhaps a modern Galileo. He was quick to point out hypocrisy and fairly impatient with stupidity, but had an astonishing gift for unearthing areas of science, especially biology, cosmology, palaeontology and geology, separating them from spin and arriving at radical new conclusions. He, like some other gifted people, has had more than a fair share of misfortune and misunderstanding; but I believe his time will come. I think the Earth History website deserves a PhD. Many have been awarded one for much less valuable work. Steve had also designed or edited most of the large farm displays and the technical part of our own website, which needed his particularly accurate supervision and input.

Over the next two years Adam installed more computers and the building team made the end part of the classroom barn into another office, enabling eight people to work in two offices at once – at least be there when some of them were working! It is also a place for good constructive discussion. We have continued to encourage team spirit with an all-team meeting every day at 10.00am. This includes news of the day such as animal births or arrivals, new plans and dates of events, worries over safety, hygiene, etc. We also have a short Bible reading and a prayer, as we have had since we opened. I would like to help all our staff and visitors get to heaven, and this is a small way that might contribute to that. We also need everyone's prayers, for blessing and protection for our visitors and health and guidance for the team and the animals. The meeting is a top priority for everyone, including all staff and volunteers, work experience students, 'Keeper Experience' visitors and those with appointments here at the zoo.

As our grounds were growing, especially the grass mowing and the new maze, we took on a full-time groundsman, Jon Jutsum. Jon was highly qualified and the maze would be a big challenge to his talents: 14,000 young beech trees were being vandalised by visitors and by rabbits, moles and in places by a mysterious slow death syndrome! Jon also set to work on me, persuading me that we had to do lots more planting of trees and improving our wildlife conservation and green credentials generally. Over the next few years Jon put up 10 boxes for birds of various sorts and for bats. He became a village bat warden and surveyed the farm's five different bat species using a bat detector; which I also found very interesting. We also had lots of fences to improve or build from scratch. Jon had a higher standard of fencing than me and was excellent (though more expensive). We later took on an apprentice and the park rangers join the grounds team at quiet times of year.

53

2005: Absorbing the Rhinos, Battles with Bureaucrats

Our rhinos arrived in January 2005. Our son Larry went with a young photographer to Stansted Airport, not far from where he lived, to see them arrive and transferred to a lorry in their crates. They all then made their way to us, arriving after dark so the rhinos slept the night on the lorry. We had arranged for the press and TV to come the next morning along with a 10-tonne crane and enough regulation bump hats for all the press who were going to be near the crane. (Would a bump hat be much help if a rhino crate fell on you?) The crane lifted each crate over the rhino house to lower it down at the door. The female, Rumba, came out first, as quiet as a lamb; we shut her in the second pen. Then it was the male, Rumbull's turn; he was in a bit of a state. He kept smashing against his crate with his horn and backing out without leaving the crate entirely. Rumba seemed to realise his problem and called out to him. He was reassured immediately, backed out and joined her. It was reassuring for us to have the South African vet, Charles Van Niekerk, travelling with the animals; he had been delivering other rhinos to the other zoos. He advised us that one wall was not high enough – despite my having seen walls that high at lots of other zoos – and he was right. Young rhinos from South African safari parks were much more feisty than those from European zoos. The following morning Rumbull had both his front feet on top of a six-feet door! He could have got himself over the lower wall with no difficulty.

Our staff and lots of local photographers and TV cameras were present at this exciting event and all kept silent to avoid upsetting these gentle giants. Rob Smith, our local assistant vicar, came to offer a dedication prayer for the rhinos and their future, including for babies, which we had heard was difficult in a herd of two. Noah seemed to have success though. The press were very excited as ours were the first rhinos in the Bristol area since the Ice Age, and of course lots of media coverage helps what the marketing folk call 'brand awareness'. Our numbers were up 75% in the first month.

The rhinos arrived to a half-finished enclosure which took much of the year to finish, including working out how big the net mesh should be to allow the public to touch the rhinos without getting too close. The first mesh was too big and one day, after a knot in it had broken, we found a mother holding her tiny child half through the hole stroking the rhino! We quickly made the required changes.

We also said goodbye to Lucie after five years. She had set a high standard in animal love and care and had been so good at organising the diets and management sheets of our growing animal collection, and at deploying lots of young staff; all accompanied by her shining Christian faith. She had also reared our famous baby camel, Callum, who became a celebrity at his next home among Martin Lacey's trekking camels. and in pageants at Christmas. Lucie seemed so much a part of the place that I awarded her a season ticket for life – at least my life!

We decided that Chris Wilkinson, who had grown up on the place as a volunteer since 14, and had known the farm as a dairy farm, was ready for the job of head keeper. Chris had a diploma in animal management and had spent a while in Africa and I felt that, though he was very young, he had shown the leadership skills in organising volunteers that made him ready for the job He also had the gift of speaking, from doing presentations, to take some of the animal shows, a willingness to learn and practical skills to lead from the front. He soon started and finished a demanding, in-service foundation degree, with college weeks taken at quiet times of year and spare-time study.

Sadie Garland had also arrived the previous year. She was very friendly, cheerful, smiley, highly qualified in horse care and with a good knowledge of small animals; she also had a budding ability for looking after the young helpers. Sadie soon reorganised the young 13-year-old volunteers, who were by now applying to us in large numbers, and she arranged a training schedule in animal care for them to make progress. We also had an increasing number of year-10 pupils wanting a week's work experience. Schools have an increased responsibility to make sure their placement is properly supervised. We needed to weed out those who were just dumped on animals because they were no good at anything else. Sadie drew up some forms and our standard of school pupil rose. Many have gone on to higher education colleges and to be keepers elsewhere. Sadie went on to do in-service training and was awarded a top regional prize in her group.

This was also the year of our second zoo inspection. The bar was raised higher for this one as we now had more animals. We needed a treatment room, with two separate sinks, a table for operations and the medicine cabinet in it. We also needed better food preparation areas with separate sinks for washing hands and utensils.

With expansion there was pressure, not only on the toilets which we had expanded, but now on the café. We had applied for planning permission and had built a covered veranda with open sides next to the café. One day in April

2005, when a planning officer was looking at it, I said to her 'We have planning permission to build an animal shed over there, would it matter if we kept the same footprint but made it a bit higher? We are planning to bring in some giraffes and a mating giraffe needs 22 feet to eaves of his building.' She did not appear to have much sympathy for the male giraffe getting a headache on a low roof, but she took note of the height when I said 'There is a man with a drain pipe standing over there; the building comes to the top of the drain pipe.' She looked at it and said that the present plans would be fine. I was very keen to do the right thing by the planners and particularly did not want to have to go for retrospective planning permission after having built the shed. So now I knew all was well.

We went ahead, with an engineering firm designing a timber building to suit. We started work on the enclosure fence and the yard and had started digging away the bank behind to lay it all out. The engineer's drawings arrived. They had cost £4,000. Three months later I heard from the council: we probably did need fresh planning permission. Thus we were doomed to apply for retrospective planning permission – a situation that press and councillors later suggested we had deliberately provoked.

On July 4th I suddenly heard that a road through the back of the farm was being closed for repair for three weeks. We had needed to take water across this single lane road to replace a pipe that had crossed the road, tied to a tree branch for the previous 30 years, and which the water authorities were not happy with. I thought this would be an ideal way of avoiding closing the road again and inconveniencing the locals. I found that I needed to get a license, which included checking there were no wires or pipes under the road. I had farmed the land for 45 years so knew there were none there; but when I met the gas inspector I asked him to double check with his instruments. He said there was nothing else there signed his own letter to me. I rushed the completed forms, cheque, and maps down to North Somerset Council offices, explaining that a window of opportunity had arisen.

A week later I had heard nothing so went to the on-site contractors, Ringways, and asked them to check our work. We dug in two pipes and put them in a four-inch drainpipe as a conduit. We tamped it down. Job done. Or so I thought. I had a phone call from Peter Butcher, in charge of highways, saying the paperwork was not correct because we had not obtained clearance from 14 utility companies to say that their apparatus was not under that bit of road, and that our man was not licensed. I said the job had been supervised and completed by North Somerset's own contractors, Ringways, and that we had done a test to see there was no apparatus under the road – and anyway the job was now finished and no problem had been encountered. Furthermore, I had now found an old Avon County Council license to do the same job, and that did not require special contractors.

Peter Butcher sounded furious! He said the old license was not valid (he had not seen it), and that I would need to rip it all out and start again, or he would send someone to destroy it at my expense. He confirmed this in writing the next day. This was the only time I had ever found a North Somerset Council officer fast and enthusiastic about anything! I wondered if he had a special cause to fight, against apparently arrogant landowners, who did not grovel to him enough. Barry then rang him. As Barry spoke Bristol better than I do he had a politer reception and was told to open up the pipe at each end to show it was deep enough. Barry duly did that.

I consulted the NFU legal department to see if they thought my previous license was valid. They thought it was; so I wrote again to Peter Butcher, with a copy to my councillor, laying out all the details and saying I had no intention of causing offence, but only wanted to use an opportunity, to save inconveniencing the public with yet another road closure; could I assume he was now happy, knowing I had this old license, that I had also paid for, and that the NFU legal department thought was valid? I also said that I had heard from Barry that if he opened the pipe up all would be well. So please would he tell me if I needed to do anything else? I heard no more. Every day I expected a letter, or a phone call; we could easily withdraw our pipe from its conduit if we received one; there would then be no water apparatus under the road. The contractors, Ringways, then asked did we want some all-tarmac peelings from the road. I said yes, it could come in useful. To my horror, they tipped 100 tonnes of mainly earth from the sides of the road they were widening, as well as ten tonnes of peelings in our car park; it was unusable and we had to employ someone else to dispose of it. Ringways also finished the tarmac road so that all the run-off water went straight into our field gateway. We had to repair the gateway, but I said nothing.

A few weeks later a spring dried up, and so we urgently needed water in the fields below the road, where our new pipes were supposed to provide for the sheep and cattle there. We rapidly dug a mile of new pipe in and connected it up to the pipe we had previously dug in under the road. No water reached the sheep and cattle, so we wondered where, on the one mile of pipe, we had left a loose fitting. We dug up all the connectors; this took nearly a day. Then we wondered if Peter Butcher had sent someone to secretly destroy our pipe, and so that we did not have a chance to withdraw our pipe that he must have been informed was in a conduit. Surely no one could do that and not say so? When we looked closely, the tarmac had been carefully cut and restored, and our pipe with its conduit had actually been damaged and re-buried, so that we would not know about it. I then received a bill from North Somerset Council, for £606, for breaking up our pipe! At that moment I understood why some council civil servants were so unpopular with the public, whom they were meant to be serving and whose rates paid their wages. They sometimes actually experience abuse at their own homes. Our district council had been made into a county council 'unitary authority'. Had the staff been promoted to jobs beyond their ability? It appeared so to me.

What should we do? Thoughts about murder, bulldozing down the council's offices, and a few other unhelpful options came to me… then I remembered that Jesus said 'return evil with good, and pray for those who do evil things to you'. So I asked my staff to patiently write for the 14 letters from the utility companies and the rest of the paperwork and find someone else (but definitely not Ringways, who had done us such harm) to spend another £1200 to dig the pipe in again. The NFU said they would undoubtedly back me and pay for a court action.

First, I wrote an official complaint to the council. Another member of North Somerset Council replied, predictably closing ranks, saying our pipe was not deep enough nor with the right ballast, so they destroyed it. I wondered why they had not told Barry that when he opened the pipe up at each end. Their subsequent pictures showed they were not telling the truth. I wrote to the Local Authority Ombudsman, who asked to see my old license. The council wrote a made-up a story about having telephoned us on the day, to say they were coming to destroy our pipe; the ombudsman believed this story, and they believed the council's word that our pipe was not deep enough, despite photographs clearly showing to the contrary, and they said our paperwork was incomplete without the 14 utility companies' letters. The ombudsman then did not send me back my license, despite my repeated requests. Without it I could not make a court case.

By this time I had decided the whole issue was wasting too much of my precious time and I should do no more. I knew there was a spiritual battle in the universe; I wanted to remain on the side of good, and progress and no revenge. So with the help of a friendly councillor I agreed to drop the case but not pay the council's £606. That was at least their partial admission of guilt. I reflected how much things had moved in 45 years. Paper trails had replaced relationships.

We had also applied for membership of BIAZA, the British and Irish Association of Zoos and Aquaria, with two other zoos to sponsor us and an inspection; we were accepted as provisional members, Bristol Zoo and Slimbridge WWT very kindly agreed to be our sponsors, with Neil Bemment of Paignton Zoo as our mentor. I did not want to be a rival of other zoos. We wanted to keep different animals from Bristol Zoo because we had lots of space for big ones; and some enormous indoor and outdoor playgrounds. There is also the fact that if one zoo provides a good day out, it encourages people to go to others as well. Miranda Stevenson was the excellent director of BIAZA, keen on the highest standards of husbandry and enrichment of the animals. She came from the conservation charity side of BIAZA, but was good at putting the case across for all zoos to have the highest standards to allay public criticism. She and I were never going to agree about Darwin; but at least she heard some joined up science on that subject.

There were others who did not agree with us. An article appeared on an atheist website, warning about us. They decided to bombard us and the press with complaints, hoping to wear us out and close us. I am glad to say that most of them couldn't be bothered, but half a dozen persisted and complained about our website – how ridiculous it was to suggest God being Creator was a scientific proposal, where was my evidence? I patiently answered them as politely as possible. One resorted to a brief 'Anthony you are a c—-'. I wrote back that he had got my gender wrong, and please could he unpack his objection a little? Others became politer. It faded out after a few months. A note appeared on the website later saying 'be careful about these people; they have done their homework'.

At this time also, Barry wanted to build a finch enclosure. Barry's parents had looked after dozens of finches at their house in Bedminster, when he was a lad. It seemed a good idea. Darwin had said finches pointed to evolution. Creationists agree with that evolution, but say God made a few pairs of birds, and perhaps a pair of ancestors of finches and other Passeriformes, with genetic potential to spread out into lots of them – 1,200 or more species in the group. These are unlikely to be related to penguins, flamingos, owls or parrots. Barry built an outside enclosure attached to our old covered bull pen, which became the inside enclosure. We bought Whydahs and Weaver Birds and Zebra Finches; 17 sorts of finch in all. There was recycled running water and a bird bath and lots of plant life and nest boxes galore.

In 2005 our attendance rose to 94,500, a further increase of 20%.

54

2006: Giraffes, Alligators and Boundaries

When the planners had changed their minds and told us we needed permission for the taller giraffe house, plans were too far ahead to stop. We went ahead and applied for new planning permission but knowing the speed North Somerset worked at, we knew it would be retrospective planning permission by the time it was through, and that to wait would damage us economically. We also thought giraffes were on the way soon. We had decided to build in steel and use the excellent steel-frame specialist John Wyatt, from mid-Wales, who had built our arable barn. Our son Caspar had shown us his new under-floor heating in a cottage he was renovating in Cornwall which seemed quite easy to install. So I enquired of his plumber who made us some plans and did the final fittings; Barry and his team duly laid the under-floor heating pipes and finished off under John Wyatt's building. Andy Raines did the extra gates and fittings.

I designed our giraffe house to include features I had not seen together at any other zoo. There is a fixed, indoor crush for a giraffe to walk through each day, to hold and treat it with minimum stress. There is an electronic weighing platform for daily weighing. This crush is linked by gates to a doorway for loading animals persuasively and easily and there are electric winches for raising browse. I had felt it most important to have a weldmesh wall on the keeper floor and on the top floor for visitors, so that the giraffes could be seen at all times. I had been to other new enclosures where it was very difficult for anyone, even keepers, to see the animals. This may have kept them private, and perhaps a bit wild; but we were hoping for animals that could be seen and that were relaxed with the public. We also introduced silage barrels of tree leaves. Woburn Safari Park were trying it for the first time that year, in place of the frozen oak browse they had used for years. I had made up to 2,000 tonnes of grass and maize silage for many years and knew it could be exactly right. I had heard that some people thought it was a good thing to open the barrels regularly to kill the mould that they heard grew on silage. I told them on no account to do that, because it was introducing oxygen that added to the mould! The barrels had to stay tight shut all the time, to keep them saturated in carbon dioxide.

I knew from the latest Lincoln Park working group in America that most zoo giraffes were not being fed the right ration. Giraffes are very fussy eaters and are often spoilt by rations that were not good for them. They need an average of 18%

protein – higher than the total diet fed to a high yielding cow. They also need linoleic acid, found in linseed, and lots of fibre in proportion to their concentrates. So we ordered linseed lozenges and decided to use 18% sheep concentrates as well. We also discovered that high protein Lucerne haylage (hay that was not quite dry enough, so was packed into polythene silage wrap) was available for horses and we fed that also, along with the browse. We decided to feed all the browse and haylage on hay racks (boards actually) outside, but attached to the weldmesh wall. There was no waste, nor sticking out bits of hay rack to hurt the giraffe. Their tongues could reach through the weldmesh and pull the food through. We subsequently discovered that if giraffes do not have enough work for their tongues to do, they spend a lot of time licking. Sometimes in zoos they lick entire holes in timber planks. We had thus satisfied this need for tongue exercise as well.

We also decided to weigh the daily food intake of all the types of food and also weigh the giraffe daily. It was probably unique to have only one giraffe in such a modern enclosure and so it was an opportunity to do this. We also incorporated a viewing platform at giraffe head height for the public to get close. We also incorporated two toilets, both with disability assistance and baby changing, and a new septic tank. We made a long ramp for all visitors, including wheelchair users.

We had been laying down all these plans but still currently had no giraffe. I had tried to procure giraffes through BIAZA. I was told we had to join EAZA to get animals that were in European Endangered species Programmes (EEPs). So we applied. We were told we might have to wait two years. So I tried all the dealers. One in Holland said he had high hopes of getting some females in from South Africa, where they had a surplus, like our rhinos. He negotiated with the EEC authorities for seven months; along with a Spanish zoo which was in an area that might be suitable for quarantine. Then the EEC authorities said they had to be quarantined off-shore to prevent Foot and Mouth. We were not clear why a blood test in South African quarantine, then in Spain, was not enough, but it wasn't. The EEC had no off-shore quarantine station, apart from Pierre et Miquelon, a small island off Nova Scotia, where no aeroplane big enough for a herd of giraffes could land. So the entire EEC has no quarantine accommodation for large animals. This meant the promised giraffes could not come from South Africa. So we were stuck with no giraffe and a nearly completed house. What could we do? We all prayed and told the Lord that as we had tried all avenues to no avail, please would He help.

I rang our friendly dealer, Trevor Lay who had always been helpful; he rang a European dealer, and within two weeks a giraffe arrived! It was a male and we called him Gerald, after a close friend Gerald Bonington, who had spent much of his youth on our farm, like an older brother to our family, and who with his wife Rachel and children Ruth and James, had been friends ever since. We also had two good Send a Cow friends and trustees called Gerald so the name was imperative, especially as there is a book called *Gerald the Giraffe*.

The press were duly informed of Gerald's arrival and, on the day he arrived in a wooden trailer behind a lorry. I transferred the trailer to my Landrover to take him along the narrow, bumpy roads to the door of the house. We opened the crate. He was much too shy to come out, but ate a banana. Eventually, and it took a long time, he became convinced that his best option was outside the trailer, and so stepped out into his new house. We had been warned how dangerous a giraffe could be, by kicking in all directions but Gerald was, and still is, very quiet and friendly. Our staff watched his entry with complete and quiet fascination. His amazing shape and size, yet perfectly balanced movement, were mesmerising. The press were there in force; there are no other giraffes in Somerset, Gloucester or South Wales. We asked our friend, John Backhouse, ex-navy flyer, now our church curate, to pray publicly for him at the dedication of the enclosure; we thanked God for such a lovely animal and prayed for a mate to come and for good health.

We felt one animal on his own was not a good thing so gave him a tall Anglo Nubian goat called Arthur, but they did not get on and were both frightened of each other. So we swapped Arthur for Steady Eddie, an English goat. They immediately bonded and were good friends for the next four years, to the amusement of the press. It is not unusual for male giraffes without a harem to wander on their own in the wild, but they like to team up with other males for mutual protection. In zoos they do a lot of fighting (neck banging) which appears disturbing. As we are Noah's Ark we wanted a male and female.

A year later we managed to find a male zebra who we called Zebedee. He became good company for the Gerald and Steady Eddie. We monitored Gerald's weight day by day; he put on a steady one pound a day for two years, except for the first month that Zebedee was with him when he put on no weight at all! He then regained his appetite.

I was to discover the politics of zoo world. Three years later we had still not been inspected by EAZA and did not qualify for a female giraffe; meanwhile it had been decided to weed out all hybrid giraffes and not breed from them. I thought this was crazy and said I did not want a female if we could not breed from her. I then thought I had found a female through a breeder but, having paid a deposit on her, the EEP demanded she stay in their programme. A court case ensued. Meanwhile the EEP was sending three female hybrid giraffes to a north country zoo provided they did not breed them. I protested to BIAZA, suggesting hybrids were an asset that should be bred, if on a separate stud book. The protest was ignored. Those who had giraffes did not want other people to have them. The rich charity zoos closed ranks, with a few older safari parks. They had forgotten that in the '70s lots of giraffes were imported from Africa; without which there we might now have none in Britain. There were quarantine facilities at Plymouth and Chester at that time. I warned that, without new blood, the gene-pool would get weaker. No one was interested.

Other important things happened in 2006 at Noah's Ark. We completed a perimeter fence that the previous year's inspection had required. It cost £25,000 but was worthless because footpaths crossed the farm. For two years we had been trying to move these footpaths. In building this perimeter fence we had left provision for a new footpath, by leaving a set aside strip outside the fence but inside our land on which walkers could then travel without any stile for a mile. This could also be a bridle way, in the unlikely event of walkers wanting horses on their footpath. It now became a priority to move the footpaths on to this new and better path, on which we had also installed picnic tables at three beauty spots. The footpath officers came and looked at it and agreed that it would be better – only time for objections to be satisfied now stood in the way of moving them. I met with the footpath officers, health and safety officer and planning officer in December 2006; everyone was united that the footpaths had to be moved from the danger of a zoo area.

We also built an alligator pool and pen in the old milking parlour building; and bought in two young alligators, which we kept tame. The end of 2006 also saw changes to the rest of that building as we made more tanks for a larger reptile collection. I had done a study of reptile classification and it appeared there were perhaps twelve, but possibly as few as five, distinct and unrelated groups of modern reptiles, depending on how many of the lizard families could evolve by variation over time. We wanted representatives of as many of these as possible and we now had snakes, tortoises and alligators, chameleon, geckos, monitors, iguanas and skink. We also included some invertebrates, like leaf-cutter ants, tarantula and giant snails.

More reptiles meant more electricity; we needed to upgrade lots of our electrical circuitry. Chris Moulding, a very meticulous, conscientious and hard working young electrician, had been spending his holidays working on these and building up expertise under two different electricians; he now wanted to be our four-day-a weekelectrician, while he studied for further qualifications. He was very careful and thorough, good at the design work and research we needed to do for each electrical project. He was another of God's gifts to us.

In 2006 our attendance rose to 107,000 a rise of 13%. This put us past the 100,000 visitor mark for the first time and was a cause of great reassurance and celebration. We were filling a need. Even better news – North Somerset's tourism department awarded us their County's Top Leisure Attraction trophy. This was the first time we had won a top prize and we celebrated with a meal out with all the staff, whose brilliant, consistent work this marked.

55

2007: Gibbons, Tapirs and Zoo Politics

We had applied in good time for planning permission for a new gibbon gallery. It was quite a challenge for the team to build this, as the outside exercise area was 22-feet high and quite large, built in an L-shape round a very luxurious house we had designed. The house consisted of two tiled gymnasiums with central heating; the stud bookkeeper thought it was the largest indoor area in Europe for a pair of gibbons. I had been concerned as I looked at others, that outside areas were often good, but in our climate the gibbons, which are the most endangered of all the apes and all come from the Far East tropical rain forest, spent most of their time indoors. So we went for a big house. It was eventually built and in good time. It was opened in front of a crowd of our visitors, by our building team leader, Barry, whose team had built the enclosure. Our son, Larry, prayed the dedication prayer.

With the planning permission for the gibbon gallery came a requirement from North Somerset Council to offer a five-year plan of everything we had in mind to do. We met with all the team leaders to pray and to decide our dreams and priorities. We had been asked to build a new café by the council, so we put that in the plan and had a topographical survey done. Everyone also thought that big cats would be very interesting for visitors, and an increase in birds of prey and even bears could be easily absorbed. Elephants would be expensive, but as a long term plan they were worth putting on the map, along with a tropical house, for keeping tropical animals in a purpose-built building. We hurried everything along to get the whole plan in by August '07. To our dismay we later found it then sat on the planning officer's desk for seven months!

Animal procurement is also a problem. When we joined BIAZA I soon discovered that it was a coalition of private enterprise zoos and charity zoos. Many of the older ones of each were also members of EAZA (European Associ-

'By our last Christmas, Lord Wraxall had become very friendly': Anthony and Christina with Lord Wraxall in 1995, the year they bought the farm from the Tyntesfield Estate

Anthony and Christina at the machinery dispersal sale. Memorabilia of 35 years of dairy farming finding new homes

Christina and Anthony: humble beginnngs of Noah's Ark Zoo Farm

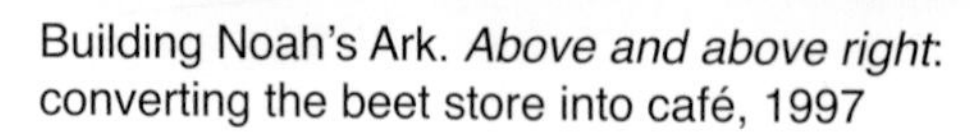
Building Noah's Ark. *Above and above right*: converting the beet store into café, 1997

right:
Anthony laying ground work for a cattle grid

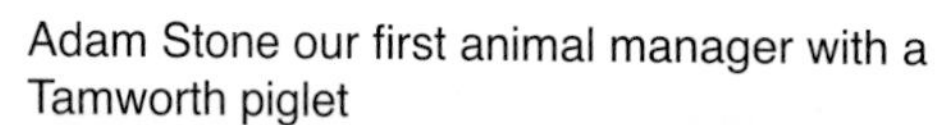
Adam Stone our first animal manager with a Tamworth piglet

'God's gift to us': animal manager Lucie Guilbert, with her 'baby' Callum the camel

Dr Liam Fox MP opens the slides

'Would you like two Shire horses?' Roy Juggins was the answer to our prayers – though more than we had prayed for

Our Nativity performed by Trendlewood Church, Nailsea

The Ugandan ambassador at Send a Cow Day, Noah's Ark

The X7 arrives at the gate, 44 years' late. It took a story in the press about a young girl walking on a dangerous road, and three hours later we had the promise of a stop

James Emly with Rumbull in the holding crush

Gerald gets his hooves cleaned by Sadie Garland

From top right

Barley, Anthony and Rumba. Barley has had 22 puppies in three litters (the singer George Michael bought one of them) and is adored by visitors

Barry, Max and Tim building the Gibbon Gallery

Visitors with special needs accompanied by Clifton Rotary Club volunteers

All the family at Anthony's 70th birthday, 2008

One of the family: with Tanvir, our once timid male tiger

Our staff, 2010

Anne Harley, chair of North Somerset County Council, opens the new play slide, 2010. Anthony and Barry Baker look on

Colin Hall, Chair of Clevedon Town Council and *(left)* Dennis Croome, Reader, opening the new ring-tailed lemur enclosure, 2010

Staff, volunteers and friends, summer 2011

Ann Widdecombe with Anthony and Christina 'strictly come digging' for our new Elephant Eden, September 1st 2011

Our 50th wedding anniversary February 24, 2012

ation of Zoos and Aquaria) and so could acquire animals for nothing, indeed paying for animals was not allowed. Swaps, however, were allowed. The law of the land and BIAZA regulations allow sales of animals. 'Conservation by commerce' is wholly legitimate, indeed essential so that all the small private collections can feed into the zoo world to everyone's advantage. The charity zoos also had the advantage of being exempt from paying VAT on entry tickets and being able to claim gift aid on all value-added entry tickets. So Cotswold Wildlife Park, in private ownership, in a comparison they did with Marwell Zoo (of similar visitor numbers but a charity founded at about the same time) found that charity status earned Marwell £1.2 million more per year than Cotswold. A charity zoo can also appeal for charity funds, and even lottery money, to build new enclosures and get Gift Aid on all donations. Yet their standards are not required by the DEFRA zoo inspectors to be higher, nor their giving away to conservation work abroad any more than private enterprise zoos. I suggested to our zoo inspectors that this was not fair, to which they replied 'there is a lot that is not fair', so we needed to get over it.

We had also put up a prefabricated temporary tapir house, and tried to acquire Brazilian tapirs through the EEP and BIAZA. None were available for the next two years. So I had to buy two, which did not come until the end of the year. Part of the outside of our gibbon gallery was not needed for gibbons, until we bred or acquired some more so we found some coatimundis, this time a surplus male group was available through BIAZA as these are fairly plentiful. Coatis are busy little animals, which climb well and are interesting for visitors; they are in the Procyonidae family with racoons and red pandas, a family that we had not got represented. We also bought a male zebra we called Zebedee. We had an inspection by three BIAZA zoo inspectors, to accept us as full members of BIAZA; after our provisional membership period. We were grateful for the time they spend on BIAZA matters and for their helpful comments towards our improvement.

Christina was worried about our keeping big cats. She was very nervous that they might get out and eat us. Very reasonably so, it seemed to me; I was too! So in the winter of 2007/8 we went on a tour of ten zoos that kept big cats. I enquired about all the details of locking the doors and cutting and keeping the meat, what escape-procedures and guns were needed and what emergency procedures involved, how high their fences needed to be and of what design, and lots of details of management. Most of the detail was quite similar to other dangerous animals, like rhinos and gibbons; only more so. We heard of one zoo where a tiger had seen a dead bird outside its (poorly constructed) pen. In the night it chewed its way through the wire, squeezed through the hole and took the bird, then squeezed back through the hole! Tigers are nervous and territorial; they spray their enclosure as they are 'retromingent', like all the cat family, and the males spray their urine backwards. They can spray 20 feet! One tiger keeper I spoke to had been hit full in the face, deliberately and accurately, by a male tiger's urine. At a safari park a male tiger often sprayed at open car windows!

In the middle of all this we heard of a tiger at San Francisco Zoo that had got out and killed someone, and of a (closed at the time) British zoo where there had been two big-cat escapes. Whatever the press said about these escapes the word in the zoo world was that they were all caused by doors left unlocked. It was a challenge to get the designs right, the key protocols right, and not to employ keepers who arrived drunk to work. In the end Christina was willing to sacrifice her freedom; she could see that we needed to expand or close, to stop the continuing losses of keeping going with (comparatively) low visitor numbers, and preferred tigers to lions as they were nicer to draw or paint and did not seem to roar so much. The tiger is also in desperate need of help as there are only 3,000 left in the wild and being poached at perhaps one a day, so it was important that potential breeding stock were retained in as big numbers as possible in captivity.

I therefore drew up plans that were, I thought, better than all that I had seen, and cheaper than all but the most basic. Our zoo inspector added a few thoughts to remind us that some zoos, which we were planning to copy, were operating with old enclosures that would not pass inspections today, or that were off-show to the public. It was clearly going to be more expensive than I had hoped.

We also needed a new farm road. Every year we had the challenge at harvest time of gathering 500 tonnes of crops from our fields while visitor numbers were at their highest, then sending the crops away in huge bulk grain lorries, 30 tonnes at a time. Harvesting work is, at least half the time, out of visitor hours, often starting with straw hauling at 7.00am. In July or August combine harvesting continues till the dew comes down at 10 or 11pm. Most of our fields could be reached without conflict with cars or visitors. The main approach to the grain store for all tractors, combines and lorries was through the entrance that visitors used. So we applied to the council for a Determination Order for a new track and also a new straw barn. As this was not on the tourism part of the farm it did not need full planning permission, so was much quicker with very little paperwork.

Much of 2007, therefore, was spent on the boring work of upgrading an old track into a farm road and in improving the car parks to handle coaches better.

We had little to show for either and yet they cost £35,000. The water authorities had also invented some new rules, which meant lots of temporary water pipes above ground that now needed to be buried, and our reservoir water was no longer legal for the public to drink or wash their hands, even though it was fed by mains water only. These new rules were well meant, to save the nation's water and make it cleaner for the public, but they were expensive to us.

In February we installed a play Kidbineharvester for children to climb on and pretend to drive. We had had our old Ferguson tractor – which the children had loved climbing on – condemned by the safety officer, so the new installation meant the children could have great fun and in safety.

Another first in 2007 happened when we were approached by Pete Blake, owner of a shop called The Reptile Zone and world authority on all things reptile, asking if we would like to host a 'Venomous Snake Week'. It was clear that Pete's venomous snakes, which he kept off-show at his house, were going to need a glass room for him to show off. Barry and his team made one. Pete and his colleagues are seriously brave and they handled, gently but firmly, a dozen or more of the most venomous snakes in the world. He told us how important these creatures were in keeping the rodent population down, and were not to be feared unless they felt threatened. Pete returned on subsequent years and increased the week to a fortnight for a growing audience.

2007 was also another warm summer after a warm winter. At a farming conference we attended, the figures showed a steady rise of 1.5°C in the mean winter temperature over the last 30 years. This meant a survival of insects and fungal diseases instead of them dying of cold. It also gave evidence that was helpful to those who were trying to convince us of climate change. There was also doubt about continued warming in the last few years, which appeared to be cooling. We were told the atmosphere contains 385 parts per million of carbon, a rise from 350 ppm which was considered safe; and that our emissions have done it. So why had 1940-1970 produced a cooling of temperatures at a time when we were burning coal and oil at a huge rate? This conference led some of us farmers to doubt the global warming message that was being given us in the press.

In the 1970s a hole in the ozone at the South Pole had been spotted; CFC gasses were banned around the world; the ozone hole mended. Perhaps this carbon could be a correctable problem. As is so often the case, there is as much spin as science; so those of us who have been damaged by government spin about the dangers of BSE, or the lack of danger with Foot and Mouth, would like more science. Some people are good at convincing government that they deserve funding for a band wagon they are riding. I have since read several books by informed scholars with no vested interest either way and have become even more sceptical about global warming. It seems to me they have become a bullying movement that is based on several falsehoods and is likely to misuse huge amounts of money here and abroad. However, much of the low-carbon movement was just encouraging lower consumption and less waste. These had to be good for us on the farm as with all businesses. For further concerns about carbon issues see appendix 2.

Science moves on in our understanding. It has become clear that many things in science are less clear than people are led to believe. New ideas are proposed, some of them are taken up by textbooks and they become enshrined by teachers and lecturers as a paradigm. Einstein's theory of special relativity (which deals with motion in a straight line) and general relativity (which deals with gravity and accelerated motion generally) have widespread acceptance by mathematicians, partly because they are complicated; and complicated is clever, so it is also probably right! At Oxford we used to be told that many mathematical ideas are difficult to understand, like the concept of 11 dimensions; 'you don't need to understand it, but just to accept it' we were told. I am suspicious of statements like 'scientists say…' Were people just manipulating us for control or money?

Most people do not realise that SatNav has put one of Einstein's assumptions in doubt. The clocks in global positioning satellites at 20,000 km above the Earth, run 46,000 nanoseconds a day faster than on the Earth's surface, because the gravitational field is thinner; but they are ploughing their way through that gravitational field at 3 km per second and so are 7,000 nanoseconds a day slower. The GPS clocks are slowed, therefore, before launch, by 39,000 nanoseconds so that they tick at the same speed as Earth's clocks. In this way our position can be calculated accurately. Had Einstein's suggestion, that nothing travels faster than the present speed of light, been applied to GPS, we would have had a very complicated system which was found not to be needed. But we have a bigger challenge when we add the thought that gravity is assumed to travel 'instantly'; or 20 billion times the speed of light (Tom Van Flandern, 1998).* So it is wrong to suggest nothing can travel faster than the current speed of light; gravity most definitely does. Does that mean that light once travelled much faster also? If so the Earth is much younger and put the 'millions of years' dating under threat (see chapters 41 and 44 and appendix 1).

In 2007 our attendance rose to 122,500, an amazing 14% increase which vindicated all the hard work and new investment which was happening. We

* 'The speed of Gravity, what the experiments say', Tom Van Flandern; *Physics Letters A*, December 21st 1998.

were also very excited to achieve a Finalist award in South West Tourism's Large Leisure Attraction competition. This was our highest accolade yet, as it put us in the top four for the whole of the South West, which stretches from Gloucester to Cornwall and contains scores of old established attractions and expensively founded ones, much better known than Noah's Ark Zoo Farm.

This was Adam Beaumont's last submission for us. We were very sorry to lose his great talents as he moved to his long-awaited fast track in the civil service, which we had been preparing him for since his arrival! In his place came Samantha Cordrey, fresh from a marketing degree; pretty, vivacious and full of enthusiasm and ideas, and capable of getting things done. Hayley Walker had also been to see us in April, just before she finished at Cambridge and was about to be married and become Hayley Lung. Hayley was petite, very bright and attractive with a strong faith and a surprising sense that we might need an education officer! Christina and I were so surprised, and so pleased with Hayley, her qualifications and Christian maturity that we felt she was right to create a job for. When she arrived she set about creating an education department, offering workshops, improving our displays and began taking animal shows, with three others of us. Sadie's job of supervising work experience students was also growing, from 42 in 2006, to 65 in 2007 (then 78 in '08, and 96 in '09) so she needed her own desk and telephone space. Sadie also took over the contacting of holiday volunteer youngsters from Christina, who had been doing this since we began, from her further list of 50 or so 13-year-olds and upwards.

2007 had been a landmark year for us. Not only in attendance and competition but the whole place seemed such a wonderful place to live and work in. Every day there were coaches arriving full of excited chattering children and their teachers or parents. The valley was filled with laughter and shouting as youngsters discovered so many new exciting things to see and to do. There were screams of joy from the zip lines and slides in the adventure play grounds and little people ran and jumped and skipped like spring lambs on all the grassy areas. Even the chicken joined in the fun as they often chased the young visitors while the parents rocked with laughter. I saw a little boy one day sitting solemnly for five minutes with a chicken on his head. The big rhinos and giraffe were an undoubted wow-factor, but the visitors' book said 'the chicken rock!'

56

2008: Celebrations, Developments and Very Wet Weather

EARLY IN 2008 WE BOUGHT TWO FEMALE ZEBRAS, TO LIVE WITH ZEBEDEE. We called them Zara and Zoe. Zoe was sent to us almost guaranteed pregnant, because she was fat; but could not be confirmed pregnant because almost all zoos have no way of containing animals for scanning. The BBC was interested in installing a web-cam, because no live baby zebra had been televised at birth, and very few are born in this country. The first night I suggested the web-cam was not high enough to escape the giraffe's attention, but was not heeded. Gerald the giraffe duly licked the camera to death! The next web cam went up a little higher; and we waited for two months for the zebra birth, to no avail. The zebra had been over-fed. On the right diet, and with a big paddock for exercise, she had shrunk! The BBC were disappointed, I was very upset, too. The zebra had cost a lot of money. It confirmed my plan that is universal in the farming world but rare in zoos, to build containing crushes for all major animals in future. The giraffe race was now adapted to control the zebras, to inject or examine them.

We also decided to get some ostriches. These are the world's biggest bird, but they lay the smallest egg in proportion to their body; a 150kg bird lays a 1kg egg. By contrast the world's smallest bird lays the biggest egg in proportion to its body – the bee hummingbird weighs 1.6g and each of its one or two eggs weigh 0.41g, this is a very slightly greater effort, at 25% of its body weight, than a kiwi whose egg is over 20% body weight Most zoo keepers are afraid of ostriches, but I knew that ostrich farmers handle them all the time, so I asked an ostrich farmer if we could buy a male and two females from him and if he would give three of the keepers, Chris, James and Mark, training on handling them. We took a horse box down to Devon on the day; and learned how to catch an ostrich by the head and pull its head down below its knees, while backed against a wall, at which point it cannot not kick (unlike a rhea or emu, which can). At this stage you hood it by holding its beak in one hand and sliding a spare sleeve off your arm and over the ostrich's head and letting go. As soon as an ostrich is hooded it stands still and can be pushed to a suitable place, examined or treated.

We also put them with the giraffe and the zebras in the enclosure next to the rhinos and called it the Africa section. Chris, the electrician, spent a lot of trouble installing African music for when people arrive. We had already put other animals together in continental groups. Zoning the park was one of those God-guided things we cannot claim to have consciously planned, but we discovered that our animal enclosures were zoned with almost no re-arrangement. We named areas Africa, North America, South America and Australasia and Hayley, our Education Officer made display boards to add educational value.

For much of the winter Barry and his team, helped by the grounds team, had been building the new 0-5's playground, mainly designed by Barry, with some exciting new outdoor play equipment; we called it the Termite Mountain Playground. It was opened and dedicated on my 70th birthday by Bishop Peter Maurice, of Taunton. We gave free entry for all over-70s. Lots came, and being older and polite they said thank you afterwards!

We had also had a party for 60 local friends that day in our classroom barn, and had held a party for all our children and grandchildren and some old friends of all of us, at Redwood Lodge Hotel a few days earlier. I often led meetings and spoke publicly, but usually try to hide behind the subject I am speaking about so that my presence is secondary. On this occasion I was unavoidably the centre of attention for a while, which was very nice but was even better when all our children and grandchildren joined in a birthday song they had written, with more than a dozen musical instruments which they had kept secret from me. I felt so proud of each of them as they contributed to the performance in front of all our other guests too. What a family to know are out there doing their best.

When we had brought the Siamang Gibbons into the collection the previous year, I had made a display, as I have mentioned, in consultation with my friend and farm consultant, Professor Stuart Burgess, about the 20 major differences between apes and man, with the proposal that these were so different that they should not be in the same classified order. This year I produced the draft of a leaflet and sent it to the director of BIAZA for checking. She sent it to other zoologists. Their conclusion was that all but a few small details of the differences were true, but so what? We say they are related. Why do you want to make such a fuss? I should not try to let facts get in the way of a good story, apparently! We made another display and printed a leaflet. Some more atheist websites photographed the display and once again treated it with derision and mockery, but never a word about the science. I wonder why?

This was also the year for our next DEFRA Zoo Inspection, this time with two Inspectors because we had too many animals for one. All the animals were deemed well kept, but we needed to upgrade our feed rooms; these were also in the public area, so should ideally be moved, along with the treatment room.

However, I strongly disagreed with one inspector over the handling of our alligators. We had been handling our young alligators for the last two years; they were very tame and we put sticky tape round their jaws to bring them to the public, then washed it off afterwards. We later replaced the tape with cotton tape and velcro; the alligators showed no sign of stress and visitors were very pleased to be close to, and look closely at them. They are unlike any of the lizards and have many special design features: ossioderms down the back for helping control their temperature, eyes, ears and nose on the same plane for keeping above water, unique and powerful immune and digestive systems, five front and four back toes, three of which have claws. Alligators are capable of growing to be the largest reptile and are very dangerous. The inspectors (more precisely, one of them in particular) objected to us bringing them in to animal shows on the grounds of an alligator's right not to be displayed, not on safety grounds!

We were undoubtedly being treated unfairly, as other zoos are allowed to train and handle exotic animals. We feel it very important that all our animals are kept in a good environment and are friendly and as close as possible to the public. We continued to catch our alligators each week to weigh them and put a cloth strap mask on their face now to do this; our 'keeper experience' people can be close to them, but we have had to stop bringing them in to animal shows. Unfair? Absolutely. There is no right of appeal.

We had started two 'keeper experiences' this year to allow the public to get close to the primates and reptiles in one and the big zoo animals of rhinos, giraffe and tapirs in the other. It also increased our revenue, which goes towards staff training and new staff facilities. The keepers enjoy it and judging by the comments by the increasing numbers booking in, so do the customers. It is truly awesome to be touching the big animals and only at a zoo like ours can anyone get to feed and be close to the smaller exotic ones.

Importantly, the zoo inspectors had repeated they did not want any more expansion to our zoo until hikers were being kept out of the protective zoo boundary fence. This gave added impetus to the matter of diversion of the existing footpaths on to our new one. Very little had happened with our footpaths in over a year, apart from the great irritation of the council insisting we install disabled access deer-fence height kissing gates into our perimeter fence, in place of the Cotswold-style ladder stiles we put in two years before. This was despite the fact that they were to be moved within a year, and despite the fact that only a miracle would get a disabled person past several ordinary stiles to reach these new ones. As the council provided the kits, we installed these.

Meanwhile, our five-year plan had been with the planners for seven months since August 2007. Its production had taken six months and in total cost over

£10,000 to have it drawn up, including the details, a topographical survey for a new café and plans for the rest of the zoo area. It was not even to be 'received' by the planners for a long time yet. They have targets for dealing with a planning application in eight weeks, or thirteen weeks for a commercial development; so, disgracefully and as I have mentioned, they just left our five-year plan sitting there for months, despite many requests, because it was not a planning application! Eventually after complaining to several councillors, another planning officer was given our file, in February 2008. To our astonishment he immediately started asking for more things that the five-year plan requirement did not mention. Why was there no joined up thinking? So we were asked for first an access plan, then a few weeks later, an energy plan, an ecology plan, and a health and safety plan; some of these were already in the five-year plan, but to tick some boxes we should have been told about, they had to be in separate document form. Our application was yet to take many economically damaging months to complete, as we were clearly their guinea pigs to try the procedure on. A couple of months later (!) they wanted a list of staff qualifications, a disability access audit and a response to a health and safety audit done a few weeks earlier.

By this time, May, I was keen to put in an application for building our big cat enclosure, because I knew it would need thirteen weeks to pass it and we needed to start work in August, while the ground was dry. We put in the application, but found that it could not be dealt with until the five-year plan had been received. We then received a demand for a flood risk assessment! The farm is at 450 feet on a ridge overlooking wetlands on each side! Then, as late as December 15th 2008 we received a request for a waste disposal policy, for food waste, animal waste and human waste! This was in response to a new Government regulation in October requiring such in planning applications. I replied within an hour but the Christmas holiday meant the application wasn't registered until after Christmas – too late for the planning meeting on January 7th. This was yet another delay to our tiger enclosure. By the end of 2008 our five-year plan had become a three-year plan, as two years had already passed since January '07, when permission was first requested!

Moving the footpaths was even slower. There are two ways of moving a footpath; by Town and Country Planning Act, i.e. when a development receiving planning permission requires it, or by Highways Act, which usually takes longer, when the development does not necessarily require it, but there are other reasons (in our case the zoo inspectors' health and safety requirement) that do. We went for both permissions at the same time, just in case. Hikers are notoriously obstructive in not allowing even the most reasonable changes to be made. I don't blame them; most landowners hate footpaths because a tiny minority of walkers are very difficult. Walkers have been known to complain to the RSPCA if they see a lame animal, or even if they see after-birth hanging from a cow's back end! We would all prefer no footpaths. Footpaths were originally used by farm staff to get to work or to the village church, shop or pub; now they are used entirely for leisure, often by people who cannot read a map, or do not even carry a map. Often people walk anywhere they want and apologise if accosted far from a footpath. We have had animal rights people walking in by a footpath and quickly leave it when no one was looking, to go into the visitor area to take photographs to try to incriminate us.

Consultations lasted 18 months until our application was finally registered, in July '08. The footpath diversion actual job was then given to a man who was sick for six months! I wondered what would happen if the person required to feed my animals or milk cows was sick that long. Paperwork is apparently an unimportant job and requires no deputy. The result was, our tiger arrival was put off again and again. Then when the planning permission was actually granted, formal consultations on footpath removal could begin. I began to think we were becoming a site of special persecution. The council officers' paper trails were again jeopardising the economic life of the community they were paid to serve. I felt sure the council's delays would cost us between £50,000 and £100,000 in lost visitor attendance next Easter and told them so. It made no difference.

2008 will go down in the record books as the latest harvest since combine harvesting began. Combining on the majority of farms began in my lifetime; I can remember all the exceptional harvests. By September 7th, the farming community had received seven weeks of rain; almost no wheat harvest had been done, the forecast was poor. That Sunday I felt I should ring three local vicars and asked if they would pray in their churches for fine weather, and especially for the Azores anticyclone to come and sit on Britain. I had been praying daily for fine weather for many weeks; often we had a fine day but wet night. Our visitor numbers are very dependent on fine weather; our numbers were down quite badly, but not disastrously. However, God had not sent us the stretch of fine weather farmers needed, yet He had promised to Noah and his descendants – who include, as far as I am concerned, all of us now – that 'seed-time and harvest will not fail' (*Genesis* 8:22). We prayed in the churches on Sunday 7th. On Monday 8th it was wet. On Tuesday the weather was poor but on the weather forecast chart a finger of high pressure came out for 500 miles from the Azores anticyclone towards mid-UK; this built over two days and by Friday 12th the weather was sunny and all the combines in the country were rolling. That anticyclone stayed there for three weeks; time for everyone to get their harvest in, but then mysteriously it went, and there was wet, or at least dull, again for three months. At Christmas 2008 a third of the West Country's next year's crop was not planted. But we had been given the weather we had urgently needed for the harvest.

I felt that despite the summer's poor attendance and poorer than expected receipts, we still needed to expand with big cats. So in September, despite delays in planning permission and because I thought the permission was bound to come very soon, we used the same weather window and started doing work below ground on the tiger enclosure, which should not offend the planners. We started by digging in the water pipes, including a large underground tank for harvesting rainwater. This water was to come from land drains and from the gutters on the tiger house roof. We dug two ponds and their circulation systems; drainage pipes and electricity conduits, including laying the concrete pad that the tiger house would be bolted to. We also erected the 105, 4-metre-high poles of the tiger fence. This was the wettest field on the farm; I was relieved to have this wet job done in reasonably dry weather. We worked down the ground and planted the tiger surface grass on the last day before it rained hard at the onset of winter. We did not want to upset the planners, no matter how inefficient they might be. Perhaps God was in the delay.

While Barry was putting in an underground rainwater collecting tank, a hiker who was clearly an enemy saw the underground work and reported us to the council's planning enforcement officer. I wrote to our planner, with copies to five councillors, saying that although this was underground work related to the big cat enclosure, as the five-year plan was not passed this was still agricultural land. I was putting in a pad of concrete that could be used as a sheep folding area and the underground tank could be a sheep dip if the tiger plans were refused. I did not need planning permission for either of these on agricultural land. Eventually they were placated, but not before the Planning Enforcement Office had been sent out. We hoped that planning permission might be hurried along by this. We were wrong. Nevertheless, I still felt planning permission could come by Christmas, so I ordered the building in October and it arrived a month later, in pieces, which we stored on the concrete pad ready for permission to start. I felt sure we could have tigers in by Easter '09 to help our finances. In the meantime we switched our attention to the new meat kitchen and cold store and to moving the treatment rooms as the inspectors had asked.

In the wet summer of 2008 we also brought prairie dogs into an enclosure we had built the previous year. We had been asked to set up an ethics committee under the Zoo Licensing Act, to consider matters to do with finding and managing the animals; these meetings had to be minuted. I asked a retired clergyman at our church, Paul Pike, if he would be chairman of the ethics committee. Paul had been a missionary in Japan for many years and had a good background knowledge of animal life and of the Christian issues related to keeping them. I also asked our vet, Claire Tibbs, head keeper Chris Wilkinson and Hayley Lung as education officer to be the other members. I wanted to discuss tiger procurement, elephant procurement and details of the enclosures we had planned. They all suggested that prairie dogs could dig downwards a long way, so we should put weldmesh across the entire surface of their enclosure, and build an earth hill over the top. An expensive decision, that very few zoos had done, but then we wanted our enclosures to be bigger and better than most zoos.

Christina and I decided to go to Martin Lacey's Great British Circus, in Colchester in September 2008, where Martin, as one of the few DEFRA licensed animal trainers in the country, showed us round. Martin is a real animal lover and has a saying 'a day without animals is like a day without sunshine'. As we went to each tiger pen the tigers came to him and each gave him an affectionate lick in the face through the weldmesh. Martin said 'my tigers are all in love with me'. We then watched them performing in the ring, where they were treated totally differently from the old fashioned circus shown on BBC and ITV where whips and chairs in the faces of the big cats to taunt them were universal. Martin was very disparaging of such bad techniques, which glorified the animal handlers for being daring. Here the emphasis was on wonderful animals, which were encouraged to do what they wanted to do by nature. The six tigers all seemed very pleased to do what they were asked to do, ending in three of them lying on the ground and rolling over together. They were rewarded with a treat after each command.

Martin is not only a DEFRA (the government ministry responsible) licensed animal trainer, but his circus is subject to all the inspection requirements of DEFRA. Furthermore, an academic body appointed by DEFRA, the Circus Animal Working Group, produced a report in 2008 saying 'there is no scientific evidence against the principle of animals in circus'. They found that the circus gave the animals far more stimulation than zoos, but zoos gave them more space (usually). This left circuses on a level playing field with any farm or zoo. Clearly any animal owner could be cruel and would deserve to be prosecuted for that. Martin, like us, was hotly opposed to any cruelty; which is counterproductive anyway, as cruelty just makes animals become frightened and unpredictable. So Martin encouraged his circus audiences to visit the animals afterwards in their sleeping quarters. He was not trying to hide them away. Animal rights protestors ignored these facts and the scientific evidence, and instead used old films to pretend nothing has changed in circus, as they did with battery hens. They were being deliberately deceptive, it seemed to me, as they had been when I was young and in the League Against Cruel Sports. I doubted whether they care about animal welfare anyway.

We were also shown Callum, the baby camel that Lucie had reared back in 2002, and whom I knew well, because I saw him every day that year. He had been born by surprise in his mother's first winter with us. We did not know whether she was pregnant on arrival as camel pregnancy is 15 months. One morning a friend riding her pony through the farm spotted a steaming mass in the camel pen early one frosty morning and rode back quickly to tell us. Camels do not have the same maternal instincts that cows do, who lick their calves immediately. Camels' tongues do not come out further than their teeth so they abandon their young, only to return and bite their heads or kick them into action! Sometimes they 'talk' to them. As Callum was not getting up he appeared to be abandoned without milk or care.

So Lucie had taken him in hand, fed him some artificial colostrum (first milk) and mothered him all day, then slept the night with him and with Barley the dog, under a lamp to keep them all warm. The press and TV companies were fascinated by the story and very soon he was a celebrity, responsible for helping raise our visitor numbers that year. We brought him into animal shows and even into the Christmas nativity, accompanied by a wise man! The next spring he had become a bit of a handful so went back to Martin, who used him in his camel trekking business and hired him out to pantomimes and theatre. We heard that he had gone on a stage in Birmingham with other camels.

I had also seen Callum in 2005, when Martin hired him to our daughter, Annie, to do a Christmas nativity pageant among Anthony Gormley's beach statues at Crosby near Liverpool, called 'Christmas in Another Place'. I had helped Annie take the now adult camel to several schools, advertising the nativity. Now in Colchester I wondered if Callum would still remember me. I gave him some carrots. When we were later sitting beside the ring, every time Callum went round the circus ring in the interval with his passenger, he turned his head towards me as if to say, 'Hi dad, how am I doing!' Callum looked in top condition, as did all the animals, including all the tigers.

As I reached 70, Christina and I decided to start drawing our pensions. We had never taken anything from Noah's Ark receipts; but now we hoped that the profit from the rest of the arable farm could also go into growing the Ark. As our very modest annuity matured we decided to invest the lump sum into part of a wind turbine. On the basis of wind figures published for our area and projections by the turbine company we decided that it was probably a good economy, would save a little of the world's energy reserves, and also be a reasonably good investment, perhaps to eventually install three 15 KW wind turbines; each big enough to produce a third of our energy requirement. We obtained planning permission for two turbines surprisingly quickly; the government does not allow opposition to these if appearance alone is the objection. The cynics were quick to point out that these would only turn for some of the time and are not very efficient. We knew that, but energy costs were such that if we used all the turbine energy ourselves it would be a reasonable return, at our average wind speed of 6.5m/s, even at 13.4% of maximum output, which they are expected to run at. It would also show our visitors and our grandchildren that we wanted to do what we could for the planet.

At the end of the season we also managed to procure some Azara's Agoutis and Maras, which were surplus to other collections within BIAZA. But our attendances and income were a great disappointment. All rural tourism in the west was feeling dejected. Some were 30% down on last year. We were expecting, needing and hoping our attendances to be up, to reflect our added investments. Instead we were about 11% down. But, because we were offering keeper experiences, had put our prices up a little and the shop had done quite well, the total receipts were 1% up. God never promised us honey and roses everyday, but He said He would meet our needs, and he said He would never leave us. George Muller, renowned for his prayerful life and for opening his Bristol orphanages was once asked 'George do you find God always answers your prayers first time?' He replied 'Oh no. He likes my company much too much for that!'

57

2009: Frustration and Excitements

The press were hyping recession as if there was no other news. Everyone seemed to agree that lack of confidence was causing lack of spending, causing recession. The press seemed bent on sapping what little confidence was left. I always felt the oil producers deserved more blame than they received. When oil rose to $140 a barrel oil producers were warned the price could plunge the world into recession, but they kept production low anyway. It was very bad news for us farmers, as the prices of fertilizers and oil for drying the harvest all soared in the summer to autumn of 2008. All commodities that needed oil the most, like steel, heating gas and all transport costs, rose depressingly fast and far; it all began a loss of confidence. A highly inflated property market became exposed as confidence suddenly collapsed, which in turn eroded borrowers' ability to repay loans. This then, but only then, led to American and British building societies and banks being found to be lending money they did not have to buy property that was valued far too highly. The government had to step in with our tax money to pay for everyone's greed; and to keep bankers in jobs they should have lost, but which paid far better than our own. Why did servants of the banks, those who were managing them, get bonuses for bad work? And how dare the board members, on behalf of the owners who were the share holders, reward incompetence? All bankers came out of the crisis with very bad reputations. A cartoon summed it up; with a sign in a dark alleyway 'Beware, bankers operating in this area'!

Most of the early recession happened when we were closed, from November '08 onwards. God seemed to be shaking everything that was shakeable. This was the banks' turn to be shaken; along with wealthy investors, property owners and lots of other people by consequence. These things are usually a challenge to us to pray and ask God questions. Then expect some answers. Were we all listening?

We clearly had two responses we personally could make. Do we act with caution and not appointment two replacement staff and a further two new staff, put the tiger enclosure and wind turbine on hold, batten down the hatches and wait for it all to pass? Or do we try to set an example of confidence, in our case it would be in God caring about our every prayer and every move, and keep investing for growth. I spent much time in prayer in late 2008 and early 2009, trying to be certain this was faith not optimism; that God was in this, not just my ambition. Christina and I both felt we should press on and set an example of continuing the investment the country needed so badly, to recover from the recession.

Our five-year plan had clearly caused us serious delays. The tigers that could have arrived in 2008 slipped to March 2009, then June. So tigers were not going to help our early-season publicity. By October '08 we decided we needed to introduce something new for 2009 and began work on our Bird Water World and Wellie Splash Pool.

Jon and the grounds team had removed the six-year-old aviary fences, which did not look good as a first impression of the zoo. They mechanically dug out several hundred tonnes from our old silted-up ponds; lined them, poshed them up, and reinstated them on five levels. We had started pumping well-water to keep the ponds topped up, some years before, to save treated water. Now we bought a bigger pump and pumped the water to start in the new Wellie Splash Pool; from where it gravitated down to the other ponds, via four waterfalls. The grounds team built a pathway through the ducks and hens for the public to have good access to these, which were very popular with small and big people alike. The keepers had removed all the aviary birds to the arable barn for the duration of building this, as the aviary was not now fox proof. When it was finished, and the heaviest snows for many years had melted, and the staff teams had sorted out all the mess, the birds were brought back. We procured some white peacocks, Reeves pheasant, Tufted Aylesbury, endangered-in-the-wild Carolinas Teal, and Guinea fowl to add to the ten or so varieties of birds that were in it before. The grounds team put up a 20-feet high netting roof to keep the flying birds inside. The keepers helped the whole project along too, with their specific bird housing buildings. The peacocks now had perches 15 feet high.

The Wellie Splash Pool was designed to provide moving water for children to have fun damming up and letting go, splash themselves and others with, and with a lot of stepping stones across a very shallow wide pool. This was constructed in appalling weather by Barry and Tim, Barry's cheerful brother-in-law and highly skilled builder who had joined the team on a full-time basis a few months before. They put up a tent in sub-zero temperatures, over the main part of the Wellie Splash site, put a gas heater in it to raise the temperature and avoid the cement freezing, and built it to try and be ready for half term. In the event the builders excelled themselves, despite two younger members of their team being off injured for a month. They did not quite have it ready for half term as it was more complex than originally intended and was ready for opening on a beautiful fine day, on March 2nd, by some teachers, parents and children, from the brand new Trinity Primary School, Portishead. Several newspapers were represented. I reminded the parents and children that water was vital to us; God had made us out of more than half water, men were 60% and women 55% water, that 71% of the Earth's surface is water, and water comes in the form of vapour and clouds, ice and snow, rain and streams and oceans. Now let's have lots of fun with Wellie Splash. Christina read a prayer of dedication and Mrs Carter, the form teacher, cut the ribbon.

We had been wondering for some time why our application to join EAZA (European Association of Zoos and Aquaria) had been so seriously delayed. In January, Samantha rang the EAZA office in Amsterdam to ask what had happened to delay us by three years. They told us that BIAZA had told them first we had been provisional members with them until September 2007, then that our Christian beliefs were not compatible with EAZA!

The consequence of EAZA's decision for us was that we could not receive a female giraffe. A few weeks later I wrote back to Mr de Boer, the EAZA Chairman as follows:

> Dear Mr de Boer,
> A few weeks ago I wrote to Alex Rübel asking why we had received no reply to our application to join EAZA, three years ago.
> After some correspondence he wrote this email:
>
> Dear Anthony,
> Your website is how you communicate with your visitors and one way in which you transfer the education message. In line with our code of ethics, this education message has to be based on accepted scientific facts. What Noah's Ark is doing as education/communication is not based on scientific facts, what you are doing is putting a question mark to accepted science and comparing it to the creation narrative, based on the poor science of so-called 'creation scientists'. Your whole website is based on this, your links are carefully directed to creationist websites, and throughout the education section you make explicit mention of a creator.
> Therefore we will not reconsider your application as we do not consider Noah's Ark to be a good fit for our organisation.
> Alex Rübel
> Chair Membership & Ethics Committee

I had previously mentioned that we were building a new website, for several months. We now have that website up and running. As it so happens it answers his criticisms. First, all our education is based on scientific facts; second, he complained about a 'specific mention of a creator' on our education pages. That is no longer there. But of course there are many Christian schools in the UK, who expect us to provide scientific Christian education, so there is a link for them to other pages, now included under 'Creation Research'. All our presenters of Animal Shows and Education classes base their presentations on scientific facts.

I was a little alarmed about Alex suggesting it was wrong to be 'putting a question mark to accepted science'. Is that not what Copernicus, Galileo, Darwin and Pasteur and many other Europeans were doing in their day? And was that not what was wrong with recent European dictators; that no one questioned them? Ironically the reason Europe is free of the fascist dictators is because countries like UK and USA, that believed in God, in prayer, and with the creation narrative took up arms to oppose them! That freedom was won in my lifetime, so I am keen that it is not lost by a younger generation, naïve to the consequences.

In the UK at the moment, despite no contrary view to Neo-Darwinism being allowed on British television, '40% of the public believe creationism or Intelligent Design should be taught alongside evolution in schools' (MORI poll, Institute of Ideas, 4th Feb 2009); and 20% of science teachers likewise (*Times Ed Supplement* Nov 2008). We at Noah's Ark are convinced that there is evolution everywhere, from bacteria to galaxies; and are doing research to discover more. Yet among Zoos I think we are the only one to put all scientific views of origins on display, whether we agree with them or not. They are appreciated as fair by visitors of all faiths and none.

As I think EAZA will be enriched by having us, I am writing this to you and to our representatives from UK on your council, to appeal against the above decision as being unfair. I would be pleased to discuss this wider, or in more detail, in closed or in open debate.

Yours sincerely

Anthony Bush Owner/CEO

I received a reply a few days later that EAZA were not allowing our membership; I replied to it with a longer, more reasoned argument, asking our BIAZA members of EAZA for their support in this. It all fell on deaf ears. Meanwhile what were we to do about female giraffes? BIAZA and its influence of the Stud Book Keeper, refused to let us have hybrid females, but offered males. I did not want fighting males at Noah's Ark, even if it was natural for males in the wild to keep together. And how could we ever get breeding tigers in an EEP programme?

One cloudy morning in January a fox apparently killed one of our female ostriches! We had found the ostrich dead and without a head one morning, but otherwise it had been healthy. A post mortem revealed that the ostrich had died of a huge blow to its abdomen. Something, perhaps the fox, had clearly frightened her and she had run till she hit a wooden fence post with a big crash. When she died the fox must have eaten her head. Jon, the groundsman, called up the fox at the same spot the next night, and shot it. We concluded that female ostriches on their own do not have the instinct to chase off foxes. We had to get a male quickly.

The press heard about this story and rang me and asked if the ostrich could have been killed by a wild puma or other big cat. I replied that 'it is possible, but unlikely, as it was probably a fox'. They took the 'it is possible' part of the story and quite a few column inches then described local sightings of the beast. The story was a bit of fun for a few days, as local 'experts' had clearly decided it couldn't possibly be a fox!

We had previously purchased a male ostrich with the females a year before. He had been an old male, but recommended for being fairly quiet. We had not been told he was in love with an emu! When he arrived with us he could see three emus about fifty yards away. We wondered why he kept running at the fence. He got past the protective inside fence and damaged himself on the outer fence. We repaired the fence and the vet sewed up the ostrich. Then I rang the previous owner to find out why the ostrich wanted to get out towards the emus. He told us the story of ostrich/emu love. So we removed the emus, which we needed to anyway, in to our Australasia Zone, 400 yards away. Unfortunately an ostrich has a very small brain, smaller than its large eye; which meant he could see better than he could think. He then tried running at the fence on the other side of his big field, nearest to the new emu field. Eventually he appeared so frustrated that he ran round and round the field one day till he collapsed with exhaustion. The keepers carried him in to his shed on a plywood stretcher, where he died. After this, with hind sight, we should have bought another male to replace him, who would have seen off the fox. But we hoped for a quieter life, and already had two females for company anyway.

But we now needed a new male, so, after locating one over the phone, Christina and I took a day off (well, half one anyway) and drove to an ostrich farm on the edge of Gloucester to collect him. The ostrich keepers rounded up all six ostriches from one field into their shed to hood the male; but unfortunately he broke away, taking the yard gate with him. The ostriches were extremely upset and the owner and keeper both wondered if the birds were now too hyped-up to get in again that afternoon. I suggested we ask God to help; and then prayed aloud with them that the ostriches would quieten and go back to their shed. You cannot drive a flock of ostriches, they run in all directions! I then said 'give the Lord time'; and we waited and had a good conversation about ostriches and God and other things. After a short while the ostriches did indeed go back in their shed for food and the keeper said 'It looks as though your little prayer was answered'. The male ostrich was then hooded; pushed to our car trailer, and we were away.

February 2009 had been heralded from the previous year as being a time when Darwin's 200th anniversary would be celebrated. It certainly was. There were several major BBC programme series, each advertised for many weeks, in which the big Darwinist guns were wheeled out and given monopoly air time. No dissent was allowed; no programme with any other view. 'He transformed our understanding of life on earth' was a frequent excuse for Darwinian adoration. Did he? What they seem to be referring to was the suggestion that life could happen and develop without God. Shame on them. Charles Darwin was a very moderate man, who was still a creationist when he left the Galapagos Islands and remained a deist till the end! I wrote this letter, which we posted to all professors of geology and biology in the whole country and to the press:

> Dear Scientific colleague,
> Open letter: Darwin 200; a new paradigm;
> Creation plus evolution.
> I have recently sat through three of the BBC's 'Darwin 200' series. Framed in some of the best television our license fees have made possible, have been some shameful claims that I feel sure would have made Darwin himself cringe.
> In both of the first two programmes Darwin's last paragraph of *Origin*, had been misquoted. 'There is grandeur in this view of life, with its several powers; having been originally breathed by the Creator into a few forms or into one…' Both programmes had removed 'by the Creator'. In the third, Attenborough claimed Darwin had turned away from his earlier belief in God, in later life. But Darwin wrote this, three years before he died; 'In my most extreme fluctuations I have never been an atheist in the sense of denying the existence of a God…..It seems to me absurd to doubt that a man may be an ardent Theist & an evolutionist.' (Letter to John Fordyce, May 7 1879; *Spencer; Darwin and God*, SPCK, 2009).

Then, all the programmes invent creationist beliefs; who, they insist, believe in immutability of species, as Owen and other 19th century scientists did. No wonder Owen et al did then; for example the goldfinch and the chaffinch species are from the same environment but look very different; they seem to remain unaltered. But this was their science, not their Bible. No creationist believes fixity of species now; some of us accept that the Genesis 'kind' points to a vastly wider evolution; of perhaps 350,000 species of beetle from one pair; and stick insects appearing first with no wings then with complete wings; these point to a creation with huge potential to evolve. A few phyla, orders, or perhaps families have been created to evolve. Mendel's work hinted at these pre-programmed genes. DNA appears to be a language, which we can read, and that I expect God can speak. The scientific quest is to discover if this is so; and the limits of evolution.

Meanwhile, the BBC's robust-looking facade of a neo-Darwinist tree of life remains on shaky foundations. Biogenesis (already pre-armed with DNA) 'crawled out of Precambrian ooze' (Leroi); or 'started in the sea' (Attenborough). It conveniently assumes the design and properties of the atoms, and laws of physics were just 'there'. Then 'life' somehow acquired mutational properties that helped it change into single celled eukaryotes, then sponges and 'bodies strengthened by an internal rod' (Attenborough), etc, till we arrive, by unguided accident. So is that more scientific than Genesis? Why are the BBC and educationists presenting these ideas as the only explanation for the arrival of the vast array life forms both now and in the fossil record? Why is dissent censored off air and out of classrooms?

As Richard Dawkins has said 'next time somebody tells you that something is true, why not say to them: "What kind of evidence is there for that?"' So what kind of evidence is there for biogenesis and genetic diversity without a creator?

This zoo is sponsoring a website; written by a man who I think is a modern Galileo; with a new paradigm, probably as unpopular, yet as correct, as Galileo's. It is www.earthhistory. org.uk It suggests that both American Creationism and neo-Darwinism are wrong, because both are dogma-driven; not studying the empirical age of sedimentary rocks, layer by layer. We propose that there is a completely different explanation of the fossil record; and invite examination and discussion. This is a scientific enquiry.

We look forward to your reply.

Yours sincerely,

Anthony Bush. Curator/Owner

The subsequent silence from academics was deafening! It was difficult to know what to do about this incessant output about the origins of life on earth; in which its writers only wrote from one view, which would be easy to refute, if only that was allowed. I had written to the BBC on this many times to no avail. Meanwhile, they seemed oblivious that 'the idea that changed the world' was only the idea that there was no God, so people could do what they wanted. The social distress of the moral vacuum it generated and of its subsequent sex without responsibility, I have already outlined. The Darwinists are reluctant to admit to Darwin's influence on Hitler, Stalin, Mao Zedong and Pol Pot; but all these men were profoundly influenced by him to see people as disposable animals, rather than as beings created in God's image.

Alfred Nobel, the inventor of dynamite, had read his own obituary accidentally printed prematurely, in a Paris newspaper before he died: 'L'Agent de Mort, est Mort', the agent of death is dead, it said. Nobel was so shocked that he rewrote his will, depriving his family of most of their fortune, and endowed the five Nobel Prizes as his legacy. Darwin, on the other hand was told by his teacher, Professor Adam Sedgwick that if he published his *Origin of Species*, the world 'would suffer a damage that might brutalise it and sink the human race into a lower grade of degradation than any into which it has sunk since written records tell us of its history'.* Sedgwick realised that without belief in God, British people like all others could easily revert to total selfishness and moral anarchy. Darwin ignored his advice. Sedgwick was proved horrifically right. Much of the world went on to believe we were merely naked apes, so instead of behaving nobly, self-sacrificially, as made in God's image, they willfully followed their worst instincts. The world suffered one of the most violent centuries of all history. Sexual anarchy became widespread, with its bitter harvest of unwanted pregnancies, abortions, sexually transmitted infections, adulterous marriage breakdowns, dysfunctional broken families. Behaviour is clearly every individual's responsibility, but Darwinism had encouraged man to behave at his animal-worst; it was mainly the God-fearing that kept conscience alive. Some argued with me that Christians had been violent at times, so were just as bad. They may have been, but Jesus clearly states 'love your enemies; do good to those who hate you'; so Catholics who had burnt Protestants or Muslims at the stake, were not obeying Jesus. Whereas Hitler's godless attempt to make his supreme race survive was a Darwinian idea and legacy. So too is man behaving sexually like a promiscuous animal.

I also sent the letter to 24 groups and individual Creationists, with a plea for

* Clark, *Darwin Before and After*, Paternoster, 1950

more unity among us. This has begun to bear fruit. Many people mean well, yet there is much disagreement between Creationists that needs discussion, some of it substantial. In the meantime I hope we can disagree without being disagreeable.

In March a fresh group of apparently angry atheist opposition sprang up, called Sink the Ark on a Facebook site. This time they wrote to BIAZA, complaining that we were creationists, teaching creation and therefore not teaching good science to children, and complaining that our website article about Charles Darwin made deeply offensive allegations about his legacy. What were BIAZA going to do about us? Miranda Stevenson, BIAZA Director, distanced herself from our position, but sent their emails on to me to deal with. She was also angry with them for the concerted attack they were making, with so many sending her the same email. She objected strongly that humanists, who should want freedom of speech, should now be opposing it.

These emails were not just *against* us, they were also very rude and abusive. So much so that some of the staff were upset. This was good for us as it was an opportunity to toughen up and learn to reply to evil with good. That was not easy. We were less than brilliant a few times, but have been learning! I answered each of the writers in detail; almost all of them shied away from scientific arguments and reverted to a religious rant against Christianity before long. I began to treat the correspondents like an angry Alpha Course, who were asking all the furious questions that perhaps others should have answered years before. I include some in appendix 6.

Their Facebook site, which our staff followed, also implied they were going to write to schools warning them about us. And they started saying things that were untrue. The office team complained to Facebook that they were libelling us, so their page was closed. They promptly hacked into our own Facebook site, which was telling children about new animal arrivals and chatting about the animals; instead, the atheists started libelling us on our own site! So we closed that too. They also raised a petition on the 10 Downing Street website, asking for the government to withdraw their support from us (which was uninformed, as we received none) and saying how disgraceful it was for Enjoy England to give us a Red Rose of the Visitor Attraction Quality Assurance Scheme (VAQAS). They achieved 1,470 signatures, including Richard Dawkins and several of the people who had been writing to BIAZA and us. I don't know how credible petitions like this are. Noah's Ark Zoo also appears on their list! And several names appear twice. See the No. 10 website for the petition and list of names.

The head of VAQAS came to visit because he had received so many complaining letters about us. He told us that Gordon Brown had 20,000 signatures asking for his own resignation! He also had a good look round and was impressed by our visitor's book, which was full of unsolicited compliments about all aspects of the zoo and its output. He thought we had nothing to worry about, but that our opponents had probably not visited us to see what we did, or if they had, were being very unreasonable.

It appeared most of this atheist frenzy came from a website of Bristol Professor of psychology Bruce Hood: 'A blog where science and superstition meet'. He had rung me and asked if he could bring a Michael Schermer to see me, a former fundamentalist Christian, the American founder of the Skeptics Society and editor of a magazine, *The Skeptic*. He sounded as though he might understand science and be open to a fellow sceptic like me. I agreed, but it appeared in a very short time that his background was history more than science and he was quickly out of his comfort zone in biology and geology, as was his friend. He and Bruce Hood later resorted to ridicule rather than intelligent argument, when Hood described their visit 'we went to visit the delightful but completely delusional Anthony Bush'. 'Delusional' I have since discovered is atheist-speak for 'believes in God'. Archbishop Rowan Williams was also called delusional on another atheist website. You might think it was the reverse was true, that it was delusional to think that everything comes from nothing, or indeed that anything can come from nothing!

At about the same time a Wikipedia article was written about us by a Bristol mechanics PhD student, Richard Craig and allies. It began totally against us, drawing heavily on Schermer and Hood, until our supporters modified it to contain some history and truth about awards and animals. The 'delusional' sentence and more has stayed on Wikipedia for three years, despite perhaps 25 attempts to modify it, which doesn't say much for Wikipedia's impartiality. My personal email address was at the bottom of the Bruce Hood blog, hence the torrent of abusive emails. I like robust argument and I am sure some atheists are different but none of those we have come across behave well. They seem to encourage rudeness, lies, half-truth, slander and anything else they think they can get away with to further their cause, whatever that is. Perhaps it is because they know that their argument is weak.

2009 was also the year for us to go yet more green. The globe is in trouble we are told; too much carbon is reaching the Earth's atmosphere. The debate raged over whether it is all our fault, or whether the sun is largely responsible. It is certainly true that renewable energy would reduce what we are putting in the atmosphere. Lots of other things could help clean up the planet a little. Green Tourism Awards were being offered in a scheme that awarded bronze, silver, gold, or unclassified. We felt we were ticking lots of the boxes so Samantha, our marketing manager, and Jon our head groundsman, got busy telling the rest of us what we should do to be even better. The new wind turbine was a huge start, and recycling roof water in the tiger enclosure and spring water in the Wellie Splash helped too. Planting 20,000 trees, including about 2,000 more trees each year right up to 2009, added to it as well. We were installing double glazing and good insulation in all our new buildings, putting in low energy light bulbs, collecting all the animal dung for composting and recycling on to the wheat fields. Our conservation areas for helping our native species, with ten or so bird and bat boxes, were also a part. We had been buying fair trade coffee and tea for the staff for years. We bought all our supplies locally where possible, but we still had to work on rubbish separation.

As I have mentioned I have grave doubts about global warming (see appendix 2). My biggest concern is that all major weather events that used to be called 'Acts of God' and caused us to turn to God for help and guidance (see *Amos* chapter 4), are now lumped together as 'climate change'. Hot, cold, wet, dry, hurricanes, gales, there is no need for a cause any more because an impersonal climate did it. Added to that, it is now all our collective fault, with no atonement except obeying all the edicts from control! If we are not careful we will be diverting money meant for the poor, like our Send a Cow African partners, into carbon-reducing projects, with poor scientific justification. My reading of the Bible points to God being very much in charge of both the weather and human decisions. If a sparrow does not fall without God, how can a billion tonnes of rain or snow? There are huge self-correcting mechanisms in nature. And He is very concerned about our attitude towards the poor.

There are also some very dubious things being said about extinctions of species based on a somewhat fanciful book by Norman Myers. He said in *Sinking Ark*, 1979, that one species every four years had gone extinct till 1900, and then quoted a 1974 conference 'guess' that 100 per year were disappearing. He then changed this, with no apparent justification, to 100 species per day! This figure reappeared like Chinese whispers, in one of the BBC series by Andrew Marr in 2009 as 27,000 species per year, without any supporting evidence. It is time this was confirmed by some science rather than just stated by conservationists wanting to justify their funding. There is a relative importance between species, too. If polar bears disappear it would be tragic. But 5,000 species of frogs cannot each have the same importance! We have actually tried to eradicate some insects, like warble flies, and are fighting several others, like mosquitoes, tsetse flies, locusts and many internal and external parasites.

Our 2009 visitor season opened in the snow. We cancelled the first day, a

Saturday, because icy roads made driving very dangerous, and it was due to snow that day. The following week was warmer but snow was around every day; attendance was 2,200 down on the previous year. The next week and subsequent fine weeks saw us overtake the previous year by March 20th.

But we were making no progress on the tiger enclosure. Just after February half term, North Somerset Council took up my request to come and visit us, before the planning committee meeting when they would be deciding about the tiger enclosure. We gave ten of them coffee in our café and explained how we had been their guinea pigs with the first five-year plan they had ever requested. No one had known how to do one. It had taken two years for them to finally receive it, and we were feeling economically damaged by it. I did not think I should tell them we were likely to make the biggest loss of my whole life this year; it might just mean they would lose confidence that we had a future. They seemed impressed with what they saw and wanted to help by speeding everything up as fast as possible. The following week, March 14th, their committee voted unanimously for permission for our tiger house to be started.

The footpath department were also now being helpful and had already begun informal consultations to move the footpaths, perhaps by May. A site meeting immediately arranged by our agent, Rebecca, proved sticky because, when we had been given retrospective planning permission to become a zoo in 2002 they had insisted on a zoo license but had not officially recorded their permission for us to be a zoo! So we were not a zoo. This meant that the footpaths could not be diverted under the very quick Planning Act route; but needed now to be diverted under the Highways Act. Council naivety (or was it ours?) in not knowing that having a zoo license did not make us a zoo, would cost us another £5,000 (plus £5,000 in agents' fees) for moving the coach park by five metres, installing a further 200 metres of boundary fence and six more disabled kissing gates, all to link with Nailsea.

Applying under the Highways Act also meant objections would be much more likely and possibly drawn out; an immediate threat to tiger arrival in May, and there were several objectors to placate. Meanwhile, visitors were driving in to the car park, enquiring about tigers and driving out again. Lack of tigers was harming our cash flow!

However, on March 14th when planning permission finally came through, our whole building and grounds team could focus on the new tiger enclosure; we hoped to have it ready for a June opening. Risk assessments had all been done, especially complicated by the site, which was under two sets of overhead electricity cables. The building contractor, John Wyatt and his family of three building sons erected the building frame and did the internal metal frameworks, doors and weldmesh walls; our grounds team worked on the five-metre high fences and gate fittings, the electric fences and the 3.5-metre stand-off barrier. The building and maintenance team worked on the water and electricity supplies, the ponds, the viewing platforms, two tiger platforms, and the internal concrete walls, windows, ceilings, kitchen fittings, automatic water troughs in each den and piecing everything together. The keepers did the internal tiling and painting, made five tiger beds indoors and two of the outdoor tiger climbing platforms. I was officially site manager and architect and Barry was the supervisor, so we had site meetings most days to discuss the details. The materials and outside contractor's costs were about £260,000.

At the other end of the farm our new wind turbine was erected by contractors on March 17th, on foundations that Barry and Tim had expertly laid a month beforehand, while we waited for planning permission for the tiger enclosure, and connected to the supply that Chris Moulding had spent days (and nights) connecting all the way (100 meters via three buildings) to our meters. It looked like a beautiful moving sculpture, giving us the promised clean energy. It was activated on March 20th by Liam Fox, our MP and dedicated in prayer by Rosie Lunn, the Rector of Wraxall. I spoke as follows:

> Wind power has been harnessed for at least 5,000 years, perhaps first by sailing boats on the Nile; the first windmills were pumping water by 200BC in China, Persia and the Roman Empire. By WW1 the USA were installing 100,000 wind pumps per year, mainly for pumping water, 6 million were working by 1920. Windmills have been used in Britain at least since the 14th century, to pump water, and grind grain.
>
> The first wind generator was made in Scotland by Prof James Blyth in 1887, who made a cloth-sailed one to light his cottage. He offered to use surplus power to light the village street, but his offer was turned down because the villagers (of Marykirk) thought electricity was the work of the devil. His third model powered his home for 25 years.
>
> In 1927 two Americans went commercial with wind generators and started a technology for remote areas of America, Africa and even Antarctica. Britain's first wind farm was in Delabole, Cornwall in 1991.
>
> The UK is the windiest country in Europe. We have put this one up because this is one of the windiest land sites in the area, with an average wind speed of 6.5m/sec or 14mph.
>
> According to the manufacturers a 15Kw turbine in our wind conditions, should produce 45MW of electricity per year; saving sending 45 tonnes of carbon from coal fired power stations into the atmosphere, the equivalent

to 12 cars a year (@ 0.36kg CO_2/mile), 2,150 mature trees (@21kg CO_2/tree/year.)

We have planted 20,000 trees in the last 5 years; these are still small but are probably 3 or 4 more turbine–equivalents.

We are going to see how this turbine performs; we will be delighted to tell people even if it a total failure. It should pay for itself in about five years. If we were a charity or school, we could have got a grant for it. We did not receive anything.

We unashamedly need God's help here; so we always pray for our new animals and installations. Rev. Rosie Lunn, Rector of Wraxall parish, will now pray a dedicatory prayer for her newest and perhaps tallest parish resident.

The press and TV were all there. Liam Fox MP cut a ribbon as there was no wind that day to activate it! In its first three days after full activation it produced 360kW, then hit a calm time, so it took 32 days to generate the first megawatt (1,000 kilowatt hours) but only 17 days for the second MW. By September it had produced at an average of 11% of full capacity. But perhaps a windier winter was to follow? It also helped towards our Silver Award in the Green Tourism Business awards, which Jon Jutsum had encouraged us to work towards and achieve. Sadly, it broke in a November gale, despite being the only turbine of its size with a British Kite Mark. It was out of action until the following October.

We had taken on Sammi Luxa as our events manager, a pretty and bright history graduate who had worked for us in her holidays for over two years, and three park rangers who also helped out with other things around the farm. Park rangers had grown to be our front-line people, meeting the public, doing tractor rides with commentary, and being humble enough to clean toilets and collect rubbish. Jon Woodward had a degree in evolutionary biology and was a rugby player; he helped with all the science on the website, in displays and answering emails. Dav Bennet became senior park ranger and helped on grounds at other times, and Chris Collier, a former teacher from South Africa now turned electrician student, helped Chris Moulding with electrical work. We also took on Catherine Tisdall, a qualified vet, who had taught veterinary students, to replace Hayley as education officer during Hayley's maternity leave. Will Bradbury, who had been with us for a while as a builder, came back to further his career as an apprentice keeper. All these excellent staff members were much needed, but required us to expand visitor numbers to cover the costs.

On a bright and clear Tuesday morning, June 23rd, we were awaiting the new tigers. They had started their 200-mile journey to us at 6am, from Martin

Lacey's Linctrek farm, whose camels we had kept since 2001. Suddenly a large white van with its maroon and grey horse box came into view, creating its little dust cloud down the rough stone farm track. Almost the whole staff were present to welcome them, with quite an air of excitement; except for a few who had to look after the 300 school children that were with us that day and who knew nothing of what was happening. As one of the tigers could possibly be quite heavily pregnant, we thought it should be a quiet welcome, followed by a press call the next day to unveil the new tiger dens and the pussy cats themselves. The van backed into the enclosure and the first crate, with Tira on board was duly lifted off by four members of staff, being careful not to put fingers through the mesh! The maroon red crate was rolled down the concrete back area and tied to the tunnel leading to den 1. As soon as the sliding doors were opened Tira walked calmly out, turned and snarled at us, to warn us she was not just a pretty face.

Next the trailer was unhitched and rolled away, the van opened and the second red crate containing Kushka was unloaded. One TV camera crew was allowed to be present for this. They were filming Michaela Strachan's 'Animal Road Show', and doing a one hour programme on our zoo animals. They took a good shot of Kushka staring out of her crate through the mesh, calm but full of menace. When her crate was secured and the doors opened she walked calmly out too, looked at Tira in the next den, then hopped up on her five foot high solid wooden bed. Kushka was laid back from day one. She seemed to accept it as home straight away.

These were undoubtedly some of our most exciting zoo moments. These huge magnificent animals left us in no doubt that we only had one chance to know we shouldn't have done that! We had written our risk assessments and our keeper procedures, which the keepers concerned, Chris Wilkinson (who as head keeper and who had written the procedures), Emma and Mark, had all signed. Chris was the only one of us who had met the tigers personally. He had spent a week in February doing his tiger training with them; learning their diet and seeing how big cats were handled, including some babies. He was going to be their exclusive keeper for their first week while they settled in and learnt to recognise the other keepers. Then Emma would take over. Emma had worked at several zoos, including the Isle of Wight Big Cat Sanctuary, and had a long interest in big cats, which culminated in her doing a masters degree in animal management, including big cat enrichment. She was therefore probably one of the most highly qualified big cat keepers in the country. Emma and Mark had been for a week to Whipsnade and London Zoos to update their tiger knowledge. Mark and Chris would be relief tiger keepers.

We had done an escape procedure with Sadie acting as a tiger with a mask on; we had to set out in six cars and tractors to find her and tranquillise her. We had done a gun practice on a big plywood target against a tree stump, using three shots from each of us who were licensed to fire the shot gun, using single slug shells. Our performances were photographed. We each, Chris, Will Bradbury and I, had about the same sized group, kept on file as log of the practice. The zoo inspectors required us to shoot-to-kill any escaped tiger, as we would only be likely to get one shot at it; tranquillising was too at-risk of not working.

The things that were not quite ready were mainly cosmetic and were finished over the next few weeks, ready for the official opening on July 25th. But before then we had three press calls; one the day after the animals arrived, for six cameras, and another at turn-out day to see how they liked their new enclosure. Four more cameras came, but apart from one brief walk down the track to the waiting press 50 yards away and back the tigers refused to come out again. The press took some magnificent pictures of Tira growling from about two feet away; she didn't get up, she lay there and snarled! The third press call was for Tanvir the magnificent large, slightly pale, two-year-old male tiger, who was delivered two weeks after the females. We had hoped he would be bold and courageous and lead the females outside but in the event he was more timid than they were, and hid at every opportunity.

Our next tiger press day was the official opening, on July 25th. All the teams had worked very hard to get everything ready. The little ice cream log-cabin, with sinks, work tops, drains and hygienic walls and surrounding fences, was a lot of work for the builders and a couple of days' work for the electricians, too. The paths and fencing and reed bed drainage were all finished.

The day coincided with the tenth anniversary of our opening in 1999. It was a beautiful sunny Saturday and a record number of visitors came, including nearly 200 specially-invited locals and officials and all those involved with building the Tiger Territory. Our newest Conservative MEP, Ashley Fox, cut the ribbon. He told us his family were regular visitors to us. Our son Caspar read a dedicatory prayer; and everyone was allowed all round the path on the outside of the enclosures for the first time, to see the ponds, the platforms and the vegetation growing. To anyone who asked where the tigers had come from I wondered whether to say Martin Lacey; to which the enquiry would have followed 'who is he?' So for brevity we told them 'a private collector in the East of England'. This also avoided the long discussion that might ensue about tigers used in the zoo-inspected private collection of a DEFRA-licensed circus owner. (see chapter 50). I hoped it would not look any more secretive than camel ownership; and hoped for intelligent discussion if people enquired more.

To our relief our pregnant-looking tiger Tira gave birth three days later, five weeks after her arrival; but all was not well. She started, unusually, in the afternoon. Tigers usually give birth at night. By 6.00 pm she had produced four cubs but three were dead. As CCTV was broadcasting the event from our own and several other websites, Chris, the head keeper, who was watching her, switched off the camera, discreetly removed the dead babies, leaving the one live cub in the nest calling to its mother for milk. Tira paced past it for another hour ignoring it, until we were afraid it was going to die of cold. So after a brief discussion with me, Chris switched off the CCTV again, removed the tiger by sliding a stick under her door; locked her out, collected the baby and rushed it to some heat and milk to see if he could save it, while I locked up and switched on the CCTV again. I felt sure, and told the keepers so, that the baby would not survive long, so if it died on day one it was not their fault. Over 17,000 people had been watching Tira give birth.

In the event Chris and his wife Clare, Mark and Will by night, and Emma joining by day, fed him first half-hourly then hourly, then two-hourly, then three hourly until, after three weeks, he had become stronger and seemed to be doing well. He looked strong enough to be seen briefly in our animal show, so visitors could learn about baby tigers. He came into the show in his box, for a ten second appearance twice a day, held by a keeper in rubber gloves and feeding overall. We had installed a web-cam and discovered 8,400 people/computers were watching it by day, often by minimising the baby tiger's picture on their computer screens at work; then maximising it whenever the keepers fed him! He received several press visits and was given the name Tumkur. Then sadly, after a full and hopeful 3½ weeks he suddenly died in the night. The keepers were all surprised, very shocked and upset and even tearful; especially as he looked stronger. So were the public who had become attached to him. It was a very difficult time.

Meanwhile, Tira continued to be unwell. We boarded up her window so that she was off-show to the public. The vet came and we consulted by phone almost every day. Following a week of treatment, but of no eating (which is not altogether unusual), Tira finally stopped pacing round, so we knew something was so wrong that intervention was essential. We had been reluctant to tranquillise her because tranquilliser drugs sometimes prove fatal. On a Sunday afternoon our vet, Clare Tibbs was called, Chris tranquillised Tira and samples were taken. But Tira never regained consciousness. For any animal keeper death is always a terrible time. There is the sadness over losing an animal you had bonded with, and yet you can't do anything about it and wonder what you should have done that wasn't done. We had called the vet 18 times in August.

We knew we had done all we could.

We now had two fresh problems. Tira's body belonged to Martin Lacey, but we were required to provide a post mortem and dispose of the body. We decided that Catherine, our education officer and qualified vet, helped by Tom, who had previous experience working with carcasses, should do the post mortem using the body hoist in the new but unused Tiger Kitchen. I felt this was our best solution, especially as we had just taken some live body fluid samples the day before.

I had also hoped we could save the entire skin, including head, tail, and feet, for our education exhibition. All tertiary education institutions had collections of body parts because they are so much better than pictures in books. We had permission from Martin Lacey, Tira's owner for this. On the black market a dead tiger was probably worth £50,000 and I did not trust everyone at places where we might have sent the body. We offered it to Bristol University, who did not want it. So we put the body parts we were retaining in the deep freeze to await the taxidermist's return from holiday. The organs were photographed for an article by Catherine in a vet journal. Catherine's final conclusion was that the tiger died of liver and lung failure caused by cancerous masses that overwhelmed those organs. I asked the staff to bury the tiger in a place where we could dig it up again in a year or so, to recover the skeleton as an educational exhibit. The NFU reassured me this was not only traditional for all non-food animals, including horses, but remained legal, despite the requirement for all food animals to be incinerated, since 2003. There is no risk, if an animal is correctly buried and not near a water course. It has happened throughout history and is still done all round the world. We also needed a DEFRA CITES (Convention on International Trade in Endangered Species) Article 10 certificate to keep tiger parts for display; they had to be kept somewhere while we waited for this.

In August the same atheist group that attacked us in February did fulfil their threat and wrote to schools in the Bristol area, warning them that we were 'creationist' and therefore did not teach proper science, but myths about a creator. They also wrote to education officers in neighbouring counties with the same warning asking them to write, too. Worcester County's Mr Colin Weedon wrote to all his county's schools, warning his schools against visiting us with the atheists words repeated 'they withhold their creationist message until visitors arrive'. The facts are that we call ourselves Noah's Ark and on the list of things we do, on our ¾ million leaflets each year we put 'Exhibition about Evolution and Creation'; and 'Exhibition of Noah's Ark to Biblical scale'. As we distance ourselves from what we feel is the inaccurate geology and timescale of 6,000BC Creationists, we could not say we were creationists. So what were we?

A governor from one of the schools wrote to us with a copy, incensed on our behalf, but asked for his name to be withheld. Such is the intimidating power of the atheist extremists, that, having frightened many Christians in science away from speaking out that they believe in a Creator, they are now rounding on little us!

In August they issued a general press release warning anyone who would listen that this 'creationist zoo' existed. BBC West listened immediately! For some reason in the last year they had refused to publicise anything we sent to them (apart from online) but took this up. It was as if their local editors were part of Sink the Ark. For this programme they did some excellent footage of our animals; they are always technically excellent. I insisted on a live interview on 'Points West' (rather than a recorded one) because I did not trust them. It seemed to go well from my point of view. I reminded viewers that in the Second World War the whole country believed in and prayed to God for deliverance. I was alive then. So what had happened that atheists now thought they could stop our freedoms and silence everyone who still believed in God? The next day was our all time record attendance! Attendance for August was also up, by 55%. Various local and national papers and radio stations echoed the atheist view. Twitterings went round the web, mainly shedding more heat than light, worried lest there should be any credible mention of God in science.

The first two weeks of September were once again harvesting weeks, due to an all time wet July and a wet end to August; but in these two September weeks our attendance was 80% up on the previous year. Then E-coli was reported as coming from first one, then four farms. A press scare followed. Professor Hugh Pennington who had made the wild forecast about BSE in 1986 (see chapter 36), was reported as saying no child under 5 should ever touch an animal! Open farm attendances plummeted (we heard later by 80%); ours dropped by a third. The E-coli proved to be a press scare about 100 children who had been to some farms, but especially one, in August where they allegedly contracted the illness. 27 were hospitalised, but no guilty animal was found on any of the farms, and there were no human fatalities. Our attendance drop worried us. We prayed about it as a team on Monday morning, wondering what to do.

Suddenly on the same Monday morning our young male tiger, Tanvir, decided to follow a meat trail up to the top of his timber tower and became too nervous to come down for his supper. We were immediately very concerned, but while anxiously praying about this, I realised it was a press opportunity. Our keepers knew that once he was hungry enough, Tanvir would forget his anxieties and come back down. The staff were wary, knowing our enemies would put a blaming-us slant on it. I insisted we go for it – please! In the event it was the national news story of the next day: big wussy-pussy, timid tiger still up his tree… Tanvir was on TV, radio (but not local BBC), websites and in lots of papers . There were the usual whingers about Christians not being able to look after animals, but it was mainly lots of fun. Tanvir came down half an hour after the last press team had left on Tuesday evening. Our numbers recovered the next day and for that week!

Then just as we were expecting a quiet life BBC West challenged us with an all-out attack. Alastair McKee, producer of 'Inside Out West', wrote saying 'we would like to interview you about your links with the Great British Circus, in particular any animal loans. We intend to reveal that a tiger carcass was buried on the zoo grounds without a proper post mortem, in contravention to environmental health legislation'.

Some of the staff were worried about the buried tiger, despite my wanting it for display with an Article 10 certificate, so while I was away on a conference and by a week before the time of the interview, they had dug up the tiger body and sent it to Newton Abbot incinerator to deal with any remaining uncertainties. We were ready for the BBC. No buried tiger, proper post mortem and any dealings with Martin Lacey were completely legal, because his premises were fully inspected and licensed. Martin was probably the best tiger keeper, with the healthiest, fittest looking tigers in the country. Did the BBC really want to make a fair balanced programme, or were they atheists siding with animal rights fanatics and determined to damage us? However, gross their behaviour, I was not about to abandon Martin as a friend, or tell lies.

I refused to do a recorded interview, especially because on a contentious issue like this I needed to have a fair hearing. After two weeks of the producer, Alastair McKee working on Samantha our marketing manager, charming her with stuff about his professional integrity ensuring me a fair say, very, very reluctantly I agreed to a recorded interview – but only if the whole thing was recorded by my own cameraman. I kept the transcript. How false McKee and his promises proved to be!

The 'Inside Out West' programme, aired on October 19th, was a disgraceful attack by the BBC using, contrary to their own guidelines, mainly secret film taken by an extremist, vegan, Captive Animal Protection Society (CAPS) journalist 'Sarah'. The woman had lied her way into being allowed to volunteer with us, saying she was a vicar's wife and desperately wanted to work with animals. She had secretly crept into our freezer room, taken the polythene bag out of the freezer that held the tiger skin and head so that she could film it. She then asked a temporary staff member (falsely described by the BBC as a senior member of staff) questions about a subject upon which she had not been briefed.

Two weeks before the programme aired a BBC crew had bought entry tickets quietly and done a piece to camera on our site without permission, proclaiming we had broken the law in burying a tiger, that we had tigers from the Great British Circus and any young born would be sent to a circus.

My 30-minute interview was exactly as I had predicted of BBC West: all but 1 minute and 5 seconds was cut. If McKee and the BBC had been impartial they could have fairly represented the views for or against the circus. They would have mentioned all the safari parks' connections with the circus and Martin Lacey's DEFRA license, or the eight academics in the DEFRA working group who found no scientific evidence against animals in circuses, or the fact that circuses more than zoos enrich tigers' mental stimulation. They could have included that private collectors are keeping up the numbers of highly endangered animals. But McKee had already sided with CAPS and decided Martin Lacey was guilty. They could have explained the educational reason we kept the tiger head in the only place it was legally allowed – the freezer. In interview they asked me 'why was the decision taken to keep the tiger's head?' which I answered. In the programme they inserted a more emotive question they had never asked me 'why did you cut Tira's head and feet off?', using her name as if she was alive at the time. This caught the ear of the press more than anything else.

They stated that we had buried a tiger illegally, which was not only untrue as we were applying for a CITES certificate, but there was no tiger buried even at the time of the interview, let alone the programme. They claimed we had not done a proper post mortem. We had done a long and thorough one, which I have on file.

In their 'Inside Out West' programme they included secret footage by CAPS. BBC guidelines state that, for secret filming, there should be antisocial behaviour or a serious illegal act. In our case there was neither and therefore no justification to film on private property without permission, and no cause to use CAPS' secret film. The CAPS reporter was later totally discredited as a liar and all their allegations were dismissed by the zoo inspectors. As for the 'balance' that the presenter Josie D'Arby spoke to me about, it was clear Alastair McKee, whether for atheist reasons or not (he dodged my question about this in the interview) and his line manager Roger Farrant just wanted to shock the public against our squeaky-lean image.

With hindsight we should have done what other zoos do, and kept quiet when animals are born in case there are still-births or early deaths. Our wish to further the interests of science by showing births in public (as we had done successfully with our tapir on a web-cam a few months earlier) will now have to stop. But it was curious that a few months later when Bristol Zoo had a female lion die in its very small enclosure, all the news around that and its replacement was positive for Bristol Zoo especially on BBC 'Points West'.

For us though, the result was a nightmare. One member of staff was in tears because she had allowed the spy to volunteer without a CRB check. Another was in tears because she had had her private conversation recorded without her permission on a hidden camera. Some newspapers, who should have known better, put us on front and whole page spreads, shocked at a tiger head in the deep freeze (the very place it was legally required to be!) and implying we were being cruel to our animals.

The BBC interviewed, out of 18 professors of biology they could have chosen in Bristol, Professor Steven Harris, a well-known critic of zoos, saying we were disgraceful for keeping tiger body parts. What a hypocrite! His university had one of the biggest collections of dead animal parts in the country! We had angry emails from our enemies.

I was urged by three upset BBC producers who were embarrassed at the outrageous BBC breach of trust, to write to the Editorial Complaints Department stating that their producer and his line manager had broken their own editorial guidelines many times over and told several lies about us and asking for an apology. One of them wrote to the BBC himself, complaining about the 'mood music' that was played at the time to imply guilt. However, I was not expecting justice, the complaints procedure requires two sets of correspondence with the producer, then a further one with the Editorial Complaints Unit, all of whom, when I did this just said they disagreed in their defence. If we wanted justice it would mean using a lawyer and going to the BBC Trustees. I felt that would be pouring away £50,000 of good money after bad and the best that we would get would be an apology a year later, to remind everyone of the bad news all over again. Alastair McKee deserved to be sacked, but would probably be promoted by an amoral, self-seeking BBC staff structure. A long time has passed since Lord Reith set high, moral, Christian standards for the BBC at its founding.

The very next day after the programme, another animal rights group, Western Animal Rights Network, empowered by the BBC's programme that they had been clearly told would include their footage (actually CAPS footage, but CAPS is a charity so are not allowed to demonstrate publicly, so informed their militant wing), sent us an email saying:

> I write to you on behalf of the Western Animal Rights Network, to announce we will have started a campaign aimed at closing down Noah's Ark Zoo Farm. The campaign will be peaceful and will include regular pickets outside

> asking people to boycott the zoo. We will also be asking your suppliers, advertisers and the schools who visit your zoo to stop working with you. Activists involved in the campaign range from Anti-vivisection activists who have worked on campaigns such as SHAC (Stop Huntingdon Animal Cruelty) and Speak (the campaign against Oxford Uni), to hunt saboteurs and more internet based activists. We will all be calling on our large range of previous experience to ensure that the zoo is shut down and that animals will no longer suffer at Noah's Ark Zoo. If you have any doubts about why we want to see your zoo closed just visit this website page which will be up within the next few days.

If the attacks we suffered from Sink the Ark in February, the Humanists in August and the BBC across the region were not enough, we were now under attack from the shadowy, violent world of animal rights activists. My reaction that morning was to take the email, as King Hezekiah in the Bible had taken his letter from a lethal enemy, and 'spread it before the Lord' at our team meeting. We told God that we did not know what to do, if anything, so please would He show us? A lady rang a little later and said we were in a spiritual battle; if we did what we would normally do we would lose. We should fast and pray and God would show us. OK.

The demonstrators arrived on the same day as their email, a very wet Tuesday (my late father's birthday) when there were almost no visitors to witness their placards saying 'Animal Hell'. I decided to take the battle to them and went to speak to them in the pouring rain. It was clear they had read the Sink the Ark atheist material, which was probably their main motivation, and knew almost nothing about animals. They complained, as their website did, that we were cruelly bottle-feeding our lambs past a month old when they could no longer digest milk. (But every lamb drinks from its mother for 5-7 months. And every open farm bottle feeds lambs for the whole season.) Their 'Sarah Litton' had reported baby rabbits were just thrown into a dust bin (she omitted to say the litter in question had all been born dead, except one which was almost dead so had been euthanised). A mouse had been found by a keeper with a tumour on its back, but instead of taking the mouse to the vet (and prolonging its suffering) it had been professionally euthanised ('I felt sick', was 'Sarah's' emotive description of it). We had been reluctantly persuaded to take four goats from an old lady who could not cope with them, so we had put them in quarantine and off-show. One of them tested positive to Johne's disease, which is dangerous to humans, so had by law to be put down. As was permitted, we fed the body to the tigers. 'Sarah' reported we had fed all the donated goats to the tigers. They were extremely shocked that Tira, the tiger, had died, implying cruelty; as if cancer was our doing. They said we had 'decapitated' the tiger (it was dead, so why use this expression?), and its head and skin were being prepared for the taxidermist to make an educational exhibit.

These folk as well as being strongly atheist trusted their 'Sarah' as revealing the truth (or close enough to justify a demonstration). They suffered a real downpour of rain and left, bedraggled, two hours after they arrived, damaging our sign with their own as they went.

Emails flew round the country answering accusations, including to BIAZA who decided to suspend us pending an investigation about the BBC allegations. The BBC quickly saw this as an opportunity to imply we had done something illegal to offend BIAZA, so announced this suspension as well on the main local news. North Somerset's Health and Safety Department also announced that CAPS had complained of 16 allegations of animal cruelty (but refusing to give us more details than CAPS website), which they would be investigating. Then one day in half term we found our boundary fence had been cut in seven places; and no sooner had we mended it than they painted KILLING on our TIGER TERRITORY board at the front gate, and a papier mâché tiger head planted on a stick beside it. The BBC had been successful in persuading a few people we had killed and decapitated the tiger.

Two days later Jon, the head groundsman, was out in the grounds late at night when he heard a male intruder coughing a few yards away. He called out to the intruder (unfortunately), then rang me on his mobile and I suggested he dial 999. The police had prioritised our calls because of the tigers and possible attack by animal rights protestors, whom they deal with in their counter-terrorism department. The police procedures were triggered. Within ten minutes the police helicopter was overhead with its heat-seeking camera; at the same time as six riot squad police, who spread out into their rehearsed counter-terrorist positions. The intruders had fled. When the police drew a blank they sent a tracker dog and handler later to search the wood next door; they followed a trail to the nearest road but the car had gone. They promised to return on other nights to check us out.

Half term had begun with us all feeling decidedly battered and two of our staff needing therapy. I had finished writing a hymn called *Lord of the Mountains*, to the tune *Highland Cathedral*; the last-but-one verse came to me at Friday breakfast when I was feeling at my lowest (see appendix 3).

Finally, in the middle of our last day of the season, our main gates were shut and locked in the middle of the day by protestors, preventing visitors from coming or going (for a few minutes until we sorted it), then a few days later all our 17 varieties of finch were released or stolen from their aviary overnight. Our church and farming friends were very supportive and we also received lots of email, phone calls and letters of support.

Our half term attendance was well up on the previous year, and the whole year was 21% up! So true to His promise, God was looking after us. But He also promised that people would persecute us, and there were two final twists to come. BIAZA clearly panicked in the face of the attacks we were suffering, so decided to permanently suspend us, and without the promised 'full investigation'. They evidently tried me at their membership meeting in my absence. I was shocked at BIAZA's betrayal. Such a thing would be unthinkable for the NFU or CLA, who stood by their members enduring unfair attack. This would also mean we were on our own as a zoo against every animal rights activist in the country, who would doubtless attack us for being suspended. Defending us and risking the animal rights terrorists, was clearly not a comfortable option for the other zoos, most of whom kept animals in smaller enclosures than we did. So on the grounds that a breakdown of trust had occurred, due to my not being straightforward over telling them our tigers were coming from Martin Lacey, they abandoned us.

BIAZA were right about the breakdown of trust, but it was I who did not trust the director of one BIAZA zoo, nearby, whom I suspected was behind some of our trouble, not that they did not trust me. Miranda Stevenson and David Field, two senior BIAZA officials, had stood in our tiger house two months earlier and said 'Anthony, we know these tigers have come from Martin Lacey, so tell us where they came from'. I asked if it was confidential and was told, no. So I declined saying that I thought a nearby BIAZA member would deliberately betray us to animal rights activists or to the press. BIAZA's procurement policy allowed us to procure or return animals from most sources, including Martin Lacey. In fact, Miranda Stevenson told me she had visited Martin's Great British Circus a few months before and admired his animal keeping and handling. Both DEFRA's Zoo regulations and BIAZA regulations require our ethics committee to be happy about procurement and should be satisfied if our ethics committee are. The final outcome was that the local BBC West were delighted to tell the world a second time about dismissal from BIAZA, once again without asking me to do a live interview – great impartiality once again. They could have added that only about a quarter of Britain's 350 zoo-licensed wildlife collections were members of BIAZA, and some of the biggest were not members – like two of the collections nearest to BBC West – Longleat and Cotswold Wildlife Park, also Howletts and Port Lympne among the bigger zoos.

As a consequence of all this and under pressure from the staff who were receiving emails from friends and enemies about their views, I decided to ask Martin to swap his breeding tigress for a donated one. I was especially sad because the numbers of tigers are under severe threat, with only 3,000 left in the wild, and being shot by poachers at one a day. If we did not keep a healthy captive population they will be as extinct as the Tasmanian tiger (a pouched dog), which finally died in a zoo in 1936 and is probably extinct in the wild too. I would like to have helped keep the UK tiger numbers up by breeding, but we changed our big cat enclosure to a sanctuary. I have nothing but admiration for Martin, but it was clear that irrationally emotional people were going to terrorise our visitors if we kept the breeding link as it stood. What a lot had changed since, as I have mentioned, Billy Smart started Windsor Safari Park and Jimmy Chipperfield provided circus breeding lions for Knowsley, Woburn, Blair Drummond, West Midland Safari Parks, as well as Longleat, where ironically the 50 lion extras in the film Born Free were placed, which inspired the animal rights group of that name. And all this despite Martin's excellent tiger training and shows now. Part of this animosity may be because old films, like *Pussy Galore* and *The Greatest Show on Earth* show old fashioned circus with whips and chairs in the faces of lions, so although cars and telephones are different now from in old films, people assume that circus is the same. That was now Martin's battle not ours.

The Bristol atheists delighted in adding this to the Wikipedia article against us. They had signed the Sink the Ark petition earlier in the year, and presumably felt it was their duty to try to destroy our reputation and extinguish us from being the only God-believing zoo in the country.

The miscalculation of public opinion had been mine entirely. I had been brought up a modernist and rationalist in the age of reason, and thought I could explain my actions coolly and be involved in rational debate. We are in a post-modern, post-rational age, both for faith issues and for this; for a growing number of people if it feels good, do it or believe it, if not, either ignore it or kick up a storm, whatever feels best.

The final blow was probably the worst. It was from our own council. First, North Somerset Health and Safety questioned whether our animal disposal policy allowed us to just send a tiger back to a circus owner. They had believed the BBC and their animal rights protestors' accusations against Martin Lacey. So our ethics committee had to meet to confirm what we had decided two years before, that Martin's business was licensed by DEFRA, very well run in accordance with the highest animal welfare standards and it was the right step. Peter Sampson, our oldest and best friend within BIAZA, kindly promised three lion cubs for the beginning of our new season. Then in November the same council officials announced to the press we were 'under investigation for alleged animal cruelty' because, they said, they are obliged to take all allegations seriously. As they knew us well and visited us often, we assumed this would be over very quickly. We were terribly wrong.

What a season 2009 had been! We had never had such opposition, nor had we had such amazing support and all-time record attendances. With hindsight we could thank God for late planning permission and late arrival of tigers, to come exactly when they did. It meant that the inevitable protests against us came right at the end of our season, not when they could have harmed us, in August.

I was still trying, with Steve Robinson, to present a new paradigm to the scientific world, gently but clearly. This was going to be altogether more difficult than I had expected. Four new pieces of evidence had come to light during the year supporting our proposal. First, some scientists working on the DNA of a variety of life forms, had announced that the tree of life so proudly presented by the atheist BBC's Natural History Unit as a wall chart and distributed to hundreds of schools and others was 'a figment of the imagination, torn to pieces by an onslaught of negative evidence' ('Uprooting Darwin's Tree', *New Scientist*, 24th Jan 2009, p34). Though they are now suggesting a web of life, still linked (in unspecified ways and unconvincing mechanism) to a single ancestor.

Secondly, the asteroid storm that cratered the moon (Late Heavy Bombardment), was confirmed by further evidence to be the result of a storm that lasted only one and a half rotations of the moon, i.e. 40 days or so. (The author of this work is looking for a publisher courageous enough to publish it.) Thirdly, a search of more distant galaxies, whose light has taken longest to reach us, suggests that galaxies are denser and more active the further back in time we go; they are also more numerous and brighter. It is quite possible that galaxies evolved from huge and active quasars, not from collapsing clouds of dust particles. ('The Quasar that built a Galaxy', Phil Berardelli, *Science Now*, December 1st 2009.)

Fourthly, there is yet more water reported throughout the solar system: the moon is yielding more evidence of water, Saturn's rings are made of water-ice, and its moon Enceladus, which has ice on it has a striped and volcanic South Pole region spouting huge jets of hot water vapour into space. Water was being found on moons and asteroids all over the solar system. This would support our proposal that on day two of Creation, God surrounded the solar system 'expanse' with water vapour, out at the Kuiper Belt, which could have been involved in the Late Heavy Bombardment of the solar system, as ubiquitous rain, falling wherever gravity drew the water/ice droplets (see appendix 1).

There is also evidence that new scientific theories do not take over quickly.

Old theories need to die with the people who support them. Then when a new generation arises to accept a new theory and other supporting evidence as fact, it takes hold. So science may take a while to change its geological timescale, from the long one based on the rate of radioactivity always having been the speed it is today, to one consistent with the empirical evidence of the rocks themselves and astronomy as we see it – with faster radioactivity in the past and a much shorter history. And God our Creator will be at its heart. Unembarrassed, we will think back to a Genesis we can identify with, and walk with our Maker once more in the cool of the day.

58

2010: The Coldest Winter for 30 Years, Expansion and Challenges

NOT SINCE 1978 HAD IT SNOWED SO MUCH. IN 1978 AND FOR SEVERAL winters up to then, the press had been full of dire warnings of the oncoming Ice Age. This time the prophets of global warming just went quiet. The truth was that weather is not the same as climate. They had used every weather extreme to bolster a climate change claim. Somehow this extreme cold and frequent snow seemed hard to fit in. Washington DC had the cold too, because the jet stream that should have sent snow on the Vancouver winter olympics, moved, and sent the snow on the East Coast of the USA in record depths of two feet everywhere. Whereas the Winter Olympics imported snow by hundreds of lorries for the skiing; 9,000 cubic metres of it.

We had begun several large projects on the farm. The keepers were building a large vulture aviary. Barry and his team were re-building the old and tired outside play area by the café with a bigger play ark and taller climbing apparatus. We moved office in a major upheaval in February, to the Old Stables, with room for seven people upstairs and seven downstairs all with phones linked to computers. It cost over £50,000 to do, including phone links to the shop and ticket office.

Early in the New Year the animal rights protestors were at us again. In characteristic North Somerset Council fashion their inspectors had done nothing since their announcement in November. You might think that as the county's biggest and currently Top Leisure Attraction we deserved better than that. We asked and asked again what we were supposed to be guilty of. Astonishingly, no one would tell us. As the protestors at our gate had produced nothing but false accusations it was pretty obvious the council were giving credibility to liars. They had bowed to a concerted email campaign against us by vegan protestors who object to farm animals, zoo animals and most pets (but not their own dogs).

Following the BBC's triumphant announcement that BIAZA had excluded us, many of our faithful season ticket holders and others assumed we had been closed or were about to be; even our MP thought we had been forced to close. Our season ticket sales were cut in half. (Or could it be the recession, or the very cold weather?) Sympathy was being passed to us for our plight. We denied the disgraceful allegations of cruelty, of course, but usually got a weak paragraph at the end of a lurid press article saying 'Noah's Ark spokesperson strongly denies cruelty allegation'. Was that read or believed? Some journalists should have done better. We planned as far as possible to keep a low profile. Most people had probably not even heard of us, let alone the allegations, so why tell them by arguing? We were sure the inspection and our troubles would all be over by the end of January. But our county is special. Their handling of our footpaths and planning had each lasted six months longer than anyone could have thought possible. Now this investigation for cruelty was to drag on from November to March.

Samantha, our marketing and office manager, had left us for a bigger job in Bristol so we decided to divide her job in half and promote her two deputies to take her place. This was not the time to be taking on new staff and both Jon Woodward, who became communications and office manager, and Sammi Luxa who became marketing and events manager in charge of front-of-house, were extremely competent and intelligent young graduates, who Christina and I had confidence in. With some external training days and with supervision from us we were sure they would rise to the challenge; though it must have seemed to them like a mountain to climb. We had asked the experienced Rosie Inge, recommended by the Country Landowners Association, to be our PR specialist to help get us out of our bad cycle of publicity. She helped our new young team organise a really good press day on February 2nd. Three new lion cubs had arrived in three crates from Linton Zoo the day before, by the very kind actions of Peter Sampson, our BIAZA ally and owner of Paradise Wildlife Park and Wildlife Heritage Foundation. The cubs were a bit nervous on this their first day, but about 18 sections of the press were represented. However, there was still the tendency for them to write 'this troubled collection', or 'this collection under investigation for cruelty', so part of Rosie's help was to show us how to challenge the press, and encourage them to report good news rather than false gossip.

Two policemen arrived one day and two inspectors with clipboards. They were from DEFRA's Convention on International Trade in Endangered Species (CITES), who had insisted they inspect us with priority over North Somerset Council. This inspection was mysterious; they were checking to see if our endangered species had microchips that matched their paperwork. Had someone told them we were dishonest and importing illegal animals? There were no illegal animals; all our micro-chips were in order and nothing was dishonest, of course. Chris Wilkinson was finding it difficult persuading other collections to send the CITES documents to us in time, so that the document was actually in our file (rather than just in existence) before we showed the animal. Why was that necessary? Because it was! A ponderous and unnecessary system needed attention so that less paperwork was needed. Two sorts of CITES certificates were possible – one specimen specific and one transaction specific. Why would anyone want to get a new piece of paper with every movement, when one that would be valid for the life of the animal would be better? To have the first but not the second was a very serious offence, apparently, subject to police action. It was high time the transaction only certificates were abandoned. We eventually made strong recommendations to the new government.

At the start of the season a third animal rights group, the Bristol Animal Rights Collective took up the case against us, with placards at our gate announcing we were exposed for animal cruelty, and showing pictures of a tiger skin in a bin liner and implying we had killed a tiger! They were very intrusive and stopped our visitors' cars whenever they could, to give them a leaflet that told many lies about us. Libel aside, this was also an accident waiting to happen, as the cars backed up onto the main road when one stopped. We solemnly warned the police about this, but they refused to intervene, saying they couldn't until the accident happened. BARC was a tiny single issue group wanting no animals in captivity. They were vegans; against all intensive animal farming and most pet keeping. They did not care about animal welfare, except insofar as it made a case against captivity. They were also apparently atheists, because they also wrote to all schools in the area telling them 'PLEASE DON'T VISIT NOAH'S ARK ZOO FARM, NOW UNDER COUNCIL INVESTIGATION'; complaining to schools in the words of an Oxford Professor Harvey found on the internet:

> The zoo is conflating science with religion. They are proposing a two-stage process of initial creation followed by evolution through natural selection. The first is not open to scientific testing while the second is. This is educationally unacceptable.

We thought the allegations were insufficient to convince schools, especially as the letter was unsigned and from no address, merely signed 'Bristol Animal Rights Collective', with an address where they met, of the Kebele (anarchist) Café in Bristol. They also wrote to businesses dealing with us with much the same letter. (We were given both by well-wishers.) We were wrong. We later heard that one school did take this seriously and a Bristol head teacher believed the lies he was told. However, a Christian teacher who knew us intervened with the truth about us. In another school one parent was enough to put off a whole school trip, but when we heard about this we offered the parent a free trip to reassure them and expose the lies.

March 2010 began on an all-time low for me. I was feeling sorry for myself for ten reasons:

1. The weather was the coldest for 32 years. This was uncomfortable for the staff and animals and obviously a real deterrent for visitors, especially small children, who cried in the cold. It was also a very expensive time for keeping all the animals and staff warm.

2. Our attendance was down by 40%; how much of this was the recession that was having an effect all over the country, or the terrible weather?

3. E-coli had depressed our attendance by half at the end of the last season. It probably was still.

4. The accusations put to North Somerset last November were still under investigation. Why so slow? Many people believed the press reports that our keepers were guilty of cruelty. 'There's no smoke without fire', as one of our season ticket holders had suggested to me over the phone. Some press reporters were still giving us an unpleasant twist of accusation.

5. Demonstrators with lying placards and leaflets at our gate, saying we were guilty of extreme cruelty and animal abuse, were irritating. Some of our young visitors were being frightened by megaphones and cars being stopped. I needed to encourage the staff to treat them kindly despite our opponents' disgraceful behaviour. Atheists may feel they can lie, terrorise or steal our good reputation, but Christians must return evil with good, and must love our enemies. I received many suggestions of what unpleasant things some of our supporters were willing to do to them, but I firmly discouraged hostility.

6. Send a Cow trustees when thanking me for 20 years as President in December had decided we should put out a joint press release from Noah's Ark and Send a Cow about Prince Charles taking over as president in my place, and me standing down. But now we were tainted by allegations so we were asked to keep quiet.

7. I was not asked to preach as a Lay Reader in our church after 18 years. The reasons were unspoken, but were they the same?

8. Our bills were mounting with the inevitability of 25 paid people doing their jobs in our quiet season; we were doing repairs and 'off-show' improvements to keep up with latest health and safety standards, but visitors would never notice most of these.

9. Our wind turbine, which we had chosen because it was the only one that was up to British Standards, broke last November through bad workmanship, and was not going to be mended until next July at the earliest (actually October finally).

10. Our arable crops had suffered badly from the very cold and frosty winter; the pigeons had cleared half the oil seed rape fields, so they looked from a distance as if nothing was there.

As with all depressing situations, we also need to think of all the good news! Count your blessings; name them one by one is always good therapy. The blessings almost always outweigh the gloom.

1. We were all alive and healthy.
2. All the animals looked terrific.
3. The staff were happy and united by opposition, and by the encouragement of all our happy visitors.
4. We had received 3,000 visitors over a very cold, dull and wet half term, and 500 season tickets bought, who all seemed delighted we were open for a new season.
5. Other tourist attractions were down by even more than us.
6. The whole park looked better than ever.
7. Snow is beautiful.
8. Difficulties can add interest!

9. I was explaining the Christian faith to some of the demonstrators, and exposing veganism's hypocrisies and explaining morality to some of them who needed to hear our view.
10. The oil seed rape had lost all its big outside leaves, but the pigeon always leave the growing point at the top of the plant; so disease in the leaves is less likely. When the sun and warm rain come, yields may not suffer.
11. Jon and Sammi were showing themselves worthy appointees to publicity and marketing jobs and were beginning to win the PR battles and had good ideas.
12. Jesus had said we were to celebrate when people spoke lies about us for His sake, because they had done the same to Him. We couldn't expect to build a Noah's Ark on a hill without some opposition.

As someone has said 'We may grumble about the air we breathe, but it is all we have, so get on with it and do the best you can!'

By April, Barry and his cheerful building team had built a magnificent replacement play Ark and two high play towers complete with high balance beam, traversing climbing wall and huge scramble net. Jon and the grounds team had planted 11,000 more willow trees, built a new road through the old adventure playground and made the grounds smarter than ever. Our Christian friends were reassuring us that God had not abandoned us; in fact trials and difficulties were being used to make us stronger than ever. As I had learnt before, an oyster is designed to use the irritation of a grain of dirt to make a beautiful pearl. Indeed St. Peter's letter tells us to 'rejoice in the sufferings of Christ!' Lord, help me do this. I wanted to believe it.

Eventually, on March 2nd the DEFRA Zoo Inspectors arrived, with two health and safety officers, and spent six hours with us looking at allegations of cruelty. They worked through each allegation in detail and found none of the animal welfare allegations to be true and they could see the long list of other allegations evaporate before their eyes. They were not totally happy that we had taken the baby tiger in its box to show the public, but only because it had died; had it lived that would have been fine. Oh for hindsight! However, they still needed three weeks to make their report. This ordeal had more weeks, indeed months, to run!

I continued to speak to the BARC protestors each week for an hour or more. They were mainly ignorant of farming. They did not know that their food (organic, they were pleased to point out) was usually fertilised by manure from intensive agriculture (where animal welfare might well be at standards they would normally protest about); nor that all crops have to be protected from predators by killing rats, mice and pigeon, not to mention insects. They wished that their food did not exploit animals, but their purism was disillusioned. They were doing their best, they insisted, which was apparently OK for them, but not for us. They also relied on importing their tastes from around the world, so veganism, if it was to be an adequate diet, was a choice for the rich Western nations. The BARC's leader kept a rescue dog she had to get back to – was this a captive dog kept locked in a small flat, I wondered aloud to her? Was it better than our big cats in fields and dens that she was so insistent ought to be in the wild?

Eventually, on March 22nd, the inspectors' report arrived. They found 'first, there is no doubt that the animals in NAZF are generally well cared for by experienced and dedicated people. Allegations of cruelty on the part of them or of Noah's Ark generally, are in our view grossly unfair.' The undercover investigator had complained that she had received no initiation training at Noah's Ark; yet she had signed a form that she had received training from us! 'This throws into doubt the truth of a number of statements made on the basis of her evidence', they said. The staff were jubilant that at last it was recognised that we had been lied about and falsely accused. The calls for revoking our Zoo License were described as a 'considerable over-reaction'. It also showed that the BBC West programme had backed a liar, and lost. But it was a waste of time seeking redress. Who remembers TV programmes anyway? So why remind them? It was considerably galling that we were then sent a bill for £2,125 for the inspection by North Somerset Council. Does that mean anyone can dream up a charge, persuade rent-a-crowd to sign an online petition and such a penalty is inflicted? Ironically, this means that sum of money is not now available for improving our zoo.

I knew the inspectors had wholly exonerated us. They said so at the time. Unfortunately the wording of their report was naively ambiguous. 'Generally well cared for' was meant by them as 'viewed over all', but our enemies took it as 'mainly, but not entirely'; so several people, including me, had to write in our defence to each paper, attempting to put the matter straight. This was also good for our PR. However, they gave the animal rights protestors a linguistic reason for continuing their protest for the next seven months. They refused every invitation to come to look round our animals, but just continued to protest with banners at the gate. Our visitors and local council members were now becoming upset with them, for ignoring the proper investigation. People were stopping to tell the demonstrators they were accusing the wrong people of bad practice. 'Why not stand outside Bristol Zoo, where their large animals are in tiny enclosures and they had a lioness die recently?' 'Because we are trying to close Noah's Ark.' (And visitors drive in without intimidating the demonstrators, unlike Bristol Zoo's pedestrian visitors!)

One of our visitors saw that the demonstrators had stolen one of his estate agents boards and were using it. So got out and grabbed it and was punched by the demonstrator. A local land owner blocked them from parking their cars, with rocks and branches. So I decided to be as nice as possible to them, and continued to visit them beside our gate, coolly discussing all the issues, to try to educate them, for sanity and for God. I offered them tea, but was refused. Eventually the protestors took up my offer of a free look round with me, at the end of July.

Three of us spent an hour and a half with three of them showing them the large animals and the huge enclosure for elephants that we were planning. They remained implacably hostile, insisting that our animals did not have as much room as in the wild. We pointed out that the wild was not such a great place if you were being attacked by a lion, or eaten alive by wolves. We protect all our animals from hunger and thirst, from disease and fear of predators but no, we were not as big as the Serengeti. However, we did establish on the last week of the season that they were not at all interested in animal *welfare*. They were only interested in preventing captive animals. So animals can kill and eat each other, be ill or injured, they did not care, as long as they were free. This had to be idolatry; of worshipping and preserving nature at the level to which it has evolved now. I suggested we needed to consider the claims of their Creator and mine on our lives and remember He had given us the world of creatures to rule with Him and for Him.

In April we had a visit from the owners of an award winning farm in the north of England, who had been next on the hit list of 'Sarah' the CAPS under-cover reporter. At last we rumbled her tactics. First, she has to discover where any dead bodies are kept, then she creeps in when no one is looking and takes pictures. Next she alleges cruelty and implies bad management are the cause of death. The press falls for it because if she moves around the country a new section of local press can be shocked by death. The fact that every animal will die sooner or later is overlooked, so is the fact that 10% of births are stillborn and have to be put somewhere, to await disposal. In our North of England colleague's case, he had a partial nervous breakdown under the press allegations. He lost two stone, was afraid to meet anyone and felt the world was against him. He was just like two of our own staff. In the North of England attraction's case their county stood with them, and soon awarded them a Top Attraction prize. Opposition vanished. We were sad that our county had been more harmful than helpful for so long.

However, the inspectors report coincided with a change in the weather. Our numbers rose and, as a test of confidence in us, our season ticket numbers rose too.

Christina and I had met several times during the 2009/10 winter with the new North Somerset Rural Business Forum, where we had been very grateful for support in our plight from many fellow farmers and country people, who knew the violent and unreasonable face of animal rights activism. One of the speakers was Professor John Webster, who gave an excellent talk encouraging beleaguered farmers to feel good about the job we are all doing, especially where animal welfare was good. We invited him to Noah's Ark to look at our welfare, as he is probably the top authority on animal welfare in the country, having invented the Five Freedoms as a standard of welfare:

1. Freedom from hunger and thirst;
2. Freedom from discomfort;
3. Freedom from pain, injury & disease;
4. Freedom to express most normal behaviour;
5. Freedom from fear and distress.

John Webster visited us one day and had a good look at our enclosures and enrichment practices then, in answer to my questions about what he thought of our animal welfare and also Professor Hugh Pennington's comments about E-coli, wrote to us:

> I know Hugh very well and respect his views. However I believe that his suggestion that children under five should not be exposed to farm animals betrays a quite unrealistic understanding of the nature of risk. Absolute freedom from risk is impossible. Moreover attempts to avoid exposure to risk can often do more harm than good. There is good evidence that our middle class attempts to protect our children from exposure to common germs in the natural environment have increased the prevalence of asthma and allergies. These disorders arise from mistakes made by an immune system that has not received a proper education in early life.
> Another essential element of a proper education is to teach children respect for animals based on a proper understanding of their needs and their behaviour. Pets can help in this regard, but it is not enough to fall in love with the few animals that are lucky enough to be members of the family. Children need to learn respect for all animals, on farms and in the wild. Farms where

children learn to handle animals have a very important part to play in this. Only in this way can we expect our children to grow into adults that support humane farming by buying high welfare products and recognize our responsibility of stewardship to the wild animals that share our living environment.

On animal welfare he added:

> …in the worst of zoos, animals have simply been put in cages so that we can watch them fade and die. However we can do it properly. We need to provide them with a rich social and physical environment wherein they can get what they want, food, comfort, companionship (as appropriate to their species), so far as possible through their own natural actions. This is the art of good zoo husbandry and it requires a lot of skill and a lot of understanding. The aim, in short, should be to make each day a pleasant experience for every animal. I believe that you are succeeding in this aim.

We felt that our hard work and compassionate animal keeping had at last been recognised and by the top authority in the land. What a contrast with the unthinking protestors who refused for months to even look round our animals and the selfish BBC producers who attacked us in such an unbalanced way.

Our season took off better at the Easter Holidays. Although the weather was much colder than last year, our numbers began to recover. By the end of April we were experiencing several days with attendance up on last year. The visitors' book recorded 'much better than Bristol Zoo', 'much better than London Zoo', 'better than Longleat', 'better than Chester Zoo', 'excellent value for money', 'a magical place', 'the chicken rock!'

Late in April two white-headed vultures arrived to fill our now beautifully finished aviary which the keepers and ground staff had worked so hard on. Then three little fluffy owl chicks (South African Eagle, barn and burrowing owls) came to replace an owl we lost to a poisoned mouse, which had crawled into its enclosure last autumn. Chris managed to find eight pairs of finches to replace the 15 pairs of finches that had been stolen or released last November. Our drop slide that I had installed 11 years ago needed and received a new £3000 surface, and a huge tube slide arrived, to complete the outside play area.

On May 18th Ann Harley, the new chair of North Somerset Council, opened the Vulture Enclosure and the refurbished adventure play area, while (Rev) Paul Pike, our ethics committee chairman, prayed for their blessing and dedication. By the end of June our numbers had just crept ahead for the month including half term.

We had a bigger range of chicks than ever hatch out under Mark Walters' supervision. We had both the world's smallest and the largest nidifugous (leaving the nest at hatching) bird: the Chinese quail and the ostrich; and lots of ducks, rheas, finches, bantams, peafowl, and Guinea fowl.

One day we spotted an unusual event, which we reported to the press as follows:

> Doris the duck, had sat patiently on her eggs for 28 days. Then one by one they hatched. Eight little ducklings hurried after their mother to the water that sunny May afternoon; to the safety Doris knew she could expect from the tranquil pond, just ten metres from her nest. Safety at last in the middle of the deep pond, from all the predators she knew could harm her babies. But this was no ordinary pond. Little did she know but Doris had been sitting on her eggs inside a tiger enclosure at Noah's Ark Zoo Farm. Now there was a very large threat hiding in the grass and creeping towards her floating family. A pause. Then a flash of orange with open jaws and a seven foot tiger lands in the pond just half a metre from this new duck family. Tiana the Tiger had been watching tantalised, every day, as she had hunted round her enclosure. Behind an electric fence protecting some bushes was this wonderful smelling duck aroma. Day after day she smelt her. Now was Tiana's opportunity.
>
> Splash! The little duck reacted in a second. She took off from the pond like a missile, centimetres from Tiana's outstretched paws. The ducklings scattered as Doris duck, circled above Tiana's head quacking loudly and temptingly, landing on the ground a few yards from the pond. Doris pretended her wing was broken and limped along shouting to the tiger. There was a furious splashing as Tiana abandoned the babies and leapt out of the pond towards the apparently helpless juicy looking duck. Only to find that the duck took off again, once more centimeters from the tiger! Doris quacked loudly and circled back over the pond and landed once again amongst her ducklings on the pond. Again Tiana pounced with a furious splash, only to find little Doris was again too quick for her. So Tiana this time laid low in the pond among the ducklings. The ducklings were too small to tempt the tiger, but surely the mother would come and try and rescue them again. Once again little Doris pretended her wing was broken and quacked even louder, and struggled even more temptingly. Again the great tiger fell for the simple trick and chased out of the pond, only to find the little duck beat her in the air and circled round, this time landing outside the enclosure. By this time Emma, the Big Cat Keeper, had heard the

commotion and called Tiana in to her supper. The little ducklings rallied, heard their mother calling and made their way through the weldmesh fence to their mother, who this time took them to another pond a few yards from the tigers' fields.

Hatching had been a safe exercise for Doris the duck behind the electric fence and in a totally fox-free area. She proved herself more than a match for one of the world's most dangerous predators.

I also used a quiet April and May to push forward our plans for installing elephants. I have always wanted elephants in our collection, ever since I had visited Pittsburgh in 2003 and heard that there was a Noah's Ark show running nearby which included live elephants in the cast. Elephants, it seemed to me were the ultimate animals to have in a serious collection. So they had been on our five-year plan because we could provide proper amounts of space for them, indoors and out. Some collections have historically kept elephants in tiny yards and stables, because they are better than circus elephant conditions. We however could give an elephant herd a real attempt at natural behaviour with the biggest enclosure in Europe. So we applied for and obtained planning permission for what we knew was to be the biggest enclosure and most modern elephant house in the country. But this was not without the usual anti-zoo pressure groups complaining to the council's planners and to us at every stage. Barry, Chris Wilkinson and I visited two elephant collections. Both were excellent for very different reasons. Dublin Zoo had a new £6.5m covered sand yard, with open sand yards and pools 4 m deep. They were very hands-on, but their keepers used 'protective contact' through bars. They kept the three females and two babies busy all day and night with feeding and enrichment techniques, burying food, hanging it from poles, hiding it in holes, sometimes on time-switch opening, for night feeding. They water-cannoned the elephants because that encouraged them into the water to swim and find treats. They seemed very busy, happy elephants. The other elephant herd was the biggest outside Africa at Howletts Zoo in Kent. Here 15 elephants were kept on 'no contact', in as natural a way as possible, on eight acres. In the summer they were kept out of doors day and night, with the male running with the females all the time. He had sired 10 babies, so the system was the most successful at breeding in Europe. So there were things we could learn from each of these collections. I had drawn up plans which we discussed with Dublin's Gerry Creighton, who was extremely helpful and encouraging, offering to help us all the way through our process.

The RSPCA had written to the planning authorities to oppose permission to keep elephants. I decided to contact them to find out why they opposed us. Were they more atheists? Eventually Rob Atkinson and Ros Clubb, both PhDs, came to see me and I showed them our proposed site. They explained that the RSPCA was opposed to keeping elephants (and dolphins) in zoos. I asked why. They said longevity in zoos was less than in the wild. Why did they think this was so? Because of obesity and poor feet and lack of social stimulation for what was a highly social animal and mental stimulation.

They gave me a big pile of research papers to prove their point, along with a copy of the 'Best Practice by the Coalition for Captive Elephant Wellbeing'. I told them I was surprised they were so negative, instead of encouraging us to do the job properly. As a former cow-boy I was used to looking at management problems and sorting them out. In zoos elephants were clearly being fed a protein-rich ration of old bread, fruit, veg, and good quality hay, when in the wild they ate browse (tree leaves and branches) and poor quality rough grass. This was inevitably going to lead to obesity, and boredom, then poor feet from too much protein and too little exercise. We were planning to feed huge quantities of tree browse, low quality hay or haylage; we had in mind big fields, sand yards, a swimming pool for three to swim at once, and protective contact training regularly. They admitted this was all in the Best Practice and would be a huge step forward on what was going on now.

We issued a press release saying the RSPCA had visited us, but although they were opposed to keeping elephants in captivity they had also given us a copy of Best Practice. We assumed therefore that they wanted us to keep them well, much better than was the case now in almost all zoos. They then counter-circulated the press, linking themselves with Born Free and the Captive Animal Protection Society, just saying they were opposed to our elephants. I replied that they were uncharacteristically negative and needed to 'lighten-up', stop being two-faced and admit that elephants were going to be in British zoos, so why not support us when we were trying to do as their Best Practice recommended? It made good press coverage and we came out of it well.

Then suddenly, over three days, in August I received 450 individual emails from a Please Stop the Elephant Enclosure at Noah's Ark campaign, then later another 250 from a campaign against elephants in captivity. Each one was 'horrified and saddened' by the information posted on, guess where, the BBC West website. I decided to write (copy and paste) patiently back to all 700 of them with the following letter:

> Thank you for writing to us about our proposed elephant enclosure.
>
> As you are asking us not to proceed with our elephant enclosure, you are

presumably content with the standard of elephant keeping in existing zoos in UK and Europe. I am surprised. When the RSPCA recently visited us we both agreed that, although they were totally opposed to keeping elephants in captivity, for those that would continue to be in captivity a radical change in their management was needed. It is very difficult to modify an existing site, but much easier to put up a new one.

We are well aware that elephants at their very best are in the wild and I would not wonder if you wanted to give lots of money to keep as many elephants as possible living in ideal situations, especially keeping poachers away and keeping the elephants from being unwelcome neighbours to hungry hard-working African farmers.

Unfortunately not all elephants can live like that. Many are poorly kept in zoos around the world. Some are threatened by culling in their native land. Our own plans are to take poorly kept elephants or otherwise dead ones and give them a life that is like no others in the UK. Most animals other than elephants live longer in captivity than in the wild. There are reasons. The RSPCA admit that obesity (caused by, in my view, a terrible diet), bad feet (caused by obesity), space (currently set at less than an acre in UK), and lack of good social interaction between the elephants (which are kept in small and unnatural herds) are among the reasons.

There is a Best Practice of the Coalition for Captive Elephant Wellbeing, which no zoo in the UK has signed up to, but which was handed to me by the RSPCA (though I already had a copy). We hope to be the first in UK to attempt Best Practice.

Actually I don't think the wild is all that it is cracked up to be. We are told about the best herds, but not the hungry ones, or those threatening human habitations and those maimed by poachers or unable to keep up with their herd. And we don't know how far elephants walk for preference if they had adequate food and water where they were and no lions. Some people assume elephants want to walk for miles, but I doubt it. We will see here, where they will have further to walk than any other UK zoo and much more than if they were dead!

So like Noah we are rescuing elephants from a worse fate and will be trying for the very best.

Again, thank you for writing to us.

Several of them replied apologizing for the misinformation they had received and wishing us well.

There is a huge mountain to climb in funding, building and stocking what we hope will be Britain's (perhaps Europe's) biggest and best elephant enclosure. We spent £25,000 on the project by the final planning permission stage for what has been our most meticulous preparation by far; the opposition has also been the greatest by far.

Late in July our education team, Hayley and Catherine, in between teaching dozens of school workshops and animal shows, had been trying to achieve a 'Learning Outside the Classroom' Quality Badge. We were given a thorough examination of all our output and achieved it with flying colours, at the first attempt, for our excellent range of National Curriculum workshops and our hands-on animal education. We announced it to the press, had good coverage and arranged another day for teachers to come and look round. Our opponents had been shown up for lying about us. When it eventually reached the ears of the Richard Dawkins website, they got in a real fluster. They sent a very rude email about us to the HQ of Learning Outside the Classroom in which Professor Dawkins, sounding all too like an Atheist Gestapo, wrote:

> Dear Sir or Madam
> Undoubtedly your unwitting blunder in awarding your Quality Badge to the Noah's Ark Zoo Farm has already been drawn to your attention. To be fair to you, the fact that it is a creationist front rather than a bona fide educational institution is somewhat deeply buried on their website. This is doubtless how you managed to overlook it. I have no doubt that you will already be putting in train the necessary procedure for withdrawing the Badge, and I congratulate you in advance for doing so. You may be sure that the sooner you announce the withdrawal, the less the embarrassment will be.
> If there is anything that I, or the Richard Dawkins Foundation for Reason and Science (RDFRS), can do in the future to assist you in the difficult task of vetting the true credentials of would-be recipients of the Quality Badge, do please let us know. We'd be delighted to help you to avoid such embarrassing mistakes in the future. And in general, as an educational charity with a special interest in science, we'd like to assist you in any way we can to achieve our shared aims of improving the learning experiences of children.
> With my best wishes
> Richard Dawkins FRS, Emeritus Professor of the Public Understanding of Science, University of Oxford

It would have helped if he had bothered to find out what we taught or believed. But I suppose his bullying tactic had worked before so why not try again? The LOtC folk resisted him robustly, telling him that their award went to a wide range of people, including Canterbury Cathedral and an interfaith organisation. They want youngsters exposed to a breadth of beliefs so they can make their own minds up. This argument was then taken up widely; first by the *Times Educational Supplement*, then the *Daily Telegraph*, the *Daily Mail* and the *Sunday Times*. At last a little bit of the science we were proposing was filtering out too. Ann Widdecombe was among our defenders.

August 2010 will go down as the wettest for 20 years (175 mm of rain) and the worst for tourism. I again wrote to our local church leaders in mid-August asking for prayer for fine weather for the harvest and for the holidays. A week later the Azores anticyclone once again arrived and stayed for 10 days. The harvest was saved and on Bank Holiday Monday we had our biggest ever attendance, as well as a rowdy 'national' animal rights protest. A lady wrote the following letter to the *North Somerset Times*:

> I was driving to Noah's Ark Zoo Farm on Bank Holiday Monday to collect a friend and unfortunately met the protestors at the gate on the way in and out. As I drove in they shouted verbal abuse at me, using phrases such as 'Christians are nutters', and tried to block the car but on the way out one woman stood in front of my car making it impossible for me to move. Again the verbal abuse started. 'I didn't see you coming – you're trying to run me over', and as I carefully edged through the 15 or so protestors one of them kicked my car, whilst another tried to dismantle my rear wiper and all I was doing was trying to leave.
>
> I had my six-year-old daughter in the car and she was absolutely terrified, as was I as they surrounded the car on all sides. Although I had heard and read about the protestors before, I have never seen them in action; I am completely shocked and outraged by their behaviour.
>
> How can a group say they care about animals yet at the same time terrify a six-year-old child is beyond me – just who do they think they are?
>
> All this makes me want to support Noah's Ark Zoo Farm even more than I have in the past. I think they deserve an award for putting up with this despicable behaviour in such a gracious way!
>
> I am delighted to hear that on Bank Holiday Monday they had their highest ever number of visitors; surely that says it all.
>
> Mary Bush (No relation to the owners)

In August we heard that at last we had found a female giraffe for our male, Gerald. She could not come to us until the second week in October, but we could prepare for her. My 50th anniversary of starting in business at Moat House Farm also seemed worth celebrating. We decided mid-October would give us good publicity for half term. We celebrated with a Wurzels concert, a fun-day with fund-raising stalls for Send a Cow and a party for some of our older friends and fellow business ancients. The day went really well (apart from two turn outs from the animal rights protestors, one in the morning and one for the concert). We also publicised the giraffe arrival the same week and received a huge amount of interest, even going on national TV and European and USA press. The bachelor giraffe who had waited four years for a mate and who fell in love at first sight, wrapping his neck round hers and giving her a gentle lick, was the heart-warming story. Along with the goat-for-company who had turned marriage counsellor!

During the autumn we had been offered a family of ring-tailed lemurs, which we were glad to install in the spare side of the Gibbon Gallery. We needed to re-home the coatimundis. We had a place in mind in the South America section, so very quickly the builders, grounds team and keepers made a very imaginative, highly-visible enclosure with high climbing beams, nest boxes, catching room, and very elaborate multi-stranded electric fence round it. This was opened for us by our own Colin Hall, in his capacity as both chair of Clevedon Town Council and deputy chair of North Somerset. A lay Reader colleague of mine prayed for them, Dennis Croome. We had underestimated how very agile and seemingly impervious to 8,000 volts these little racoon-like animals are. One by one they all got out several times. Eventually we built a perspex ceiling one foot wide at the top of their 4 feet-high perimeter fence, which finally contained them.

After (what turned out to be) the last escape I emailed our eldest granddaughter, Hannah, at University:

> Yesterday we had a naughty coati get out and climb into the 50 ft tree beside the maze! We tried luring him down with food. Not interested; so the groundsman climbed up with his tree-surgeon ropes and with various sticks and ladders we tried to encourage him down. Two hours later no joy! I joined the fun and after a while realised we had not prayed. So we paused and asked God to help us get him down. Ten minutes later trying much the same as before he came down to the ground and promptly disappeared into two miles of maze!! It was getting dark by now. While eight keepers and work experience folk disappeared into the maze, with Holly the dog, I realised we had actually only asked the Lord to help get him down from the tree, so the two of us left by the tree prayed 'Father, thank you for bringing

> this coati down, please will you help us actually catch it now'. Suddenly there was a phone call from the car park to Sadie 'Have you lost a ring tailed lemur, there is one crossing the car park now?' A parent of a work experience girl had spotted this strange animal in the nearly dark, 400 yards from where we thought it was. The keepers quickly ran and rounded it up by the Arable Barn!
> Where would we be without the Big Boss's help eh?

Our October numbers were up for the first month since June, albeit a modest 5%. All tourist attractions were badly down during the year taken as a whole (16%). The recession was probably part of it, but for outdoor attractions the very wet August meant nine wet days affected attendances enormously in those vital summer school holidays. We were down nearly 19%, including 2000 school children, so our Council's unhelpfulness, spurring on our enemies, had provably harmed us in addition to the weather. This drop meant we could not find as much winter work for our seasonal staff as we would have liked. We did go ahead with a soft-play area which gave the building team lots to do indoors in the snows and frosts of November and December. Compared with the opposition many Christians experience around the world ours, though financially and spiritually real, was trivial.

59

2011: Our Thirteenth Year, Our Millionth Visitor

As our year began I was aware that our financial reserve had dropped to almost nothing, yet our essential staffing costs and animal costs had never been higher. I had been to a Churches Together meeting at Nailsea School where I met a young church leader with a word for us. He said he felt God was bringing us a year of His favour. I thanked him for his encouragement. The bills and cost commitments were still there, but 'hope' is an essential requirement for happiness. If God had called us into this huge enterprise, He was with us for good not bad.

Our season began with us all feeling very thankful that the lies told about us by so many people last year had stopped. At least the press had stopped believing and publishing the 'allegations' that had been so soundly refuted and condemned by the zoo inspectors. We were no longer referred to as the ambiguously worded 'troubled' attraction. This year, as usual, we had lots of good news. Our Siamang gibbon had a baby boy, so we announced it and it reached the press on a day when there was little good news, so it was probably one of our widest ever publicised stories, even reaching Europe and America. We then had a naming competition and chose Sydney from 70 names sent in. Dora the donkey gave birth to baby Derek. The marmosets and the tamarins produced babies, so did a capybara, both coatimundis for the first time, the ring tailed lemur, the African porcupines for the first time and prairie dogs along with our usual goats, lambs and chicks. Spring was in the air, the whole place was looking stunning, which was also good news readily taken up. We changed the alligators for dwarf Caiman crocodiles, which were slightly rarer and took delivery of the very rare world's longest lizard, a crocodile monitor, but a juvenile.

The local animal rights extremists came back every week with the same libellous placards, banners and leaflets as last year. I sometimes went to speak to them. They were there until the end of April when on Good Friday, by stopping cars, they caused the accident we had warned them and the police would happen. Sadly someone crashed into a car that was trying to get into our gate and was lying unconscious on the road. This empowered the police to exclude the demonstrators from an area each side of our gate. They stopped coming at the end of April, returned once in June with anti-zoo and anti-elephant literature, and twice more in the autumn. The last of was a silent protest, when they refused to speak to me. Bad mistake, because it gave me the opportunity of explaining to each of them in turn why their protest was very ill-informed, and what we were really trying to do to help elephants. I had a chance to explain the Christian gospel to some of them without the unthinking interruptions that were often used.

For the first time in many years I agreed this year to travel to speak at outside meetings. Of the eight speaking engagements which I accepted one was at Trinity College, Dublin to speak about the different sorts of Creationism to their Theological Society. I requested they open it to all the faculties, especially scientists. It was apparently their fullest meeting for a long time. This was the first time I had presented our Recolonisation Model to the academic community. It stood up to scrutiny well and I had some good conversations with undergraduates, graduates, PhDs and two professors, who agreed that apparent scientific certainty was often open to question. The organiser kindly emailed me a few days later:

> I have to say Anthony, I think that your talk was easily one of the most successful we have had due in no small part to your presentation and approachable manner. I cannot thank you enough for an excellent lecture.

The BBC produced a series of programmes, all attempting to explain the origin of life on Earth. In each series illogical conclusions were drawn from some excellent TV science. In all cases 'millions of years' were essential. Professors Brian Cox and Jim Al-Khalili came first, in both cases everything came from nothing. I wrote to Brian Cox suggesting that in the same programme he had said that the energy could not be created or destroyed, he was proposing that at the Big Bang the energy was all created. Where did it come from? He also insisted we were made by the stars in one programme, by gravity in another, and how 'light breathes life into us' in a third. He had stood in Karnack Temple explaining how the Egyptians used to worship Amun-Ra the sun-god, but now we build machines to study the light from stars. Is Brian now suggesting we worship light as our Creator? Is that better than Amun-Ra and the sun? It sounds very like more worship of the creation rather than the Creator.

Jim Al-Khalili assured us 'there is a profound connection between the nothingness from which we originated and the infinite in which we are engulfed'. Jim may want a God-free science, but I am so glad to know that Jesus is that connection. He also reminded us that mathematicians, like the Bristol-born Paul Dirac and Albert Einstein (born a Jew in Germany) are clever people putting equations to theories. He gave me no reassurance that these widely accepted theories are correct. In fact he left me extremely concerned that a whole generation was being taught that anything with an equation to it is true.

David Attenborough then presented a BBC series 'First Life'. Charming and gentle as he is I am continually astonished at David's science; he seems happy that life, with all its complexity, can just bubble into existence by chance in the sea somewhere. He said: 'after billions of years of single celled life, something amazing happened in the deep sea – some cells are sticking together…' At least he admitted the very thought is amazing. Then he said that this clump of cells has become a sponge. Is that repeatable, observable science for lots of single-celled creatures to become a new joined-up creature? Which then remains the same life-form for 600 million years. Like the old whirlwind-in-a-junkyard making a motor car, Attenborough's is the latest 'once upon a time' fairy story claiming to be scientific. In this case the time was millions of years long, long ago.

Dr. Adam Rutherford's 'The Gene Code' on BBC4 was no less simplistic. By suggesting that because all DNA is similar in all life on Earth, it must have evolved from a single cell, is merely making a statement not offering proof. DNA is incredibly complex and no one has come close to suggesting how the amino acids, not to mention the information in them, could self-assemble to produce DNA, let alone a living creature. The same DNA in every creature could much more reasonably point to a common Designer, of genius beyond genius, who made all living things to be inter-dependent. Rutherford and Attenborough, like Cox and Al-Khalili, seem little more than good story-tellers and all seem reluctant to come to terms with their Maker.

By February, our Jungle Den Soft Playbarn, which Barry had designed so imaginatively and on which his team of Tim, Dav and Will had worked so hard, was complete and ready to open. Christina had also added huge animal paintings opposite the murals she had done in 1999. It was officially opened by David Pert, a former head teacher and schools inspector, then chair of the Diocesan Board of Education of Bath and Wells Diocese. He called our work 'a wonderful educational context in which to proclaim our commitment to God's Creation in a wholly inclusive and sensitive way.' Our friend Rev. Ruth Legg, Rector of Portbury Parish in which part of the farm lay, led our prayer of dedication. Hundreds of parents and toddlers immediately loved the Jungle Den and we began to hold special Jungle Tots mornings on Mondays to attract newcomers with a good offer. We put up a notice on the wall:

> Jesus said 'Let the little children come to me and do not hinder them, for the Kingdom of Heaven belongs to such as these.' *Matt.*19:14.

The wet summers of 2008 and 2010 were very bad for us but could not compare with Japan on March 11th, 2011. Their east coast was devastated by a force-nine earthquake and three subsequent tsunamis that left 30,000 dead. The tsunamis began with a huge waves at Sendai crashing through sea walls and damaging the 'earthquake-proof' nuclear reactor as Fukushima. As usual God uses the world's disasters to bring out the best in people and many stories of love and courage emerged, some of which we heard about through our friends Paul and Janet Pike who had been working in Japan for 25 years.

On March 19th we welcomed our millionth visitor. It seemed quite a landmark despite so many people trying to close us down, economic uncertainties and huge weather challenges. Our excellent team were achieving progress and lots of people seemed to appreciate what is here. The weather was amazing, too. April was the driest and warmest for many years, so by the end of April our visitor numbers were 62% up on last year and was our best ever attendance.

We joined in the morale-lifting national celebration of William and Catherine's wedding on April 29th. We bought a TV license and connected TV to our Ark Arena Screen for three hours of the wedding, processions and kisses on the balcony, and put flags on the animals for the animal show. It was such a relief that the Duke and Duchess of Cambridge had avoided the disaster that so many others fall into who like them live together before marriage, because they were sensible enough to be faithful to each other in their temporary separation. It could otherwise have all been so terribly different. Theirs seemed to be a God-blessed meeting and marriage.

Our elephant planning continued throughout the summer. Following the granting of Planning Permission we then heard we had been awarded a £267,000 grant from the Rural Development Agency. This had originally been sought and promised at £400,000, but the election in May changed everything, with the new government committed to tackling a huge fiscal deficit. I employed a fund-raiser for a morning to see what ideas she might have, but, although she had good ideas about what information we needed to gather together to convince donors that we were the sort of organisation that deserved donations, she was convinced that charities and businesses were no longer supporting major projects such as this.

In early June we invited Alan Roocroft, a consultant elephant expert from the USA, who advises 40 elephant collections around the world, to come and talk about our proposed enclosure. Alan was very pleased to be consulted before we began work and had some excellent ideas which he shared with Chris Wilkinson, Barry Baker and our preferred building contractor John Wyatt, who had worked with us so well in four previous projects. During the meetings we decided that if we made 15 acres available, we could include a two-acre willow plantation and some arable cropping to be strip-grazed by the elephants; ours might be the only collection in the world where elephants were shown migrating round different sorts of naturally growing food every day – grass, growing crops and willow. Together with huge sand yards, ground-sourced heat extraction, water harvesting and swimming pool this could become a new bench-mark in elephant-keeping.

In July Lord Henley of DEFRA wrote to BIAZA requesting urgent attention from elephant keepers to the improvement of their welfare, concluding with 'I should say that such is my concern about the welfare of elephants in UK zoos, that I have not ruled out the option of looking at the scope for phasing out the keeping of elephants in the UK in the future if there is little or no evidence of improved welfare'. At the same time Alan Roocroft wrote to us 'I believe you have a very good foundation for the keeping of elephants correctly at Noah's Ark following the recommendations from myself that we discussed during my visit. Letting the world know now that you are designing, planning and ultimately building an elephant sanctuary where elephants will have space and habitat, will represent a high standard of welfare. Anthony, I think you have a very good chance of attracting attention towards you goals.' Time will tell if we achieve the million pounds needed to begin the work. I had also taken the matter for prayer to our men's prayer meeting one Wednesday at 6.30am, and one of my colleagues felt God was telling us 'step by step, piece by piece'.

One of those steps was to send Chris Wilkinson to the Elephant Management School in Hamburg, run by Alan Roocroft with 12 lecturers from around the world, all very experienced elephant authorities. It was a very expensive course at £3,000, but I thought Chris as head keeper ought to be well informed and fully conversant with all aspects of elephant care. The course dealt with the practical details of elephant training in all its forms, as well as a wide range of other topics such as daily care, diseases, nutrition, behaviour, mating, births and transport. He returned fired-up and ready for us to take on elephants, so we tweaked our enclosure and barn plans to be even better.

Part way through the year it was clear that our training of young people was getting out of hand. Sadie took and passed an Assessors qualification, so that she could properly test how well our students were doing. We now had 63 work experience students, with another 25 on the waiting list and 50 volunteers on the books. Schools needed paperwork and we needed CRB checks and safeguards too. This was far beyond what we needed to do and beyond what any other zoo that I had heard of was doing, but I felt we should do it for the young people's sake if we possibly could. We also increased our number of apprentices to six during the year, four on animals, one on grounds and one on the buildings team, to try and do our bit to take some of the million youngsters out of unemployment.

On September 1st, Ann Widdecombe kindly accepted our invitation to endorse our Elephant Eden appeal and to do a 'strictly come digging' of the first turf on a pond that would both serve the tapirs now and as an elephant wallow in the future. As I have mentioned, I had first met Ann when her brother Malcolm invited me home when we were 18 and she was nine.

It was a beautiful, sunny day with a big crowd of visitors turning out to see Ann on a late, last day of the school holidays. I described how and why we had planned the enclosure. Ann was very encouraging in her speech as well as being cheerful and smiley and, though I announced that as I was no Anton du Bush and was not going to lift her into the digger cab, she took my hand and did a quick dancing twirl! She also fed a tiger and a giraffe. Paul Pike prayed for God's blessing and guidance. Lots of the press, including three TV camera crews were there. Most media coverage was very positive. Predictably the BBC turned up with some hostile pre-recorded comments from animal welfare people for me to counter. I refused to do a pre-recorded interview myself, only the live lunch-time slot (of two, 15-second sound bites). By the evening the BBC presenter had become better informed and a fairer 'Points West' piece was broadcast.

I suggested our opponents were being hypocritical for either supporting or writing 'Best Practice' standards and then attack us for trying to do what they suggested. They had all decided that as they did not want elephants in captivity in Europe, the best way of achieving their aim was to oppose breeding and only support non-breeding sanctuaries. Yet breeding was an essential part of Best Practice. By wanting elephants in single sex groups and denying them the right to breed and interact with their young, they were depriving them of a major part of their welfare. I also invited BIAZA's director with the head of the elephant welfare group to discuss our proposals. To their credit they came, stayed to lunch, but refused to endorse what we were doing:

> Anthony I hope you understand that I cannot be seen to 'welcome' or 'support' any institution currently planning to hold elephants in the UK. It is of utmost importance that in my role as Chair of the Elephant Welfare Group that I am impartial and focused on driving forward improvements in the welfare of elephants currently housed in the UK. I will however watch with interest the progress of your project and wish every success with the park.

So we were still on our own.

We invited several elephant charities and writers of anti-elephants-in-zoos reports over the next few months to the farm to see the proposals for themselves. Jon Woodward wrote a brochure, some leaflets and lots of letters to individuals and the press trying to explain what we wanted to do. Our son Larry came down from Newcastle to chair our Elephant Fundraising and Development committee, so that he could begin to take ownership of some of the direction and expansion we hoped to see. The staff were very impressed with him, as was I.

The Elephant Stud Book keeper controlling all the zoo elephants in Europe took note that we wanted elephants but suggested none would be available for 10 years, apart from a possible male. However Chris had heard on his training course that retired and confiscated female circus elephants were available. This was not the best news for stocking Europe's biggest and best enclosure; but God is in charge so we will see what we are helped to.

It became clear once again that our café, under the Hall's management, was struggling on busy days in the summer. Queues were stretching out of the door, as they had every summer for several years. We had put a new café in our five-year plan; in June we had another ground survey and agreed a final plan for full planning permission. But, because of another wet summer, numbers were not quite where we wanted and instead we decided to give the old café a new kitchen, food-prep area and store for the coming year. This would speed up the queue at a tenth of the cost of a new build. An old building attached to the café and ripe for redevelopment was rebuilt by Barry, Tim and Dav that autumn and winter.

A year earlier we had decided that the staff tea room was much too small, as it had been built for a staff of 5-10 and we were now 24. I had told the staff that profits from our Keeper Experiences, which the keepers had made so popular, could go towards staff training and new staff facilities and so, as and when time and money allowed, an old dairy heifer building was transformed. It was re-floored, insulated throughout, and poshed up with central heating, a shower, toilets, lockers, sofa, a computer room, tables and chairs and automatic lights. We had a celebratory meal there for 26, on December 6th and everyone agreed it was a wonderful new staff room. Planning permission for the new café arrived the same day, but that would now wait until our numbers grew again.

The BBC continued putting out some excellent science programmes, about botany, apples, weeds and another by Professor Jim Al-Khalili on July 13th as part of, he proudly announced, 50 years of science from the BBC, this time about the Big Bang. He fairly pointed out that many scientists, including the late Prof Fred Hoyle have opposed the Big Bang, preferring the 'Steady State Theory', of the universe always having been as it is now. Al-Khalili complained that Steady State puts the origin of the universe 'out of sight, where it can never be challenged by a direct appeal to science.' He then went on to assume that retreating galaxies point to having been 'created out of nothing by an almighty explosion'. But there is a problem, he said, 'dark matter' is required for galaxies to gravitate into being. 99% of matter is required to be 'dark', and there is none anywhere to be seen. The £9bn CERN collider, set up and finally running in November 2009 to try to 're-create the big bang' has done 200 trillion collisions and 'dark matter remains elusive' the programme concluded. As I have shown (see chapter 39) I am sceptical of big bang theory, not least because of the vital and apparently non-existent 'fudge factors' of dark energy and dark matter required to make it work. One wonders why only two theories are considered as being possible, carefully leaving out the possibility of God providing the input of the laws of science, energy, matter and design. The question 'did the universe come from nothing by chance, or by an energy-giving, matter-creating God?' can clearly only be answered on a BBC programme with 'by chance'.

Professor Brian Cox was back again in December, this time in the Royal Institute with lots of TV comedians and actors lecturing them about Quantum Theory. At the end of a very entertaining lecture, after quoting his hero Humphrey Davey 'nothing is so fatal to the human mind than to suppose our views of science are ultimate…' Brian declared 'Quantum Theory doesn't allow mystical healings, or ESP, or other manifestations of new age woo woo. Remember this is physics and physics is usually done by people without star signs tattooed to their bottoms…nothing strange, no woo woo, just beautiful physics!' I partly agreed with him, that astrology and new age superstitions have nothing to do with physics, but his view did sound rather 'ultimate'. His physics explores the amazing world of atoms with their totally reliable laws without giving a thought to how they arrived out of nothing, yet apparently designed with a purpose. You and I and Brian Cox seem to be part of that purpose.

Every zoo is on the look-out for animal news stories. Our opportunity came in June when we were offered three beautiful white halter-trained female Bactrian camels from the Netherlands. They appealed to us all so much that I accepted the purchase price immediately and Barry and Tim switched their programme to build an extension to the camel house to take them. However, I had underestimated lethargic bureaucracy again. A disease called Blue Tongue was the issue. The camels needed vaccination against it, despite both countries being free of Blue Tongue for two years. Vaccination could have been done in a day, but the British Government's Animal Health at Chelmsford, insisted on a vaccine that had been proven for camels. There was none, because there were not enough camels to demand research, but why would a vaccine that suited cattle not be sufficient as there was no Blue Tongue in either country? Three weeks passed while first Trevor Lay, our importer, then I, emailed all concerned to get permission to vaccinate the camels. The shed was built and we were all ready for them when, finally, we heard that a cattle vaccine would be sufficient. But by now the Dutch had despaired of British bureaucrats as being not fit for purpose and sold the vaccines elsewhere.

Meanwhile our babies born earlier in the year had become news for us. The coatis left their nests and began to explore their high balance beams in their enclosure and the baby porcupine was cute. The prairie dog babies are always compelling as are our usual cheeky and playful lambs and kids. The ostriches hatched out not just one clutch, but in September a further chick in the exceptional mild weather. We put it in the warm incubator room, where it fell in love with a chicken, which used to sit on the ostrich's back.

2011 was a huge encouragement to us all. By the end of the summer term we were 15% ahead of our best-ever year and 37% up on the very wet 2010, with more schools than ever and more secondary schools than ever. Up to 22 coaches were parked each day in our car park. Even after quite a wet summer holiday we were still 21% up on last year and 8% ahead of the best ever 2009. This was apparently unlike most tourist attractions, who were the same or down on last year. There were only three fine sunny weeks in July and August; in the first we made hay, in the second we harvested our oilseed rape and in the third we harvested our wheat. We finished at 8.30pm on Saturday 3rd September after a hectic day with two combines and three bale teams to bale and cart the straw. Then the heavens opened and over the following three days we had 31mm of rain to remind us how right we had been to use what fine weather we were given. To my astonishment our oilseed rape harvest was almost double what we had ever grown before and the wheat crop about average. So these along with a record high price for them and good visitor attendance for the whole season, had meant that God had indeed blessed us, as had been promised at the Churches Together meeting in Nailsea School in January.

At our team meetings in August and September I was encouraging the staff to think about evolution. It is everywhere of course, but the question was how many creatures did God need to create at the beginning? Was it just one, or were there quite a lot? For example all dogs are related, but are they related to cats? Answer – yes, there are no differences between dogs and cats that could not be pre-programmed in the DNA, and all the carnivores are built with a similar digestive system, head and legs to dogs and cats. The evolution from within the DNA which God creates with the potential to evolve, is a very different proposal from the secular proposal that an original bacterium's DNA is added to by mutations and viruses by chance, until it becomes all of nature. Which sort of evolution fits best with both biology and palaeontology? The fossil record, though much fuller than 150 years ago, still does not link together the phyla of life by the tiny changes that folk like Richard Dawkins say exist. Biologists were now talking about a 'bauplan' or 'structural plan or design'. For example the authors of *Invertebrates* (2002)* are not stated Creationists, but describe the phylum as 'these are more than a body plan, they include a structural range and architectural limits, as well as the functional aspects of a design.' So I wrote on an Invertebrate display 'This appears to accord with Genesis where the text states God made everything according to its 'kind'. Thus biology and faith can go hand in hand.' The question many ask is how many groups are there?

So in our morning meetings we looked at all the phyla of invertebrates, of which there appear to be 24 groups, with, in my view, the arthropods being subdivided into at least three more subphyla. The literature appears to put vertebrates into: 15 mammal groups, 21 groups of birds (or perhaps less), five groups of living reptiles and a few extinct ones included two dinosaurs and one pterosaur. There are three fish groups, jawed, jawless and bony. The fungi were in seven phyla and the single-celled protists in perhaps a further 30. The plants were in 11 flowering super-orders and six sporophyte (seeding by spores, not seeds) divisions. So Creation theory would suggest that our Creator had about 120-150 different groups to bring into existence with the inbuilt potential in their DNA to evolve and diversify into the millions of species that fill the world today. By the time of Noah, some of this irreversible evolution would have taken place so that must be the reason for such a huge ship, 150-yards long, being needed.

By October our oldest four grandchildren were at university so now were beginning to make their major life decisions. In December two TV series showed the differences in attitudes to sex that exist. A series about the Amish people in America showed six British teens meeting Amish teenagers and experiencing their way of life without electricity or cars, at work and at leisure. The devotion to God and prayerfulness of the Amish impressed the British teens. So did the way the Amish chose their spouses. No kissing until they are engaged was the firm Amish rule, which first surprised the British, then strongly appealed to the girls as taking the pressure off them and allowing them to talk, socialise and discover the character of the dating man. Amish people marry when they are

* *Invertebrates* Brusca & Brusca; Sinauer 2002, p41.

young, but 'pure', as they described it and after serious thought.

By contrast the pretty young Geordie comedian Sarah Millican, raised a big laugh on 'Live at the Apollo' by saying she didn't want her vagina described as a 'baby-passage', because she never intends to have babies, but as a 'make-a-cock-happy-passage'. She probably really meant 'make-two-people-happy- passage' and was right that we have sex parts for fun far more than for babies. But without some Amish-like faithfulness it may not last long. Speaking at National Marriage Week in 2011, Ian Duncan Smith, Secretary of State for Work and Pensions had said that 90% of British young people aspire to marriage and of those who marry, only one in ten separate by their child's fifth birthday, compared with a third of the cohabitees. The Amish divorce rate is virtually nil, at less than 1%.

In December we heard that after a lot of hard work by our grounds team and others, we had won another tourism award. This time we were finalists in the Sustainability Award for the South West. It reflected the fact that we had only missed a Gold award in Green Tourism by two points. There were things we can do, all with money of course, so we must try these.

Our 10.00 am meeting times with all full-time and volunteer staff have continued everyday in-season and most of out-of-season days since we began. The pattern continues to be:

1. Notices about the day; which groups are coming; and meet the Keeper Experience people.

2. Information about a topical subject like conservation, weather records, animal arrivals, a history anniversary, agricultural or current affairs news, or a staff member's special interest subject.

3. Bible reading with a comment from a staff member on how they find it helpful.

4. Prayer for the day.

Sometimes we say everyone's name round the room and repeat them back; sometimes we introduce our name and job.

A little while ago we finished the New Testament as far as *Revelation*, as our Bible reading. It was timely. In *Revelation* our Lord Jesus is revealed in all His glory to John, the writer. Jesus urges the seven churches to stand firm, stay awake and alert in the face of growing opposition. A new heaven and earth are waiting for us if we are faithful. Then we catch a glimpse of God on the throne of heaven, surrounded by a choir of millions of singing angels. The elders are there, representing God's faithful people who have received all the rewards promised to the churches. Suddenly the Lamb of God, Jesus, appears and takes the scroll of the future and unfolds it seal by seal. The seals represent the authority of God, from whose hand come the warnings and the judgements of the horses of the apocalypse, white, red, black and pale. These four horses have been riding throughout history bringing 1. deception of counterfeit religion* 2. war 3. famine and disease and 4. death foreshadowing the coming judgement.

Then heaven is seen, filled by people from every race and language who have been under pressure and difficulty. The whole scene is very far from a world abandoned by a forgetful God to bad things; this reveals a sequence of disasters from the very hand of our Maker, to test us and help us get to heaven. In heaven the sickness, tears and sadness end, to be replaced by the unimaginable beauty of a vast, priceless, golden city, with gates of pearl, where God is obeyed willingly by the faithful, and millions go about their work happily. We were never told this life would be easy, only that it is preparation for the next life, which lasts forever, and it will be worth it. I would so love it if all who visit, or work on this farm, or who read this book could be there in heaven.

* Billy Graham in his *Storm Warning*, Nelson, 2010, p30 says 'the first horse symbolises the deception through counterfeit religion and secular anti-God and anti-Christian belief systems. It is a white horse, seemingly pure but bent instead on conquest.'

60

Retirement and Work

2009 WAS THE CENTENARY OF THE OLD AGE PENSION. BEFORE 1909 YOU worked until you dropped, sometimes working or living with a kind relative. But the last hundred years has seen a life expectancy at birth in the UK rise from 53 to 77 for men and from 55 to 82 for women. There were always older people, of course, but not nearly as many. A report by the *Daily Telegraph* in April 2011 suggested that a quarter of under 16s are expected to live beyond their 100th birthday.

One challenge we all now face is how are we going to spend those extra years, and where will the money come from for old people to live on? To increase the retirement age has been one very sensible government response. Many people will want to go on working in a paid job well into their 70s, as we have. Many others will have an opportunity of being useful in an unpaid way to all manner of needs and causes. Without a doubt God who brought us to this life as human beings in the first place, has plans for deploying each of us usefully until He calls us home. He is also quite capable of leading us into that plan. We may well need to ask Him for this. There is a horrific thought of a world where euthanasia becomes legal, so by public pressure a slow death when it appears difficult is not allowed. There are some medical procedures that have artificially extended life for the good. To withhold such medical procedures may be legitimate and even wise, but to encourage overdoses and poisons to end life, however ghastly that ageing process may be for some, is a very dangerous route. The prospect of the fit and able dictating the fate of the ill and weak, would usurp dreadfully the place and the purposes of God at death.

We are humbly grateful for the amazing opportunity we have had of at least appearing to be useful, long past our normal sell-by date; although it has been much busier than I have often wanted, more repetitive and tiring than I expected and much more spiritually and emotionally challenging than I had ever imagined. All this is despite guarding our 'closed on Sunday' rule carefully, for physical and spiritual reasons. We are so grateful to all the over 65s and over 70s who have been working here, both voluntarily and paid over the last decades, and those who have cheered us on by letter, email and personally. Life would have been very much the poorer without them, especially those who have worked here. Our young staff have benefited from talking to them, seeing their reactions to different crises, and hearing stories of how life used to be. We hope many other older folk will come forward to help at Noah's Ark in the years ahead.

It is an irony that when older people keep mentally and physically active they seem to raise their quality of life for longer. To rest and do nothing is a seductive destroyer. Whoever first said 'old age is not for sissies' was right. The older we get, the more of a challenge it seems. My mother's 'use it or lose it, darling' slogan at 91, has been found by many to be a good aim and a blessing.

61

Conclusion

AS EACH OF OUR LIVES DRAW TOWARDS THEIR INEVITABLE CONCLUSION CERTAIN things stand out as important achievements. They can seem fleeting in our influence over them. Christina's and my greatest joy and achievement, if we can call them that, are our children. There is nothing better than a family going in the right direction. With God's daily help we could only try to be examples they could copy and lay foundations on; the children then have to find God for themselves and follow close enough to build for themselves, with parental cheering from the touchline, down the phone, or whenever we meet. We are so proud of them.

It was a very busy life raising four children, which in one sense happily for us, never completely ends; but it was remarkably easy having fourteen grand-children! We are so proud of each of them, too and so happy to be linked to our four lovely in-law families too (though for three of our children's families I am now the only grandpa).

Helping people to find God through Jesus Christ remains a top priority to me. I have heroes of faith who have remained faithful Christians to their last breath. Billy Graham and George Muller both reached old age. A much younger friend of mine and fine example was Peter Birkenhead who died in his forties and whose family we are in touch with still. When he was dock missioner at Avonmouth he used to try to help all sorts of seamen, who were often lonely, short of suitable clothing for Britain and far from home. On one occasion he spoke to a ship's boatswain, who was a Muslim and sceptical about Jesus. At the end of a conversation Pete said to him 'I am going to pray that Jesus Christ gives you a dream'.

A few days later Pete saw him again and asked 'Has Jesus given you a dream?'

'Has he given me a dream?! Last night I dreamt I was driving my car down the road and there in front of me was a cross of fire. I tried to swerve to miss it, but which ever way I turned to avoid it, it was still in front of me. I hit it and smashed it into a thousand pieces, and then I knew at that moment that Jesus Christ knew everything I had ever done'. Muslims set a lot of store by dreams and visions. As a consequence I have prayed for many Muslims in the last thirty years.

For twelve years a variety of members of seven different churches and our own staff, have worked hard at putting on nativity plays here, to remind people of Jesus' birth and life. At first they took place in barns; then for the last ten years in the arena, all with live animals. Over 25,000 people have watched and participated in them; of all colours and walks of life. A young Mary receives a vision from the angel Gabriel that she is to be the mother of the Son of God, a disapproving Joseph receives angelic reassurance, they travel with a donkey to the inn where an unwelcoming innkeeper (knock, knock, 'Go away, we're full') eventually finds them a space among the lambs and cattle at their manger. Shepherds are on a hillside of bales, with their munching sheep when suddenly the angel appears and tells them the son of God is born and they must hurry to find him. Meanwhile magnificently clad, wise men (and women) are searching the sky and spot a new bright star (I have always felt this was a travelling and supernatural light, not an astronomical body) which they follow, as it moves to wicked King Herod (boo, hiss!) who wants to worship the new king too. The star/light moves to Bethlehem, here there is a combining of shepherds and their sheep and wise people and their shire horses, camel or llamas on the manger scene, with always a live baby waiting for them, sometimes held by its own mother, Mary, or carried from the mother behind the scenes to Mary by Gabriel, or blinking up at them or waving its little hand. I am always moved as big men and women bow before the infant Jesus to acknowledge God had begun the biggest rescue of all time; Jesus had started his 33-year journey to put us in touch with God. Wise men and women still seek Him.

These nativities have been very simple; put on in a cold arena, with no refreshments for the public, no Santa for children to come for, just the heart of the Christmas story, perhaps made all the more real by absence of comfort. Yet each year hundreds of new people, out of the thousand each day, come by recommendation or with friends who have seen one before. Some young children have never seen live animals before. So far, all but two performances have been free to the public; with a charity collection at the end for Send a Cow, or the Crisis Centre's work among the homeless in Bristol. It actually involves huge commitment by the churches who perform and who usually have to hire extra PA and lights, not to mention our own staff and volunteers. But they, as we do, feel it is well worth it, as a unique way of helping people remember that the Lord Jesus is vital to Christmas and to all of life.

On a wonderful visit we paid to South Africa, we stayed with our good friends Charles and Nina Baber on their 20,000 acre farm in Transvaal, where our son Caspar had spent half of his year out before university. We had been, while with them, to visit several safari parks including their own, run by their son and daughter-in-law. I had thought how wonderful it would be to live in a safari park, surrounded by magnificent exotic animals. I never dreamed at that time that 15 years later we would be doing just that. It is amazing to look out of the window at rhinos, bison, camels, giraffe, tapirs, zebras and ostriches, and to hear the loud calls of gibbons, lemurs, geese and cranes, not to mention tigers and lions. We feel more vulnerable than ever to economic pressures, the weather, our legal duties and responsibilities to our wonderful staff, the animals and thousands of visitors. But as a retirement job it is difficult to imagine a more interesting and exciting one. I would love my legacy to be of pointing lots of people to their Creator who is real, made close, forgiving and empowering them through Jesus, Son of God. A wonderful life after death can then lie ahead for all, with those challenges of the New Earth that we are told about in the New Testament. It sounds infinitely better than the alternative oblivion of the second death. Someone once said 'you are immortal in the place God wants you'. It will be for others to see when the Boss no longer wants us here and others are ready to take it all on.

Appendices

Appendix 1 Creation and destruction; Genesis and science

In my lifetime there has been a sustained attack on the Bible by both secular intellectuals and some theologians. For example, many Christians feel they cannot believe the creation story in *Genesis* as a scientific possibility, not because an alternative is more believable but because no suggestion has been put as to how these ancient texts can be understood in the light of the latest science. They have usually been taken as a story with spiritual meaning. This seems to me to be poor theology because, as has been found so often with Biblical history in the last 50 years, the text *has* been confirmed. Does it matter which view of *Genesis* we hold? I think it does, because there are stated many of the foundational truths of how to live, such as men and women equally carry the image of God; all people have common ancestors and all races are of equal value; men and women were created to rule the Earth on God's behalf; marriage is for life; and many more. When Thomas Jefferson wrote in the American Declaration of Independence 'we hold these truths to be self-evident, that all men are created equal…', he owned 250 slaves and 'self-evident' for over a hundred years meant the inferiority of women, slaves, Indians, poorer non-voters and minors. Biblical-evidence is what Jesus constantly referred to, especially *Genesis* from which He quoted more than any other Old Testament book except, and equal with, *Exodus*.

The newly developed theory of Creation, found in much greater detail on our website www.earthhistory.org.uk, suggests that like *Genesis*, the discoveries of space research and in geology tell the story of a created world and solar system. The surfaces of the solar system have been profoundly changed by asteroid storms; in particular the one on our earth-moon system known as the Late Heavy Bombardment (see below). In the case of Earth, the earliest rocks are missing, apparently lost in the Earth's mantle; subsequent rocks tell the history of recovery following this period. Fossils do not tell the story of the origin of life on Earth. So we are considering two distinct events, a formed Earth followed by a transformed surface. This is, of course, just as it is described in *Genesis* chapters 1-8.

The Bible begins in *Genesis* 1:1 In the beginning God created the heavens and the Earth. Now the Earth was formless and empty, darkness was over the surface of the deep, and the Spirit of God was hovering over the waters. And God said 'let there be light' and there was light. God saw that the light was good and he separated the light from the darkness. God called the light day and the darkness he called night. And there was evening and there was morning the first day.

The creation of the heavens by God is stated, but not exactly how, or when, or how vast. The way it is worded 'In the beginning' may indicate this was before God's creation week. Nine times in the Bible we are told God stretched out the heavens. His energy applied here, perhaps at many times the present speed of light, might explain the missing dark matter and dark energy, which are so elusive. We know for certain that by the end of Day One the Earth was in existence, described as covered by 'the deep', somewhere in the heavens. It was rotating before a light, and 'let there be light' was the first of ten creation commands. This source of light, as Earth rotated into evening and morning, would probably have been the primeval quasar, or Active

Galactic Nucleus (AGN) at the centre of our present Milky Way galaxy; the text states our sun was not in place until Day 4. Quasars were vast, high-energy, balls of hydrogen which formed the luminous centres of active galaxies and rotated like Catherine wheels propelling hot hydrogen at high speed. This condensed to form stars.

Big Bang theory says light arrived by 'a dominance of photons 10 seconds after the bang' with no explanation for the creation of photons from either nothing or from the bang. Is that a more scientific proposal? In the 21st-century branch of physics known as quantum chromo-dynamics, the vacuum is not empty space but a sea of energy from which matter particles draw their mass. The speed of light is a function of the state of energy in the vacuum. In transit, the photons of light (which are mass-less, but still subject to gravity) continually recharge their energy just as particles draw their mass from the vacuum. If the vacuum were emptied of zero-point energy, the result would not be light travelling at infinite speed but not travelling at all. So at God's command 'Let there be light' came the creation of photons and the energising of the vacuum, perhaps much stronger than it is today. Light, in all its electromagnetic complexity from gamma rays via visible light to long-wave radio, had arrived.

The light from our Milky Way's AGN is described as having arrived at the Earth at God's command before evening. Assuming our AGN was at the centre of the Galaxy (now a black hole) and was 25,000 light years away at today's speed of light, that would imply the speed of light was very much faster at Creation (and atomic rest mass, since $E = mc^2$, very much smaller). If this was so, it would also greatly shorten the apparent age of the universe; since radioactive decay, by which the earth is conventionally dated, is proportional to the speed of light (see chapter 43). Many people are surprised to know that the speed of gravity is always assumed to be instantaneous, so why was not the speed of light the same as the speed of gravity, or at least much faster once than it is now? There is room for more open-minded research here.

Day Two is even more mysterious. *Genesis* 1:6 says God commanded some water to be separated beyond a firmament or 'expanse'. The Hebrew word is sometimes translated as 'sky', but verse 14 clearly states various celestial bodies are to be set in it. So the waters above would have started as a thick spherical shell of water vapour beyond where the Kuiper Belt, the outside rim of the solar system, is now all that remains. This shell of water protected the Earth from cosmic rays before it had built up a magnetic field. The water would have soon begun spreading inwards throughout the solar system by gravitational attraction of the sun and the planets, it collapsed by rotation towards the ecliptic plane in which the planets rotate. There is evidence from our solar system that large amounts of water vapour once filled it, and water in various forms is everywhere still. It is found, as I have mentioned, in the distant reaches of the Kuiper Belt where those 'dirty snowballs', the comets, begin. Mars has been deluged in water. Venus had seas on it which are now dry. Our moon has water on it. Saturn's rings are water crystals; many planetary moons and asteroids have water on them.

On Day Three the Bible states the land was commanded to appear, after the water had been gathered 'in one place'. I am persuaded this means the land was on giant rock columns as the water was gathered into deep underground 'seas' (surface seas would have produced rain clouds and a rainbow). These seas may only have appeared above ground as large lakes rather than the oceans we know today. The text implies, by the later appearance of a rainbow as a promise, that there was neither rain nor a rainbow at first. The land was watered by streams and moisture from below. Furthermore, this water needed to be very deep. Psalms 24 and 136 mysteriously imply that God formed the land upon the deep waters, disclosing a Hebrew tradition that this was so. At the time of Noah we are told 'the fountains of the Great Deep burst forth' and were responsible for the inundation, caused by so much more than rain and which left the whole Earth's surface deep under water at the end of the earliest geological epoch of all, the Hadean.

Later, on Day Three God created seed-bearing plants and trees of various kinds. DNA is a language we can read but I suspect God can speak it. When the text states 'And God said 'Let the Earth produce vegetation ... according to their various kinds' it implies He spoke a small number of plant kinds into existence, each with the potential to evolve into thousands of species to fill all present and future ecological environments of the world.

On Day Four God creates unnamed 'lights' in the firmament, or expanse, which we now know as the solar system and there would have been more planets than now, perhaps 12, as well as the Sun and Moon. Some of these planets subsequently exploded into asteroids and some may have been given moons. The text describes the creation of these 'lights' to separate night from day; and to mark the seasons and years we now know and to shine light on the Earth.

On Day Five winged creatures ('birds of the air') and water creatures were created. It is likely that 'birds' refers to a variety of winged animals including insects as well as the feathered birds. Sea creatures would include the water invertebrates also. God 'breathes life into' a few creatures, giving them the potential to evolve into enormous groups of creatures.

God's command here is to be 'fruitful and increase in number'. They were created with the far-sighted genetic ability to evolve, reproduce, diversify and fill the range of environmental niches which were or would become available. This would provide the genetic changes from which natural selection could select.

On Day Six the final acts of creation were the formation of terrestrial animals, with mankind the pinnacle. The Biblical account names animals as 'livestock', 'wild animals' and infers creeping insects, land invertebrates and reptiles ('creatures that move along the ground'). There is a clear distinction made between Man and animals. We are a deliberate and separate act of creation by God, whose image is found in the maleness and femaleness of mankind. Adam noted the similarities to Eve before their differences; and was given the command to fill the Earth, to live from its fruitfulness and to manage the whole of creation on God's behalf. The *Genesis* 1 and 2 differences, it seems to me, are best understood as God's account given to Adam in chapter 1 and Adam's own story in chapter 2.

Resurfaced Solar System, the time of Noah?

For decades I, along with other Christians, have speculated on where the evidence lies for the flood of Noah. Clearly a local flood in Mesopotamia or the Black Sea would not need a huge ship to be built for rescuing the animals. The traditional proposal is for the whole geological column from the Cambrian layers to the Cretaceous to have been laid down under it. However, for reasons touched on in chapter 43, there is too much rock worldwide to be laid down in the short and devastating cataclysm the Bible refers to. In 1997 Steven Robinson, to whom I am indebted for most of the interpretations above, proposed that the Late Heavy Bombardment was the worldwide cataclysm we had been searching for, at the right time and with the right effect.

Here is a summary of the information scientists have discovered since the Apollo space mission. The ages are from radioisotope dating, though we think the real length of time is very different. Whatever that initial solar system of our sun and planets was like, it is different now. It has been resurfaced, probably at different times on the rocky planets, by both water and asteroids since its creation. Astronomers observe that our Earth/Moon system experienced the Late Heavy Bombardment (LHB) at the end of the Hadean Eon 3.9 Gya years ago (giga = one billion). Asteroids issuing from an explosion of a planet between Earth and Mars seem to have been the cause. This would have been after the main asteroid belt we see now, of which the conventional radiometric age appears to be 4.6 Gya old, created by an earlier explosion or collision. Water has been abundant on the Earth from as far back as datable minerals can take us, as early as 4.4 Gya. At the beginning of the next eon, the Archaean (3.9 Gya), the entire planet was under water and it was to remain largely submerged for another 1.3 billion years. (Flament *et al* 2008.)*

Asteroid activity is also everywhere, perhaps from different periods. It is possible that almost all the moons in the solar system except our own are captured asteroids (Jupiter has 63 moons and Saturn 62). The giant gas planet Jupiter is continually absorbing asteroids; according to the most recent computer simulation it could have an iron core as much as 16 times the mass of the Earth (Militzer *et al.* 2008).** The sun's emissions of elemental spectra also point to its having absorbed many asteroids. We know any object above a metre in diameter in orbit round the sun level with the Earth gravitates into the sun within a short time. There have also been huge impacts on the rocky planets, Venus and Mars. Mercury has also been resurfaced and may have lost part of its mantle as well as its entire outer crust. The moon's orbit was probably further away once; and it is possible Earth's tilt came about at this time. Uranus, although a gas planet, also appears to have had its direction of rotation altered, with an axial tilt of 98°.

The dust from a planetary explosion would have encouraged the precipitation of water vapour to gravitate towards every extant planet and asteroid, including the Earth. This precipitation would have been the rain described in the Noah story, when the 'windows of the heavens were opened' and which continued for 40 days and nights around the world. The Earth's atmosphere could not have held anywhere near enough vapour for such rain.

On the Moon this LHB has left 80 giant craters between 300 km and over 1,000 km across. Some work that is waiting to be confirmed and published, suggests this bombardment lasted perhaps less than two Moon rotations at the end of the Hadean period. It has been estimated that if 80 giant asteroids hit the Moon at the same time a total mass of 2×10^{17} tonnes would have hit the Earth with an explosive force of

* Flament, N, Coultice, N & Rey, P F, 2008 A case for late-Archaean continental emergence from thermal evolution models and hypsometry, *Earth and Planetary Science Letters* 275:326-36.

** Militzer B *et al*, 2008 A massive core in Jupiter predicted from first-principles simulations, *Astrophysical Journal Letters* 688:L45-L48.

one trillion H-bombs, totally destroying the Hadean Earth's surface. This would seem confirmed by there being no Hadean rocks on the Earth's surface, while their successor rocks, the early Archaean, appear as an up-welling of magma burying the Hadean land; and all forming under water. Such would fulfill God's description in *Genesis* of the destruction of people and place (the *mabbul,* a Hebrew word used only of this event) – the destruction of 'them and the earth' (*Genesis* 6:13).

It has been suggested that the seas would need to have been at least 4 km below the land surface, to prevent the water being boiled dry by a 40- to 50-day bombardment of the Earth of a similar magnitude to that which hit Mars and our moon. All these things seem to point to this being the time of the Great Flood, when God delivered his judgement on the Earth with a devastating cataclysm of asteroids – releasing the waters of the Great Deep to be joined by 40 days of rain from the Solar System through the 'floodgates of the heavens' (*Genesis* 7:11). If so, Earth's fossil-bearing rocks, the Phanerozoic, would record the story of recovery of life after this resurfacing, with the first Earth surface (the Hadean) totally buried and lost. Chapter 43 deals with the important time-scale issues.

We are told little else in the Bible about the hugely changing world after the Flood. Noah planting a vineyard and the animals having habitats to survive in, would indicate that the Ark probably landed on part of the Earth's surface that had not been covered in volcanic larva, and so had soil and recovering plants (the olive is mentioned). This, Noah called Ararat, or Holy Land. The area was subsequently subducted under Archaean rock and no trace remains of it or the Ark. The rest of the Bible indicates that God took a profound interest in people of every nation, all of whom descended from Noah; disapproving strongly of violent and exploiting people, while sending messengers and prophets to many nations with good news. Finally, Jesus comes to His rapidly-changing world and reveals His loving heart by healing us, befriending us and helping us to be the bearers of good news to a violent, frightened and lost world. The hairs of our heads are all numbered, Jesus tells us, and He healed all who came to him who were sick. 'I will put none of the diseases on you which I put on the Egyptians' (*Exodus* 15:25) probably also means He and His angels know where every harmful bacterium, virus and parasite are found. Few believe Him and fewer still call on Him for help, but His wonderful plan and offer are there for us.

Appendix 2 Global warming?

There have always been compelling reasons for Christians to care about the environment. God has charged us from *Genesis* 1 onwards with ruling the world as His managers, and His initial relationship with Adam showed that He plans being alongside us in all the challenges. For centuries mankind has been taking short cuts, by pouring sewage into rivers and industrial chemicals into rivers and seas and CFCs and other gasses into the atmosphere. This had to stop. Fossil fuels have been discovered to be a wonderful blessing and driver of an Industrial Revolution which could raise everyone's standard of living beyond our ancestors' wildest dreams, but cheap oil and gas supplies are beginning to dwindle. Our wholly honourable inventiveness and search for more varied and cheaper food, timber and metals has put pressure on some species of wildlife. Mankind has responsibilities to God and future generations in all of this.

Margaret Thatcher kick-started interest in global warming in the 1980s by setting up the Hadley Centre under the Met Office. She had a special interest in countering our dependency on coal. A few years before the press had been printing alarmist articles about an impending Ice Age: *Time Magazine* (24th June 1974), *Newsweek* (28th April 1975) and *National Geographic* (150:5, 1976); following a 30-year period of global cooling (1940-70) during the post-war economic boom. The International Panel on Climate Change (IPCC) was set up in 1988, which happened to be a very hot year in the USA with drought and fires consuming Yellowstone Park. So Senator Al Gore's Senate Committee on Science Technology and Space, in 1989, had good alarmist reasons to think about it. Gradually the band wagon grew and was fed by assertions more often than facts. What's new?

I have heard some very wild assertions made about climate, made by stringing together the last ten weather extremes around the world and saying 'look what we are bequeathing our children'! The cold winters of 2009/10, and 2010/11 dampened this down somewhat.

The truth is much more complex than we are led to believe. Professor Ian Plimer, an earth history scientist, published a well-researched and referenced book in 2009 to explain the complexities. The Sun has the most profound influence on our climate; tiny changes on its constantly moving surface make big differences on Earth. None of the 23 IPCC climate models include this (I. Plimer, *Heaven and Earth,* 2009, p101). Plimer argues that although carbon-dioxide levels have been rising, there are several causes and warming may also come from other sources. Even if warming is taking place (which, since 1998, may not be true) there is historic precedent for a much warmer northern hemisphere producing great advantage. For example, the Roman Warm Period, 250BC-450AD, was 2°C higher than today; populations and forests grew, citrus and vines were grown near Hadrian's Wall. Then followed a cold spell from 535–900AD when glaciers grew in long, bitter winters and populations dwindled. This was followed by the Medieval Warm Period (900-1300AD) when European economies boomed, Greenland was peopled and grew grain, sheep and cattle. In Britain we had wealth enough to build many of our greatest cathedrals. Then came the Little Ice Age (1280–1850AD) with variable but colder times leading to fairs on the frozen Thames for at least 20 winters. There was also population decline, crop failures, disease epidemics and the depopulation of Greenland. Then we had a warmer

20th century with a dip from 1940–1970, those very years when we were burning coal and oil as never before.

Plimer argues that thermometers globally do not show a temperature rise; that carbon dioxide of human origin may be increasing but is certainly not approaching a dangerous level. Carbon dioxide has been ten times higher in a previous ice age! Higher sea temperatures do not produce more hurricanes.

The graphs below show the famous 'hockey stick' graph, (top graph) that has become iconic to the IPCC, and infamous to others; it does not record the medieval warm period (900–1280AD) nor the Little Ice Age (1300–1880AD) with short lived warm pulses, that are drawn from hundreds of studies (lower graph).

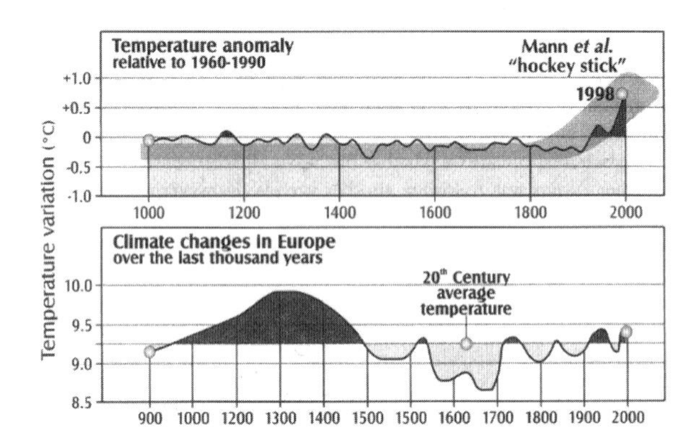

Philip Foster in his book *'While the Earth Endures' (SMP 2009)* similarly suggests there are eight baseless fears about global warming:

1. Sea levels are not rising dramatically. Only 10% of land ice is in the northern hemisphere (4% on Greenland and 6% on North America and Eurasia. In total this is hardly shrinking. Antarctica with 90% of land ice is getting slightly colder.

2. Global warming is not producing more extreme weather, hurricanes and tornadoes. If the expected warming heats high latitudes more than low, this would have the effect of diminishing the very differences that cause large-scale weather disturbance. This is confirmed by the number of hurricane strikes by decade in the USA: 1940-49: 23; 1950-59: 18; 1960-69: 15; 1970-79: 12; 1980-89: 16; 1990-99: 14. Hurricanes are not becoming more severe, only more costly, due to more expensive and denser properties being damaged. Katrina that hit New Orleans so devastatingly in August 2005 was a category three, whereas really bad ones are category five.

3. There will not be a serious shortage of water. A warmer climate will mean more water not less.

4. Tropical diseases such as malaria will not spread. Malaria is not dependent on heat but on mosquito vectors. There have been outbreaks in Siberia in 1920, and in Europe and America for millennia. It was only eradicated from the fens in the 1950s and in Holland in the 1970s. Poverty is the main cause of the spread of malaria and the criminal banning of DDT after Rachel Carson published her well-intentioned book *Silent Spring*, arguably caused the deaths of 40 million people from malaria – more than Hitler and Stalin together.

5. The Gulf Stream will not be overwhelmed by meltwater from Greenland, nor Europe subsequently frozen. Greenland is not melting any faster than it has been in the last several thousand years. There was once a time when a natural ice dam across half of America broke unleashing catastrophic amounts of fresh water, but Greenland could not produce nearly that amount. Minor shifting of the Gulf Stream caused errors of measurement that led to this speculation.

6. There will be no huge extinctions in the next 50 years. No accurate work has been done to support the suggestion, it is merely speculation. Norman Myers said in *Sinking Ark, (*1979) that until 1900 one species every four years was lost, he then quoted a 1974 conference 'guess' that 100 per year were then disappearing. He changed this to 100 species *per day*! The truth is that no one knows how many species there are on earth. Estimates vary from 3 million to 80 million. Most extinctions that do occur are for reasons other than warming.

7. Global warming will not produce mass starvation. IPCC admits a rise in temperature will increase harvests and yields. Satellite measurements over the last three decades show a 4% increase in biomass per decade. Starvation is caused by war, poverty and government incompetence; the Green Revolution of plant breeding means fewer people are starving today than 50 years ago, despite a population increase from 3bn to 7bn. GM crops may well be the next advance, along with wiser use of rainwater and groundwater harvesting.

8. Carbon dioxide levels will not go on rising indefinitely. Oceans have a limit to temperature rise due to water being a poor downwards heat conductor. The Pacific Ocean Heat Vent returns huge amounts of heat back into space.

The atheist proposal that the Earth is fragile because it arrived by chance and thus could disappear by chance is pure hypothesis. Science points to a robust Earth, created with many self-correcting mechanisms. Huge amounts of carbon dioxide are produced by volcanoes, by cosmic rays that smash into nitrogen atoms and change them into carbon-14; these fluctuate by 20%. Solar winds can disperse cosmic rays as can the Earth's magnetic field.

A rise in carbon levels is followed by an increase in plant growth and by carbon dioxide absorption into warming seas. This is assisted by a slower release of carbon dioxide from warm seas and an increase in absorption in sea crustaceans.

Summary

God has given us responsibility for this amazing Earth's future, and we should want to pass it on to our grandchildren in a shape which we and He are pleased about.

Appendix 3 Songs and poems

Lord of the Mountains *to the tune Highland Cathedral*
Lord of the mountains, streams and fields of green,
Creatures of glorious wonder fill this scene,
Sharing the beauty owned by all that thrives
Call to the great adventure of our lives.
God of the shining sun and stars of night,
Galaxies far beyond our searching sight;
Vast beyond comprehension burning bright
Giving you praise for calling forth the light.
Father of all the years of time,
We in our turn, living to serve;
Sharing gifts of your design,
Filled with your love divine.
Lord Jesus Christ for all that you have done,
Making us whole when we were almost gone,
Giving us life when in our greatest need,
We give you thanks for all you have redeemed.
Saviour from all our ills and pain,
Keeping us near, shield from our fears;
Taking all who come to you,
Healing our wounds and tears.
Hold us when we are parting from your way,
Keep us fulfilling your best plan we pray.
Let, as the evening light upon us falls,
Yours be the voice that heaven homeward calls.

To the tune of **We Plough the Fields and Scatter**
1. We plough the fields with tractors
With drills we sow the land;
But growth and yield are still the gift
Of God's almighty hand.
Some may add fertilisers
To help the growing plants;
Control the weeds, but still we need
The sun and rain God grants.
All good gifts around us
Are sent from heaven above;
So thank you Lord, oh, thank you Lord
For all your love.

2. With many new inventions
We do our work each day;
With grain and forage harvesters
And balers for the hay.
But you, Lord, now we thank for

Inventive skills and drives
To ease our daily work load
And give us better lives.
All good gifts………

3. O Lord you are the maker
Of galaxies above;
Of birds and plants and insects,
And everything that moves.
Atomic powers obey you,
By you all things are fed;
And Lord you've heard our prayer:
Give us our daily bread.
All good gifts……….

4. But Lord we ask forgiveness
When we have so much good,
So many people starve
And search rubbish dumps for food.
Please help us find the answers
For people's desperate need
And for our planet's future
For wisdom we would plead.
All good gifts…..

To the Country and Western tune
Put Your Hand in the Hand of the Man Who Stilled the Water
Put your hand in the hand of the man who stilled the water,
Follow close in the steps of the man who walked the sea.
Look at Him and you know He sees all people's hearts quite differently,
Keep your hand in the hand of the man from Galilee.
Put your hand in the hand of the man who fed five thousand,
Follow close in the steps of the man who helped men see.
Look at Him and you know He sees all people's hearts transparently,
With a love for the lost and the sick and the poor like me.
Put your hand in the hand of the man who cleared the temple,
Follow close in the steps of the man who cursed the tree.
Look at Him and you know He sees all people's hearts quite differently,
With a call 'follow close' to the Lord of Eternity.
Put your sins in the hands of the man who faced great trials,
The nail-pierced hands that were hammered to the cross for me.
Look at Him and you know He sees all people's hearts transparently,
And he died and he rose from death to set us free.
Put your hand in the hand of the man who stilled the water,
Follow close in the steps of the man who walked the sea.
Look at Him and you know He sees all people's hearts quite differently,
Keep your hand in the hand of the man from Galilee

To the tune of **Zaccheus Was a Very Little Man**

1. Zaccheus was a very little man,
and a very little man was he.
He climbed up into a sycamore tree,
for the Saviour he wanted to see.
And when the Saviour passed that way,
He looked into the tree, *and said*
'Now Zaccheus you come down
For I'm coming to your house for tea'.

2. Zaccheus was a tax collecting man
as greedy as greedy could be.
He cheated and stole and lied and worked
for the country's enemy.
But when the Saviour stayed that day
he changed for all to see, *and said*
'I'm giving stolen money back,
for it's you, Lord, I'm wanting to please'

3. Zaccheus's size didn't matter any more.
A bigger kinder heart had he.
He gave half his money to the Jericho poor
for his Saviour he wanted to please.
And as the Saviour left that day
He looked at Zaccheus once more, *and said*
'Today this man is saved, from being lost,
like others who will turn to me'.

4. Zaccheus was a very little man,
and a very little man was he.
He climbed up into a sycamore tree,
for the Saviour he wanted to see.
But when the Saviour comes our way,
He looks into our tree, and says
'My friend now you come down
for I'm coming to your house for tea'

Carol *to the tune of Three Coins in a Fountain*
1. One night long ago now
God came to us as a child;
Born our king in a stable
Laid down where the hay was piled.

2. Jesus, little baby,
Why did no one want you then?
None knew you only Mary,
Joseph, shepherds and wise men.

3. Jesus, God so holy,
Did you have to come to die?
Was all our wrong so hateful?
Did we all your laws defy?

4. Jesus, Great Creator,
Born a child but now our judge,
And yet you took for me Lord,
Punishment without a grudge.

5. Jesus risen Saviour,
Born a child and yet our king;
Humble then, though so powerful,
We will all your praises sing.
We give our all to you, Lord,
Mighty God, death conquering.

Carol *to the tune Somewhere over the rainbow*
1. Somewhere, over the mountain,
Secret, far;
Jesus came as a baby
Heralded by a star.

2. Awesome God our Creator
Chose to come;
Outcast, laid in a stable,
Only announced to some.

3. A baby born in dirt and straw;
Mere shepherds and wise Magi saw
His humble home.
Yet has He seen His welcome grow,
Does He come first or does He know
There's still no room?

4. Jesus, I'd like to thank you
For your birth
Now I'm ready for your work
Doing your will on earth.

We Thank You for the Summer Sunshine, Lord

Harvest Thanksgiving hymn

We Thank You for the Summer Sunshine, Lord

1. We thank you for the summer sunshine, Lord,
and thank you for the winter rain;
and thank you for the crops that grow our food,
for our bodies that the food sustains.
And praise you for amazing creatures, Lord,
for cats and bats and frogs and bees,
for rhinos, elephants and newts and ants,
for seals and eels and fruits and trees.

Chorus:
Raise your voice in the wide savanna – (roar!)
Sing aloud from the bottom of the sea – (boom, boom!)
Lift your antlers high; soar and call from the sky
'Thank you Lord for making me!'

2. We marvel at the gecko's feet, O Lord,
the chameleon's long fast tongue;
the crocodile and snake we fear to take
the turtle in its bony home.
What a wonder are migrating birds, O Lord,
the humming bird's rotating wings,
the Lyre Bird, Quail and the Peacock's tail,
the Skylark and the song it sings.
Chorus

3. We're astonished at our eyes and ears, O Lord,
our smell and taste and sense of pain,
our muscles, skin and bone; with nerves all grown
as wiring to our awesome brain.
We're humbled by the tiny creatures, Lord,
bacteria, spiders and fleas;
mosquitoes, ticks, lice - creepy crawlies not nice,
but we're sure you've a plan for these.
Chorus

4. How did you make the Milky Way O Lord;
great planets and their moons and sun?
How did you set their pace in endless space
while galaxies around them spun?
And thank you for the golden sunset Lord,
the silver moon that shines by night
and thank you that you're there to help us bear
the darkness and the dazzling light.
Chorus

Appendix 4 The Bush Family Tree

Including possible connection with George III and Bishop Bush of Bristol. Family trees are a somewhat artificial and very selective; usually the paternal line only is traced. In our case my brother John nvestigated for our father:

Barnard Bush (b1912), married Elizabeth Weeks, had a sister Theta, and was son of -
John Hubert Bush (b Frome, 1875), who married Edith Swanton, had four brothers and two sisters, was son of -
Barnard John Bush (b Blatchbridge, 1851) married Frances Elliott, had five brothers and six sisters, was son of -
John Bush (b Frome, 1827) married Ellen Dowling, had four sisters and five brothers, was son of -
James Bush (b Blatchbridge, 1791), a thatcher, and co-founder (with his father-in-law, John Gunning) of Warminster and Donhead St. Mary Wesleyan-Methodist meeting houses, he married Ann Marie Gunning, daughter of John Gunning and Mary Noble (daughter of John Noble, who by some tradition was the son of the youngest son of the morganatic marriage between Prince George Frederick (later George III) and Hannah Lightfoot (b 1730), c 1753. Marriage license confiscated by Chancery Court, 1766. Hannah may have been banished to Warminster and George's marriage annulled; James Bush was the son of -
Thomas Bush (b Frome, 1766), married to Charity Dowling, he was the son of -
James Bush (b Frome, 1733), married to Alathea Sutton, he was the son of -
John (Jonas) Bush (b Frome,1706), married to Alice, he was the son of
Adam Bush (b Frome, c 1680), married to Elizabeth.

There is a possible/probable connection to the following Bushs in the same area:

Walter Bush, married to Maud, widow of Christopher Bailey of Southwick Court. (Initials WB 1567 on Southwick Court)
John Bush of Dilton, mortgaged Dilton for £500 in 1566, relinquished it in 1576, descended from (or perhaps was son of) –
John Bush (Granted Manor of Dilton on dissolution of Monasteries in 1540, Married Elizabeth Fernfold. Brother of Paull Bushe, first Bishop of Bristol, Priest and Bonhomme, Edington. Married Edith Ashley, who died before Queen Mary's reign.
Both John and Paull were sons of William Bush, married to Miss Strange, Gloucestershire heiress, during reign of Henry VII.
Son of John Daylwyn (changed his name to **Bush),** probably wool merchant arriving in England in reign of Henry VII, and clothes manufacturer for the king. Married to Cecily Ryde. Descended from Evan Daylwyn, (b 1380), the Bard of Glamorgan Gorsedd (Daylwyn – Welsh, 'two bushes')

Appendix 5 The Second World War and Days of Prayer

Most Second World War histories tell of the battles between men and armies, but omit the consequences and answers to prayer. I have already mentioned General Sir Arthur Smith's experience of delivery in the heat of the battle. There would have been many thousands of others. Bishop Maurice Wood told General Synod one day of his experience on a Dunkirk beach, where he was a chaplain at the evacuation in 1940. A German plane strafed the beach and Maurice threw himself to the ground and prayed for protection. When he eventually stood up he said that bullet marks disturbed the sand all round him but his body left an outline that was untouched. Why was Maurice Wood spared? God alone knows, but I and many others were blessed by his long ministry.

When the Second World War began King George VI recalled the memory of his father George V who in March 1918 called the nation to prayer – as Old Testament kings had sometimes done. As soon as the day was announced, the enemy action, which was succeeding at the time, was halted. Then, following the day of prayer, the allies began an attack. They found enemy morale had collapsed and progressed to victory in November.

Thus George VI called Britain to prayer. All churches took this seriously. The King is after all, the head of the Church of England. A large proportion of the population went to churches and chapels. Almost everyone prayed sometimes. Why did victory take so long? Why was so much horrific killing allowed? The stories are very little different from the horrific killing that the Old Testament describes and which has happened in every century of human history. God had his reasons then and they were varied: heroism and villainy, selfishness and sacrifice, beauty and hideous ugliness co-existed for years. God must have had a billion reasons in a billion lives, because Jesus tells us 'a sparrow does not fall to the ground without your heavenly Father.' Millions went early to heaven. Age did not weary them, nor the years condemn. Others were spared for lives of service and sacrifice or for lives of selfishness. We each have our opportunity to shine, but none of us knows for how long.

Below is a list of the Days of Prayer and of certain events that followed them. There are probably many other events that could be recorded; perhaps this will be completed by others. We will never know the full consequences of millions of people praying for millions of others.

World War Two: Dates, 14 Days of Prayer and Consequences

German build up to war

1935 German rearmament achieved air parity with Britain.
Hitler/Mussolini axis as a result of British sanctions on Italy over Abyssinia.
1936 March 7 Rhineland demilitarised, announced as symbolic.
1938 February Austria occupied.
September Czechoslovakia occupied, including 35 divisions of Army and Skoda armaments factory.
1939 April 7 Italy invades Albania.
August Germany and Russia sign non-aggression pact.
Sept 1 Germany invades Poland. Britain and France issue ultimatum.
Sept 3 Britain and France declare war after rejection of ultimatum.

Sept 17 Russia invades Poland from the east.
Sunday October 1 King George VI calls the nation to the FIRST DAY OF PRAYER. Consequences:
November 24 Magnetic mines rendered useless by Lieut. John Ouvry.
Goering completely underestimates British radar and fails to order its destruction; after one failed attempt by Luftwaffe, bombing switched to London.
Blitzkrieg conquers western Europe and drives allies back to Dunkirk.

1940 Sunday May 26 1940, DAY OF PRAYER.
May 26 – June 4 338,000 Allied troops rescued at Dunkirk. Gale force winds over Flanders kept most Luftwaffe aircraft grounded; calm channel seas enabled troops to be rescued by small boats, and mainly by navy ships. Some fog added protection. Hitler failed to order the annihilation of the British and French.
Sunday June 9 NATIONAL DAY OF THANKSGIVING
Lend-lease agreement with USA agreed.
24 June Fall of France, armistice.
21 July Hitler orders planning for invasion of Russia, 'Britain is on its knees we march on Russia'.
August USA entrusted with radar secrets for joint development.
Sunday September 8 DAY OF PRAYER, Britain and USA.
September 13 Mussolini, in opposition to his generals, orders Italian attack in North Africa.
September 15 Battle of Britain won by the RAF, against the balance of power.
September 17 Hitler calls off operation Sealion, the invasion of Britain.
Sunday September 26 DAY OF THANKSGIVING for Battle of Britain deliverance.

1941 Sunday March 23 , DAY OF PRAYER.
April 6 Germany attacks Yugoslavia and Greece. Germany suffers huge losses in Crete – it is Hitler's last airborne attack. British army withdraws from Greece and Crete to North Africa.
May 9 Capture of first Enigma coding machine by HMS Bulldog
May 27 Bismarck Battleship sunk.
June 22 Hitler invades Russia, breaking his pact.
Sunday September 7 DAY OF PRAYER.
September 8 Russia announces first victory of war, at Smolensk, with eight German Divisions defeated.
September 12 Russian winter arrives exceptionally early with first snow.
October 7 Stalin lifts ban on religion in Russia to lift morale.
October 19 Stalin decides to stay and defend Moscow.
October Radar causes German U-boats serious setbacks in Atlantic.
Sunday November 16 DAY OF PRAYER.
November 18 Operation Defender leads to Rommel's defeat at Tobruk
November 20 Early fury of Russian winter hits Germans hard (–37°C 4 December). Moscow saved.
December 7 Japanese attack on Pearl Harbour ends America's isolation.
December 21 Typhus reported in German troops on Russian front.
Sunday December 29, DAY OF PRAYER.

1942 February 27 Successful raid on first German radar installation at Bruneval, almost no casualties; capture of installation led to jamming of German radar and saving of Allied bombers.
Sunday March 29 DAY OF PRAYER.
April 1 First convoy of allied supply ships to Russians, 14/19 get through, leading to 400 tanks and 500 aircraft being delivered each month.
June Americans defeat Japanese at Midway. Beginning of Japanese decline.
Germans advance on Stalingrad to the eventual loss of 250,000 troops and enough equipment for quarter of German army. Hitler says 'What is life? Life is the nation; the individual must die anyway.'
Sunday September 3 DAY OF PRAYER.
October 22 Battle of El Alamein won. Montgomery had broadcast to his troops 'And let us pray that the God of Battles will give us the victory'; after victory he wrote 'let us not forget to give thanks to God for His victory.'
November 7-8 US Army lands in Morocco, North Africa.
November 10 Vichy France, North Africa, surrenders.
November 16, DAY OF THANKSGIVING for North Africa; church bells rung.

1943 May 19 DAY OF THANKSGIVING for Victory in North Africa.
May, Battle of the Atlantic against German U-boats is won.
May/June German Russian armistice talks break down.
July 10 Successful Sicily landings.

1944 June 6King George calls for a VIGIL OF PRAYER for D-Day landings:
'At this historic moment, surely none of us is too busy, too young or too old to play our part in a vigil of prayer. 'The Lord will give strength to His people; the Lord will give His people the blessing of peace.'
President Roosevelt called the US nation to prayer:
'help us, Almighty Father to renew our faith in Thee.'
General Eisenhower's message to the allied troops before the D-Day landings:
'Soldiers, sailors and airmen of the Allied Expeditionary Force; you are about to embark upon the great crusade, toward which we have striven these many months. The eyes of the world are upon you. The hopes and prayers of liberty-loving people march with you... We will accept nothing less than full victory! Good Luck! And let us beseech the blessing of Almighty God upon this great and noble undertaking.'

For the first 24 days of the D-Day offensive allied deaths were one-third of the average for the whole war.

ADDITIONAL DAYS OF PRAYER were called on:
3 September 1944
September 1946 (for the Paris Peace Talks) and
6 July 1947 (during the economic crisis)

DEATHS

Germany	7.23million	10.38% of population
Soviet Union	23.1	13.7%
China	20	3.86%
Japan	2.7	3.78
Great Britain	0.449	0.94%
United States	0.42	0.32%

Britain and USA suffered remarkably few casualties compared with both the First World War and other countries in the Second World War.

Japan

Japan was a victim of its religion: the Japanese government forced every subject to practice State Shinto and admit that the Emperor was divine. Japan waged war at his instruction and both inflicted and received horrific damage. It was considered a social disgrace for a soldier to surrender; so millions more died unnecessarily. In the closing days of the war Emperor Hirohito said:

> Duty is heavier than a mountain; death lighter than a feather.

At the Battle of Iwo Jima 22,000 Japanese died; 7,000 Americans
At the Battle of Okinawa 100,000 Japanese died; 12,500 Americans

March–August 1945, in Japan 330,000 died and 500,000 were injured by the bombing of 42% of 62 cities, with 104,000 tonnes of American bombs dropped.
At Hiroshima 80,000 Japanese died; at Nagasaki 70,000.
The A-bombs allowed the Japanese to surrender with honour. The Emperor in a speech said:

> the war situation has developed not necessarily to Japan's advantage' and ordered the Japanese to 'endure the unendurable' in surrender.

Hitler Youth *Deutsches Jungvolk*

A quasi-religious movement by 1935 there were 3,500,000 members, by 1939 almost all youth between 10 and 18 were members. At initiation the 10-14-year-old swore eternal allegiance to the Fuhrer, and recited a vow ending:

> You, Fuhrer, are our commander, we stand in your name. The Reich is the object of our struggle. It is the beginning and the Amen.

Appendix 6

Emails from apparent atheists' groups, messages from supporters and comments from our visitors' book

Below are the texts of emails sent to us during 2009 (**in bold**) and my replies, the last of which is of several replies to the same person.

1. There is NO evidence whatsoever for the bullshit you try to pass off as fact. Face the facts: there is no supernatural creator, there is no god. There is no evidence to suggest there is.

> I expect you realize that you are giving us the atheist position that poses as science but in reality seems unwilling to discuss it. The evidence for God is both in millions of people's experience and in the events of history. Jesus Christ was a real person, whose life and death and resurrection are described by several independent witnesses; Matthew, Mark, Luke, John, Jude, Peter, as well as Paul who encountered Jesus while busy killing Christians and imprisoning some of them. For your own encounter with your Maker this side of death I would suggest you talk to Him and ask: 'God, if you are there, please convince me'.

2. I do not usually use expletives but your website deserves it, a crock of shit dressed up to look like science, I will be writing to my MP to ensure that you are not receiving any tax based funding.
A half witted cretin would recognise that evolution in virii has led to swine flue; one of thousands of examples supporting the theory of evolution; & yes I do fully understand what the word theory means in the context of evolution & other areas of science.
It is a shame that there is no god to punish you for this pile of misinformation, prevarication & outright falsehoods, if Darwin were alive he could sue you for libel & would win. Your perversion of the truth is appalling & quite frankly I actually do hope that you die a slow & painful death, preferably from a newly evolved bacterium or Virus.

> You sound angry. Who told you we don't believe in evolution? We do, from bacteria to galaxies there is a story of constant evolution.
> We think God made a few creatures pre-programmed to evolve, including viruses. It is only Richard Dawkins and some he seems to have influenced, who thinks that no modern Creationists believe in evolution.
> But we don't think you can extrapolate evolution backwards so that everything is related. Nor do we think that humans evolved from apes. We think as all Christians and many other theists do, that we are made in God's image to behave very differently. As our website explains.

3. I have a suggestion for your website. Close it down. Rarely have I read such rubbish about evolution. It is astonishing in this day and age that intelligent people should be so stupid as to believe in creationism. It certainly must not be presented to children as science. It belongs in the same category as the flat earthers. Bob

A few days ago you wrote to us out of the blue saying [the above]. I wrote to you asking for a suggestion on any one scientific inaccuracy you might like to point out. You are in a long line of people who write to us just angry that we present God as the source of all Creation. Your reply was just a religious rant, so I assume you know nothing about Darwinism and its reductionist, simplistic proposals that do not deserve to be called science. The fact that a minority (almost certainly) of scientists around the world (but a majority in UK, though some are intimidated into it) support it is probably that like you they don't like the idea of God being in control, and assume someone somewhere has worked out that Darwinism can work. It has no theory of how the laws of nature and physical forces arrive; what caused a Big Bang if it ever happened; what stuck the galaxies together; what formed DNA and life; what changed a prokaryote into a eukaryote, or into algae; what caused sexual reproduction out of asexual; what caused the 35 phyla of life in the Cambrian Explosion to appear; what gave life forms their genetic inheritance for Natural Selection to select; and so on. It is clear that evolution is everywhere, from galaxies to bacteria, butterflies to elephants, but the 'tree of life' is a lie; sometimes referred to as the palaeontologists trade secret, here are two quotes from one of our displays, put together by a geologist:

The extreme rarity of transitional forms in the fossil record persists as the trade secret of paleontology. The evolutionary trees that adorn our textbooks have data only at the tips and nodes of their branches; the rest is inference, however reasonable, not the evidence of fossils.
Stephen Jay Gould, *Natural History* 86, 1977.

Most families, orders, classes, and phyla appear rather suddenly in the fossil record, often without anatomically intermediate forms smoothly interlinking evolutionarily derived descendant taxa with their presumed ancestors.
Niles Eldredge, *Macro-Evolutionary Dynamics: Species, Niches, and Adaptive Peaks*, 1989

Bob you are a victim of a conspiracy, there is a battle going on for your soul, between God and His enemy. Believing lies will not help you. One day you will face your Maker and He will want to know what you did with your life to make a difference; and what you did about the evidence He gave you that He is everywhere. The agnostics prayer is 'God if you are there, please convince me'. He will.
With best wishes Anthony

4. I have written today to the zoo forum at DEFRA to register my objection that you have breached their rules concerning education by concealing your creationist agenda. Promoting your offensive and deluded religious belief under in the guise of a petting zoo is a grotesque abuse of young minds and it is my concern that some vulnerable children may even be taken in by your bizarre and inaccurate fairy stories. I shall do everything in my power to ensure that your wolf in sheep's clothing organization is exposed.

Thank you for writing to us. I am not completely clear why you seem to feel so strongly against us. I wonder if you have actually been here? We have won tourism awards at local, regional and national level over the last six years. We call ourselves Noah's Ark Zoo Farm, not North Somerset Wildlife Park. You get what is on the packet. Why did Noah's Ark get built? Because God told him to do it. Noah's was a historic event and the biggest conservation exercise ever conducted. We remind those people who wonder if the universe, life, including DNA and the genes, arrived naturally or supernaturally, that God is Creator and the world is not a meaningless dread-filled loneliness. He has a plan for each of us.

Where has Noah's Ark's its most credible mention? (We have anecdotal evidence from 45 countries all around the world, including the Gilgamesh Epic). In three chapters in Genesis, as well as in three other Old Testament and four New Testament books, including most notably in important teaching by Jesus Christ, himself, and by St. Peter. Having just been to a reunion at the biggest Anglican Theological College in the country, where I was a student a while back, I was intrigued that the former Archbishop, Lord Carey and other staff members whom I spoke to, all believe in the story of Noah as history.

Considering all primary schools are required to have assemblies each week that is primarily Christian, you sound somewhat alone in suggesting that our mainstream Christian position is a grotesque abuse of young minds. It is the atheists who seem to wish to destroy the Christian heritage of this country; of lifelong monogamous marriage and strong family life; of sexual purity before marriage and fidelity within it, of adherence to the 10 commandments, and of weekly worship of God. There is still a vast majority belief in God, despite the Darwinist position, with all its weaknesses, being the only one allowed on TV science programmes.

I don't think you really know what Creationism is. If you want to know why we distance ourselves from the American form, try:
www.earthhistory.org.uk/introduction/evolutionism-creationism-compared/

I regularly attend the Zoo Forum, who know well that we conceal nothing. I suspect your real hang up is that you are rejecting God, your Maker. Many of our critics are lapsed Roman Catholics who have probably been over-fathered by priests. If so, cheer up I come from a tradition that was burnt by Roman Catholics(!) but many Catholics now seem like true believers in Christ. Why not try reading St John's Gospel all by yourself. I think you will find that Jesus Christ, without whom nothing was made that has been made, can be as real to you as he is to millions of others of us around the world. Unlike every other faith, faith in Jesus Christ is about a relationship with him, not rules, traditions, superstitions, fears about what people think of us.

5. Are you aware that an official petition has been made against you and your religious beliefs propagated to innocent children? Your zoo brings shame to this nation, putting us in line with the USA and their creationist museum. Furthermore, you exploit the innocence of children by promoting your mythological nonsense. It amounts to mental child abuse.

Thank you for writing to us, we welcome all feedback, knowing many others

think as each correspondent does. We welcome discussion here from those who agree or disagree with us.
You are certainly stating your case. Mental child abuse? Hmmm. We have received a number of emails from the Sink the Ark group and those who supported the petition to No. 10 against us. They overlook a few things.
We have received tourist awards at local, regional and national level over the last 6 years, our views are displayed for all to see, including the awards judges, and the Visit England inspectors who comment on them and appreciate what we are doing.
We have researched the theory of evolution in great depth and our aim is to present a broader range of options to children, having become convinced of the shortcomings as well as truths of Darwinism, and of Creationism. We hope children will benefit from this broader debate. Many schools come here because of this.
The government does not support us in any way. It is the other way round; unlike all the charity zoos we pay VAT on all attendances here, while they are exempt.
You sound shocked that we should propose a decay in the speed of light. This is not original; others beat us to it. We are looking for an explanation for why the Radioisotope dating of rocks is different from the empirical ages, see www.earthhistory.org.uk/technical-issues/cyclicity-in-chalk/ It is a proposal, not dogma.
We are not doubting the evolution of species. Evolution is everywhere, from galaxies to bacteria, beetles to elephants. But we question the tree of life when that is presented as dogma. Surely that is brainwashing? Some palaeontologists have described the lack of evidence for the stem and major branches as 'the trade secret of palaeontology'. You will know Niles Eldredge and Steven J Gould and others disagree sharply with other Darwinists over this.
For you to say anyone who disagrees with you is guilty of child abuse overlooks a few things. All schools are required to have an assembly each week, which is 'mainly Christian'. Mainstream Christianity includes that Jesus Christ, son of God, 'without whom nothing was made that has been made' (Jn 1) is our source of wisdom, power and relationship. That God made the universe and made us (in some way) is foundational to all Christians, just as it is that Jesus died on the cross for us, and that heaven and hell await the human race after death; and God wants us to choose Him and heaven. To state or preach such things is not brain washing, any more than for you to say everything evolved out of nothing without a First Cause. We put our cases and see which people choose.

6. I have looked the so called education you are offering at the Noah's Ark Zoo Farm. You as a scientist ought to be ashamed of yourself for peddling this un-scientific nonsence [sic] about creationism to children.
It is almost beyond belief that you could have gained a scientific degree in a biological science only to then ignore all the scientific evidence on evolution and put your name to the utter rubbish on your website.

Then after our 'straight bat' response, he wrote again:

If your educational purpose is to teach to the National Curriculum, which presumably fully endorses evolution by natural selection, why is your website so full of creationism? Also your website gives links to sites such as the Earth History website which contains no real science whatsoever.
Martin
PS Can you tell me how Noah managed to get 2 members of between 30 million and 100 million species on board (by the way there would have been an awful lot of beetles)

I can't blame you for not knowing about Creationism. The BBC's script writers for David Attenborough and most programmes about Darwin are equally or deliberately ignorant. Creationists think God 'breathed life into' (to quote a Darwin phrase from Origin) and therefore gave the genes to a few creatures at the beginning, so that they were capable of evolving by natural selection into the millions of species we know now. So one pair of beetles might contain all the genetic potential to become 350,000 species. We can only guess at how many air-breathing vertebrates and invertebrates had evolved by Noah's day; but he probably would not have needed more than 300 pairs of vertebrates.
The Darwinist view, on the other hand, has no proposal for how life (a prokaryote) arose; but suggests that somehow those prokaryotes obtained genetic information by tiny changes (but no scientific explanation of how this happened) so that Natural Selection could select and evolution could happen. A bit of Lynn Margulis magic produced a eukaryote. Sexual reproduction then apparently suddenly, but inexplicably, appeared; leading to millions of amazingly complex creatures arriving quite undirected and by chance. I think you will agree that is little less than a fairy story, but is masquerades as science. How it is better to teach this to children, rather than reassure them that they have a Maker who loves them, escapes me. If children are required to have an assembly each week and mainly of the Christian faith, why is it suddenly dangerous to mention God in science? Jesus Christ, whom billions of us believe was the Son of God, manipulated nature in reassuringly amazing ways. These led me to be a believer, then into a relationship with Him.
The Earth History website is meant to explain that the fossil record appears to be the story of recovery after a wipe-out, rather than the story of the origin and evolution of life from nothing. I am sorry you did not read it enough to see it is full of the very latest science. The Late Heavy Bombardment that resurfaced the solar system in the Hadean/Noachian is an important part of the proposal. (Ironic names you might think).
In the fossil record, phyla and orders of life appear suddenly, without evolutionary ancestors. So there is a Cambrian explosion of marine life, then an explosion of spore-seeded plant life, then the insects appear in the Carboniferous, all with trachea, so they did not come from the sea, etc. Just as Darwinists have different views from each other, so Creationists do too. We think geology points to a Creation at least 100,000 years ago, to allow time for the rocks to be put in place. We think a 6,000BC Creation is as impossible to defend as Darwinism. The empirical ages of the rocks themselves, however, simply do not agree with their Radioisotope ages. There must be another so-

lution, like perhaps a decay in the speed of light perhaps due to a variation in the energy field of the vacuum. If we had a tiny proportion of the funding for our paradigm that is afforded to the current paradigm we might make faster progress.

May I suggest discussion is the way forward? Be as forceful as you like; but we are capable of constructive thought this end. I have four science graduates on my staff and a science professor as a consultant.

7. It is my understanding that there are at least a quarter of a million different kinds of beetle on this earth. Consequently there must have been at least a half million beetles turn up to board the Ark. This, to me, presents a considerable problem of logistics. Surely they could not be allowed to just run all over the place as they would have been trodden on by the larger animals, or eaten by the predators. My only conclusion is that some of Noah's children, (our ancestors of course as we are all descended from them, all other humans being drowned) collected them in pairs and put them in boxes, along with food and water. This would have required a quarter of a million boxes which would have been a rather large stack. All sorts of questions lead from this; how could the Ark accommodate them? How were they secured? How, after the flood had subsided, did they get to the remote parts of the world in which they live?

Do you have any information as to how this was handled? I would much appreciate any information you could supply.

Yours in anticipation.

I think there are nearer 350,000 species, actually Mick. Our assumption is that God originally breathed life into one pair of beetles and in their DNA gave them the ability to evolve over time into all the thousands we know today. Likewise with all 27 orders of insect, like butterflies, dragon flies, etc; and other invertebrates, plants, fungi and vertebrates. The alternative is to believe that nothing designed them. It has seemed to me more likely that God existed without a cause than that all the amazing creatures did. Jesus then shows us how, as Son of God, He had power over Creation, in raising three people from the dead and doing lots of other miracles. If you would like to look further into a credible reconciliation of science and Genesis have a look at our website at:

www.earthhistory.org.uk/creation-theory-index/introduction/

We think that, as Genesis says, God made the world and its creatures and put us in charge; to rule the world well with Him. He wants a relationship with us to help us do all that as well as possible.

8. I've just read some of the tripe you have on your website.

Polluting vulnerable young minds with religious twaddle before they are questioning enough to be able to rationalise the information themselves is preying on the vulnerable as far as I am concerned.

You should be ashamed of yourselves.

Thank you for writing to us, albeit in astonishing patronizing and unhelpful way. Four of my staff are science graduates. We understand Darwinism very well and are proposing an alternative paradigm. If you are not too old to consider something new, give it some thought. The only people to do brainwashing are those who present one view alone and will not allow any alternative to be considered; like the atheist Gestapo. The rest of us make cautious proposals and invite discussion. Perhaps you would like to be more specific about your queries.

Why propose an alternate theory when one is not needed? We have a perfectly good working model with evidence to back it up.To pollute young minds with some bizarre notion of mysticism dressed up as fact seems wrong to me.

The trouble is that the alternative theory seems to be only partially right. There is lots of evolution, from galaxies to bacteria, but it needs God to start it all off and in the case of living groups of creatures, to front load them with genetic material for Natural Selection to work on. To say that God is not part of it all would not only be unsatisfactory it would be dangerous, as the atheist dictators of the 20th Century showed the world with their very bad proposals of racial supremacy, eugenics, etc.

Belief in God is not mysticism it is part of our national heritage. As the atheist convert to deism, Anthony Flew, said 'it is more likely that God exists without a cause than that the universe exists without a cause'.

What an utter load of tosh

You will be able to say that to your Maker one day. You might then wish you had thought about it a bit longer.

Religion is one of the worst things that as humans we have invented. The suffering and misery it has caused and has continued to cause is unprecedented. If there is a maker, or something bigger (who knows there actually may be) how on earth could we possibly hope to understand what it is, let alone know what Its thoughts are?

I understand how it can look that way.

But if we examine carefully the religious material that we have been bequeathed by history, we can discover quite quickly that which has been invented – you are right, there is a lot of invention. Looking past the professionals to see what if anything is revealed by God, the Biblical witnesses stand head and shoulders above those who are trying to control us in all the religions. This was why William Tyndale spent his life trying to make them available to every ploughboy in England in the 15th century; and was burnt at the stake for it by the religious professionals and politicians, who did not want people thinking for themselves. I strongly recommend Luke's gospel as written by an accurate historian and a doctor; you will see for yourself whether it seems accurate, inspired, and a description of God coming to earth; or in your own words, a load of tosh.

I'm interested. Where would I find this?

You can get to it online at:
www.biblegateway.com/passage/?search=Luke+1&version=NIV
then follow the arrow icons at the top for the other 23 chapters, leading from Jesus' birth to his death and resurrection.

It is one of the four gospels (eyewitness accounts of the life of Jesus) in the New Testament of the Bible, if you have a copy. All four were written to help people have an accurate contemporary version of the historic account of Jesus, who was the only person ever to claim to be the Son of God, and have no burial place. We each need to decide for ourselves if it seems true. 'God, if you are there, please convince me' is a good prayer to say any time. I am sure He will. *(I also enclosed a slide show about flying geese)*

I believe and have noticed that the world is amazing and I think that the slide show is lovely and very inspirational.
I'm still of the opinion that if there is a God, or a bigger picture, I don't believe we really know what it is as it is so vast and so removed from where we are we cannot really comprehend it.
Maybe it's just life or consciousness itself that is the amazing thing.
I still am of the opinion that we are simply intelligent/dangerous animals that have developed a higher consciousness over many hundreds of thousands of years and we have tried to explain this by coming up with stories of gods and divine intervention.
My thoughts on God would be that, if there is one, it would be far more universal than we have given it credit for. I was looking at pictures from the Hubble Telescope and the enormity of what is out there is truly quite mind numbing! What is the universe? How does it work? What is it a part of? Why does it even exist?
I think Man and Earth are likely to be a tiny little insignificant spec of something so vast we cannot even begin to comprehend what it is. It is our own vanity that makes us think that God takes a minute interest in us and our tribulations. I think he (if there is a he) creates the conditions and rules about how things work and where the right building blocks exist life is the eventual outcome. Anyhow, after our last email I visited Canterbury Cathedral and I have bought a 100 minute Bible to have a read of as I am interested in gaining an understanding of what it has to say about things and I am very happy to continue to hear from you should you be interested in corresponding.

Thanks for your thoughtful email. You are clearly in the big quest so many of us have embarked on to discover God and His plan for each of us. My own search took a great leap forward when I suddenly realized that God the Creator, who is mega and out there, was also, according to Jesus Christ, interested in us personally. It was a mind-blowing time, but I began to pray to Him personally and read from His book, the Bible, as so many had done before me; and found Him to be spiritually real.

This is something no one else can do for you, D——-. If you have read Luke's gospel to satisfy yourself with the facts of Jesus coming in real time and real geography and doing real miracles to satisfy Luke the medical man, I would recommend John's gospel next. John was a Jewish fisherman who became a disciple, then church leader. He lived a long life, finally imprisoned on Patmos Island, where he wrote the last book in the Bible, Revelation. But his gospel, the fourth of the four gospels explains how Jesus was the Son of God and convinced his followers by well attested miracles. It is a more spiritual gospel than the others and many thoughtful people like yourself have found God speaks to them through it.

ENCOURAGEMENT

We also had encouragement during the attack, mainly by telephone, sometimes by letter. These are a sample of the ones received by email:

1. As we wanted to 'check out' the Zoo for ourselves, we actually visited yesterday and what a lovely day we had. The zoo is absolutely beautifully kept and it was a delight to see the Siamang Gibbons 'new addition' a tiny little baby! This farm zoo has lovely facilities for children of all ages, with playgrounds and trampolines as well as wonderful educational resources. The evolution of snakes was a fascinating and most informative read found in their small reptile house. I never thought I would get so close to 2 gigantic Rhinos in the 'Rhino Ranch' and it was a truly awesome experience when these guys stood up only a few short feet in front of us. We took the opportunity to talk with some of the staff (who had no idea who we were and that we would blog about our experiences) and they were lovely, friendly and very knowledgeable indeed.
2. This family zoo farm is a welcome oasis; I was particularly amazed at the sheer size of the 'mock up' of the Bow of Noah's Ark, which wasn't even full size! This zoo is a marvelous place for children to be exposed to the Intelligent Design perspective, encouraging critical thinking from our youngsters. Just one example was from the information about bird songs found by the aviary, which really raised questions as to how and why, in the theory of neo Darwinism, would birds need such beautiful and sometimes extremely complex songs?
3. We saw the programme on the TV last night which was pretty outrageous but we are hoping that it will prove to be good publicity for the farm. We are very much praying for you all and hoping for a good half term with good weather and lots of visitors.
4. I wanted to let you know how much I admire your courage and faithfulness in presenting a God-glorifying aspect to creation in an increasingly hostile academic environment. Thank you so much for the 2 years of enjoyment our children and we have had as season ticket holders. The educational aspect has been wonderful for our home educated children, as well as all the good clean fun that the children have had in the various playgrounds.

I am writing to offer the farm my support and best wishes at this difficult time. I have written to the Evening Post making my views very clear and I hope they publish my letter. I think you have been wrongly vilified and I am sure that the zoo will come through this trial and will be vindicated. Please pass on my best wishes to Christina and Tony Bush at this time. They will come through this and the this attack on their integrity will be shown for what it is, a lie! They must know that people are standing with them at this time.

5. I would like you to convey my sympathy and support to Mr and Mrs Bush in the wake of the recent adverse publicity re the zoo farm.
6. I hope this was the appropriate place to send this type of comment! I visited with the group of (zoo) staff that came to your attraction in November. Just wanted to compliment you on your biblical stand with the way you run things, I saw evidence of this on our short visit, and I think it's quite a brave thing to make such a stand,

particularly with the spiritual climate in this country. I'm sure you get strong opposition to your ideas, but well done on standing firm.

COMMENTS

We had lots of comments in our visitors book, too. Here are some:

What a fantastic day! So many animals I love them all. But I love the sheep the best.
Great day out! Fun for all the family. Everyone very helpful, thank you!
10,000 times better than Bristol Zoo. Makes cocktails out of them!
A fantastic day despite the rain. Absolutely fantastic staff! Very, very helpful. Would recommend here to anyone.
Great day out and value for money.
I touched a giraffe and a rhino and it was amazing. I will definitely come back.
Amazing! Everything you want and more. Really impressed.
I had a brilliant day. The zip wire was fab.
Staff are not in any way rude – I found them lovely. Thanks for a great day – miles better than London Zoo.
Excellent – informative shows, helpful staff, friendly animals! Lots of space indoors and out – the perfect school trip venue! Thanks!
Very good the best day ever.
Brought disabled 6 year old and everyone was very welcoming and helpful. Thank you.
A wonderful visit. Loved the show and the tractor ride.
Raining – loved the llama and the camel. He is cool. Hay barn = awesome. Monkeys rock! It was wicked!
Noah's Ark is FANTASTIC!! I'm really glad I came. My favourite bit was feeding the camels and llamas.
The fact that this place is growing is testament to your hard work and faith. All other zoos put across Darwin's Theory. It is nice to have the Bible version of how we came to be. God bless you.
I loved all the animals and just mucking about having fun.
Enjoyed holding reptiles. Nice to come to a zoo where you can get up close to the animals. We travel to come here again from Midlands.
Saw two lambs born today! Amazing!

Appendix 7 Bibliography

I have 1200 books in my library. These are some on Creation and Evolution:

Alexander D 2008 *Creation or Evolution Do we have to Choose?*
Atlas R 1995 *Principles of Microbiology*
Attenborough D 1995 *The Private Life of Plants*
Back P 2003 *Darwinism and the Rise of Degenerate Science*
Bahn P 1996 *The Story of Archaeology*
Balouet J-C 1990 *Extinct Species of the World Lessons for our Future*
Baratay E & Hardoun Fugier E 2002 *Zoo A History of Zoological Gardens in the West*
Behe MJ 1996 *Darwin's Black Box*
Benton MJ 1993 *The Fossil Record 2*
Benton MJ 1997 *Vertebrate Palaeontology*
Berry RJ 2009 *Real Scientists Real Faith*
Briggs M & P 2006 *The Natural History of the British Isles*
Bright M 1997 *Intelligence in Animals*
Brusca RC & Brusca GJ 2003 *Invertebrates*
Bryson B 2003 *A Short History of Nearly Everything*
Burgess J, Marten M& Taylor R 1987 *Microcosmos*
Burgess S 2000 *Hallmarks of Design*
Burgess S 2002 *He Made the Stars Also*
Burgess S 2007 *Origin of Man: The Image of an Ape Or The Image Of God*
Capula M 1990 *The MacDonald Encyclopaedia of Amphibians and Reptiles*
Carroll S 2006 *The Making of the Fittest*
Clarkson ENK 1998 *Invertebrate Palaeontology and Evolution*
Darwin C 1872 *The Origin of Species By Means of Natural Selection*
Dawkins R 1997 *Climbing Mount Improbable*
Dawkins R 2006 *The God Delusion*
De Waal F 2005 *Our Inner Ape*
De Waal F 2002 *Tree of Origin Primate Behaviour*
Dembski WA 1998 *Mere Creation; Science Faith and Intelligent Design*
Dembski WA *Uncommon Dissent Intellectuals Who Find Darwinism Unconvincing*
Downer J 2002 *Weird Nature Science is Stranger than Myth*
Ensler E 1998 *The Vagina Monologues*
Forshaw J 1998 *Encyclopaedia of Birds*
Fortey R 2000 *Trilobite! Eyewitness to Evolution*
Foster P 2009 *While the Earth Endures Creation, Cosmology and Climate Change*
Foster S & Johnson RL 2006 *Desk Reference to Nature's Medecine*
Gitt W 1998 The Wonder of Man
Gotch AF 1995 *Latin Names Explained*
Gould SJ 2002 *I have landed*
Greenaway T 1999 *The Plant Kingdom, Guide to Plant Classification and Diversity*
Haines T 1999 *Walking with Dinosaurs*

Haines T 2001 *Walking With Beasts*
Halliday T & Adler K 2002 *The New Encyclopaedia of Reptiles and Amphibians*
Hawker LE & Linton AH 1979 *Micro-organisms, Function, Form and Environment*
Hawking SW 1989 *A Brief History of Time*
Herron EM 2003 *The Dead Sea Scrolls*
Heywood VH 2001 *Flowering Plants of the World*
Hoyle F 1983 *The Intelligent Universe*
Johnson H 1993 *The International Book of Trees*
Johnson PE 1994 *Darwin on Trial*
Judson O 2002 *Dr Tatiana's Sex Advice to all Creation*
Kardong KV 2002 *Vertebrates*
Kuhn TS 1996 *The Structure of Scientific Revolutions*
Lambert D 1993 The *Ultimate Dinosaur Book*
Langone J, Stutz B & Gianopoulos A 2007 *Theories for Everything*
Levin H 2003 *The Earth Through Time*
Le Fanu J 2009 *Why Us?*
Lubenow ML 1994 *Bones of Contention*
Macdonald DW 2006 *The Encyclopaedia of Mammals*
Martinez FG 2000 *The Dead Sea Scrolls Translated*
McIlhaney JS & McKissic F 2008 *Hooked: How Casual Sex is Affecting our Children*
McIntosh A 1997 *Genesis for Today*
McKenna MC & Bell SK 1998 *Classification of Mammals Above the Species* Level
Middleton JR & Walsh BJ 1995 *Truth is stranger than it used to be*
Midgley R 1993 *The Visual Dictionary of Dinosaurs*
Moller L 2002 *The Exodus Case*
Morris D 1967 *The Naked Ape*
Morris D 2004 *The Naked Woman*
Nieman DG, Allen ME, Thompson KV, Lumpkin S 1996 *Wild Mammals* in Captivity
O'Hear A 1999 *Beyond Evolution Human nature and the Limits of Evolutionary Explanation*
Paxton JR & Eschmeyer WN 1998 *Encyclopaedia of Fishes*
Perrins C 2003 *The New Encyclopaedia of Birds*
Phillips R 1983 *Wild Food*
Plimer I 2009 *Heaven and Earth Global Warming, the Missing Science*
Potter C 2009 *You are Here A Portable History of the Universe*
Prothero DR 2007 *Evolution What the Fossils Say and Why It Matters*
Rohl D 1995 *A Test of Time The Bible – From Myth to History*
Ryan W & Pitman W 1998 *Noah's Flood*
Shuker KPN 2001 The *Hidden Powers of Animals*
Sibley CG & Ahlquist JE 1995 *Phylogeny and Classification of Birds*
Sobel D 1999 *Galileo's Daughter*
Sodera V 2003 *One Small Speck to Man*
Sparks J 1999 B*attle of the Sexes*
Stanley SM 2009 *Earth System History*

Stove D 1995 *Darwinian Fairytails; Selfish Genes...and Other Fables of Evolution*
Strobel L 2004 *The Case for a Creator*
Tarbuck EJ& Lutgens FK *Study Guide to The Earth an Introduction to Physical Geology*
Toghill P 2003 *The Geology of Britain, an Introduction*
Whitcombe JC & Morris HM 1994 *The Genesis Flood*
Wilson DE & Reeder DM *Mammal Species of the World, 2nd Ed*
Woodward T 2003 *Doubts about Darwin*
Zimmer C 2001 E*volution The Triumph of an Idea*
Zuk M 2002 *Sexual Selections*

INDEX